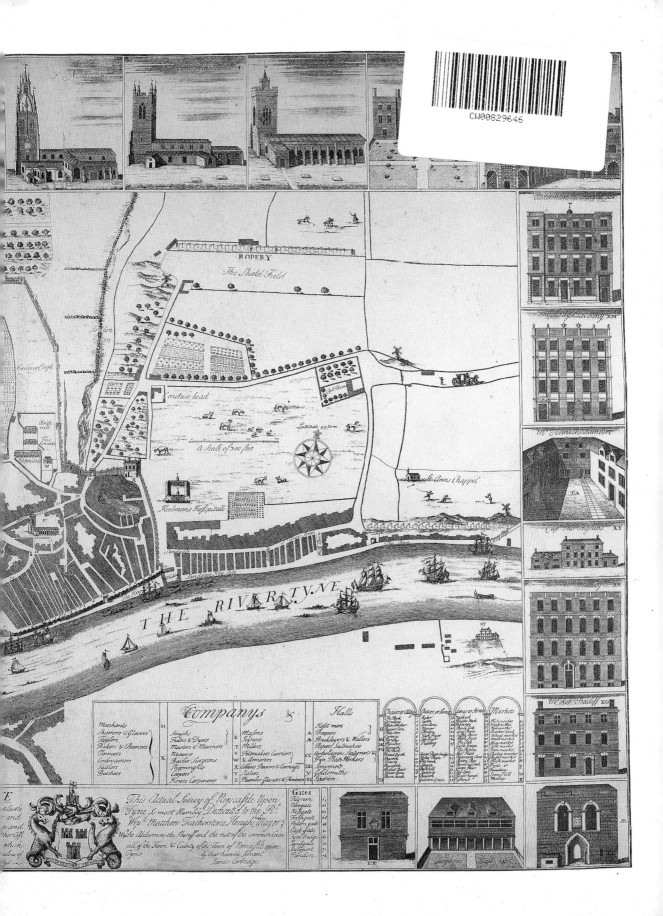

CW00829646

St Nicholas

All Hallow Church

THE RIVER TYNE

ROPERY

The Shield Field

Panden Dean

Carling Crofs

Bridewell
Free Schools
Hospitall

Conduit head

Latitude 55:00 m

A Scale of 300 feet

St Anns Chappel

Keelmens Hospitall

Aldernam Fenwick

The Lady Clavering

Mr Fenwick Lambert

Capt Tho Hopkins

Mr Rob Bailiff

Companys

Merchants
Skinners & Glovers
Taylors
Bakers & Brewers
Tanners
Cordwainers
Sadlers
Butchers

Smyths
Fullers & Dyers
Masters & Mariners
Weavers
Barber Surgeons
Shipwrights
Coopers
House Carpenters

Masons
Joyners
Millers
Feltmakers Curriers
& Armorers
Saddlers Paviors & Carriage
Slaters
Plumbers Glasiers & Pewterers

Halls

Hostmen
Drapers
Bricklayers & Wallers
Ropers Sailmakers
Upholsterers Stationers
Tyn Plate Workers
Scriveners
Goldsmiths
Fixiners

Chaires or Alleys

Chaires or Lanes

Lanes or Streets

Markets

This Actual Survey of Newcastle upon Tyne is most Humbly Dedicated to the Rt Worpll Matthew Featherstone Hough Mayor & Worple Aldermen the Sheriff and the rest of the common Councell of the Town & County of the Town of Newcastle upon Tyne by their humble Servant James Corbridge

Gates

Surgeons Hall

NEWCASTLE AND GATESHEAD
BEFORE 1700

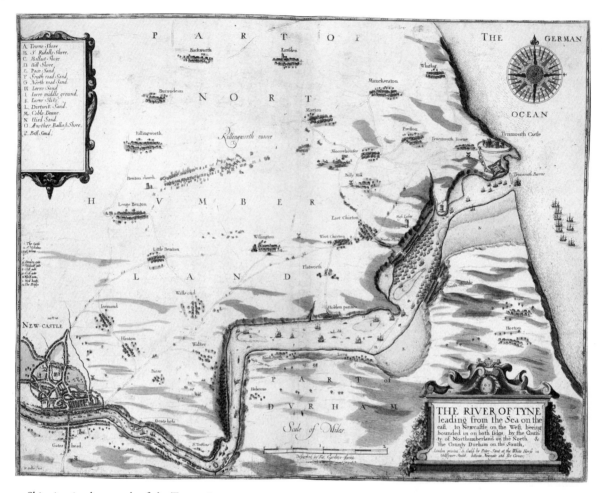

Shipping in the mouth of the Tyne, 1655.

Newcastle and Gateshead
Before 1700

Edited by
Diana Newton and A.J. Pollard

PHILLIMORE

2009

Published by
PHILLIMORE & CO. LTD
Chichester, West Sussex, England
www.phillimore.co.uk
www.thehistorypress.co.uk

© Diana Newton, A.J. Pollard and Contributors

ISBN 978-1-86077-579-6

Printed and bound in Great Britain

Contents

Acknowledgements

This collection of essays, the prequel to *Newcastle upon Tyne: A Modern History*, edited by Robert Colls and Bill Lancaster in 2001, was conceived at a meeting held in Newcastle at the instigation of David Rollason, then the director of the North East England History Institute in 2004. We would like to thank those that gathered then and the other contributors who subsequently joined us for helping to make the intention a reality. We could not have done so without the help of Richard Higgins and Sarah Mulligan in searching out and supplying illustrations from the Special Collections at the University of Durham and the Local History Collection at Newcastle Central Library, or the generous grants made by Tyne and Wear Archaeology Service and Gateshead Borough Council to pay for them. In addition, we would like to thank Anthea Lang of the Libraries Arts and Community based services of Gateshead Council for her support and Adrian Green for his constant encouragement. Finally it is a pleasure to record our thanks to Noel Osborne for taking it on, to Simon Thraves at Phillimore for keeping us at it, and to Sarah Pavey for seeing it through the press with him.

Diana Newton and A.J. Pollard
North East History Institute
Michaelmas, 2009

Illustration Acknowledgements

British Library, 75 and frontispiece (074978, Maps.1.Tab.18,41)

Durham University Library, Special Collections, 3, 4, 7, 9, 14, 28-32, 34-7, 50, 54, 58, 62, 64-5, 68, 71, 82-4, 90, 92, 94, 96-7, 99, front endpaper

Anthony Goodman, 40, 39, 43, 56

Barbara Harbottle, 10-12, 15, 17-18, 20, 22, 24, 48-9

English Heritage, 8, 23, 63, 78, 85, 88, 91

Hunter Blair, C.H., *Northumbrian Monuments*, Newcastle upon Tyne Records, vol. IV (1924) p.83, 33

Lewis, S., *A Topographical Dictionary of England* (1831), vol.2, p.216, 57

The National Archives (MPF 1/333), 74

Newcastle City Library, Local Studies Collection, 6, 16, 21, 25, 26, 38, 41, 42, 45, 46, 51, 66, 67, 70, 72, 76, 86, 89, 93

Oxford University Libraries, 69

Peter Rushton, 55, 98, 100

Tyne and Wear Museums, 2 and jacket

The Society of Antiquities of London, 1, 5, 27, 44, 47, 52, 60, 77, 79, rear endpaper.

Abbreviations

AA	*Archaeologia Aeliana*
APC	*Acts of the Privy Council* (London, 1890-1964)
BL	British Library, London
Brand, *Newcastle*	Brand, J., *History and Antiquities of the Town and County of the Town of Newcastle upon Tyne*, 2 vols (1789)
Bourne, *Newcastle*	Bourne, H., *History of Newcastle upon Tyne* (1736)
CPR	*Calendar of Patent Rolls* (London, 1895-1909)
CChR	*Calendar of Charter Rolls* (London, 1903-27)
CJ	*Journals of the House of Commons, 1547-1714* (London, 1742)
CSPD	*Calendar of State Papers Domestic*
DRO	Durham Record Office, Durham
DUL	Durham University Library, Durham
EHR	*English Historical Review*
Hist. Parl.	Roskell, J.S., and others, *The History of Parliament: The House of Commons, 1386-1421*, 4 vols (1993)
LJ	*Journals of the House of Lords, 1509-1767* (London, 1846 onwards)
LP	Brewer, J.S., and others, *Letters and Papers, foreign and domestic, of the reign of Henry VIII* (1862-1910)
NRO	Northumberland Record Office, Woodhorn, Northumberland, now Northumberland Collections
Rot. Scot.	Macpherson, D. and others, *Rotuli Scotiae*, 2 vols (1814-19)
SS	Surtees Society
TNA	The National Archives, Kew, London
TRHS	*Transactions of the Royal Historical Society*
TWAS	Tyne and Wear Archive Service, Newcastle
Welford, *Newcastle and Gateshead*	Welford, R., *History of Newcastle and Gateshead in the 14th and 15th Centuries* (1884)

Notes on Contributors

Diana Newton is Reader in early Modern History at Teesside University and Director of the North East England History Institute. Her publications include several works on the history of the North East in the late 16th and early 17th centuries, including a contribution to *Northumbria, History and Identity, 547-2000* (2007).

A.J. Pollard is Emeritus Professor of History at Teesside University. He has written extensively on the history of northern Yorkshire and County Durham in the later Middle Ages and was editor, with Adrian Green, of *Regional Identities in North East England, 1300-2000* (2007), as well as a contributor to *Northumbria, History and Identity*.

David Heslop is the County Archaeologist for Tyne and Wear. His particular interest is in Iron-Age archaeology, but he has concentrated recently on the medieval and post-medieval archaeology and buildings of Tyneside.

Barbara Harbottle, former County Archaeologist for Tyne and Wear, is an independent scholar and archaeologist of medieval Newcastle who has led several excavations of medieval sites.

Constance Fraser, formerly a Senior Staff Tutor in the Centre for Lifelong Learning at Newcastle University, has published extensively on the medieval history of Newcastle and Northumberland.

Anthony Goodman is Professor Emeritus of Medieval History, University of Edinburgh. He is interested in the social and religious history of later medieval England. He has published widely, including *Margery Kempe and her World* (2002).

Anthony Tuck, Emeritus Professor of History at the University of Bristol is a late-medievalist who has written, among other topics, on the history of Northumberland in the 14th and 15th centuries.

Richard Britnell was formerly Professor of History at Durham University. He has specialised in towns and trade. His most recent publication is an edition of late medieval court records from Crossgate, Durham.

Grace McCombie, an independent architectural historian, was co-author of the second edition of Pevsner's *Northumberland* (1992) and is author of the forthcoming Pevsner *City Guide to Newcastle and Gateshead*.

Christine Newman was assistant editor of the Victoria County History of Durham, and has published on the religious history of north-east England and the towns of Darlington and Northallerton.

Simon Healy is a researcher for the History of Parliament. His particular interests include Crown finances, the confessional state, relations between central government and local society, the North of England, and Welsh history in the early 17th century.

Keith Wrightson is the Townsend Professor of History at Yale University. He has published extensively on the Early Modern British economy and society.

Peter Rushton, Reader in Historical Sociology at the University of Sunderland, specialises in the history of crime and society in the 17th and 18th centuries, with particular reference to County Durham.

Introduction

A.J. POLLARD AND DIANA NEWTON

A visitors' guide in 2007 declared that 'Newcastle and Gateshead have joined forces to become known as "NewcastleGateshead", a destination that's brimming with energy and culture.' The cynic might conclude that in the early 21st century Newcastle had finally achieved its objective of taking over its smaller neighbour across the Tyne. For the history of the two mismatched towns has always been a fraught combination of cooperation and conflict: cooperation symbolised by the bridge between the two which has existed since the early 12th century and conflict by the division between jurisdictions that ran down the river and across that bridge. Yet the graceful millennium bridge, providing a new link, and the iconic Angel of the North sited in Gateshead, stand witness to a new spirit of harmony centred on the river.

This collection of essays focusing on the early history of both Newcastle and Gateshead is the third of a trilogy. The first volume explored modern Newcastle and the second the region of which it is the centre.[1] In this volume 12 archaeologists and historians have contributed essays on aspects of the histories of both towns from the earliest evidence of settlement until the end of the 17th century. Gateshead is included alongside its larger and more powerful neighbour not only because in the 21st century a new partnership has been developed, but also because the history of the two has been so inextricably linked, a reality acknowledged by at least two of the earlier histories of the area.[2] While Gateshead has had its recent historian, no comprehensive history of Newcastle has been attempted since 1950.[3]

The essays that follow reflect the interests and expertise of the contributors in the history of the two towns up to 1700. Some originated as contributions to an

---

[1]   Colls, Robert and Lancaster, Bill (eds), *Newcastle upon Tyne: a Modern History* (Chichester, 2001) and Colls, Robert (ed.), *Northumbria, History and Identity, 547-2000* (Chichester, 2007).

[2]   MacKenzie, E., *A Descriptive and Historical Account of the Town and County of Newcastle upon Tyne, Including the Borough of Gateshead* (Newcastle upon Tyne, 1827); Welford, *Newcastle and Gateshead*.

[3]   Manders, F.W.D., *A History of Gateshead* (1973); Middlebrook, S., *Newcastle upon Tyne, its Growth and Achievement* (1950).

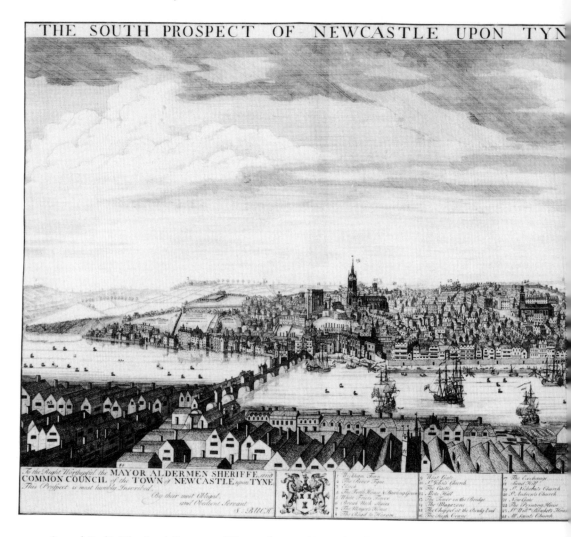

1   Samuel Buck's 'The South Prospect of Newcastle upon Tyne taken from Gateshead Church Steeple', 1745.

earlier projected collection for the history of Newcastle. A considerable amount of research has been conducted since 1950 on the early history of Newcastle, as the many editions of documents and learned articles that have been published testify. It is hoped that all this work, including the essays brought together here, will pave the way for a much-needed new history of Newcastle upon Tyne and Gateshead. The editors did not in this collection attempt to bring together a comprehensive history before the 18th century. The historian of Newcastle before 1500 is hampered by a dearth of evidence, especially the lack of borough

records which have survived for many other towns. There is also still much more that can be done, especially on Restoration Newcastle between 1660 and 1689, which remains an almost untouched field. This introduction, however, seeks to draw out from each of the essays in this volume an overview which encapsulates the development of the urban settlements that grew at either end of the Tyne bridge from their beginnings to the dawn of the modern age.

Origins and Growth

The histories of both Newcastle and Gateshead are conventionally traced back to Roman settlement, the building of forts on both sides of the river and a bridge, *Pons Aelius*, connecting them. But as David Heslop points out there was Iron-Age settlement along the Tyne long before the Romans came and the river side is studded by sites of ritualistic significance to its inhabitants. The crossing point at which both Newcastle and Gateshead developed was already and was long to remain a significant ceremonial and religious centre. The Romans established themselves where there was already a significant ritual centre. For them, however, the site was one end of the far northern frontier of their empire. They created settlements for military reasons. Hadrian's wall originally ended at a fort on the castle hill in Newcastle. Perhaps the Romans were given too much significance by early antiquaries who liked to emphasise a civilised past before the barbarity of the Middle Ages overwhelmed the far north.[4] What tends to be forgotten, and emerges from Heslop's essay, is that the sites were abandoned in the fifth century, the bridge was swept away and the countryside reverted to scattered agricultural settlement. There is fragmentary archaeological evidence of occupation in the site of the fort, but no indication of enduring construction until three centuries later, when a cemetery was established there. Perhaps, near the end of the Anglo-Saxon period, a church was built on or near the site. Remarkably not one of all the excavations in the city that were undertaken in the 20th century has revealed evidence of any Anglo-Saxon settlement, apart from a fish weir on the river. For six centuries after the collapse of Roman rule, there was no identifiable urban settlement.

The sparse historical, as distinct from archaeological, evidence we have suggests, in fact, that Gateshead was more important in Anglo-Saxon England than the site that became Newcastle. The name is found in Bede's *History of the English Church* as the site of a monastery in 653. There may also have been an ancient hall there as well. Gateshead might have had a defined existence as a pre-Norman estate belonging to the Community of St Cuthbert. Certainly it was well enough established to be the ill-fated meeting place of men of Northumbria (Northumberland) and the Bishop of Durham which led to the murder there of Bishop Walcher in 1080.[5] Indeed this crime against William I's servant could have helped to trigger the building of the New Castle on the hill across the river, dominating the site. But as yet there was no bridge and no traceable urban settlement on either side of the river.

---

[4]   For which see below, pp.1-22 and Sweet, Rosemary, '"Truly Historical Ground": Antiquarianism in the North', in Colls, R., *Northumbria*, pp.107-11. But one might also note that the Italian scholar, Aeneas Piccolomini, later Pope Pius II, who passed through in 1435, learnt that Julius Caesar had built the castle and, perhaps because of that association, expressed relief at having returned to civilization when he reached Newcastle from the Scottish borders (Gabel, Leonora C., *Memoirs of a Renaissance Pope: the Commentaries of Pope Pius II* (1960), pp.35-6).
[5]   See below, p.137.

2 *The Building of the New Castle* by William Bell Scott. Robert Curthose, with coronet and crossbow, inspects the plans. The wooden bridge and Gateshead appear in the background.

Both followed, one suspects, almost immediately. St Nicholas' Church was built outside the castle within 14 years. A market place probably already existed between castle and church; and a bridge, wooden like the first castle, probably followed soon after, though it is impossible to be sure when. What is certain is that within 50 years of the building of the castle the laws and customs of the royal town of Newcastle, in effect the first borough charter, were acknowledged by Henry I. Gateshead, at the southern end of the recently erected bridge and owned by the bishops of Durham, followed in its wake. The first recorded development was on Pipewellgate between 1154 and 1160; the High Street was built up by 1183; and the first borough charter granted by Bishop Hugh du Puiset (1154-95). Britnell suggests that urbanisation could even pre-date 1150.[6] It is therefore only from the late 11th/early 12th century that we can confidently date the continuous urban history of 'NewcastleGateshead'.

Growth between 1150 and 1300 was spectacular. Newcastle was a boom town as the north-east frontier was opened up, agriculture expanded and population exploded. It no doubt benefited from the confirmation of the disputed border between England and Scotland. Under the terms of the Treaty of Durham in

[6] See below, pp.24-6, 41-2, 140-4.

3   Newgate in the early 19th century, by T.M. Richardson, snr.

1139, Northumberland, with the exception of Newcastle, had come under the rule of the Scots; and even Newcastle was conceded to them by Henry of Anjou in return for support in 1149. Thus for eight years until Henry, now King Henry II of England, was able to recover Northumberland, Newcastle lay in the kingdom of Scotland. Following the repossession of the town, he began building the stone castle, which was completed by Henry III. A new stone bridge was put up following a fire in 1248. The Anglo-Scottish border was not finally settled until the Treaty of York in 1237; and it was not immediately certain that it would prove enduring. Nevertheless, in the long peace that followed, Newcastle prospered.

By the mid-13th century Newcastle was a major port and already one of the larger towns of England. Its international trade, as Fraser shows, was founded on the export to northern Europe of wool, wool-fells and hides, and to a lesser extent coal and lead, reflecting the predominantly pastoral nature of its rural hinterland. It imported grain, timber, wine and spices. Newcastle also served a wide hinterland both in the products brought in for export (wool came from as far afield as northern Yorkshire) and in the distribution of luxury goods, especially

the wine and spices that it imported. The town became the head customs port for
the coast between Berwick and Whitby and in time the northern wool staple.[7]

At first, ships which came upstream as far as the bridge were beached for
loading and unloading. Excavation has revealed that reclamation of land was
begun at the end of the 12th century and a series of piers were built during the
13th. These were then linked together in one long waterfront that was pushed
out three times into the river between the 13th and 16th centuries. After the
acquisition of Pandon it extended downstream, creating what has remained the
quay ever since. As the waterfront reclaimed land from the river, streets and
houses were laid out behind. Above the waterfront, the town expanded. During
the 13th century five houses of friars were established on open ground on its
fringes. Until the middle of the 13th century Newcastle was an open town. Work
did not start on building a town wall until 1265, which cut through some of the
friaries' lands. Completion of the landward arc was hastened by the renewal of
war with Scotland in 1296, and the quayside was finally protected in the early
15th century.[8] Gateshead expanded in parallel with Newcastle. It was never fully
urbanised, but as Britnell shows it flourished as a suburb on the route into the
town from the south. By 1300 the population of Newcastle was something of
the order of 7-8,000, that of Gateshead some 1,200. Newcastle itself had come
from nowhere in just two centuries to be the fourth town of England, after
London, Bristol and York.[9]

Bust followed boom. A series of shocks hit England as a whole, and Newcastle
in particular, in the first half of the 14th century. First there was the conflict with
Scotland, which in the second decade of the century frequently drew the Scots
to the gates of the town and led to serious, if short-lived, disruptions of trade.
Secondly, in the same decade, deep agrarian recession impoverished the town's
hinterland. Thirdly, from 1349 successive outbreaks of plague led to a halving
of the population. Estimates for 1377, based on poll tax returns, suggest that
there were only 3,500 to 4,000 inhabitants in Newcastle and 600 in Gateshead;
and this may have fallen further to 3,000 and 500 by 1400. In Newcastle tithal
income due to St Nicholas' Church collapsed from £77 6s. 8d. in 1291 to £33
6s. 8d. in 1402.[10] This was not only an economic disaster, but it also changed the

7   See below, pp.42-3.
8   See below, pp.29-37.
9   See below, pp.58, n.37, 150.
10 See below, pp.57, 69, 157-62 and Palliser, D.M. (ed.), *The Cambridge Urban History of Britain: vol. 1, 600-1540*
(Cambridge, 2000), p.758. The calculation is based on 2,647 taxpayers. For Scottish threats see McNamee, Colm, *The
Wars of the Bruces: Scotland, England and Ireland, 1306-1328* (East Linton, 1970); Grant, Alexander, 'Disaster at Neville's
Cross: The Scottish point of View', in Rollason, David and Prestwich, Michael (eds), *The Battle of Neville's Cross,
1346* (Stamford, 1998), pp.15-35 and Macdonald, Alastair J., *Border Bloodshed: Scotland and England at War, 1369-1404*
(East Linton, 2000).

character of the Tyne towns. Leaving aside the social, cultural and psychological impact, to which we will return, the mid-14th-century crisis made Newcastle and the Tyne what it was to be for the next five centuries; the centre of the English coal trade. Coal, hitherto a secondary commodity, rescued Newcastle from the worst consequences of the slump. By the end of that century it was heavily slanted to the shipping of coal to domestic outlets, especially London.

Nevertheless, the mid-15th century witnessed a slump even in the coal trade, which virtually came to a halt, and both Newcastle and Gateshead passed through a severe recession. In both towns properties were unlet and rental incomes declined drastically.[11] The coal trade, and Newcastle's fortunes, revived after 1470. Until the mid-16th century some 15,000 tons a year was shipped from the Tyne. Thereafter they took off: c.50,000 p.a. by 1590, 400,000 by 1660 and 600,00 by 1700. The mid-15th-century slump, particularly marked in the North East, consolidated the structural change in Newcastle's economy. From the predominantly independent port with an international market it had been before the 14th century it became a port whose trade was largely with domestic markets as a supplier of fuel, and whose fortunes were bound to those of London and the South East until the 19th century. By the early 17th century, 80 per cent of its trade was with other English ports and most of that with London.[12] William Gray, who proudly boasted in 1649 that it was 'The Harth that warmeth the south parts of the kingdom with fire', unwittingly acknowledged the Tyne's dependence on the metropolis.[13]

But this trend hides serious disruptions to trade caused by war on land and sea. The Scots had posed a threat since the early 14th century. Their descents into the Tyne valley from time to time thereafter, for example in 1341 and 1388, caused stoppages, both through destruction of pits and interruption of shipping. In 1640-1, when the Scots occupied Newcastle, trade collapsed. A year later, when the Civil War broke out, Newcastle was under Royalist control. Parliament imposed a two-year blockade until the Scots took the town in October 1644. War at sea, the action of privateers and the preying of pirates also caused problems occasionally, especially in the first decades of the 15th century, the later 16th century, in 1626-9 and during the Dutch Wars later in the century. But, however serious such periods of disruption were, production and trade always quickly

---

[11]   See below, p.259; Butcher, A.F., 'Rent, Population and Economic change in late-medieval Newcastle', *Northern History*, 14 (1978), pp.66-77. For the slump in north-eastern England, see Pollard, A.J., 'The North-Eastern Economy and the Agrarian Crisis of 1438-40', *Northern History*, 25 (1989), pp.88-105; idem, *North-Eastern England during the Wars of the Roses* (Oxford, 1990), pp.50-2, 71-80.

[12]   Wrightson, Keith, 'Elements of Identity: the re-making of the North East, 1500-1760', in Colls, *Northumbria*, pp.136-7.

[13]   William Gray, *Choreographia, or a survey of Newcastle upon Tyne* (Newcastle upon Tyne, 1649), pp.37-8.

4 The market place in Newcastle in the early 19th century, by T.M. Richardson, snr.

resumed. Coal shipments were back up to their previous levels within a year or two after the Scots captured Newcastle in October 1644.[14]

Short-term disruptions notwithstanding, the economic history of Newcastle and Gateshead from the middle of the 14th century was driven by the coal trade. Although it predominated, it was not the only product traded on the Tyne: Newcastle merchants grew rich through the continuing export of wool, lead, grindstones and later glass and through the import of grain and a wide range of luxury goods as well. It was a distributive centre of consumer goods, eventually developing its own specialist shops in the later 17th century. When Celia Fiennes visited the town she found that the shops there were 'of distinct trades, not selling many things in one shop', as was the case in most provincial towns. Yet the image of both Newcastle and Gateshead in England and abroad was shaped by the black gold, whether it was the local poet's celebration of Newcastle as the new Peru in 1651 or Defoe's more jaundiced description of the town in 1727 as 'not the pleasantest place in the world to live in', partly as a consequence of 'the smoke of the coals'.[15]

[14]   See below, pp.290-2 and Howell, *Puritan Revolution*, pp.121-68, 274-8.
[15]   Morris, Christopher (ed.), *The Journey of Celia Fiennes* (1949), pp.210-11; *News from Newcastle* (London, 1651), BL E. 622 (15); Defoe, D.A., *Journey Thro' the Whole island of Great Britain* (1727), vol.3, p.158.

Control of the Tyne

The economic crisis of the 14th century probably exacerbated rivalries on the river, and especially the tensions between Newcastle and Gateshead, that continued through to and beyond 1700. The source of this rivalry was the initial grant to Newcastle in the 12th century of a monopoly of all trade in and out of the river. That monopoly was challenged at North Shields by Tynemouth priory, at South Shields by the priory of Durham and by the townsmen of Gateshead, a seigneurial borough of the bishop. It was single-mindedly and relentlessly defended by the citizens of Newcastle. At first concerned with rights to trade independently, in the 16th century conflict extended to the authority to maintain, and profit from, the navigability of the river. All sides assiduously lobbied the Crown, and then Parliament, from whom both the citizens of Newcastle and their rivals received from time to time contradictory grants, which served only to make their lawyers happy.

The conflict with the prior of Tynemouth over North Shields first erupted in 1267, was pacified in 1305, and resurfaced at the end of that century. It continued to be unresolved and rumbled on until Newcastle secured a Parliamentary settlement in 1510. But this was still not the end, for in the 17th century an issue of reinforcing the shores with ballast dumped by ships coming into the river to load coal arose. The dispute with the prior of Durham over South Shields was first recorded in 1256, and recurred periodically thereafter. Concessions were ultimately won by the two priors, restricted largely to permission to fish and produce salt, but at both places they were not permitted to erect quays. In respect of North and South Shields Newcastle retained its monopoly largely intact.[16]

The most significant conflict was between Newcastle and Gateshead. It focused on three issues; the right of the bishop to hold a market in his town, possession of the southern part of the bridge; and the entitlement of Gateshead to ship coal and maintain a quay on its side of the river. Newcastle lost the first battle. Gateshead market was first recorded in 1246. Thereafter Newcastle claimed in vain, throughout the Middle Ages, that the bishop had no authority to license a market in one of his own towns. Rights on the river were more intractable. Not long after the establishment of Newcastle, a settlement was reached between the liberty of Durham and the people of Northumberland, dating from the episcopacy of Ranulph Flambard (1099-1128). It laid down that the northern third of the river belonged to Northumberland, the southern

---

[16] See below, pp.43-6 and Howell, Roger, *Newcastle upon Tyne and the Puritan Revolution* (Oxford, 1967), pp.300-11. For the 18th century see Ellis, Joyce, "'The "Black Indies": the Economic Development of Newcastle, *c.*1700-1840', in Colls and Lancaster, *Newcastle upon Tyne: A Modern History*, pp.15-21.

5   A detail of the old bridge from Buck's map.

to Durham and the middle third was common to all. This was confirmed in
the reign of Henry II. St Cuthbert's stone on the late medieval bridge marked
the point where the traveller south entered the palatinate of the Bishop of
Durham. By the 14th century the bishop was claiming that his right extended to
the middle of the river and insisting that he had an immemorial right to trade
freely on the south bank. This inevitably brought the citizens of Newcastle into
conflict with Gateshead, especially as the economic slump in the 15th century
deepened. In 1314 Edward II ruled for Bishop Beaumont; in 1384 Richard II
granted Bishop Fordham the right to maintain a quayside at Gateshead. Both
grants were contested by Newcastle and a veritable war on the Tyne ensued.

In 1344 the bishop prosecuted Newcastle men for preventing his ships from docking at Gateshead and for seizing them. Forty years later Fordham claimed that since the beginning of his episcopacy he had been prevented from receiving any profit from his coal, presumably by the same means. At the same time the men of Newcastle regularly destroyed the fish traps which Gateshead maintained on their side of the river. Newcastle's response to Fordham's victory of 1384 had been to build a tower on the southern half of the bridge, effectively laying claim to its entirety. In 1414 Bishop Langley successfully appealed to the Crown against this infringement of his liberty and the tower was formally surrendered to him at the beginning of 1417.[17] It would appear that Gateshead successfully withstood this sustained assault. Not only did it continue to trade on the Tyne, it was also able, as Britnell makes clear, to exploit its fisheries and to maintain its own staithes.[18]

But tensions between Newcastle and successive bishops of Durham did not subside. The citizens of Newcastle remained determined to make good their claim to the monopoly of trade on the river. Moreover, they resented what it viewed as the existence of a tax haven on its doorstep. In the 16th century Newcastle developed new strategies. For an all too brief moment in the mid-16th century, when the bishopric was temporarily dissolved, they secured an Act in Parliament incorporating Gateshead in Newcastle (1553). But this was repealed in the first Parliament of Mary's reign. A year later they secured a 450-year lease of land east of the town upon which they built their own quayside. In 1576 Newcastle petitioned the Crown again for possession of Gateshead on the grounds of disorder across the river. Gateshead retaliated by informing the Crown that they were all Papists in Newcastle. Newcastle finally achieved its aim more indirectly by securing the 'Grand Lease'. Originally a grant from Bishop Barnes of a 79-year lease on all the coal mines in Gateshead and Whickham to the queen in 1578, it eventually ended up in the hands of an 'inner ring' of Newcastle burgesses, in 1583 for 99 years. The politics of this is discussed in greater detail below, but the Grand Lease effectively put Gateshead into the pocket of the oligarchy who also controlled Newcastle. Another old battle was won by 1647, at which date there were no longer any markets or fairs being held in the town. Only when the lease lapsed in 1682 were Gateshead's leading townsmen once more able to assert their independence.[19]

[17] Holford, M., King, A. and Liddy, C.D., 'North-East England in the Later Middle Ages: Rivers, Boundaries and Identities, 1296-1461', in Green, Adrian and Pollard, A.J. (eds), *Regional Identities in North-east England, 1300-2000* (Woodbridge, 2007), pp.30-5; Liddy, Christian D., *The Bishopric of Durham in the Later Middle Ages: Lordship, Community and the Cult of St Cuthbert* (Woodbridge, 2008), pp.181-5.

[18] See below, pp.165, 167, 169; Liddy, *Bishopric*, p.34.

[19] See below, pp.220-7, 277-81, 299-304.

But the relationship between Newcastle and Gateshead was more ambiguous than the story of their rivalry suggests. Newcastle men had always owned property in both towns, they served as bailiffs and later in the vestry which dominated town government in the 16th and 17th centuries, and they entered into partnerships with Gateshead men in the management of collieries. It worked both ways. Thomas Cole, a Gateshead cordwainer, acquired property across the river and by 1608 had a half-share in the mines at Whickham. His nephew became a Hostman. As Rushton shows below, notwithstanding the Grand Lease and the closure of its market, Gateshead prospered and expanded during the 17th century, perhaps because of the opportunities the Lease opened up as well as the general boom on the Tyne. There was an underlying mutual dependence between the two, in good times and bad, which had existed ever since the building of the bridge.[20]

Population, Society and Town Governments

The wealth generated by coal after the mid-16th century led to an expansion of Newcastle's population. But, by 1563, it had barely recovered to its early 14th-century level of 7,500-8,000. Gateshead had perhaps grown proportionally more with a population estimated at 1,500 in 1563. A century later, hearth tax returns suggest that the inhabitants of Newcastle numbered over 13,000 and Gateshead over 3,500. But, this broad canvas hides a dramatic demographic dynamic. Repeated plague and high mortality was the cause of population decline in the 14th century. In Gateshead, it has been estimated that 50 per cent of its population died in the very first outbreak of plague in 1349 and there is no reason to suppose that it was any less severe over the river. Visitations in 1369 and 1379 were equally terrible. Epidemics swept through Newcastle and Gateshead all too frequently over the following two and a half centuries. In 1380 Newcastle town petitioned the Crown for financial relief on the grounds that 6,054 of its inhabitants had died in an outbreak of plague in the preceding year. Given the poll tax returns of three years earlier, this looks like an exaggeration, but one cannot doubt that the town suffered severely that year.[21] Most information is available for the outbreak of 1636, discussed in detail by Wrightson, and this shows a death toll of almost 6,000, probably representing 47 per cent of the population. What kept both Newcastle and

[20]   See below, pp.271, 302-4.
[21]   See below, pp.76, 150, 313. It is possible that the 1377 poll tax return hides a larger number of exempted poor in Newcastle than elsewhere, thus leading to an underestimate of the population two years before this outbreak.

6 Surviving medieval/early modern houses as sketched in the early 19th century.

Gateshead going was continuous inward migration, especially into Newcastle, rather than a compensatory rise in the birth rate. Indeed in the 14th century, recovery from the Black Death in 1349 was prevented by outbreaks of plague in 1360-1 and 1379 which in effect removed the replacement generations. In the late 14th century a surge of bequests to religious institutions and intensification of provision for souls after death may reflect not only the traditional fear of God, but also a shared response to the punishment He seemed to be inflicting upon them. Three centuries later, Wrightson shows, the strength of communal association held society together under the appalling blows dealt by the outbreak of 1636.[22]

In 1636 the poorest wards, especially the slums of Sandgate, suffered worst. By the end of the 17th century Newcastle was notorious for the scale of its poverty. The hearth tax return of 1665 suggests that the houses of over 40 per cent of its inhabitants, concentrated most markedly in Sandgate, were exempted from paying on account of poverty. Here lived the keelmen, casual labourers, and sailors; and here were found 'the lewd and disorderly houses'.[23] At the other extreme the great merchants lived, as they always had, in the Close in Sandhill along the river above the bridge, and in newer developments in Westgate and Pilgrim Street. For the population decline and recovery over four centuries had also had an impact on the topography of Newcastle. Throughout the later Middle Ages and well into the 16th century there were empty plots and undeveloped land within the walls. Infilling proceeded and by 1638 ribbon development had begun outside the walls beyond Newgate, Pilgrim Street and Westgate. By 1700 it was further advanced, especially along the river to the east beyond Pandon.[24] Meanwhile, the evolving development from 1431 of one of these sites on Broad Chare resulted in the complex of buildings and houses which became Trinity House, the home of the Master Mariners which is delineated below.[25]

Ever since the mid-14th century, Newcastle had been marked by its extremes of wealth. When the town's general prosperity collapsed in the 14th century, a small elite of super-rich emerged. These were the merchants who prospered from the coal trade and quickly established a narrow oligarchy controlling both it and the government of the town. The most famous and reputedly wealthiest late-medieval Newcastle merchant was Roger Thornton (d.1430), whose career crops up in more than one essay below. By the 17th century, local myth claimed that Thornton had become the recipient of the first charter from the hands of a grateful King Alfred, the first mayor, and builder of the town walls. He was Newcastle's Dick Whittington and his charitable deeds, detailed by Goodman, were on a par with those of his London contemporary. He was, however, just the most prominent of a generation or two of fabulously wealthy merchants who spent money rebuilding and beautifying the churches of Newcastle even when

---

[22] See below, pp.78, 85, 258-63.
[23] Howell, *Puritan Revolution*, pp.10-13. Howell also suggests that 76 per cent could be classified as poor; Ellis, 'Black Indies', pp.13-14, on the lewd and disorderly houses and the prodigious number of the poor concentrated in the same district right through to the 19th century.
[24] Howell, *Puritan Revolution*, pp.4, 8-9.
[25] See below, pp.171-9.

7 An 'exact representation' of an equestrian statue of James II, pulled down and thrown into the river during the Glorious Revolution, as text relates, by 'a few soldiers as drunk with Loyalty as with Liquor, assisted by the well known hot-headed genius of Sandgate'.

the town was passing through serious financial difficulties. The only conclusion that can be drawn is that in the late 14th and early 15th centuries the reduced wealth of Newcastle became concentrated in a remarkably few hands.[26]

This concentration of wealth matches what we know about the consolidation of an oligarchy in the control of Newcastle's government. The details of the town's complex medieval constitution, and the adjustments made to it over the centuries, are spelled out below. The charter granted to the burgesses of Newcastle by King John on 28 January 1216 confirmed the liberties and free customs that they had enjoyed in the time of his ancestors.[27] Later, those who traded in coal belonged to one of the three principal guilds of wholesalers – mercers, wool merchants and corn merchants – who later merged as the Merchant Adventurers, in 1480. There were also Hostmen, who were responsible for entertaining merchant strangers and supervising the sales and purchases of their wares and merchandise. The first reference to hosting in Newcastle was in the 14th century and by 1508, according to Fraser, it seems that whenever a ship left the river with coal in its cargo an 'ost' was named.[28] The role of Hostmen in the town's governance is usually dated from the charter of Queen Elizabeth I incorporating the guild or fraternity of Hostmen on 22 March 1600, giving its members a monopoly on the sale of coal and grindstones from the Tyne. By this time they were largely drawn from the same pool as the Merchant Adventurers and they dominated the affairs of Newcastle.

An ever more exclusive governing elite (or inner circle) appeared, from which Newcastle's mayors, sheriffs and MPs were usually drawn. By the end of the 16th century an inner circle within that inner circle emerged, focused on those who were themselves the grand lessees of the Gateshead mines, which created more internal tensions. Not surprisingly the oligarch's grip was challenged from time to time, such as in 1305, 1341-2, 1515 and the 1590s. But on every occasion, after the intervention of the Crown, it survived.[29] What happened in Newcastle was mirrored across the river. In the later Middle Ages Gateshead was governed through a complex overlap of manorial court, borough court and Episcopal officers. This was simplified after the Reformation when the vestry of 24, overlapping in personnel with the manorial court, emerged as the governing body. It, too, was narrowly based and contained many men

[26] See below, pp.54-7, 74, 78-81, 101-5, 118-19, 121-3; Howell, *Puritan Revolution*, pp.4-6
[27] Dendry, F.W. (ed.), *Records of the Newcastle Merchant Adventurers*, ii, SS, vol.93 (1899), pp.xx-xxi, 281-2; below, pp.41-2.
[28] *Records of the Company of Hostmen*, SS, vol.105 (1901), pp.xiii, p.xxviii, pp.10-17 and below, pp.59-60.
[29] See below, pp.48-51, 280-1.

with Newcastle roots and connections, especially during the 99 years of the Grand Lease.[30]

In the 1630s opposition from the excluded, comprising not just the general body of the lesser merchants but also some of the greater ones, built up. But when the government of Newcastle was purged, in the Interregnum, there was no internal revolution. The lesser merchants still found themselves excluded. The beneficiaries were those greater merchants who had not been a part of the inner circle and who were favourable to a Parliament who had no desire to open up the closed shop. They, in their turn, lost out in 1660. The upshot was merely a game of musical chairs, which left the town still firmly in the grip of the inner core of leading merchants. Twenty years later the same elite rejected the attempts of Charles II and James II to amend the charter for electoral purposes. James's 1687 purge designed to secure the return of more pliable MPs was firmly resisted, and the King's last minute *volte face* did not prevent the town declaring for William of Orange, 'the protestant religion and a free parliament'. It equally declared for the old oligarchy, which remained firmly in control after the Glorious Revolution. It had withstood royal intervention at the end of the 17th century as successfully as it had more popular attempts at reform over the centuries before. The *ancien regime* in Newcastle was to remain unreformed until 1835.[31]

The oligarchic grip on Newcastle's affairs is symbolised in the Guildhall on Sandhill, described below by Grace McCombie. Inside the later additions and adornments lie the foundations of the original 'town house', where the mayor, aldermen and council met and, next to it, the Maison Dieu, later St Katherine's hospital founded by Roger Thornton. Part of this building was already used by the town before the Reformation and was then taken over by the Merchant Adventurers. It was described by Leland as a 'square hall place'. Severely damaged during the siege of 1644, it was rebuilt and remodelled at great expense during the Interregnum.[32]

External Relations

One reason why a narrow oligarchy was able to maintain its grip on Newcastle over these centuries was that it was a royal town, with a royal castle in its midst. Until 1603 it was close to a hostile border and it had a deep interest in remaining on good terms with the Crown. It was, the Crown needed no reminding, a

---

[30] See below, pp.302-4.
[31] Howell, *Puritan Revolution*, pp.35-63, 169-77; Speck, W.A., 'The Revolution of 1688 in the North of England', *Northern History*, 25 (1989), p.200; Callicott, Maureen, 'The Governance of the Victorian City', in Colls and Lancaster, *Modern History*, p.71.
[32] See below, pp.182-8.

bulwark against the Scots. The Crown's overriding concern was with stability and security. Newcastle burgess ceaselessly lobbied the Crown, its MPs able to promote its interests during the sittings of Parliament. Kings themselves came to Newcastle, usually on missions of war or peace. Because of the renewal of war with Scotland, the first three Edwards visited no fewer than 14 times between 1292 and 1341. In 1311 Edward II took refuge in the castle from the Duke of Lancaster, and in 1334 Edward III received the homage of Edward Baliol in the Dominican Friary. For 50 years Newcastle was more central to the politics of the realm than it ever has been before or since. Thereafter royal visits were few and far between, usually linked to campaigns against the Scots: Richard II in 1385; Henry IV in 1400, on which occasion he granted the town county status in recognition, one suspects, of its support the year before in deposing Richard II. Thornton and his fellow citizens continued to provide this support during and after the Percy rebellions of 1403-8. Edward IV visited in 1461, the last reigning monarch until James I passed through on his journey south in 1603. No Tudor came as far north. The early Stuarts, because of their peaceful obligations in Scotland, passed through occasionally; James I again in 1617; Charles I in 1633, 1639, 1641 (not with such peaceable intent towards his Scottish subjects) and finally for nine months in 1646-7 as a prisoner in the town.[33]

In 1642-6 Newcastle was itself caught up directly in Civil War, for the first and only time in its history. It had come to its gates in 1463-4 during the Wars of the Roses when the Lancastrians briefly held a front line along the Tyne, up to the walls of the town. But in 1640 it was seized by a Scottish army, which left in 1641 after the Long Parliament had been sitting for six months. The Scots were back again briefly in 1643 and then again in 1644 when they laid siege to the Royalist town. After three months Newcastle fell. Some townsmen of Gateshead may have felt a frisson of delight that the Windmill Hill was used as a point from which to bombard the town across the river. From 1644 Newcastle was in Parliament's hands. The first two years of the war had been costly, not only in terms of physical destruction, but also in the complete stoppage of the coal trade because, for as long as it remained in Royalist possession, Parliament had maintained a blockade.[34]

In more normal times, the town had been a frequent mustering point for English armies, led as often by great lords as kings. The Tyne was an assembly point for navies, in which Newcastle ships were impressed, to support land

[33] Http://museums.ncl.ac.uk/keep_timeline.htm. There were more grisly reminders of royal power when body parts of the king's fallen enemies were displayed in the town. One does not know whether the inhabitants were delighted or sickened by the sight of William Wallace's right arm. Charles I was accommodated in Anderson's Place, the new mansion built on the site of the Greyfriars.
[34] Pollard, *North-Eastern England*, pp.226-8, 298; Howell, *Puritan Revolution*, pp.144-66.

operations. And Newcastle was an advance supply base. All of these factors may or may not have been to its economic advantage. On the one hand, being a military base stimulated trade; on the other shipping was disrupted and soldiers were not necessarily well behaved. The royal victualler's account of 1322-3 reveals that in that year he hired cellars and granaries in which to store his wine and corn. The Duke of Norfolk was based in the town in the winter of 1462-3, supplying the armies of Richard Neville, Earl of Warwick, then besieging Scots and Lancastrians in the castles of Alnwick, Dunstanburgh and Bamburgh. Norfolk's presence in the town at the end of 1462 was no doubt as good for business as the victualler's a century and a half earlier. The Earl of Warwick was back in Newcastle in December 1465 to negotiate with a Scottish delegation. But Newcastle had probably been glad to see the back of John de Warenne, Earl of Surrey in 1341, whose troops had caused damage at the Blackfriars and probably more widely in the town.[35]

Newcastle and Gateshead were at the heart of a wider regional society. As several contributors show, over the whole period from 1300 to 1700 the northern peerage and gentry had multiple connections with the town. Those with lands near the Tyne developed coal mines. Many had town houses. The Neville family town house was reputed to have stood at the site of the present Bolbec Hall, close to the Neville Tower on the wall; the Percys possessed an 'Inn' on the Close. Durham and Northumberland aristocrats used St Nicholas', other churches and religious houses for christenings and as places in which to reach formal agreements; they put sons into trade there and married daughters to the sons of merchants; they patronised the religious houses, especially the friaries. In the second decade of the 17th century, Thomas Chaytor of Butterby, County Durham, regularly spent Christmas there in his mother's house.[36]

Just as the gentry and nobility frequented Newcastle, so the great merchants of Newcastle acquired estates in Northumberland and Durham and themselves merged into the county gentry. Roger Thornton, who acquired significant country property, remained all his life first and foremost a Newcastle burgess, but his son became a country gentleman. Thomas Riddell and Henry Anderson, grand lessees at the end of the 16th century, acquired property in Durham. Liddell's descendants became lords of Ravensworth. Thomas Chaytor's grandfather was a Newcastle merchant; his father a lawyer. It is an old story, and one aspect of

[35]   Prestwich, M.C., *Armies and Warfare in the Middle Ages: the English Experience* (New Haven, 1996), p.253; Pollard, A.J., *Warwick the Kingmaker: Politics, Power and Fame* (2007), p.179; below, pp.48, 52-3, 89. Goodman. Among the royal ordinance in the late 15th century was a great gun named *Newcastle* (Hicks, M.A., *Warwick the Kingmaker* (Oxford, 1998), p.247.

[36]   See below, pp.108-9, 128-35, 258-70, 272. Hicks, *Warwick*, p.253; Newton, Diana, 'Borders and Bishopric: Regional Identities in the Pre-Modern North-East, 1559-1620', in Green and Pollard, *Regional Identities*, p.67.

the way in which Newcastle acted as the centre of a region focused between the rivers Blyth and Wear.[37]

Beyond the North East were London and Europe. The leading Newcastle merchants had long maintained establishments in London. Roger Thornton held property there and by the 17th century London offices were an integral part of the business. Newcastle's MPs were usually drawn from the ranks of the greater merchants; Healy documents below the many hours spent by some of them on committee work on behalf of the town in which they were engaged in the early 17th century. Links with the court and a presence in Parliament were essential for promoting its interests, as is witnessed by the negotiations concerning the Grand Lease. It was not just London. Newcastle men established links with the principal ports in northern Europe. One example, explored by Newton, is that of Henry Riddell, who died in Elbing in 1597. And men came to Newcastle from the continent, not just the merchants who were hosted, but men who settled, from Hugo Geradino of Lucca in the late 13th century to George Ritschell, a native of Bohemia, in the mid-seventeenth. Ritschell was a leading European scholar who had enjoyed a distinguished career on the continent before he was enticed to Newcastle in 1648 by its puritan leaders to become master of the school.[38]

Religion and Culture

The appointment of George Ritschel reminds us that there was one major break in the continuity of the post-1300 history of Newcastle and Gateshead: the Reformation. Newcastle, as Goodman points out, was remarkable as one of England's leading towns in being but one parish and having no major monastery within or just outside its walls. In this respect it was no different from Gateshead except that St Mary's cared for only a fifth of the number of souls. St Nicholas' did have the support of three dependent churches, technically chapels, serving different parts of the parish, but the structure created an unusually homogeneous religious culture. In addition, with the exception of a monastery, the town enjoyed the full panoply of religious institutions, discussed below, supporting some 60 secular clergy and at the dissolution a similar number in its nunnery, four friaries and hospitals. The living of the vicar of St Nicholas' was one of the best rewarded in the North; the church a mini-cathedral. The unique ecclesiastical structure of the town enhanced its civic identity, as did the cycle of mystery plays, now almost

---

[37] See below, pp.268-72; Newton, 'Borders and Bishopric', pp.67-8; Wrightson, 'Elements of Identity', *passim*.
[38] See below, pp.47-8, 227-39, 265-6, 275-8, 286-9.

entirely lost, which were almost as magnificent as those of Chester and York. Newcastle may have been overshadowed by Durham, but it had its own distinct if more secular religious identity.[39] Newcastle was heir to the distinctive religious and ceremonial significance of the Tyne crossing point that Heslop identifies and traces from the earliest, pre-Roman settlement of the valley.[40]

Newcastle also fostered two religious thinkers in the later Middle Ages, the recluse John Lacy and the Dominican preacher, Richard Helmslay. Helmslay developed various unorthodox ideas that led to his condemnation and recantation in 1385, including the notion (tongue in cheek perhaps) that the requirement that everyone of both sexes was obliged to make confession applied only to hermaphrodites. Helmslay was no Lollard, but Ricard Wyche, an unlicensed preacher in the town, was examined and condemned as a heretic in 1402. Wyche would appear to have enjoyed little success. Newcastle's vigorous religious life remained staunchly orthodox until the Reformation swept over the diocese in the 16th century.

The first change was the dissolution of the religious houses in 1536-9, followed a decade or so later by the chantries. The nunnery and Greyfriars were eventually acquired by Sir Henry Anderson who built a grand house and garden for himself on their sites: a country seat within the walls of the town. Three of the friaries eventually passed into the possession of the Corporation: the Austins for a while as an office for the Council of the North and the Blackfriars as accommodation for nine of the guilds. The hospitals survived, being refounded by James I in 1611 as alms houses, along with St Edmund in Gateshead. The exception was St Katherine's, which in the 17th century was absorbed into the rebuilt Guildhall. The chantries all went. The main beneficiary of this massive transfer of property was the Corporation. The school to which Ritschel was recruited was founded by a bequest to the Corporation for that purpose by Thomas Horsley who died in 1545. Maintained by 1561 in part from the income of the Hospital of St Mary the Virgin, it moved in the early 17th century from St Nicholas' churchyard to premises on the site of the hospital in Westgate.

Besides the physical and institutional impact on Newcastle, the most dramatic legacy of the Henrician and Edwardian reformations was the reduction in the number of secular clergy and religions living in and serving the community. Their presence fell from some 120 (friars, nuns, parochial priests and chaplains) to barely more than six after the Elizabethan settlement: the vicar and five curates, including lecturers and preachers who also served as curates.[41] The removal of a significant

---

[39] Or this and the following paragraph see below, pp.65-114 passim.
[40] See below, pp.3-7.
[41] Mackenzie, E., *A Descriptive and Historical Account of the Town and County of Newcastle upon Tyne, Including the Borough of Gateshead* (Newcastle upon Tyne, 1827), pp.118-56.

8 The restored Blackfriars, home of nine city guilds after the Reformation.

ecclesiastical presence transformed Newcastle. It became a more secular society, more obviously dominated by the laity and by the Corporation in particular.

Both towns were slow to convert to the new religion. The first reformers to be active in Newcastle were the Scots, John Rough and John Knox, in the reign of Edward VI. Plans for radical reorganisation of the diocese of Durham collapsed with the King's death in 1553. Mary's accession put an end to the hopes of some, and the fears of considerably more, of doctrinal change. Reforming bishops of Durham after 1560, Pilkington and Barnes, did their best to impose the Elizabethan settlement by installing protestant vicars. Lectureships were established and a line of distinguished preachers invited to the town. By the end of the century both Newcastle and Gateshead were more securely Protestant. The new regime was helped by the fact that Newcastle, like Gateshead, was one parish under one bishop and that the ruling elite was more concerned to conform to government policy than stand out for religious independence. They were steadfastly loyal to the Crown during the major uprisings of 1536 and 1569. Obeying the powers that be remained essentially the policy throughout the succeeding century. The Corporation made no objection to the Arminianism promoted by Bishop Neile, lived happily with Puritanism after 1644 and accommodated itself to the Restoration of the Church of England in 1660. Business came first.[42]

[42]   See below, pp.189-218.

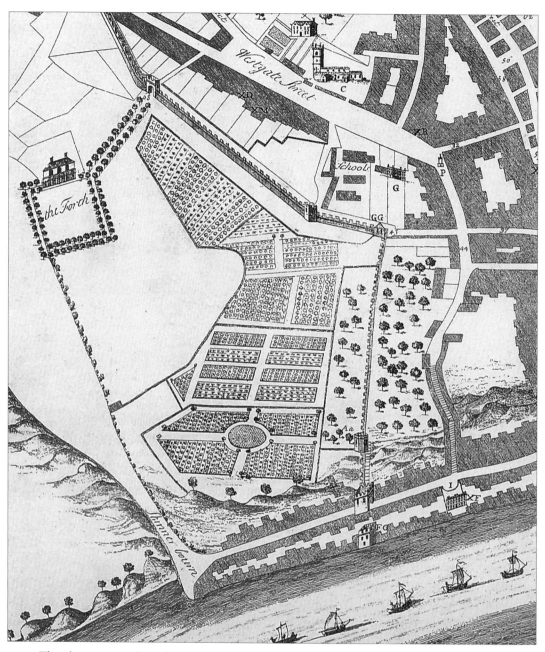

9　The pleasure grounds to the west of the city visited by Celia Fiennes in 1698, as shown in James Corbridge's map of Newcastle. The sites of the town houses of the Nevilles and probably the Percys are marked at 'G' and 'XE'.

Yet Roman Catholicism survived in the face of intensifying persecution. Similarly, after 1660 the authorities were not able to prevent the growth of non-conformity, both of unrepentant Congregationalists and Presbyterians who had held sway during the Interregnum, and Quakers who first emerged in 1653. Quakers in fact gained an earlier foothold in Gateshead than in Newcastle. When Defoe visited Newcastle in the third decade of the 18th century he found that there were now six churches in the parish and six dissenting meeting houses.[43] The impact of the Reformation on the religious life of Newcastle was not simply that it became largely Protestant, but that as elsewhere in the kingdom a single religious authority and identity was fractured. The homogeneous religious culture that had characterised Newcastle before the Reformation gave way to diversity. Nevertheless it is likely that the town played an important role in the propagation of Protestantism in the region and thus continued to be, as it was before the Reformation, a distinctive focal point other than Durham for Christianity in the diocese.[44]

One consequence of the Reformation was the discontinuation after 1581 of the Corpus Christi plays mounted by the trade guilds. They were replaced by visiting players from London and elsewhere. Newton calculates that 39 touring companies visited the town in the 40 years between 1575 and 1615. But even these visits came to an end after 1640. Another impact of the Reformation was the dissolution of parish fraternities that had flourished throughout England in the later Middle Ages. The trade guilds remained, however, with their annual feasts and other rituals as the principal sites of conviviality and recreation. They continued to be the focus of associational life until the later 17th century when new, less formal aspects of sociability emerged, including pleasure gardens laid out beyond the walls where the 'Gentlemen and Ladies walk in the evening'.[45] But it was not until the early 18th century that the first coffee house is recorded, the first newspaper was set up (*The Newcastle Courant* in 1719), the earliest assemblies were held, a playhouse reopened and subscription concerts were organised. Although horse races had been held at nearby Killingworth since 1621, and since the Restoration more gentry had acquired town houses and more of them had been joining the trade guilds as honorary members, a full social season running between the races in July and the assizes in the autumn did not

---

43 Howell, *Puritan Revolution*, pp.261-73. For recusants see below, pp.202-6, 292-3.
44 Collinson, Patrick, *The Birthpangs of Protestant England* (1988), p.40.
45 Morris, *Journey of Celia Fiennes*, p.211

emerge until after 1700.[46] With its shops for separate trades, as Celia Fiennes observed on her visit, Newcastle was emerging as not only the centre of polite society in the North East, but also the regional focus for an emerging consumer society. Moreover, new industries bringing new wealth and new spending power were developing on the outskirts of both Newcastle and Gateshead. They were entering into the modern world.

Celia Fiennes came to Newcastle and Gateshead on a hot Saturday in July 1698. As she approached from the west she noticed the coal pits all around. It was 'a noble town, though in a bottom, most resembling London of any place in England, its buildings lofty and large of brick or stone'. She was impressed by the system of conduits and fountains that supplied fresh water, by the broad, handsome and well pitched streets, by the Guildhall, by the Key and the shops and markets (it was market day) where she lingered in the shade because of the extreme heat. She took in the pleasure gardens and the curiosities in the barber-surgeons hall. She admired St Nicholas' Church, noted the ruin of the castle and commented on the number of ships in the river. She crossed the bridge, 'with 9 arches all built on as London bridge is, which enters you into the Diocese of Durham'. On the Durham side of the bridge, she remarked that there

> Are so many streets and buildings, just like Southwark. Its a little town, but is all in the Liberty of the County town of New-Castle and so called, but it is in the diocese of Durham. Through part of this you do ascend to a great height and steepness which is full of rocky stone steps and afterwards the hill continues when out of the town.[47]

Celia neither heard the name of Gateshead mentioned nor realised that it was a separate town. Had Newcastle informants misled her? As far as this early visitor was concerned, NewcastleGateshead already existed by 1700.

---

[46]   See above, pp.272-4; Ellis, Joyce, 'A dynamic society: social relations in Newcastle upon Tyne, 1660-1760', in Clark, Peter (ed.), *The Transformation of English Provincial Towns, 1600-1800* (1984), p.196; King, Rebecca, 'The Sociability of the Trade Guilds of Newcastle and Durham, 1660-1750', in Berry, Helen and Gregory, Jeremy (eds), *Creating and Consuming Culture in North-east England* (2004), pp.57-72; Berry, Helen, 'Creating Polite Space: the Organisation and Social Function of the Newcastle Assembly Rooms', in Berry and Gregory, *Creating and Consuming Culture*, pp.121-2. We are grateful to Dr Fred Milton for information on the early history of coffee houses in Newcastle and Gateshead.

[47]   Morris, *Journey of Celia Fiennes*, pp.210-11. In the passage on Gateshead, Fiennes confuses the diocese and the bishopric. However, she began her description by stating that 'Newcastle is a town and a county of itself standing part in Northumberland part in the Bishoprick of Durham, the river Tyne being the division'.

I

Newcastle and Gateshead before A.D. 1080

D.H. HESLOP

The Prehistoric Period

The most recent comprehensive account of the origins of Newcastle confidently opens:

> THE HISTORY of Newcastle upon Tyne began, over 1800 years ago, with the building of a bridge across the river by the Romans in the reign of the Emperor Hadrian.[1]

Urban development certainly starts in the second century A.D., but was there no activity of importance here in prehistory? Certainly, the catalogue of prehistoric finds from Newcastle and Gateshead isn't extensive. There are less than a dozen objects spanning the period from the Neolithic to the end of the Iron Age. Many of these are stray finds, without detailed contextual information, and none are securely related to a contemporary settlement site. Given the nature of the evidence, much of what can be said is, of necessity, inference, but, by fitting what little we do know into the wider picture of prehistoric research, we start to see glimpses of economic and religious practices associated with the river/ roadway nexus, that help explain the trajectories of later development. Central to the argument is the suggestion that the Great North Road, known to have been in use from the Middle Ages, is of considerably greater antiquity.

The reasoning used here is an argument by extension. Looking south, Blaise Vyner has argued that the line of the A1 through Durham and Yorkshire links a series of Neolithic (4200-1800 B.C.) ceremonial enclosures positioned at crossing points on the major east-west flowing rivers of the Pennine dales.[2] The modern road, he suggests, has ancient antecedents. Prehistoric routes of this sort were

[1]   Middlebrook, S., *Newcastle upon Tyne: Its Growth and Achievement* (1950), p.6.
[2]   Vyner, B.E., 'A Great North Route in Neolithic and Bronze Age Yorkshire: The Evidence of Landscape and Monuments', in *Landscapes*, 69 (2007).

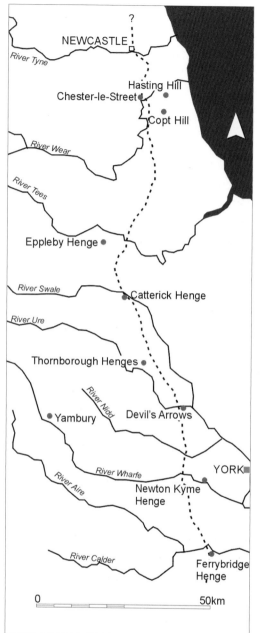

fundamentally important features of the landscape, facilitating the congregation of a widely spread population, in the numbers needed to construct and populate the Neolithic monuments on the Aire (Ferrybridge henge), Wharfe (Newton Kyme henge), Ure (Devil's Arrows and Thornbrough henges), Swale (Catterick henge), Tees (Eppleby henge) and Wear (Chester-le-Street ?Neolithic enclosure). Bradley and Edmonds point out the role of these monuments in facilitating exchange of exotic items procured from considerable distances,[3] in this case Great Langdale polished axes from the Lake District which cross the Pennines and spread across the North East and Yorkshire.

Vyner goes on to suggests that the sequence of congregational monuments should continue north, with a further example awaiting discovery (or having been destroyed) on the banks of the Tyne at Newcastle/ Gateshead.[4] Within Tyne and Wear, a parallel north-south routeway linking the Neolithic complexes at Copt Hill[5] and Hastings Hill[6] later became the A19; the difficulties of crossing the Wear are noted and led to the establishment of an ancient ferry at Hylton.

While it is true that we have not discovered a major Neolithic monument on the north

10   The prehistoric route to Newcastle (after Vyner, 2007).

    [3]   Bradley, R. and Edmonds, M., 'Interpreting the Axe Trade: Production and Exchanger in Neolithic Britain' (1993).
    [4]   Vyner, B.E., *The Tyne Gorge Study* (2003), 13.
    [5]   Tyne and Wear Historic Environment Record (hereafter T&WHER), 100. The reports are available on line at www.twsitelines.info.
    [6]   T&WHER, 109.

side of the Tyne at Newcastle or on the south side near Gateshead, such a discovery in the future is not impossible; a banked and ditched enclosure of comparable size, but of Bronze-Age date, was recently found beneath the former Vaux Brewery site on the south side of the River Wear in Sunderland.[7] This came to light through the routine application of archaeological reconnaissance techniques on a development site. There remains much to be discovered.

In later prehistory, and particularly the late Bronze Age (1100-700 B.C.), our principal source of information comes in the form of finds from the river and its tributaries. There has been much discussion about the meaning of prehistoric metal objects that have been found in rivers and other wet places.[8] Single finds have usually been explained as losses of one sort or another, perhaps during fighting, in the case of weapons, as casual accidental loss for ornaments, or, in the case of finds recovered from river gravels, as a component of ballast brought here by colliers from the Thames or one of the North Sea ports. At this distance in time it is impossible to discount these possibilities, but recent research has highlighted the very restricted chronological span of the objects and the narrow range of artefact types that have come from rivers, marshlands and bogs. Major rivers, like the Thames, tend to produce huge numbers of objects, many in a condition that shows they were not broken or worn-out with use.[9] The balance of evidence would lead us to argue that the objects were deliberately deposited without the intention of subsequent recovery. The possibility that votive deposition of weaponry may have continued into the Middle Ages is now widely recognised.[10] The River Tyne, as a major arterial route inland, a possible boundary between tribal groupings and, within the belief systems of the period, as a sentient, active entity in its own right, appears to have been the focus of ceremonial activity by communities gathering here from considerable distances.

The Late Bronze Age was an era of major change.[11] The Late Bronze Age was an era of major change. The period saw a radical alteration in the character of settlements, and the development of new forms of buildings and agricultural

[7] T&WHER, 7111.
[8] For example Bradley, R., *The Passage of Arms: an archaeological analysis of prehistoric hoard and votive deposits* (1990), p.99.
[9] Needham, S. and Burgess, C., 'The Late Bronze Age in the Thames Valley: the metalwork evidence', in Barrett J. and Bradley, R. (eds), *Settlement and Society in the Late Bronze Age*, BAR, British Series, 83 (1980), pp.437-69.
[10] Stoker, D. with Evison, P., 'The Straight and Narrow Way. Fenland Causeways and the conversion of the landscape in the Witham Valley, Lincolnshire', in Carver, M. (ed.), *The Cross Goes North. Process of Conversion in Northern Europe, A.D. 300-1300* (Woodbridge, 1980), p.271.
[11] Barrett, J. and Bradley, R. (eds), *The British Later Bronze Age*, British Archaeological Reports, 83 (Oxford, 1980).

systems which continue through the first millennium B.C. until the dislocations arising from the Roman Occupation. In the north, there seems to have been an increase in long distance exchange and a rise in the total number of metal objects in circulation. While settlements and objects are more common, there is a significant decrease in the number of burials known from this period. Instead of the practice of interment of the body into the ground, either as an inhumation in a cist or as a cremation with the ashes being placed in a funerary urn, human remains are disposed of in an archaeologically unrecognisable way. Instead, we see a recurring pattern of metalwork deposition in watery places. It is possible that the metalwork offerings accompanied a new burial rite, which saw the final act of disposal taking place within the river.[12]

The majority of objects recovered from the river, where records are precise, are described as being dredged from the Tyne. Looking at numbers alone, the River Tyne seems to have been the pre-eminent location for such ceremonies in Northern England; there are more bronze swords recovered from the Tyne than any other river in England, except the Thames and the Witham.[13] The concentration of votive objects from the Tyne at Newcastle/Gateshead suggest that the area between the suggested major river crossing and the King's Meadow island, at Elswick, was a place of congregation for ritual ceremonies from at least 1000 B.C. The concentration of objects around the small island of the King's Meadow has parallels at Runnymede on the Thames.[14] At just over a half a mile from the bridging point, the island may well have been visible from the point where the ancient Great North Road dropped into the river gorge from the higher ground on each side.

Another group of finds in the archaeological record may also fit into this picture. Again, mostly recovered in the late 19th century and again from riverine contexts, we have records relating to the discovery of four dugout canoes or log boats from this stretch of the Tyne and its tributaries. Where dates are available for this type of vessel, they tend to be of the Iron Age.[15] Their presence in former water channels is rarely questioned, the unstated assumption being that the vessels sunk while in use. However, at Fiskerton in Lincolnshire on the River Witham, two log boats, one unused, were found at a major ceremonial

[12]   Willis, S., 'Sea, coast, estuary and culture in Iron Age Britain', in Haselgrove, C. and Moore, T. (eds), *The Earlier Iron Age in Britain and the near Continent* (Oxford, 2007), p.118.
[13]   Cowan, J.D., 'The Hallstadt Sword of Bronze: on the Continent and in Britain', *Proceedings of the Prehistoric Society*, 33 (1967), Map B.
[14]   For Stuart Needham's excavations at Egham-Runnymede for the British Museum, see *Exploring Surrey's Past* (www.exploringsurreypast.org.uk).
[15]   For a review of 14th-century dating evidence of UK log boats, see McGrail, S., 'Celtic seafaring and transport' in Green, M. (ed.), *The Celtic World* (2004), pp.254-81.

11 'The King's Meadow Island in the River Tyne, from the Great North Road, Felling Moor, Gateshead.

focus for votive offerings, deposited into the river from a specially constructed timber platform.[16] Willis[17] has recently questioned the excavators' explanation for the sinking of the Hasholme log boat in East Yorkshire[18] by suggesting that it too was a votive offering: the bow pointing to the nearby settlement and the upright vessel being surrounded at bow and stern by prime joints of beef. The forensic aspects of the discoveries are significant; tree trunks frequently fall into rivers and become embedded in the silts of the river bed, but their presence in the river is time-limited by the destructive action of water and biological

[16] Field, N. and Parker Pearson, M., *Fiskerton: An Iron Age Timber Causeway with Iron Age and Roman Votive Offerings* (2003).
[17] Willis, 'Sea, coast, estuary and culture', p.117.
[18] Millett, M. and McGrail, S., 'The Archaeology of the Hasholme Logboat', *Archaeological Journal*, 144 (1987), pp.69-155.

agents. For the log boats to have survived, they need to be buried in anaerobic conditions, beneath the horizon where the timber would naturally have decayed. The explanation for the survival of the boats may be because they were buried in the stream bed when the streams were dry or much reduced by seasonal droughts, and that the act of burial was a votive offering in the same tradition as the deposition of metal objects in the preceding Bronze Age.

Of the examples found at Newcastle and Gateshead, the boat from Westgate Road is from a stream that was never navigable in any practical sense, being at the top of a steep bank on the level plateau above the river gorge; the channel here was no more than a gutter in the medieval town. Found in 1889, during the building work at the Westgate Road Post Office, the vessel was small (8.2 feet long and 3.2 feet deep) and contained or was associated with animal remains, including a skull and several horns.[19] The exact location was described in 1929 as near 'a very deep hollow ... in the back street south of the General Post Office and on the west side of St Nicholas Buildings'.[20] In this instance, the vessel may well have had to be carried to its final destination, which was important for other reasons, one of which may have been the immediate proximity to the ancient Great North Road. In the Iron Age, the selection of the object (a mode of transport) and the precise location (the tributary to the main river), as at Ryton, Derwent Haugh, and Blaydon Haugh, would be appropriate to ceremonies stressing the transforming property of the river and its cosmological position as being between the everyday world and the realm of the gods and spirits.

Moving on to the following period, objects of Roman date are also known from the river at the crossing point, prominent among which are the two famous altars in the Museum of Antiquities; one is to *Oceanus*, the other to *Neptune*.[21] Roman belief followed the Greek tradition that *Okeanos* was the river-stream that encircled and flowed below the known world. It was common to make offerings to this deity when beginning or ending a sea journey. *Neptune* was the Romanised *Poseidon*, a sea god usually associated with the inner seas, e.g. the Mediterranean, or fresh, as opposed to salt, water. This pair of altars are usually described as having fallen into the river from a shrine on or near the Roman bridge, the *Pons Aelius*.[22] We might wonder, in an area where the river bed has been reduced by about ten feet across the width of the channel, if the only remains of the bridge recovered are these two small altars what happened to the rest of the

[19]   *The Antiquary* (1889).
[20]   *North of England Excavation Committee Report* (1935), p.8.
[21]   Smith, D.J., *Museum of Antiquities, Newcastle upon Tyne: An Illustrated Introduction* (Newcastle, 1974), pp.9 and 20.
[22]   T&WHER, 1462, 1463.

stone structure? However, for present purposes, we can suggest that the tradition of votive offerings into the river continues into the Roman period, when the artefact range broadens to include metal vessels, and the motivation reflects the then current concerns of propitiation and requests for divine intervention.

The suggestion that an early Roman road crossed the Tyne here is put forward by Paul Bidwell, in his recent review of the geography of the Conquest period.[23] The traditional view of early military displacements on the frontier has nothing east of the Stanegate/Dere Street link, but Bidwell makes the compelling case that there must have been some secure link between the River Tyne estuary and the interior garrison. He argues for a pre-Hadrianic date for the road from Brough on Humber to Newcastle (Margery Route 806), the fort at South Shields (*Arbeia*) and the branch road that links a supply base here and Chester-le-Street, the Wrekendike. A contemporary Tyne crossing was defended by an as yet unlocated fort at Gateshead.[24] The suggestion made here is that not only did Margery 806 follow a much older route but that the location of the military presence was deliberately sited at an ancestral gathering place and cult focus. This helps explain the tactical weaknesses of the location of the later (late second/early third century) fort at the Castle Garth,[25] in the same way that the legionary base at Lincoln is now believed to have been deliberately positioned on the ground overlooking the Brayford Pool Iron-Age ceremonial site on the River Witham.[26] The parallels between Newcastle/Gateshead and Lincoln are striking – the Witham/Tyne parallel, the Jurassic Way/Great North Road parallel and the fact that in both cases the Roman presence was positioned where the ceremonial and religious centres were located, not where the population was concentrated, or where tribal authorities were found. Here, the cold logic of the siting of the military base is most apparent; in the absence of existing population centres, or, even, within a poorly organised and weakly centralised population, places of particular tribal authority, the best way of imposing military power was to appropriate and dominate the religious centre of gravity of the area.

What evidence is there for settlement on the agricultural land above the river? In 2001, excavations on High Bridge uncovered the remains of a round-house, dated by radio carbon to the late Bronze Age – the first evidence of occupation in the town before the arrival of the Romans.[27] The find was at the base of a

[23]   Bidwell, P. and Snape. M., 'The History and Setting of the Roman Fort at Newcastle upon Tyne', *AA*, 5th series, 31 (2002), p.257.
[24]   Breeze, D.J., *The Antonine Wall* (Edinburgh, 2006), Map 4.1.
[25]   Bidwell and Snape, 'History and Setting', pp.254, 257.
[26]   Stocker, D. (ed.), '"The City by the Pool" Assessing the archaeology of the city of Lincoln', *Lincoln Archaeological Studies*, 10 (2003), p.54.
[27]   Brogan, G., 'Excavations at High Bridge, Newcastle', *AA*, forthcoming.

long and complex sequence of later deposits, separated from the main medieval levels by a thick spread of dark soil interpreted as a plough-soil horizon. The palynological examination of samples from this layer produced evidence of an open, agricultural environment, quite different from the intensively managed ecology of the medieval urban landscape. It may be no more than coincidence that the roundhouse was found adjacent to Pilgrim Street, i.e. on the Great North Road, but it is possible that the course of the ancient route is making itself known through the discovery of settlement along its line. The single prehistoric house at High Bridge is not much of a return from over 150 excavations within Newcastle and Gateshead, a cumulative weight of negative evidence that surely demonstrates there was no large degree of settlement here.

Slightly further afield, the last decade has seen a transformation in our knowledge of Iron-Age settlement in the region. At East and West Brunton, five miles north of the river, a sequence familiar to archaeologists saw unenclosed agglomerations of circular buildings become overlain by the ditched enclosures that define individual farmsteads. The site has not been fully analysed yet, but elsewhere this change can be dated to the last two centuries before the Roman Conquest.[28] In the late Iron Age, the population was expanding and the landscape was becoming increasingly cleared of woodland. A mixed agricultural regime grew the early wheat species, emmer and spelt, and both cattle and sheep were herded, the latter being more important in the diet.[29] The evidence from this and other sites in southern Northumberland must fill in the gaps in our knowledge for the area of the city limits.

The Roman Age

If we know little of the late prehistoric exploitation of the riversides, our understanding of the Roman presence on Tyneside has been transformed in the last decade by the discovery of major new Roman sites at both Gateshead and Newcastle. Dating to the early to mid-second century A.D., a roadside ribbon development straggled the sloping ground to the west of Bottle Bank, Gateshead, the presumed line of the bridge approach, although frontage cellaring destroyed the chance to examine that suggestion on this site. On present evidence, this settlement is earlier than any known occupation on the north side of the river.[30] It seems unlikely that there was no Roman presence at such a

[28]   Heslop, D.H., *Excavations at Thorpe Thewles, Cleveland*, CBA Research Report, 65 (1987), p.112.
[29]   Van der Veen, M., *Crop Husbandry Regimes: An archaeobotanical study of farming in Northern England 1000 B.C. – 500 AD* 1992, Sheffield Archaeological Monograph, 3 (1992), p.8.
[30]   *Excavations at Bottle Bank, Gateshead*, Oxford Archaeology North, forthcoming.

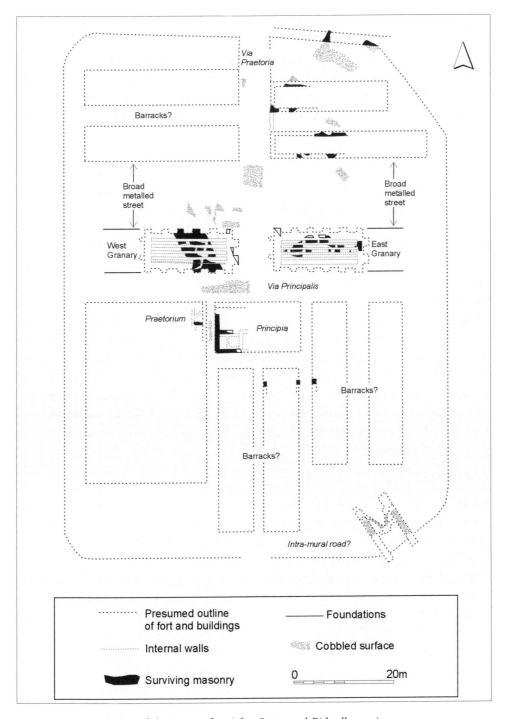

Via
Praetoria

Barracks?

Broad
metalled
street

Broad
metalled
street

West
Granary

East
Granary

Via Principalis

Praetorium

Principia

Barracks?

Barracks?

Intra-mural road?

Presumed outline of fort and buildings	Foundations
Internal walls	Cobbled surface
Surviving masonry	0 20m

12 A projected plan of the Roman fort (after Snape and Bidwell, 2007).

strategically important location on the north bank, but any such presence remains unlocated. The final phase of activity before the construction of the Roman fort may relate to buildings of an earlier date in the vicinity, perhaps associated with the traces of agricultural activity – ard (plough tip) marks, narrow rig and furrow and field boundaries – which underlay the Roman buildings.

Recent publication of the excavations on the fort beneath the medieval castle has provided a detailed understanding of the history of the site and here only the briefest summary is needed.[31] The construction of the fort, and the associated development of the *vicus* settlement, are dated to the later second or early third century. An inscription to Empress Julia Domna, the wife of Septimus Severus, that had been re-used as a threshold slab, shows that the fort was built by A.D. 213.[32] Within the 10 per cent of the interior that has been excavated, parts of a small *principia* (headquarters building) were revealed, along with the corner of the adjacent commanding officer's house (the *praetorium*), two small granaries and a series of buildings that may have been narrow barracks but are thought more likely to have been workshops. Within the restricted area available for excavation, it was not possible to establish the shape or size of the fort, but the limitations of the site suggest that an irregular plan was chosen, to allow sufficient internal area to take the unit mentioned on the Julia Domna stone, *the cohors I Cugernorum*. The reconstruction in the report has truncated corners on the eastern side, where the promontory slopes steeply to the river.[33] With almost none of the fort wall having been observed, it is possible that the plan was polygonal in plan form, like the Hadrianic fort of Bewcastle.[34] The observed portion, on the north-west side, is not quite on the same alignment as the recorded principal buildings, and the fact that the Wall here lacks the usual earthen or clay rampart suggests that compromises were made to accommodate the installation onto the narrow promontory. Building work, for example, re-paving the *principia*, continued until late in the fourth century, but as with most forts along the wall, there is great uncertainty as to the circumstances of the abandonment of the site by the army early in the fifth century.

Perhaps the most striking feature of the fort is the evidence for its use as a market in the period between about A.D. 270 and 360.[35] Commercial activity is known within military instillations across the later Empire, but at Newcastle this appears to have been incorporated into the architecture of the interior, with the

[31] Bidwell and Snape, 'Roman Fort'.
[32] Daniels, C.M., and Harbottle, B., 'A new inscription of Julia Domna from Newcastle', *AA*, 5th series, 8 (1980), pp.65-73.
[33] Bidwell and Snape, 'Roman Fort', Fig. 6.
[34] Breeze, D.J., *The Handbook of Hadrian's Wall*, 14th edn (2006), pp.146, 97.
[35] Bidwell and Snape, 'Roman Fort', pp.275-7.

space between the northern sector (barracks and workshop) and the granaries being occupied by a broad street or open space. This may have initially occurred because planned barracks or granaries in the northern part of the fort were not constructed, and the resulting space was metalled and used as an assembly area for the cohort, and then, in later years, as a public open space. Interestingly, the spread of small-change coinage, which is the main evidence for commercial activity within the interior, is absent from this space, but concentrated in areas to the north and south, even within the narrow lane between the *principia* and *praetorium*. Perhaps the assembly area retained its military significance, with its panoply of military standards and altars, and the booths and stalls of the market traders were restricted to the spaces on either side. Bidwell suggests that the importance of the location, on the north-south road and at the north end of the *Pons Aelius*, accounts for the presence of a market here.[36] Alternatively, one might suggest, this is one of the Roman manifestations of the long tradition of congregation at the Tyne crossing.

A number of small-scale development-led excavations within the ancient core of the town have added to our knowledge of the geography of the Roman settlement at Newcastle, but much remains uncertain. To supplement the discovery of the milecastle under the Arts Centre on Westgate Road in 1985,[37] the Wall and associated defensive entanglements have been found in a good state of preservation beneath an early 20th-century building, the former Coopers Auction Mart, at the eastern end of Westgate Road, close to the castle.[38] From this point, however, the course of the Imperial Frontier is not known. Two possibilities should be considered: the north wall of the fort, somewhere around the position of the Black Gate, was built onto the Wall, perhaps replacing an existing turret or milecastle, and Hadrian's Wall then plunged down the precipice to the east, in the vicinity of, or even being the precursor of, the Dog Leap Stairs; or, the Wall avoided the steeper gradients on the east side of the Castle Garth promontory by taking a more northerly line down the slope of the Side.

As Newcastle was the only fort to be placed on the line of the Wall in the third century, there are no parallels elsewhere on the frontier to assist interpretation here, where the evidence is lost or currently inaccessible. Of the two possibilities, the latter is the most likely; two or three generations before the fort was constructed, there seems no reason to take the Wall up onto the Castle

---

[36]   *Ibid.*, 277.
[37]   Harbottle, B., Fraser, R. and Burton, F.C., 'The Westgate Road Milecastle, Newcastle upon Tyne', *Britannia* 19 (1988), pp.153-62.
[38]   McKelvey, J., Jazdzejewski, L. and Garrett, F., *Former Hertz Building, 14-18 Westgate Road, Newcastle upon Tyne* (Tyne & Wear Museums, 2004), p.10.

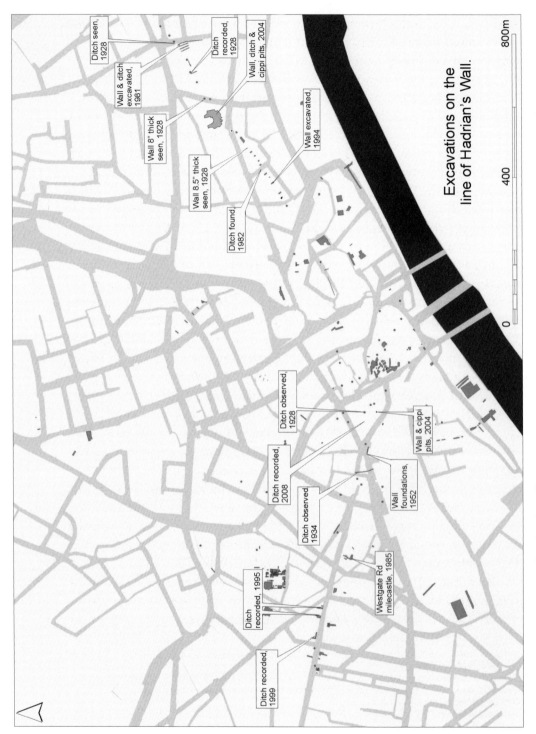

Ditch seen, 1928

Wall & ditch excavated, 1981

Ditch recorded, 1928

Wall, ditch & cippi pits, 2004

Wall 8" thick seen, 1928

Wall 8.5" thick seen, 1928

Ditch found 1982

Wall excavated, 1994

Ditch observed, 1928

Ditch recorded, 2008

Wall & cippi pits, 2004

Wall foundations, 1952

Ditch observed 1934

Westgate Rd milecastle, 1985

Ditch recorded, 1995

Ditch recorded, 1999

Excavations on the line of Hadrian's Wall.

800m

400

0

13   Excavations on the line of Hadrian's Wall.

Garth. As the other sides have very steep slopes, the north gate of the fort was the most logical choice for the principal entrance; if the Wall was attached, to progress south would require moving along the north side of the Wall and then passing through again to turn south across the river.

Nothing has been learnt in recent years of the progress of the Wall as it climbed back up to the high ground on the far side of the City Road, where foundations of the curtain were recorded in 1994 at Garth Heads.[39] In the 1,607 feet between Garth Heads and the fort, there have been no evaluations more recent than Peter Clack's 1974 trenches on Silver Street, which failed to find evidence of the Wall, which he placed between Silver Street and the Pilgrim Street roundabout.[40] The 1929 sightings of the Wall ditch with Roman pottery at Painterheaugh (where the railway viaduct crosses the Central Motorway) would conform with a line that stays to the high ground along the City Road, as did the medieval Town Wall, 1,200 years later. Further east, at Melbourne Street, an excavation beneath a modern garage in 2004 uncovered a 43-feet length of curtain wall.[41] In common with all recent sightings of the Wall on Tyneside, the site produced evidence of the presence of entanglement pits, *cippi* pits, on the berm (ledge) between the curtain wall and the defensive ditch.

How the putative road to the north fitted into this pattern is uncertain; there may have been an existing gate through the Wall at a turret which was replaced by the fort,[42] or it may have had its own gate which ignored the spacings of the fortifications, as at Portgate, where Dere Street (present A68) passed through a large gate between Milecastle 22 and Turret 22a.[43] Another area of uncertainty east of the fort is how the Wall linked to the bridge head. As the Wall originally started at *Pons Aelius*, there should be some sort of commemorative monument at the junction between Wall and bridge. This may have been located on the north-south route, the Margery 806/Great North Road. The ground to the north of the Wall would appear to have been open fields. The small amounts of abraded Romano-British pottery that occurs in later deposits is consistent with manuring the fields with refuse from settlement south of the Wall.[44]

On the other side of Westgate Road from the Wall recorded at Cooper's Auction Mart, evaluation within the rail arches in 2004 uncovered metalled and paved surfaces, structural remains and a comparatively large quantity of

---

[39] Nolan, J., *Garth Heads Industrial Dwellings, Newcastle upon Tyne: An Archaeological Evaluation* (City of Newcastle upon Tyne Archaeology Unit, 1994).

[40] Clack, P.A.G., 'Silver Street, Newcastle upon Tyne', *Archaeological Newsbulletin for CBA3*, 8 (1974), pp.2-3.

[41] Platell, A., *Newcastle, Melbourne Street* (Archaeological Services Durham University, 2004).

[42] Bidwell and Snape, 'Roman Fort', p.254.

[43] Breeze, *Hadrian's Wall*, pp.184-5.

[44] Peter Bidwell, personal communication.

second- and third-century pottery. The metalling aligns with the broad street identified within the fort and, so close to Hadrian's Wall, might equate with the Military Road, which ran along the frontier in the space between the Wall and the *Vallum* ditch. The closest sighting of the Military Road was at Pendower Hall, Benwell, in 2004, where the road was located 86 feet south of the curtain wall;[45] this is approximately the distance between the metalled surfaces in the railway arches and the line of the Wall as recorded at Cooper's, if it follows the predicted line. The structures opposite Cooper's appear to have been part of the civilian settlement, the *vicus*. This site will not lead to further excavation as the proposed new development can be achieved without further damage to these nationally important deposits, but opportunities for archaeological excavation did occur in 2008 next to the Hanover Street Methodist Church (latterly the British Electrical Manufacturing Company Building), where Harbottle recorded Roman post holes and deposits in 1965 and 1967.[46] The results of the recent excavations fully justified the belief of the city planning archaeologist that this was a key site in the historic core. It revealed exceptionally well-preserved remains of the civilian settlement in the shadow of the fort.

Evidence was recovered of both *vicus* buildings and burial plots. The open area excavation was bisected by a metalled road, 16 feet wide, flanked by substantial ditches, very necessary as the subsoil is a dense clay prone to waterlogging. The road is aligned roughly north-south, and may have run to the west gate of the fort, some 490 feet to the north-east, on the far side of the railway lines. To the west of the road, the land was divided into a number of tenements occupied by rectangular strip buildings, metalled yards, rubbish pits, wells and areas of industrial activity. One of the boundary ditches contained the broken topstone of a Mayan lava quern which, along with the majority of the pottery, would have come on to the site through the military supply network.

On the eastern side of the road, the land was free of buildings, being laid out as the burial plot of a Roman family. Two stone coffins were exposed, their position in the stratigraphy showing that the lids were meant to be seen on the surface, but the crispness of the stone carving would suggest that the grass sward covered the lids before too long. Two similar coffins were found in 1903 when the adjoining building, the Turnbull Warehouse, was constructed. Three of the four had coped lids and all were of fine quality sculpture but without

---

45   Frain, T., *Pendower Hall, Newcastle upon Tyne* (Tyne & Wear Museums, 2004), p.8.
46   Harbottle, B., 'Excavations at the Carmelite Friary, Newcastle upon Tyne, 1965 and 1967', *AA*, 4th series, 46 (1968), pp.163-218.

further decoration. One of the 1903 pair contained a Roman ceramic urn (Castor ware beaker), and charcoal.[47] Osteological preservation was very poor in all four burials, while one of the 2008 coffins had a fine Whitby jet pin and a single glass bead. It is likely that the individuals represented here are the family of one of the senior officials in the Roman Army, possibly that of the fort commander. The site also produced urned cremations. These were not grouped apart from the buildings, as the inhumations appear to have been, but were within the tenements of the properties, but whether they pre-date, were contemporary with, or post-date the *vicus* buildings is uncertain at the time of writing.

The construction of the Gateshead Hilton triggered extensive excavation across the backlands of medieval tenements aligned onto Bottle Bank. Evaluation in 1994 showed that Roman deposits survived in those areas where the terracing of the slope had led to the build-up of soil horizon, and these were more fully explored in 2000 when an area of around 7,990 square feet were uncovered.[48] This was sufficiently large to reveal the layout of the Romano-British landscape, on the slope above the waterfront, but across the river from the fort and so outside the direct control of the garrison commander.

A small quantity of pottery of pre-Hadrianic date (late first to very early second century A.D.) indicates some activity in the vicinity, but no substantial occupation in the area excavated. The settlement that developed in the early-mid second century is best described as a ribbon development laid out along the road to the river crossing, presumably an earlier manifestation of Bottle Bank. Fragmentary traces of tenements defined by ditched boundaries marked out a series of rectangular plots, several of which were furnished with substantial water cisterns, one containing a broken altar base. These resemble the allotment ditches of broadly similar date recorded below the fort in the Castle Garth.[49] A broadly similar layout of Romano-British tenements fronting onto a highway, with large cistern-like pits in the corner of the rear tenements, has recently been excavated at East Field, Sedgefield, County Durham.[50] Here the dominant economic activity was not agriculture, but craft industries, including pottery making, as discovered by Time Team in their 2002 programme on the site. At Bottle Bank, the long narrow buildings were linked to a number of metalworking hearths. The occupants of both the Sedgefield and the Gateshead sites were producing goods for a market economy, stimulated, in the early period at least, by the substantial military presence in the region.

---

[47] Rich, F.W., 'Two Stone Coffins of the Roman Period', *AA*, 2nd series, 25 (1904), pp.147-9.
[48] 'Excavations at Bottle Bank', *AA*, forthcoming.
[49] Phase 4 (Snape and Bidwell, 'Roman Fort', p.20).
[50] *Archaeology, County Durham* (Durham County Council, 2007).

In the south-west part of the site, a small length of Roman paved road was uncovered, which ran down the slope at an angle, and aligns roughly with the medieval Murk Lane.[51] This cannot have been the main route down to the bridgehead, as it was not constructed until the third century A.D.; it probably represents one of a number of subsidiary roads and tracks that divided the landscape into farms and estates in this period. How long the settlement at Gateshead lasted is not certain; the occupants were certainly not using pottery from markets that supplied Romano-British ceramics much into the fourth century. There are no instances of the discovery of architectural fragments, inscriptions or tombstones from Gateshead to support the notion that the settlement developed urban characteristics. In common with all of the other excavated civilian settlements servicing Wall forts, with the exception of Housesteads, it probably declined from about A.D. 270.[52] The fort at *Pons Aelius* may have post-dated it by a century, or a little longer; as Snape and Bidwell have concluded, 'for how long after A.D. 400 occupation continued is a question which, as at most Wall sites, can never be fully answered'.[53]

The Post-Roman Period

As the Imperial presence fades and then disappears, so too does the archaeological evidence. It is impossible to follow the history of the settlements at either end of the bridge from physical remains revealed by excavation, a problem not specific to Tyneside. What happened in the fifth century? It is possible that the auxiliary units that guarded the frontier in the late Roman period slowly evolved into the early medieval warbands that became the political authorities of the late fifth and sixth centuries A.D., sometimes occupying the former Imperial military installations, as at Birdoswald[54] and possibly South Shields and Benwell, but remaining entirely local in composition and cultural identity. The character of that identity has become the subject of considerable debate in the past decade. The certainties of Bede, who unequivocally proclaimed the Anglian origin of the Northumbrian nation, have been questioned on a number of fronts.

The traditional model of a widespread replacement of an indigenous, 'Celtic' population by Anglo-Saxon immigrants has been largely discredited. An alternative

---

[51] *Excavations at Bottle Bank.*
[52] Breeze (2006), p.84.
[53] Bidwell and Snape, 'Roman Fort', p.280.
[54] Wilmott, T., 'The Late Roman Transition at Birdoswald on Hadrian's Wall', in Wilmott and Wilson, P. (eds), *The Late Roman Transition in the North*, BAR British Series, 299 (1999), p.17.

14 'Goatshead Monastery'; the ruins of St Edmund's chapel in 1774, then believed to be the remains of Monkchester, by R.D. Godfrey.

model which would require the immigration of a much smaller number of elite warriors and religious leaders has now largely replaced the 'extinction' theory. An argument has recently been developed by Lovelock in which the transition is seen in terms of a 'native British' indigenous population copying 'immigrant Anglo-Saxon' elites, to the extent of adopting a new language, to 'maintain and enhance social position in the new Bernician society'.[55] However, even this degree of Continental, Germanic, cultural imposition probably overstates the true extent of 'foreign' influence. The development of a new archaeology of genetics is in the forefront of this debate.

Stephen Oppenheimer has recently reviewed the biological composition of the modern population of Britain and compared the complex melange of

[55] Loveluck, C., 'Anglo-Saxon Hartlepool and the foundations of English Christian identity: The wider context and the importance of the Monastery', pp.186-208, in Daniels, R., *Anglo-Saxon Hartlepool and the Foundations of English Christianity* (2007), p.187.

genetic traits with that of the other countries of Western Europe.[56] His work stresses the similarity of the populations on either side of the North Sea. There has been a long history of trade, common language and alliance maintained by a tradition of high-status marriage between the peoples of England and north-west Europe. The total amount of new genetic intrusion into England over the past 2,000 years is no more than four per cent. This can be as much accounted for by the influx of individuals and groups during the Romano-British period as after. Oppenheimer's argument has three strands: a significant, long-enduring, Germanic presence on Hadrian's Wall is attested by inscriptions left by auxiliary troops; there is considerable evidence for 'Germanic-looking' settlement in eastern England in the Roman period; and linguistic research suggests that Old English shows connections to the Germanic root language which predate the so-called Anglo-Saxon invasion of the fifth and sixth centuries A.D.[57] He believes that in eastern England, outside the currency of Celtic, Gaelic, the common language had, like the genetic signature, a Germanic character that readily absorbed the small scale, but important, influences from northern Germany and Denmark. In summary, this re-appraisal emphasises the elements of continuity within the archaeological record and re-interprets the 'Germanic' component of cultural identity as springing from deep-seated, indigenous, roots, invigorated by a constant flow of cross-sea contact. The similarities to continental material culture on either side of the North Sea spring not from the introduction of Anglo-Saxon culture into England, but from a common inheritance (including high-status intermarriage) leading to the parallel development of cultural practice and language.

Centres of local power can be glimpsed at the former forts of South Shields (*Arbiea*) and Benwell (*Condercum*), a 'recurrent feature north of the Lune, Eden and Tees valleys' as noted by Loveluck,[58] but the exact character remains elusive. From the fort at Newcastle, there is fragmentary structural evidence of occupation during this period, including water management and ditched boundaries of uncertain function, but there is no clear indication of substantial and enduring construction between A.D. 500 and the establishment of the cemetery *c.*A.D. 800.[59] Surviving the disturbance of the Saxon grave-diggers were short lengths of timber fence/building wall and a scatter of timber post holes, all cutting the demolition rubble. Across the fort, extensive stone robbing occurred, including the removal of almost all of the *principia* strong room masonry, the blocks here being 2 x 1.1 x 1 feet; the stone must have been wanted somewhere close by.

[56]   Oppenhiemer, S., *The Origins of the British*, 2nd edn (2007), p.306.
[57]   *Ibid.*, pp.358, 354.
[58]   Loveluck, 'The wider context', p.189.
[59]   Bidwell and Snape, 'Roman Fort', pp.111-27.

Elsewhere within the bounds of the medieval borough of Newcastle, over 140 excavations have intensively sampled the area, and only one further find of Saxon date has been recorded; a fish weir in the foreshore of the river at the Close. At Gateshead there is nothing that dates to this period.

Moving from the observed to the inferred, on the north bank of the river, 13th-century sources describe an early monastery named 'Monkchester' as being on the site of the 'New Castle'.[60] The absence of any reference in Bede's writings to an ecclesiastical presence here is a strong but far from conclusive argument against a monastic foundation at Newcastle. Allied to this is the lack of monastic sculpture from the castle and the absence, in the areas excavated, of buildings comparable to the well-documented monasteries at Jarrow, Wearmouth and Hartlepool. Although the evidence is presently inconclusive, the balance of the argument rests against the existence of a monastery of any size on the castle promontory. Other interpretations of the post-Roman archaeology are possible; there may have been a short-lived market site on the promontory, following the use established in the Roman period, or there may have been a political meeting place known as a moot- or thing-site.[61]

On the Durham bank, Bede describes one Adda as being the brother of 'Utta ... renowned priest and abbot of Gateshead';[62] with this in mind, undated ditches excavated at Oakwellgate beneath the medieval levels could be interpreted as boundary ditches to a religious site to the east of St Mary's Church,[63] but again, given the almost total lack of any sculptured stone or pre-Conquest human remains, in an area that has seen extensive disturbance in the 19th and 20th centuries, and with an active local antiquarian community keen to record anything that might have been unearthed, the evidence is against there having been a substantial establishment here.

What should not be discounted, however, is the continuing importance of the Tyne as the link between the religious sites in the heart of the Northumbria. We have evidence for a series of ecclesiastical sites along the river: at Tynemouth (late Saxon-period church), South Shields (possible monastery), Jarrow (major monastery), Newcastle (?church and large cemetery) and Gateshead. Upstream, the importance of Bywell (two Saxon churches) and Corbridge continues the chain to Hexham, the major religious focus of the middle Tyne Valley. The act of conversion would involve divesting the river of its ancient properties and powers,

[60]   J. Raine, *Miscellanea Biographica*, Surtees Society, 8 (1838), pp.20-1.
[61]   The evidence for the Castle Garth as a meeting site is discussed at length by Pam Graves in the forthcoming Newcastle Assessment volume, Graves, C.P. and Heslop, D.H., *The Newcastle Urban Assessment*.
[62]   Shirley-Price, I. (ed.), *Bede's A History of the English Church and People* (1968), p.177.
[63]   Nolan, J. and Vaughan, J., 'Excavations at Oakwellgate, Gateshead, 1999', *AA*, 5th Series, 31 (2007), p.160.

15 Roman sarcophagi from Clavering Place, excavated in 2008. (See p.14).

even its role in burial and the transportation of spirits; Christian practice may have made some accommodation with these deep-rooted notions. By the eighth century A.D., when interment into the ground had become the preferred burial rite for a Christian congregation, it was the ruins of the fort, overlooking the river crossing, that was chosen as the location of a major cemetery.[64] It appears that the Lort Burn promontory retained its significance as a religious focus for the dispersed surrounding population.

There is some debate as to what extent the Roman architectural remains – the fort wall, the garrison buildings, and the grid of metalled roads in the interior – were visible over 300 years after the Imperial withdrawal.[65] Whilst it is not possible to accurately locate all of the many antiquarian references to the finding of human bones in the Castle Garth, none of the well-provenanced discoveries are

[64] The full description of the excavation is in press, and so a detailed account is unnecessary here. Harbottle, B. and Nolan, J., 'The Anglo-Saxon Cemetery at Newcastle upon Tyne', *AA* (forthcoming). For other Tyneside sites see T&WHER, 273, 274, 4602.
[65] *Ibid.*

outside the presumed extents of the Roman fort wall. This substantial structure may well have been clearly discernible, if not standing to a significant height. The remembrance of the Roman legacy must have been influential in the selection of this site. Re-interpretation of the fine metalwork from the quintessentially 'Saxon' ship-burial/cenotaph of Sutton Hoo by Filmer-Sankey stress the use of Roman Imperial and consular imagery in the figurative motifs. These are used quite consciously to forge symbolic links between the present and a known and venerated past, in a way that endows the persona of the dead man with the attributes of a Roman emperor.[66] To wrap the dead in the protective arms of the fort ramparts would be to claim sanctuary in a spiritual *Pax Romana*.

Over 600 bodies were recovered among the ruins of the Roman buildings, a sizeable number but only a fraction of the whole, as mentioned above, only 10 per cent of the fort was excavated. Four types of burial furniture were recorded, in addition to the simple grave cut: plank-lined/coffined; burials with head-supports (described as 'ear-muffs' in the literature); rubble-lined graves and, lastly, well made cist burials with slab lids. It is tempting to see the latter as survivals of the North-Eastern tradition of cist burial that stretches back into early prehistory and which is strongly represented from Northumberland to the Peak District between the fifth and seventh centuries A.D., dated by association with pagan grave goods.[67] Here, however, the cists are among the latest in a sequence that stretches into the 12th century A.D., along with burials with head-supports. The densest sections of the cemetery had up to eight levels of burial, and in less densely cut areas there were path-like bands of metalling, which were in turn overlain by rubble spreads cut by later burials.

In addition to the broadly east-west orientation of the interments, fragmentary foundations of a sequence of two possible churches were uncovered, along with the foundations of a further stone building, excavated in 1977 and laid out for display in one of the railway arches, which may have been a Saxon church tower.[68] Of great importance, here, is the interpretation of the status of these buildings; was the church of more than local significance, and how does it relate to the development of the other churches in the later, medieval town? The importance of the building, in ways not immediately apparent from its excavated remains, may have contributed to the decision to site the Norman keep at this location, to complement the defensive and strategic advantages of the hilltop.

[66]   Filmer-Sankey, W., 'The "Roman Emperor" in the Sutton Hoo Ship Burial', *Journal of the British Archaeological Association* (1996), pp.1-9.
[67]   Loveluck, 'The wider context', p.187.
[68]   Harbottle and Nolan, 'Anglo-Saxon Cemetery'.

It is not inconceivable that the events leading to the murder of Bishop Walcher at Gateshead in A.D. 1080, on a site close to the present church of St Mary's, may also have influenced the positioning of the Norman tower on a vantage point that overlooked that scene.[69]

While attempting to review the results of recent research and excavation on the banks of the river, this essay has concentrated on one aspect of that story — how, over the centuries, a tradition of congregation can be glimpsed at this location, and how the cultural and ideological importance of the river crossing as a place of symbolic importance and religious practice supplemented the topographical factors that shaped the development of settlement. A longer history has been glimpsed, and the simple geographic determinism of earlier accounts replaced with a new reading of the importance of landscape in the early history of Newcastle and Gateshead.

[69] Bourne, *Newcastle*, p.168. 'AFTERWARDS this Church [St Mary's] was built, and placed where it now stands: For according to Tradition, it stood before in the Field below where Brick-Kilns now are.'

2

The Medieval Archaeology of Newcastle

BARBARA HARBOTTLE

Early Development

Although the origins of the medieval town of Newcastle are obscure, and it had no obvious beginning, it was probably a thriving settlement by the late 12th century when the castle was rebuilt, and the Burghal Customs written. The core of the town, used by the Romans for their fort, the Saxons for their cemetery and the Normans for their castle, lay on the north bank of the Tyne some 95 feet Ordnance Datum (above mean sea level), or about 69 feet above the water. Here the river was tidal but could be bridged, and reclamation of the flood plain was possible. The river bank was however very steep, and the Side was initially the only access to the upper part of the town for wheeled traffic. Burns plunged south into the Tyne, cutting deep denes through the boulder clay and making east-west movement difficult. But once higher ground was reached the slope northwards became more gradual, and meadows and the common developed to north and west.

Because the location of a pre-Conquest settlement is as yet unknown, the story must start with the foundation of the Norman castle by Robert Curthose in 1080.[1] The site on the headland overlooking the Tyne was chosen for defensive reasons, and with cavalier disregard for its existing use as a cemetery. Though the early defences are not well understood, it is certain that the headland was protected on its north and west sides by a deep ditch, and the excavated material – cemetery soil, remains of Roman structures, and clay subsoil – was spread over the interior, burying the graves but not the church, which was preserved within the defensive circuit. The result may have been a ringwork, rather than a classic motte and bailey, since there is no good evidence for a motte. The original entrance was perhaps on the site of the 'Bailey Gate' near the south-west corner of the 12th-century keep, and approached by the street called Bailey Gate.[2]

---

[1] Arnold, T. (ed.), *Symeon of Durham: Historia Regum*, Rolls Series (1885), p.211.
[2] Longstaffe, W.H.D., 'The New Castle upon Tyne', *AA*, 2nd series, vol.4 (1860), pp.90-9 and plate.

To the Right Worshipful John Erasmus Blackett Esq. Mayor of Newcastle upon Tyne. This VIEW of the RUINS of the BRIDGE of that TOWN, as they appeared after the Fall thereof in November 1771. Is most respectfully Inscribed, by his very obliged and most devoted faithful humble Servant, John Brand October 1772

16 The ruins of the old Tyne Bridge after the flood of 1771.

The second structure of importance in the early development of Newcastle was the bridge, although its date of construction is uncertain. William the Conqueror saw no bridge across the swollen Tyne in 1070-2[3] and, while it seems unlikely that the town remained without a secure river crossing for 100 years, the next suggested date is the latter part of the 12th century. As the chapel at the bridge end was dedicated to St Thomas Becket (d.1170), and so probably built soon after his death, it is thought likely that the bridge itself also dated from this time.[4] It consisted originally of 12 ribbed arches, a tower at each end, the southern one housing a drawbridge, and a third tower in the centre. There were houses and shops on either side of the southern part of the roadway, and on the south side of the central tower was the Blue Stone which marked the boundary between Newcastle and the Palatinate of Durham. The bridge was demolished after it had been irreparably damaged in the great flood of 1771,

3 Raine, J. (ed.), *Miscellanea Biographica*, SS, 8 (1838), pp.20-1.
4 Fraser, C. and Emsley, K., *Tyneside* (1973), p.20.

17   The bailey gate of the New Castle.

and all that now exists is one land arch beneath the northern approach to the Swing Bridge.[5]

The physical development of the town proceeded apace in the 12th century, both northwards away from and also parallel with the river, probably simultaneously. The rate of expansion away from the river was marked by the

⁵   Brand, *Newcastle*, vol.1 (1789), pp.35-49; Bruce, Rev. J.C., 'The Three Bridges over the Tyne at Newcastle', *AA*, 2nd series, vol.10 (1885), pp.1-11, plate opp. p.10; Bidwell, P.T. and Holbrook, N., *Hadrian's Wall Bridges* (English Heritage Archaeological Report no. 9, 1989).

foundation of several notable institutions, their locations being determined by the topography and the beginnings of a street system. The largest, though not necessarily the earliest, of these buildings was the stone castle, begun by Henry II (1168-78) and continued by John and Henry III.[6] The new fortifications consisted of a large rectangular keep surrounded by a bailey wall and external ditch. The wall was equipped with mural towers and posterns and, in 1247-50, provided with a new gate and barbican, the Black Gate.[7]

The next most significant of these 12th-century buildings was the parish church of St Nicholas, which lacks an early reference for its dedication but which contains a few 12th-century architectural fragments, and which probably succeeded the earlier church mentioned above.[8] St Nicholas' was built on rising ground just north of the castle, and occupied a central, indeed a classic, site at the foot of what became the market place. Dependent on it were the three subsidiary, but parochial, churches of St Andrew at the head of the market street, All Hallows (later All Saints') on Pilgrim Street on the east side of the Lort Burn, and St John on the north side of Westgate. While St Andrew's possesses a fine chancel arch of the 12th century,[9] St John's retains only fragments of that date.[10] For All Hallows there is no surviving structural evidence at all, and we must rely on the writings and drawings of 18th- and 19th-century antiquarians.[11] The number of churches, and their relationship to one another, is however unusual. Newcastle is, for example, distinctly different from towns such as York and Lincoln which were well established before the Norman Conquest, and had a multitude of small and independent early churches. At the same time it did not have just a single major parish church, but a complicated arrangement of churches, with their own boundaries and churchyards, administered by chaplains. This arrangement has been said to date from *c.*1220.[12]

The two major medieval hospitals, and the Nunnery of St Bartholomew[13] lying between the market street (*vicus fori*)[14] and the Lort Burn, in this northern

[6]   Colvin, H.M. (ed.), *The History of the King's Works*, vol.2 (1963), pp.745-48.
[7]   Longstaffe, 'The New Castle'; Knowles, W.H., 'The Castle, Newcastle upon Tyne', *AA*, 4th series, vol.2 (1926), pp.1-51; Harbottle, Barbara and Ellison, Margaret, 'An Excavation in the Castle Ditch, Newcastle upon Tyne, 1974-6', *AA*, 5th series, vol.9 (1981), pp.75-250.
[8]   Honeyman, H.L., 'The Cathedral Church of St Nicholas, Newcastle upon Tyne', *AA*, 4th series, vol.9 (1932), pp.96-193.
[9]   Honeyman, H.L., 'The Church of St Andrew, Newcastle upon Tyne', *AA*, 4th series, vol.19 (1941), pp.117-70.
[10]   Knowles, W.H. and Boyle, J.R., *Vestiges of Old Newcastle and Gateshead* (1890), pp.156-7.
[11]   Knowles and Boyle, pp.275-6 and plate.
[12]   Brand, *Newcastle*, p.236, note O.
[13]   *Ibid.*, p.205.
[14]   *Vicus fori* – earliest reference is before 1235, Oliver, A.M. (ed.), *Early Deeds relating to Newcastle upon Tyne*, SS, vol.137 (1924), no. 216.

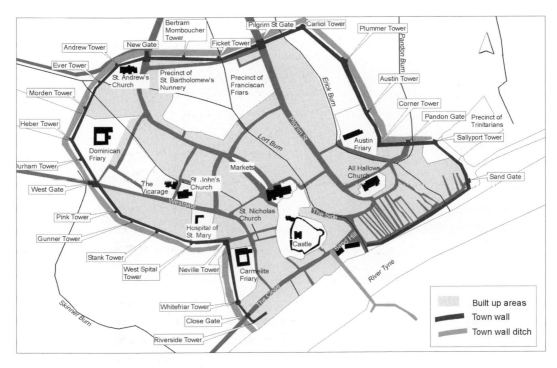

18   The medieval town of Newcastle.

part of the town, which are all believed to be 12th-century, provide three more fixed points in the development of the street system for which there is a dearth of documentary evidence. The main through street was the *vicus peregrinorum*,[15] Pilgrim Street, which ran north past All Hallows to the leper hospital of St Mary Magdalene[16] on the very edge of the town, if not outside it when built. The site was in the vicinity of the 19th-century church of St Thomas. Westgate[17] was the principal route out of the town to the north-west, and was almost certainly following the line of Hadrian's Wall, and its associated road and ditch. Flanking the south side of this street was the 12th-century Hospital of St Mary the Virgin in Westgate.[18]

During the last 10 to 15 years archaeological evidence has been recovered for 12th-century occupation in the upper part of the town. Buildings with domestic or industrial functions have been excavated on such minor streets

---

[15]   *Vicus peregrinorum* – earliest reference is before *c.*1230, Oliver, *Early Deeds*, no. 198.

[16]   *Hospitalis leprosum Sancte Marie Magdalene Novi Castri super Tynam*, said to have been founded by Henry I, i.e. before 1135. Brand, *Newcastle*, pp.424-30.

[17]   *Westgate*, earliest reference is 1251x59, Oliver, *Early Deeds*, no. 135.

[18]   *Hospitalis Sancte Marie Virginis*, founded *c.*1165. Brand, *Newcastle*, vol.1, pp.67-85; Knowles, W.H., 'The Hospital of St Mary the Virgin, Newcastle', *AA*, 2nd series, vol.15 (1892), pp.194-207.

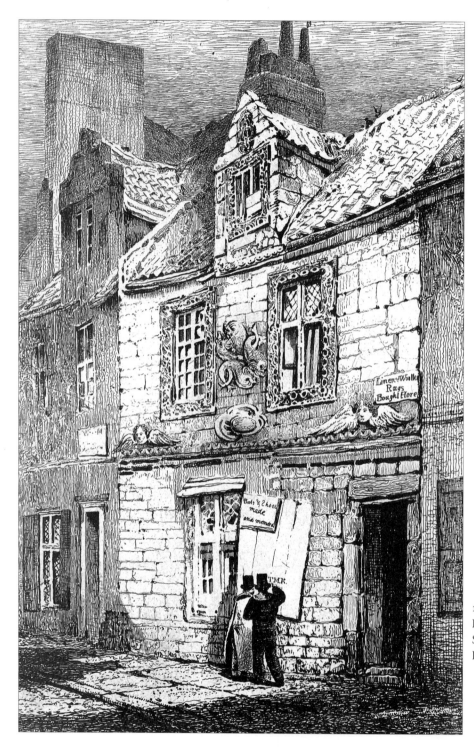

19 Old House,
Low Friar
Street by T.M.
Richardson, snr.

as Pudding Chare[19] and Low Friar Street,[20] both of which probably originated as lanes between burgages. It is suggested that the third site, Wilson's Court between the Groat Market and Pudding Chare, had not been occupied before the 12th century.[21] On the site in Low Friar Street there were two timber houses, subsequently replaced by three, the latter predating the neighbouring Dominican Friary.

The Waterfront

The southern edge of Newcastle was, obviously, marked by the north bank of the Tyne, which was tidal for some miles further upstream. The riverfront of the town in its earliest form, that is between Skinner Burn to the west and Pandon Burn to the east, was a little more than half a mile in length. It was extended eastwards to a little burn called The Swirle in 1299, when Edward I authorised Newcastle to acquire the village of Pandon,[22] and again in 1549 to east of the Ouse Burn when the town absorbed the Ballast Shores, then part of the manor of Byker.[23] These two increments nearly doubled the length of the foreshore under Newcastle's control. Its original appearance was a tidal mudflat of varying widths in front of a steep slope, said to be in places as high as 82 feet, broken by the broad and shallow estuaries of the burns. Without large-scale reclamation, however, the shore was unusable for anything except beaching boats.

The waterfront reclamation has been explored in a number of archaeological excavations of which the most informative were several in the estuary of the Pandon Burn, three above the Tyne Bridge on the Close, and three below the bridge on or near Sandgate. Evidence has been recovered for the date of the work, how the land was stabilised, and then used and re-used, how the later streets were laid out, and how the existence of the bridge resulted in different developments upstream and downstream.

The earliest reclamation so far identified was in the lower reaches of the dene of the Pandon Burn estimated to have been 130 to 160 feet wide and three and five feet deep. Here, in the late 12th century, from north of Stockbridge southwards and from west of the street called Pandon, stone revetments were built to retain dumps of stones, cobbles and flood material, so creating a

---

[19] Tyne & Wear Heritage Environment Record (T&WHER), 2001/9, 13-19, Pudding Chare.
[20] Young, Graeme, 'Excavations carried out at Newgate Street, Newcastle upon Tyne, 1997-2000', *AA*, 5th series, vol.35 (2006), pp.49-82.
[21] T&WHER, 1993/7, Wilson's Court.
[22] Brand, *Newcastle*, vol.2, p.146.
[23] *Ibid.*, p.180.

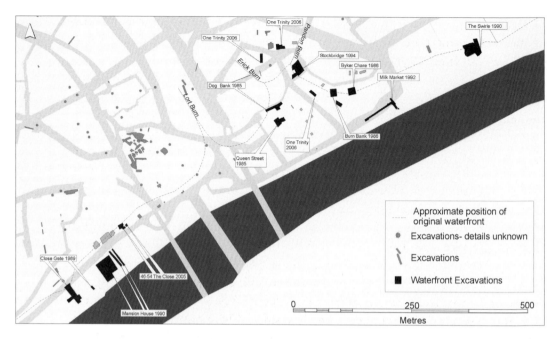

20 The medieval waterfront in relation to the modern city.

platform for buildings and reducing the width of the burn.[24] This procedure continued, one revetment succeeding another, each farther out into the river than its predecessor, through the busy 13th century, and beyond, at both ends of the waterfront. To the west, on the site of the later Mansion House, there were a succession of four waterfronts between the 13th and 16th centuries, the retaining wall of any one of them standing as much as 12.8 feet high, the land recovered varying in width from 17.7 to 37.7 feet wide.[25] The land-fill material was not confined to what could be obtained locally since flint and limestone were found in the 13th-century (phase 1) deposits below the Mansion House, and gravel from the River Thames terraces below the town wall in the Milk Market.[26] This 'foreign' material can be convincingly explained as ships' ballast dumped from the 13th century onwards, and certainly found at least as far west as the south-west corner of the town.

On the artificial platform(s) which formed the waterfront, buildings were erected and streets laid out to provide for the needs of the merchant community.

[24] Truman, L. et al., 'Excavations at Stockbridge, Newcastle upon Tyne, 1995', *AA*, 5th series, vol.29 (2001), pp.95-221.

[25] Fraser, R. et al., 'Excavation on the Site of the Mansion House, Newcastle, 1990', *AA*, 5th series, vol.23 (1995), pp.145-213.

[26] Heslop, D.H. et al., 'Excavation of the Town Wall in the Milk Market, Newcastle upon Tyne', *AA*, 5th series, vol.23 (1995), pp.215-34.

The east and west stretches developed independently from one another, though at much the same time, and were separated by the bridge and Sandhill. There are therefore three distinct units in this part of the town plan.

In the centre the bridge gave access via Sandhill to the Side and All Hallows Bank (today Akenside Hill) and so to the upper part of the town. There is no early documentary evidence for these three streets and there has been no excavation, but without them the river crossing would have led nowhere. It seems reasonable to repeat an earlier statement that 'the position of Sandhill near the bridgehead, its triangular shape, the location of the later Guildhall (town hall) on its south side, and the existence of the market cross (Cale Cross) at its north end all support the possibility of an early market place here'.[27]

West of, and upstream from the bridge, reclamation of the shore allowed north-south plots of land to exist in 1230-40 between the moat of the castle and the Tyne.[28] By the early 1270s the keeper of the bridge was able to lease to Laurence Cutellar land with buildings stretching between the highway and the river.[29] In other words, there was now a street, the Close, running parallel with the Tyne and with properties on both sides. Those on the south side were larger than those on the north, and possessed their own private quays. There was never a public quay on this length of the waterfront, one reason being that the narrow arches of the bridge prevented access by large ships.

Downstream from the bridge the chares, the long and very narrow streets which ran downhill to the Tyne, also originated in the 13th century. After the consolidation of the river bank, piers were built out towards the river, with docking spaces between them. Later the docks were filled with debris to make a continuous raised platform so that streets could be set out and buildings erected. Although by no means the whole area has been excavated, it has been proved that Fenwick's Entry and Broad Garth were established in this way in the 13th century west of the Pandon Burn.[30] To the east, in the 14th century after Pandon was taken into Newcastle, Burn Bank and Byker Chare were laid out in the same manner.[31] This very striking arrangement of the chares was not peculiar to Newcastle but was common in medieval seaports. The Key (today's Quayside) represents a joining up of the piers or jetties at the south ends of

---

[27] Harbottle, Barbara and Clack, Peter, 'Newcastle upon Tyne: Archaeology and Development', in Harding, D.W. (ed.), *Archaeology in the North* (1976), p.118.

[28] Oliver, *Early Deeds*, no. 137.

[29] *Ibid.*, p.140.

[30] O'Brien, Colm et al., *The Origins of the Newcastle Quayside* (Society of Antiquaries of Newcastle upon Tyne Monograph, Series III, 1988), p.5.

[31] O'Brien, C. et al., 'Excavations at Newcastle Quayside: The Crown Court Site', *AA*, 5th series, vol.7 (1989), p.143.

the chares to create a continuous highway, but does not seem to have been in existence until the second half of the 14th century.

There was a marked difference in the character of the two areas. The eastern, particularly Pandon, came to be densely occupied and quite industrialised. The earliest structures there were of timber, replaced in stone in the 13th and 14th centuries, and of varied function, both domestic and industrial.[32] A pottery kiln from the second half of the 12th century was found at Dog Bank,[33] there were traces of early to mid-13th-century metal working on the bank of the Pandon Burn, and a battery of lime kilns was found on the west bank of the Swirle, in use in the mid-14th century.[34] To the west, in Sandhill and particularly on the south side of the Close, rich merchants owned large houses with courtyards.

The Religious Houses

Just as there were large-scale developments in the southern part of the town in the 13th century so there were in the northern, but of a very different character. The event which was to have a great effect on the plan and the appearance of the town, as well as on its religious life, was the arrival of five houses of friars during a period of perhaps fifty years. Newcastle was one of 11 English towns which received all four principal orders, Dominican, Franciscan, Carmelite and Augustinian, as well as the Friars of the Sack. The first to arrive were the Franciscans,[35] who were closely followed by the Dominicans some time before 1239.[36] The Carmelite Friary was founded in 1262,[37] the Friars of the Sack were granted a site in 1267,[38] and the Augustinian Friars were settled before 1291.[39] As in some other towns, this arrangement did not remain unchanged throughout the Middle Ages. The first Carmelite Friary on Wallknoll was found to be in the way of the advancing town wall, and in consequence the White Friars were rehoused in 1307 in the almost empty home of the Friars of the Sack on the other side of the town.[40] Nevertheless the Wallknoll Friary was clearly reusable since, in 1360, it was taken over by the Trinitarians.[41]

[32] Truman, 'Excavations at Stockbridge', passim.
[33] O'Brien, *Newcastle Quayside*, pp.31-3.
[34] Ellison, Margaret et al., 'Excavations at Newcastle Quayside: Waterfront Development at the Swirle', *AA*, 5th series, vol.21 (1993), pp.156-64.
[35] *Calendar of Close Rolls, 1237-42*, 16.
[36] *Calendar of Liberate Rolls, 1226-40*, 368-9.
[37] *Northumberland County History*, vol.13 (1930), pp.266-7.
[38] *CPR, 1266-72*, 10.
[39] *CPR, 1281-92*, 441.
[40] Harbottle, Barbara, 'Excavations at the Carmelite Friary, Newcastle upon Tyne, 1965 and 1967', *AA*, 4th series, vol.46 (1968), p.169.
[41] *CPR, 1358-61*, 339.

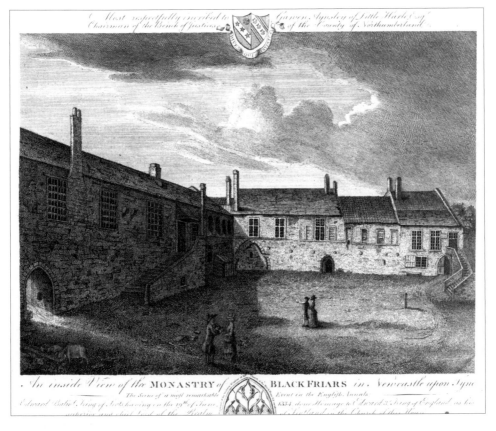

21 The Blackfriars (Dominican Friary) in the 18th century.

Because the friars arrived when the layout of the town was at least partly established, they found themselves on sites on the fringe of the built-up area. There is, however, no reason to suppose that the land was marshy or in any other way undesirable, and there is documentary and archaeological evidence that they received grants of both messuages and open land. As in other towns they acquired their sites in piecemeal fashion, the precinct of the Black Friars, for example continuing to grow until 1329,[42] the date of the last recorded grant of land, when the area amounted to as much as 11.6 acres. And in two instances the friars were the cause of the closure of streets, the Carmelites being given permission to close the Crossway on their Wallknoll site[43] and the Black Friars an unnamed street, perhaps Fenkle Street.[44]

[42] *CPR, 1327-30*, 392.
[43] *Northumberland County History*, vol.13, p.270.
[44] *CPR, 1272-81*, 397.

Although it is possible to draw a reasonably precise boundary round each precinct it is by no means certain how the particular church, claustral and other buildings were disposed within it, and this applies to the Nunnery as well as to the friaries. There is no information at all about the Carmelite, later the Trinitarian, site at Wallknoll, or indeed how much damage was actually caused there by the building of the town wall. It can be inferred from documentary evidence that the Franciscan church lay along the south side of High Friar Lane (on which the Tyneside Cinema is sited) and that its east end therefore fronted Pilgrim Street,[45] but that is all that is known. A combination of fragmentary remains, excavation and early illustrations allows more to be said about the other three.

The Black Friars is the best understood.[46] A large church with aisled nave, aisleless chancel and without a walking space, lay on the north side of a 90-foot square cloister with lean-to walks. Though the elevations of the extant claustral ranges were much altered in the 18th century their plan was fairly standard with few quirks. The chapter house and warming house, for example, survive in the east range, and the refectory in the south range. The second, western, Carmelite Friary which incorporated the house of the Friars of the Sack was on a smaller scale. The church was probably aisleless, it certainly had no south aisle, and this cloister, too, had lean-to walks.[47] The chancel of the church of the Augustinian Friary was presumably aisleless since twin buttresses were found at both its eastern angles, and a short stretch of its north wall, with 14th-century window, still stands within the post-medieval tower on the north side of the Holy Jesus Hospital. This church, however, was the only one in the town to stand on the south side of its cloister, and the only one to have at least one undershot cloister walk.[48]

The Town Wall

The building of the town wall began in or soon after 1265, the date of the first grant of murage, and dragged on into the 15th century.[49] It is not clear what prompted the town to start in the 13th century when there was no particular threat from the north, the threat not coming until the early 14th century, but

---

[45]   Hodgson, J.C., 'The "Domus Dei" of Newcastle: otherwise St Katherine's Hospital on the Sandhill', *AA*, 3rd series, vol.14 (1917), p.212.
[46]   Pevsner, N. et al., *The Buildings of England: Northumberland* (1992), pp.431-4, with plans.
[47]   See Harbottle, 'Excavations at the Carmelite Friary', pp.179-201, for an account of the excavation.
[48]   *Medieval Archaeology*, 15 (1971), p.140, and 16 (1972), p.175.
[49]   In 1989 a summary of our understanding of the town wall, with references to earlier sources, was published as Nolan, J. et al., 'The Medieval Town Defences of Newcastle upon Tyne: Excavation and Survey 1986-87', *AA*, 5th series, 17 (1989), pp.29-78.

22 Excavations at Holy Jesus Hospital (Austin Friary).

start they did and worked from north to south on both sides of the town. The western stretch of wall, where it passed through the Black Friars precinct, was described as new in 1280, the western re-entrant was probably laid out in 1311, the section from there to Close Gate dates from the second quarter of the 14th century, and the stretch to the waterfront from the middle of the century. On the other side of the town the eastern re-entrant was the result of Newcastle's acquisition of Pandon in 1298/9, and though it must be supposed that the defences were then carried on southwards there is no dating evidence for the stretch between Corner Tower and Sand Gate. Recent excavations on the waterfront showed that the wall did continue east from the Riverside Tower at the south-west corner for nearly 330 feet,[50] and that this section and that along the Quayside date from the early 15th century.[51]

The defences consisted of a wall with a ditch in front and an intra-mural road behind. Because it was built over such a long period, and on varying gradients, the wall ranged in height from 14.4 feet to 21.6 feet, and in thickness above the external base chamfers from 6.5 feet to 10.8 feet. It was surmounted by a parapet, which had a maximum height of 5.5 feet and was pierced by embrasures. There was access through the wall by six main gates across the principal streets, and by a few posterns such as the Wallknoll or Sallyport Tower. It was defended by 19 towers, of which most were D-shaped in plan, and contained a single rectangular room on one or two floors, and by turrets built on the top of the wall through which the wall walk passed. Where the ditch has been examined on the west side of the town it was found to be 37 feet wide and 14.7 feet deep, and separated from the wall by a berm 31 feet wide. Although all the large gates have long since been demolished, parts of the wall with its towers and turrets, and stretches of the road and ditch, still survive.

Because the construction of the defences was so prolonged it is not surprising that there were pauses in the work, and changes in its direction and design. While it is probable that the mayor and burgesses intended to enclose, and therefore protect, as much of the inhabited part of the town as they could, it also appears that they were trying to draw as tight a line as possible. In 1311 the people living in the area of the western re-entrant insisted that the line of the wall should be altered to run direct to the Tyne. Their reasons were not given, but this change of direction would presumably have caused less damage and, by enlarging the area, brought more dwellings within the defences. Both individuals and institutions

---

[50] Fraser, R. et al., 'Excavation at the site of the Mansion House, Newcastle, 1990', *AA*, 5th series, vol.23 (1995), pp.154-5.
[51] See note 26.

had to give up ground and buildings for the new fortifications, for which a strip some 100 feet wide was required. The Bishop of Carlisle lost a house, and burgesses in Westgate the tails of their burgages. The churchyard of St Andrew's was reduced in size, the Dominican and Carmelite friaries were cut off from a large part of their precincts. Some streets, Darn Crook, Fishergate and perhaps Fenkle Street, became culs-de-sac. The wall remained largely intact into the middle of the 18th century, and so for many years had the effect of restricting subsequent development to the roads leading away from the main gates.

Later Developments

The physical growth of the town in the later Middle Ages seems largely to have been confined to the infilling of the burgage plots within the wall. Extra-mural expansion on a substantial scale occurred only in Sandgate, the area immediately east of the Sand

23 The town wall between Close Gate and West Gate.

Gate on the bank of the Tyne. This area was used for the dumping of ballast, to a depth of up to 16 feet, from the 13th century, until in the 15th century the street of Sandgate appeared in the records as a thoroughfare, the neighbouring land was divided into plots and buildings erected. By the end of the 16th century this was a densely occupied suburb inhabited by those who gained their living from the river and its associated industries.[52]

It is easy today to forget the barrier to east-west movement across the town presented by the dene of the Lort Burn. This ran south, from the modern Eldon Square, between the market street and Pilgrim Street, and through Sandhill to the

[52] Goodrick, G. et al., 'Excavations at Newcastle Quayside: The Evolution of Sandgate', *AA*, 5th series, vol.22 (1994), pp.219-33.

Tyne. It came to be bridged in two places, by Over Dene Brig, part of which still exists beneath today's High Bridge, and Netherdenebrig. This, Low Bridge, is marked by the flights of steps on either side of Dean Street. It was created by a series of grants of land and money by beneficent burgesses at the end of the 14th century.[53]

The market street, central in every sense, ran between the New Gate, which gave access to the town from the north, and the church of St Nicholas. The earliest documentary reference to the *vicus fori* is of the 13th century when there is mention of booths, suggesting that colonisation had begun.[54] By the late 14th century it is probable that this was well advanced, and stretches of this long street had acquired specialist names indicating the type of goods sold there. The lower end, between the church and the modern Nuns Lane, was the market for food and manufactured goods, and the names of the Bigg[55] (barley), Groat[56] and Cloth[57] Markets still survive. Between Nuns Lane and New Gate was the livestock market, the dirty end, and this, now Newgate Street, was once Horsemarket,[58] Neatmarket[59] and Noltmarket.[60]

The change which marked the close of the Middle Ages was the Dissolution of the Monasteries, the five friaries being suppressed in 1539 and the Nunnery in 1540.[61] This brought to an end 300 years of communal religious use and, at the same time, rendered large areas of ground available for re-use by new owners. During the next century the Council of the North came to and went from the Augustinian Friary which subsequently passed to the mayor and burgesses, who also acquired the Black Friars and the Trinitarian Friary. The other three friaries fell into private hands, and were for a time developed as private houses.

The northern part of the township of Newcastle was, until early modern times, open land, and indeed much of it still is. Until its expansion in 1835 the town's northern edge was marked by the Crag Hall Burn, which was also the south boundary of the townships of Kenton and Coxlodge. On the east this part of Newcastle marched with Jesmond, on the west with Fenham, and on the south-west with Elswick. This huge area of originally, it is said, 900-1,000 acres, served the town as common (Town or Castle Moor, and Nun's Moor), and meadow

---

[53] *CPR, 1391-96*, 584; 'Local Muniments', *AA*, 2nd series, 2 (1858), p.13.
[54] Oliver, *Early Deeds*, no. 197.
[55] The earliest version so far found is *Beremarket* (also meaning barley) in 1388, *AA*, 2nd series, vol.1 (1857), p.30.
[56] *Melemarketgate* (later Groat Market), in 1392, *ibid.* p.32.
[57] *Clothmarketgate* in 1401, *Calendar of Close Rolls, 1399-1402*, p.267.
[58] *Horsmarket* in 1449, Oliver, *Early Deeds*, p.299.
[59] *Neatmarket* in 1430, *Calendar of Close Rolls, 1429-36*, pp.17-18.
[60] *Noltmarket* in 1521, *Northumberland and Durham Deeds* (1929), pp.1-2.
[61] *LP*, vol.14, pt.1, nos 39, 40, 43-5; vol.15, no.15; vol.13, pt.2, no.768.

24 The extent of the town and moor, *c*.1540.

(Castle Leazes). The location of the arable land is not clear, but was presumably between the burgages of the town's centre and the Moor and Leazes.

It seems certain that the rights of the burgesses of Newcastle in the Town Moor and Castle Leazes were established as early as 1213, perhaps as a gift by King John.[62] It is possible that some of this land had once been owned by St Bartholomew's Nunnery, thus explaining why part of the Moor is still known as Nuns Moor.[63] It is not clear whether this exceptionally large expanse of common could, even earlier, have been inter-commoned by the neighbouring townships (cf. Shire Moor).

The earliest representation of Newcastle's layout just after the end of the Middle Ages is Speed's map of 1610. The Lort and Pandon Burns flow, as yet unculverted, to the Tyne, the precincts of the friaries, the Nunnery and Carliol Croft are still largely open and the curved outline of the town wall remains intact, enclosing solidly built-up streets. While the amount of development on the burgage plots within the wall at this time is not known, the houses shown along the streets leading away from the gates leave us in no doubt that the expansion of the post-medieval period had begun.

---

[62] Halcrow, Elizabeth M., 'The Town Moor of Newcastle upon Tyne', *AA*, 4th series, vol.31 (1953), p.150.
[63] Oliver, *Early Deeds*, p.4.

3

The Economic Growth of Newcastle upon Tyne, 1150-1536

CONSTANCE M. FRASER

Town and River

By 1150 a trading community had developed under the shadow of the New Castle built by Robert Curthose 70 years earlier. Its bye-laws, confirmed by Henry II, are among the earliest borough laws known in England. They listed the privileges of burgesses. They would have their own town court, with comprehensive jurisdiction except for pleas of the Crown. This meant that 'foreign' merchants were subject to judgment by the native burgesses without leave of the king's bailiff. (There was not to be a 'chief bailiff' until 1216.) Especially important, the burgesses were to have monopoly of trade on the Tyne. 'If a ship have put in at the mouth of the Tyne and wishes to depart, the burgesses may buy what they will.' 'Whatever merchandise a ship has brought by sea must be landed, except salt, and herring ought to be sold in the ship.' 'No merchant, unless he be a burgess, may buy [outside] the town either wool or leather or other merchandise, nor within the borough except [of] burgesses.' 'No one but a burgess may buy webs to dye, nor make nor cut them.' Otherwise there were the usual privileges such as that the holder of a burgage who remained unchallenged for a year and a day would not need to defend his right at law unless the claimant had been a minor or out of the country. The son of a burgess should enjoy his father's freedom while he remained at home. A burgess was not required to defend himself by wager of battle but only by oath of his vouchers, except in cases of treason. There were no feudal restrictions such as *merchet*, *heriot*, *blodwit* or *stengesdint*, and a villein who stayed in the town for a year and a day without objection from his lord could so remain. Every burgess might have his own oven and hand-mill, saving the right of the king's oven. Finally, a burgess could sell his land and freely depart, unless there was a claim against him.[1]

---

[1]   Johnson, C., 'The oldest version of the customs of Newcastle upon Tyne', *AA*, 4th series, vol.1 (1925), pp.169-78; Hunter Blair, C.H, 'The mayors of Newcastle upon Tyne, 1215-1399', *AA*, 4th series, vol.18 (1940), p.1.

The 'laws of Newcastle' suggest an active trading community by the mid-12th century following the establishment of the king's castle and a bridge. The latter was functioning by 1160 on the evidence of a Durham charter, although the chapel at the north end bore a dedication to St Thomas the Martyr, i.e. Thomas Becket (d.1170).[2] The chaplain traditionally collected the bridge tolls. Other tolls were payable, some to be paid by traders on their transport (ox-waggon, horse-drawn cart, pack-horse or ship), or the commodity for sale (horse, cow, grain, flour, salt, hides, sheep, pigs and goats). The king's bailiff continued to exercise some supervision, but the burgesses were negotiating a town farm in lieu of specific tolls. In 1201 this fee-farm was raised by King John from £50 to £60, when the burgesses had to pay 100 marks (£66 13s. 4d.) and two palfreys to secure the bargain.[3] Other royal 'towns' in Northumberland were similarly coerced into negotiating an increase. This allows a comparison to be made as to relative prosperity. The farm of Corbridge was raised from £30 to £45, Newburn from £30 to £50, and Rothbury from £20 to £30. In 1215 the farm of Newcastle was raised to £100, but as part of the package the King agreed that the sheriff of Northumberland and the constable of the castle should not meddle in town affairs.[4] In 1216 a Guild Merchant was established in the town whose members were free from tolls, and Daniel son of Nicholas was elected chief bailiff. By 1233 a common seal was in existence. In 1251 the chief bailiff was allowed the style of mayor, although the title was subject to royal challenge in 1291.[5] On the national scene King John in 1203 decreed the levying of a custom of a 15th on all exports and imports, and from the dues collected at Newcastle it would appear that trade there was half the value of goods exported from Hull but twice that of Grimsby.[6]

The next opportunity to analyse trade in Newcastle comes in 1265, when Henry III licensed the collection of a toll towards the cost of building a town wall. Again we have tolls on ship-loads, herring, salmon, cod, wool, cloth, linen, horses, oxen and cows, hides, wool-fells, furs and animal skins, sheep, pigs, grain, white peas, salt, charcoal, brushwood, peat, grease and tallow, butter and cheese, sea-coal, wax, pepper, almonds, cumin, figs and raisins, garlic, onions, wine, ashes, woad, 'Rochester earth', alum, teasels, kitchenware, lead, pitch and tar,

[2] Snape, M.G. (ed.), *English Episcopal Acta, Durham 1154-95*, British Academy, record series (Oxford, 2002), p.83.

[3] Brand, *Newcastle*, vol.2, pp.131, note a, 132, 134.

[4] *Rotuli Chartarum*, pp.86-7; *Pipe Roll 3 John*, Pipe Roll Soc., new series, pp.14, 249; *NCH*, vol.10, p.42. The town successfully opposed an attempt by Edward I in 1287 to raise the farm to £200.

[5] TNA, E.159/65 m. 13, 67 mm. 17d, 31; C.H. Hunter Blair, 'The seals of Newcastle upon Tyne', *AA*, 3rd series, vol.19 (1922), pp.170-2. Other towns at that date similarly challenged for unauthorised election of a mayor were Bristol, Canterbury, Ipswich, Nottingham and Oxford (TNA, E.159/66 mm. 12, 19d, 23d, 41: 68 mm. 41, 43.)

[6] Poole, A.L., *From Domesday Book to Magna Carta, 1087-1216* (Oxford, 1951), p.96.

oil, nets, deal-boards, maple-boards and Eastland-boards, felt, steel, millstones and oars. This list can be analysed in various ways. Some commodities indicate a market in Newcastle for agricultural produce and livestock with their derivatives, wool and leather. Others suggest an overseas trade in pepper, almonds, garlic and wine. Manufacture is suggested by ashes, dyestuff, teasels and alum. Ship-building is suggested by Eastland and other types of boards. A different line of approach is to compare what might be expected at Newcastle as against commodities chargeable at ports such as Berwick upon Tweed or Scarborough. Hides were chargeable in much larger quantities at Newcastle, which in 1292 was second only to London in its exports of leather. When it came to sea-coal, Berwick charged a custom of 1d. a chaldron as against ½d. in Newcastle and ¼d. at Scarborough. With regard to lead, there was a toll at Newcastle at the rate of 2d. a cartload. The same was levied at Richmond, with the Swaledale seams, Corbridge and Haydon Bridge. Salmon was a delicacy, as can be shown by tolls charged in the various towns of the North East. At Corbridge, Croft, Hartlepool, Northallerton, Richmond, Scarborough and Yarm the rate was a farthing a fish. At Berwick and Newcastle it was a penny for 20 – presumably a tribute to the abundance of these fish in the Tweed and Tyne. (Durham was authorised to levy 1d. on a horse-load and Hartlepool 2d.) Oddly, Newcastle, which levied 2d. a cartload on lead, had no tolls on iron or other metal articles. The explanation may be that in 1265 iron was not in general production, and subsequent tariffs were not brought up to date.[7]

Relations with Downstream Communities

In 1267 the burgesses of Newcastle, confident in their status of a royal town chartered to enjoy a monopoly of trade on the Tyne, swooped down under their officers and seized ships anchored at North Shields near the mouth of the Tyne, where they were loading hides and coal. Shields belonged to Tynemouth priory, which used it to supply the Benedictine monks with fish. Tynemouth was a dependent cell of St Alban's abbey, and the abbot protested to the king against this assault on the proprietary rights of his house. A lawsuit dragged on for two years, the upshot of which was that the prior of Tynemouth was found to have extended his jetties into the foreshore, belonging to the Crown. He was forced to demolish these, and so to end his interest in general trade. At least it was ended for the next few years. Then in 1287 the burgesses struck again, to prevent the prior from buying direct

[7]   Fraser, C.M., 'The Pattern of Trade', *Northern History*, vol.4, pp.45-59 and appendix 66/7.

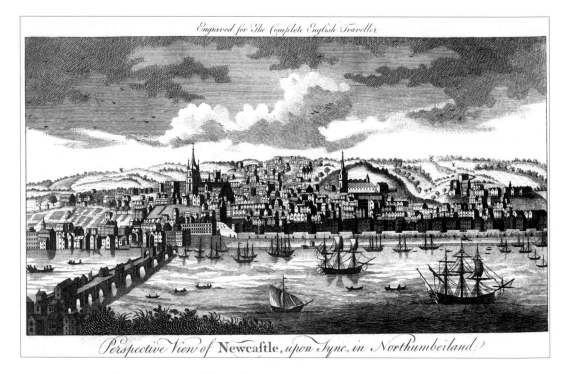

Engraved for The Complete English Traveller

Perspective View of **Newcastle**, *upon Tyne, in Northumberland*

25 Perspective view of Newcastle.

from ships off the mouth of the Tyne, where hides and coal were being loaded, and at Shields, complaining to Edward I not only of the jetties but also the establishment of bakehouses and brewhouses for the victualling of ships anchored off the mouth of the Tyne and Shields. The prior counter-complained that any purchases made by his men at Newcastle were charged tolls, contrary to exemptions authorised by the king. The burgesses sued the prior in Parliament after Easter 1290, and judgment was given in their favour in July 1292 on the grounds that the prior was attracting trade to Shields far beyond the domestic needs of his house. No ships for the future were to load or discharge at Shields. No provisions were to be sold there to merchants. All wharves below high-tide mark were to be removed. Nothing daunted, the prior in 1304 used the opportunity of a stay at the priory by Queen Margaret, second wife of Edward I, to obtain a royal charter for a fair at Tynemouth. This was revoked the following year on the grounds that it was detrimental to trade at Newcastle nine miles upstream.[8]

[8] Page, W. (ed.), *Three early assize rolls for the county of Northumberland*, SS, vol.88 (1891), pp.162-3; *Rotuli Parliamentorum*, vol.1, p.26; *NCH*, vol.8, pp.286-8; *Calendar of Charter Rolls, 1300-26*, p.46.

The prior tried again to assert his right to trade from North Shields about 1390, when land below the high-water mark was again reclaimed and a new market started. This resulted in a commission appointed in 1401 to enquire into unauthorised trade on either side of the Tyne contrary to the liberties of the port of Newcastle. The prior then diversified the trade, concentrating on fishing – reasonably for a community of Benedictine monks – although cod and ling were being sought from as far away as the Shetland Islands. In 1446 Henry VI licensed the prior to collect tolls from his tenants on grain, salt, salt-fish, leather and coal, as well as fines incurred by his tenants for infringements of the assizes of bread and ale and tolls on victuals sold to mariners anchoring at the mouth of the Tyne. This provoked an inquiry into trade on the river, which found that there were 20 fishing cobles owned by local fishermen and seven larger craft. The prior's powers were recalled by an Act of Resumption passed in 1450. Possibly taking advantage of the political situation with Edward IV's seizure of power, in 1462 the prior secured the right to victual ships at the mouth of the Tyne and import victuals free from the tolls demanded by the Newcastle Corporation. The mayor, aldermen and commonalty of Newcastle renewed their objections to trade at North Shields when in 1510 they charged the prior with erecting wharves, staiths and quays, and building thereon houses, salt-pans and mills. The prior also had salmon weirs in the river. The matter was put to arbitration, and on 23 March 1512 it was agreed that the fish weirs should stand, that the prior and his men should be free of Newcastle tolls on goods bought for their own use, and be allowed to sail with salt and fish to any part of England, Wales and Ireland. The common bakehouses and brewhouses at North Shields were allowed to remain without paying fines to Newcastle, and in time of famine the prior might have reasonable access to any corn ships coming to the Tyne before the residue continued up the river to Newcastle. It was not until 1530 that Newcastle Corporation secured the insertion of a clause in a new Act of Parliament to the effect that all items for shipment could be loaded only at Newcastle quayside itself, except for salt and fish. There could be no commercial development down river at North or South Shields.[9]

The situation at South Shields was comparable with that north of the river, with the prior of Durham mirroring the prior of Tynemouth. In 1256 the prior of Durham was charged at assizes held in Newcastle with allowing men at Shields to sell fish wholesale before offering them at Newcastle, and with supplying ships with bread and ale. Three years later the prior was forced to agree that there should be no quays there, and baking and brewing was to be

9 *NCH*, vol.8, pp.289-93.

solely for local consumption. Subsequent disputes in the 14th century revolved around fishing rights. In 1497 a prosecution was brought in the Durham court of pleas against Newcastle merchants who had seized hides from local traders. In the later 15th century South Shields commenced salt-making by boiling sea-water using small-coals.[10]

The Bishop of Durham tried to exploit the location of his borough at Gateshead, at the south end of the Tyne bridge opposite Newcastle. Whereas the king alone could authorise throughout his realm the establishment of a market, the bishops of Durham claimed that their regalian rights between Tyne and Tees entitled them to authorise a market at Gateshead, which Bishop Bek duly did. This was quickly overruled. The judges at Quo Warranto proceedings at Newcastle in 1293 flatly ignored any right to a market there and the burgesses of Newcastle man-handled any foolish enough to try to trade there or ship coals.[11] Such seizures were duly prosecuted in the Durham court of pleas.[12]

Rivalry between Newcastle and the Bishop of Durham broke out again in 1384 following the grant by Richard II to Bishop Fordham allowing him to have a quayside at Gateshead where ships could discharge and load contrary to the monopoly of Newcastle to trade on the Tyne. The commons of Newcastle petitioned for the repeal of the charter, pointing out that Newcastle paid to the Exchequer a fee farm of £100, to say nothing of taxes, customs and tolls. The Bishop of Durham in his palatinate was free from such burdens. Gateshead would be a virtual tax-haven and it would be natural for Newcastle inhabitants to withdraw south of the river, leaving the king's town 'wasted and destroyed'. Richard's Council saw the point and on 25 June 1384 Bishop Fordham was ordered to do nothing to their prejudice.[13] The next dispute between town and bishop flared up over jurisdiction over the Tyne bridge. The bishop claimed authority over the third nearest his bank of the river. Newcastle claimed sole authority. The dispute was eventually settled by arbitration in 1416, when Bishop Langley was recognised as entitled to his third of the bridge.[14]

---

[10]   TNA, Durham 13/230 m 5d; Hodgson, G.D., *The Borough of South Shields* (Newcastle, 1903), pp.38-47, 61. Cf. Brand, *Newcastle*, vol.2, p.14. Another example of high-handed treatment of its neighbours south of the Tyne was brought in the Durham court in September 1504. Here Thomas Surteys junior sued Henry Bednell of Newcastle and Margaret his wife in waste. He had leased to them land in nearby Felling for 12 years. Nevertheless the land had been exploited by the extraction of 10 cartloads of sand and clay, which had been sold. They had stripped the roofs from a 'milkhouse' and 'calfhouse', causing the timber to become rotten through exposure to storm and rain, and they had felled 300 oaks valued at 12d. each, 200 ash trees valued at 8d., 60 apple trees valued at 4d., and 40 willows valued at 4d. The case then meandered on, as it was difficult to force the defendants to appear in a 'foreign' court (TNA, Durham 13/1 m 8).

[11]   TNA, JI 651 m 25d; Fraser, C.M. (ed.), *The Northumberland Eyre 1293*, SS, vol.211 (2007), p.262.

[12]   TNA, Durham 13/226 mm 1-3.

[13]   Fraser, C.M. (ed.), *Northumberland Petitions*, SS, vol.176 (1966), pp.257-9.

[14]   Brand, *Newcastle*, vol.2, p.14, note h; Welford, *Newcastle and Gateshead*, vol.1, pp.257-9.

The special relationship between the Crown and Newcastle lay in the fact that the more the town prospered the more money could be squeezed from it by way of the town-farm, customs, tolls, tallage and taxes. The town, however, benefited from its exemption from tolls in other towns, the casual trade from periodical judicial sessions and the fact it was the county town for Northumberland and headquarters of the sheriff. Its status as a staple port provided an entry into continental trade. Hugo Gerardino, a merchant of Lucca, married the widow of Gilbert of Pandon and they appear in the lay subsidy roll of 1296 with the largest assessment of £84 in the town. He and his wife figure in the records of the eyre roll of 1293 as they sought to recover title deeds to property in town and county held by Isolda's father in trust for the son by her previous

26 The coat of arms of the Corporation of Newcastle upon Tyne.

marriage. They were exporters of wool and hides. Other Italian wool merchants were Villan Isoldi of the Black Circles, who exported 28 sacks in 1296/7, and Lupus Bouretat of the Frescobaldi, who exported 47 sacks. Herman Molle of Lubeck was responsible for 10 sacks. The presence of bankers is evidenced by the surviving petition of Jehan de Folborn. He borrowed money from the Society of Riccardi of Lucca from their agent at Newcastle, using his military equipment as pledge. The loan was to be repaid either in England or Ireland. He repaid the money a week before the expiry date but in Dublin. By the time this was reported at Newcastle the equipment had been sold and the purchaser had declined to return it although his money had been refunded. Ingram of Cologne figures on the subsidy roll, suggesting the presence of Hanseatic merchants, interested in the lead being shipped from the Tyne. In 1308 he exported 15 sacks of wool from Newcastle and a further 13 sacks in 1317.[15]

15 Fraser, C.M. (ed.), *Northumberland Lay Subsidy Roll of 1296* (Newcastle, 1968), pp.39-47; eadem, *Eyre*, 109-10, 323; eadem, *Petitions*, 87-99.

The surname of Roger Paytevin suggests a foreign ancestry, but he was well integrated into the town, being keeper of the bridge between 1282 and 1285, a collector of murage and a town bailiff.[16]

Guilds and town government

As late as 1289 Newcastle still had an undifferentiated Guild Merchant, which controlled entry into trade but not trading standards. Group awareness may be behind the law suit brought in the king's court of Exchequer by the 'poor burgesses' in 1305 against the 'rich burgesses'. The complaint was that despite the fact the town's laws entitled every burgess to trade with incoming ships the 'rich burgesses' imposed minimum quantities which penalised retailers as against wholesalers. The 'poor burgesses' were just as liable for taxation, and the action of the rich burgesses was detrimental to their business. The barons of the Exchequer accepted the argument and in 1307 found for the plaintiffs.[17]

The early 14th century was a troubled time, although Northumberland had been subject to raids by the Scots on a regular basis since 1296 and Newcastle was often the point for musters against Scotland and the depot from which stores might be distributed during campaigns. The bridge over the Tyne was breached by a flood in 1339 and it was rumoured that the money collected for its maintenance had been embezzled by various leading merchants led by John Denton. In 1341 the Scots were encamped at Heddon on the Wall, 10 miles to the west of Newcastle, overlooking the head of the tideway on the Tyne and a frequent crossing point for invaders aiming for pickings in Durham and Yorkshire. Again John Denton was suspected of undercover relations with the enemy, supplying provisions. In 1342 discontent resulted in a contested election for mayor of Newcastle. While John Denton was chosen by the 'wiser' burgesses, the 'younger' men supported Richard Acton, who won.[18] Following the ensuing riots, order was restored by the Crown imposing its own administration and forcing an agreement on the warring parties. Henceforth the town should be governed by a mayor and four bailiffs. These should be selected by a complicated arrangement whereby the 12 guilds of Newcastle should each select two of their membership. The 24 should elect a committee of four with power to co-opt a further eight. The new 12 would choose a further 12, who jointly would select

---

[16] TNA, E.122/105/4-6 (Newcastle customs accounts, 1308-17). Paytevin was an exporter of hides, assessed in All Saints' parish at £3 10s. (Fraser, *Subsidy*, p.43). Between 1282 and 1285 he had been one of the four town bailiffs (Oliver, A.E. (ed), *Early Newcastle Deeds*, SS, vol.137 (1924), pp.206-7, 66).

[17] Fraser, C.M., 'Medieval Trading Restrictions in the North East', *AA*, 4th series, vol.39 (1961), pp.135-40.

[18] Fraser, C.M., 'The Life and Death of John of Denton', *AA*, 4th series, vol.37 (1959), pp.316-19.

the mayor; this panel would then select the four bailiffs and other town officers. The 12 guilds were also empowered to scrutinise annually the weekly accounts of the mayor, bailiffs and chamberlains dealing with town revenue from tolls and the like. They would also select a panel to assess the town's tax liabilities and supervise money collected for bridge repairs.

This Charter of Liberties remained in force for only three years, when the old oligarchy resumed control, but the example stayed in popular memory and attempts at reinstatement were to be made in 1438/9 and 1515. However, the charter revealed there were 12 trade guild by 1342. Three were wholesalers, namely the wool merchants, corn merchants or boothmen, and mercers; five trades were concerned with animals and their by-products, the butchers, tanners, skinners or furriers, saddlers and cordwainers or shoemakers; two trades dealt with textiles, namely the fullers and dyers and the tailors, and finally there were the smiths and the bakers. Members of these trades continued to have a special role in the administration of the town, even if power tended to lodge with the wealthy wholesalers.[19] Many other guilds were added to the original 12 by the fourth decade of the 15th century: the master mariners, weavers, barber-surgeons, shipwrights, coopers, house-carpenters, masons, joiners, millers, felt-makers and curriers, coopers, paviours and carriage-men, slaters and plumbers, to be known as the 15 bye-trades, with subordinate rights to elect a town council.[20]

Little is known of the internal workings of Newcastle's guilds. The earliest ordinaries follow the passage of an Act of Parliament in 1436 requiring registration. These were for the smiths and for the glovers in 1436, the skinners in 1437, the barber-surgeons and chandlers in 1442, the slaters in 1451, the fullers and dyers in 1477, the Merchant Adventurers in 1480 and the master mariners in 1492. Their rules covered the length of apprenticeship, place and time of guild meetings, admission fees, fines for breaches of rules, trade regulations, duties in connection with the town's Corpus Christi plays, and social obligations.[21] Further light was thrown on the growing complexity of town trade through proceedings in Star Chamber in 1515. The action was brought by the mayor and aldermen of Newcastle against the 'artificers' of the town, who were alleged to have banded together to assert a right to trade irrespective of appropriate guild membership. It was alleged that the mayor and his officers were unable to maintain law and order and keep the sessions of the peace 'for dread of their lives'. A commission was issued by the Crown to Sir Edward Radcliffe and John Bentley to enquire

[19]   *CPR, 1340-43*, 515; Welford, *Newcastle and Gateshead*, vol.1, 114-16.
[20]   Leadam, I.S. (ed.), *Select Cases before the King's Council in the Star Chamber, ii, A.D. 1500-1544*, Selden Soc., vol.25 (1911), pp.75-118.
[21]   Brand, *Newcastle*, vol.2, pp.311-61.

into the dispute and report back to Council in the week after Michaelmas 1515. There were three articles of examination. Firstly, whether any burgess might engage in another craft to his own without prior agreement. Secondly, whether any burgess other than a merchant might buy merchandise coming to the town beyond his own immediate needs. Thirdly, whether any artisan burgess other than a merchant might sell wholesale or retail beyond his immediate needs. These claims hark back to the 12th-century Laws of Newcastle, which established the sole right of Newcastle merchants to trade with incomers, and the Exchequer suit of 1305/7 which challenged the right of merchants to bar lesser burgesses from trading retail.[22]

Various elderly persons entered depositions to the effect that they had duly served an apprenticeship and later changed their trade by agreement. A weaver became a draper, a shipwright a mercer, a mariner a boothman, another weaver a butcher, a glover a keelman and a tailor a Hostman. On behalf of the artificers it was claimed that Thomas Denton, a smith, also dealt in iron, soap, tar and flax; John Robson, a tailor, dealt not only in linen and cloth, silks and velvets, but also in hats and bonnets, knives, spices, flax and corn. Robert Wys, a smith, dealt in iron, pitch, tar, flax and coals. John Watson, a fuller, dealt in corn, flax, cloth, wax, soap, iron, pepper and saffron. Robert Sadman, baker, dealt in soap, tar, iron, hats and bonnets, flax, pepper, corn and other commodities. In short, items of trade had enlarged in variety considerably since the 14th century.

Notwithstanding such evidence, it was decreed in May 1516 that none of the crafts of colliers, shoemakers, butchers, weavers, smiths, daubers, porters, keelmen, slaters, tilers, millers, cooks, spurriers, barbers, wrights, furbishers, bowyers, arrowsmiths, glovers, coopers, girdlers, challon-weavers, masons, saddlers, shipwrights and wallers should be admitted into the crafts of mercers, drapers or spicers unless they first renounced their own crafts and paid an admission fee to their new guild. The fee was based on personal assessment of financial standing. Those worth less than £10 would not be admitted; those between £10 and £39 should pay 10s.; those worth between £40 and £66 should pay 20s. Those worth more should pay £1 6s. 8d.[23] Once again a constitution was imposed on the town. The 12 ancient guilds would again present two of their body to elect four who now must be past mayors, aldermen or sheriffs of the town, who would add eight to themselves, who would elect a further 12 who would elect the mayor, six aldermen, a recorder, a sheriff, eight chamberlains,

[22] Leadam, *Select Cases*, pp.95, 97-9; Cf Dendy, F.W., 'The Struggle between the Merchants and Craft Gilds of Newcastle in 1515', *AA*, 3rd series, vol.7 (1911), pp.77-110, where a precis of the proceedings is printed.
[23] *Ibid.*, pp.111-14.

two coroners, a sword-bearer, a common clerk and eight serjeants-at-mace. None should be admitted a free burgess unless he had lived in the town for more than a year; any such should not be a liveried retainer of a lord unless the lord himself was free of the town. An oligarchy was firmly in place and no riot would shift it.[24]

Distribution of Wealth, Occupations and the Coal Trade

There are two sources of evidence of actual trade in Newcastle. One is the lay subsidy roll of 1296 and the other is customs accounts. If one looks at the subsidy roll one finds that Newcastle was divided into four wards named by parish, St Nicholas, St Andrew, St John and All Saints. There was a suburb of Pandon, integrated into the town in 1298. The 12 jurors who made the assessment were themselves rated at anything between £3 6s. for William Ogle, a town bailiff for six years and cited in 1305 as one of the 'rich burgesses', and £14 13s. 4d. for Adam Brydoke, another 'rich burgess' with land in Market Street. Most cannot be allocated to any specific ward. On the basis of this assessment St Nicholas ward was worth over £327; St John ward, £235; All Saints, £199; and St Andrew, £65. Pandon was worth £29, with Gilbert of Cowgate, an exporter of wool, assessed at £7 11s. 8d.[25]

It is now suspect to use surnames as an indicator of occupation in the 13th century. Using such evidence there were three tanners in St John ward. There were also three goldsmiths by name, although one is known to have been an exporter of wool and hides. Some of the wealthier burgesses lived in this ward, such as Alexander le Furber (£21 10s.), Nicholas son of David (£22 1s. 4d.), Peter Sampson (£31 10s.), Henry le Escot (£28), and James the tanner (£23 4s.). The wealthiest, however, lived in St Nicholas ward, which included part of the town's waterside above the bridge. These included the partnership of Hugh Gerardino and Isolda of Pandon (£84), Samson le Cutiller (£53 13s. 4d.) and Peter Graper (£20). All but James the tanner and Henry le Escot were exporters of wool and hides, as was John Torald (£21), who lived in All Saints' ward, which included the riverside below the bridge. On the figures provided by the lay subsidy Newcastle was second in wealth only to York in the north of England, assessed with Pandon at £948 12s. 5½d. paid by 295 householders.[26]

[24] *Ibid.*, pp.114-16.
[25] Fraser, *Lay Subsidy*, pp.39-47, 76-7.
[26] *Ibid.*, xiv. Cf. Hoskins, W.G., *Local History in England* (3rd edn, 1984), p.277. This was in marked contrast to other communities in Northumberland, where the second highest assessment was for Corbridge at £159, payable by 77 householders.

27 The Key, detail from Buck's view of Newcastle. Note the town wall running between the waterside and the houses.

Once the Crown in 1275 looked to the export trade in wool, hides and wool-fells as a source of revenue, Exchequer records provide the material to measure both the volume of trade between England and the continent and the relative volume of trade between the staple ports and overseas. Apart from the brief pre-eminence of Newcastle in the export of hides in 1292 the town was never in the same league as Boston or Hull. The local wool was of inferior grade to that of Lincolnshire or Herefordshire. Its sale, however, enabled local merchants to buy foreign luxuries such as wine to resell to local establishments and men of wealth. Trade with the Baltic enabled the import of timber for ship-building and corn, particularly rye, in time of shortage. The few surviving detailed accounts name local traders, who then can be identified as mayor or bailiffs of Newcastle, representatives in Parliament or, in the case of Richard Embleton, as royal commissioner helping to maintain law and order in the North East. Newcastle ships were commandeered for national service in 1324, when there

were fears of a French invasion. Then, alongside the wool customs, accounts begin to appear on miscellaneous items such as coal. At first this appears in small quantities where the ship's master paid on what has been considered as ballast. Having discharged the grain, wine, spices, dye-stuffs and onions, the wooden ships needed a return weight to maintain stability in the water – why not coal if a market could be found for it?[27]

The first indication that Newcastle considered its trade in coal as more than a side-line is the petition to Edward III and his council from the mayor, bailiffs and commons of Newcastle for the repeal of an ordinance of 1362 prohibiting all exports from England. They were particularly concerned by the ban on export of coal, as without it they had no other common merchandise with which to trade and thereby pay their annual fee-farm to the king. In the same vein the town asked the King to allow shipments of coal anywhere on the continent, pointing out that it was not a staple commodity, and when it was shipped to Calais

[27] TNA, E.122/106, 108; Wade, J.F. (ed.), *The Customs Accounts of Newcastle upon Tyne 1454-1500*, SS, vol.202 (1995), pp.6-15, 143-86; Davies, J. Conway, 'Wool Customs accounts for Newcastle upon Tyne for the reign of Edward I', *AA*, 4th series, vol.32 (1954), pp.247-8, 282-3, 285-6, 290-1, 294.

there could be problems finding buyers and even getting the cargo discharged. The market was not in France but the Netherlands and the Baltic.[28] Where the detailed accounts survive they record ships of Camfere, Sluys, Newhaven, Horne, Amsterdam, Stavoren, Middelburg, Dunkirk and Flushing entering with linen, white herring, wainscot, brass pots, madder and spars and leaving with coal to a greater value than the incoming cargo. The incoming cargo is not always specified, nor do cargoes always balance, but an example is the *Maryknight* of Nelnyn, which entered port on 7 June 1381 and landed three barrels of tallow valued at £3, to leave on 20 June with 68 chaldrons of coal valued at £6 16s. A ship of Campe on 10 August 1381 discharged 10,000 'tile-stones', a last of potash, two firkins of *scuricorn*, a last of pitch, and linen valued at £4. It left on 18 August with 44 chaldrons of coal valued at £4 8s. Another ship of Campe the same day landed 1,000 tiles and a last of pitch valued at 21s. 8d., and left on 18 August with 60 chaldrons of coal valued at £6.[29]

Business in Newcastle was booming. This belief is supported by the fact that in 1400 the new king, Henry IV, agreed to the town being granted the status of a county borough, a privilege initially granted to Bristol in 1373 to solve the problem of this prosperous port needing to look to both Gloucester and Taunton because of its location on a county boundary. The second such grant was to York, the northern capital, made by Richard II in 1396. The grant to Newcastle in 1400 meant that the four town bailiffs were replaced with a sheriff. There were already two coroners (since 1251.) There were to be six aldermen, who with the mayor would be *ex officio* justices of the peace within the 'county'.[30]

By grafting the activities of municipal figures onto the shippers recorded in the customs accounts it is possible to pen portraits of some of the leading merchants between 1369 and 1430. The first figure to emerge in this way is Stephen Whytgray, bailiff between 1369 and 1371 and mayor in 1384. In the latter capacity he represented Newcastle in Parliament in 1385. Between December 1380 and April 1383 he exported 40½ sacks of wool, 1,566 wool-fells and five lasts seven dickers of hides. The ships were owned in the Netherlands. He was collector of the king's customs at Newcastle in 1389/90. With his wife Mary he founded the chantry of St Margaret in St Nicholas' Church, Newcastle, in 1394. Robert Raynton, bailiff in 1377 and again between 1385 and 1387, was mayor in 1388. He exported in the period of surviving detailed accounts 48 sacks of

---

[28]   Fraser, *Petitions*, pp.249-50.
[29]   TNA, E.122/106/4 mm, 3-4.
[30]   Beresford, M. and Finberg, H.P., *English Medieval Boroughs: a Handlist* (1973) pp.11, 145, 185; Welford, *Newcastle and Gateshead*, vol.1, pp.224-8.

wool, 2,034 wool-fells and 15 dickers of hides. He was followed as bailiff but preceded as mayor by Robert Oliver. The latter as mayor represented the town in Parliament in 1383, was commissioned to find a large ship for the king's navy in 1387, and was a collector of customs in 1388. He exported 74½ sacks of wool and 3,242 wool-fells. In 1393 he committed suicide. John Horton was bailiff in 1375 and 1393, and mayor in 1389. He exported 59½ sacks of wool. William Jonson was bailiff in 1390 to 1392 and mayor in 1398. He was at the start of a career which saw him as commissioner for pontage and pavage in 1409 and MP in 1407 and 1414. His exports amounted to 13 sacks of wool and a last 11 dickers of hides.[31]

Robert of Hebburn was another merchant at the start of his career, with exports of 6½ sacks of wool, 2,145 wool-fells and five lasts 13 dickers of hides. The son of John Hibbern of Hebburn by Chillingham, he maintained the landed connection. A collector of murage in 1390, he was elected sheriff of Newcastle in 1403 following the grant to the town of county status. He represented the town in Parliament in 1406 and also in the dispute over the Tyne bridge in 1412. He was elected mayor in 1414, but died in office on 3 August 1415. The Hebburns continued with this dual status throughout the 15th century. Robert's sons, Thomas, Robert and Roger, maintained the tradition with the first two representing Newcastle in Parliament in 1414 and 1418 respectively. Robert was bequeathed by his father burgages in Sandgate, while Roger had property on the Quayside and in Pandon. Thomas's son John seems to have concentrated on his country interests. His son Ralph sold land in Broad Chare in 1506 which became the home of the Master Mariners of Trinity House.[32]

Robert Hebburn already had gentry status before he entered trade in Newcastle. The link between wealth in commerce leading to acquisitions of land outside the town is developed in the career of his near-contemporary Roger Thornton, a figure of legend and hero of the couplet:

Through the West Gate came Thornton in
With hap, a halfpenny and a lamb's skin.

In a deed of 1415 he was styled lord of Thornton near Stainton in Cleveland. In 1405 he bought the estate of Netherwitton in mid-Northumberland but held other land in the county and Durham. He was a bailiff in 1396, mayor in 1400, the year of county status, was re-elected a further eight times, and represented Newcastle in Parliament in 1399, 1400 and 1416. His will was entered into the

---

[31] TNA, E.122/106/4 passim, 5; Hunter Blair, 'Mayors and Sheriffs', pp.8-9.
[32] *NCH*, vol.14, pp.32-3.

28 Sandhill, the focus of Newcastle's commercial life, with St Thomas's chapel on the left.

register of Bishop Langley of Durham and so survives. In addition to handsome legacies to St Nicholas' Church and All Saints' he bequeathed lead to the churches of St John and St Andrew for repairs, and more to the chapel of St Thomas on Tyne bridge, to the West Spital alms house, to the chapel at Wallknowl, to St Bartholomew's Nunnery in Newcastle, to the abbey of Blanchland, Brinkburn priory, the chapels on Coquet Island and Farne Island, the nunnery at Holystone, and the 'steeple' of Durham cathedral. It has been suggested that the 400 marks forgiven to the prior and convent of Hexham was a debt for lead 'upon bygging of their Kyrk'. Other charitable legacies included £20 for the Maison Dieu on the Sandhill which he had founded and £10 for the chantry of St Peter in All Saints'. His enormous brass survives, now preserved in St Nicholas' Church.[33]

The Later Middle Ages

The prosperity of Newcastle in the 15th century has been a matter of controversy. Some considered that it successfully weathered the epidemics, decline in trade and the Wars of the Roses and the more specific threats arising from proximity to the Scottish border. Others chose to interpret the paucity of documentary material as evidence of a decline in prosperity, comparable with other English towns. A curious fact is that the situation in Newcastle passed without contemporary comment, as if it lay beyond the bounds of known England.[34] The customs accounts suggest a diminution in volume of trade, with incoming cargoes consisting in the main of herring, pack-thread, felt hats, straw hats, nuts, paper, soap, figs and raisins, onion seed, kettles, iron and hops. The outgoing items were sacks of wool, shorn hides and lambskins, lead and grindstones, with the occasional chaldron of coal. Yet an Act of Parliament of 1421 decreed that keels carrying coal to ships lying in the Tyne should pay by the boatload, which was estimated to contain eight chaldrons. Presumably it was being shipped coastwise, possibly to East Anglia.[35] By 1508, when Newcastle chamberlains' accounts become available, the majority of ships coming to the Tyne originated there. Coal was used to burn limestone for the making of mortar, and church building was rife in Norfolk and Suffolk at that date. The return cargoes could be corn, for which there was an insatiable need in the

[33] Storey, R.L., *The Register of Bishop Langley*, vol.3, SS, vol.169 (1954), pp.164-7; Hunter Blair, 'Mayors and Sheriffs', p.9. See also.

[34] Dobson, R.B., 'Urban Decline in late medieval England', *Transactions of the Royal Historical Soc.*, 5th series, vol.27 (1977), pp.3-5, 11-14, 19; Butcher, A.F., 'Rent, Population and Economic Change in late-medieval Newcastle', *Northern History*, 14 (1978), pp.66-77.

[35] Fraser, C.M., 'The North East Coal Trade before 1421', *Transactions of the Architectural and Archaeological Society of Durham and Northumberland*, XI (1962), p.218.

northern counties.[36] Whether it is a hint that trade was improving or a desperate throw to stave off competition, in 1480 the three guilds of wholesale merchants, the wool merchants, mercers and boothmen or corn merchants, combined to form the Company of Merchant Adventurers of Newcastle, affiliated to the company of that name in London. Their ordinances instituted a seven-year apprenticeship, and they would meet in the Maison Dieu on the Sandhill, later incorporated into the Guildhall.[37]

On 22 June 1489 seven Newcastle ships, namely the *Nicholas*, the *Mary Huberd*, the *George*, the *Mary Harden*, the *Marken*, the *Mary Alayn*, and the *George Galaunt* set sail from the Tyne. Against the names of the shippers was the joint entry stating that they were 'governors and merchants of the merchant guild of the king's town of Newcastle of the growth of Northumberland, Cumberland, Westmorland, the bishopric [of Durham] and the counties of Allerton and Richmond'. After the scarcity of information about shipping on the Tyne and the few references to local-owned ships one can almost hear the sound of trumpets as the Newcastle wool fleet set sail.[38]

The customs rolls for 1488/9 open a new chapter about trade on the Tyne. The recorded cargoes are different. Wine is being imported again. Richard Hebburn is no longer only to be known as the provider of Dalton Place for the master mariners but as an importer of wine and exporter of wool, wool-fells, shorlings and morlings. Robert Harden, surely not the sheriff of that name in 1474, was mayor in 1492, an importer of wine and woad and exporter of wool, and likely owner of the *Mary Harden* of Newcastle. Christopher Brigham, sheriff in 1495, imported wine, iron and rosin and exported wool, lead and millstones. He was also founder of an alms house.[39]

It may be significant as evidence of a new prosperity in the town from the turn of the 16th century that the Corporation's income and expenditure began to be recorded in a special book kept by the town chamberlains. A solitary example has survived for 1508 to 1511. The fact that revenue from shipping tolls is mixed with expenditure on wages, town entertainment and even the expenses of 'the

[36] Fraser, C.M., *Newcastle Chamberlains' Accounts 1508-11* (Newcastle, 1987), pp.xviii-ix.
[37] Dendy, F.W. (ed.), *Merchant Adventurers of Newcastle*, SS, 93 (1895), pp.xxv-ix. The relative prosperity of Newcastle in relation to other English towns is suggested in tabular form by W.G. Hoskins in his *Local History in England*, where it appears as third in 1334, 11th in 1377 and third again in 1523, and in the *Cambridge Urban History of Britain*, where it is ranked fourth, 12th and fourth respectively (Hoskins, *Local History*, 277; *Cambridge Urban History of Britain, vol.I, 600-1540* (ed.), D.M. Palliser (Cambridge, 2000), pp.755, 758, 761).
[38] TNA, E.122/108/2 mm 4-8.
[39] TNA, E.122/109/4, 12, 13: 109/1. Wade, *Customs Accounts*, pp.166, 198, 205, 207, 245-6. For Newcastle's role as a distribution and supply centre for the North East see Miranda Threllfall-Holmes, 'The Import Merchants of Newcastle upon Tyne, 1464-1520'. Some Evidence from Durham Priory', *Northern History*, 40 (2003), pp.71-87 and eadem, 'Newcastle Trade and Durham Priory, 1460-1520', in Liddy, Christian D. and Britnell, Richard H. (eds), *North-East England in the Later Middle Ages* (Woodbridge, 2005), pp.141-52.

29   A busy quayside scene in the early 19th century, by T.M. Richardson, snr.

plays' suggests that although the chamberlains had long been in existence they were still unused to book-keeping. When the next set of accounts survive, from the 1560s, income and expenditure are recorded separately, and by the week instead of by the day.[40]

The growing importance of the coal trade is also underlined in the returns of the chamberlains. The role of the 'Hostmen' in the town's governance is usually dated from the charter of Queen Elizabeth I, incorporating the guild or fraternity of Hostmen in 1600, giving its members a monopoly on the sale of coal and grindstones from the Tyne. The chamberlains' accounts from 1508, however, indicate that whenever a ship left the river with coal in its cargo an 'ost' was named. As the accounts were concerned with revenue and expenditure in the town this suggests that the 'ost' was not simply offering hospitality to an incoming merchant but was informing the chamberlains of the quantity

40   Fraser, *Chamberlains' Accounts, passim.*

of coal the ship was carrying.[41] 'Hosts' in Rouen, for instance, accommodated overseas merchants, handled their business with the public authorities, served as interpreters, put them in touch with local merchants, paid accounts in their name as necessary, cashed their letters of credit and advanced them money.[42] Some Newcastle 'osts' might serve only occasionally. Others did so repeatedly. Edward Baxter, mercer, served 147 times between 1508 and 1511. John Brandling, boothman, served 101 times. He had been sheriff of the town in 1505 and was later mayor in 1512, 1516 and 1520. Christopher Brigham, another boothman, served as 'ost' 321 times. Allen Hardyng, mercer, served 280 times. Thomas Sanderson, 255 times; Edmund Jekluff, 220 times and William Winship, 153 times. Baxter, Brandling and Sanderson can be found in the customs accounts as coal-shippers. It is interesting to note that ships serviced by Baxter, Brandling and Hardyng were mainly from the continent. Brandling specialised in ships from the Netherlands, particularly Antwerp. Hardyng specialised in ships from the French Channel ports. On the other hand, most of Brigham's ships came from East Anglia.[43]

It is worth noting here the number of ships 'registered' from Dunwich, which had long ceased to be a viable harbour. The explanation for this puzzle for East Anglian historians as to why men continued to seek admission to the freedom of the lost port of Dunwich may be that it enabled them to claim the benefit of reduced tolls at Newcastle on their cargoes of coals. Whereas there was equal liability for payment of ballast dues, there was a preferential rate of 1d. a chaldron on outgoing cargoes of coal. The favoured ports of Scarborough, York, Hull, Grimsby, Great Yarmouth, Dunwich, Colchester, London, Rochester, Dover, Sandwich, Rye, Portsmouth and Dartmouth could be regarded in some sense as royal foundations, sharing a common status with Newcastle. A 'free' ship of Dunwich would normally have paid a toll of 20d. on a cargo of 20 chaldrons of coal. An 'unfree' ship would have paid 80d., namely an impost of 20d. plus 60d. toll at the rate of 3d. a chaldron. (The rate for ballast dues was a fixed impost of 12d. and a further toll of 1½d. a ton on ballast discharged on the town's ballast shores.) Again, freemen and free ships paid at a special rate of 3d. a chaldron on grindstones, against the 12d. charged to the unfree. The chamberlains' accounts indicate that unfree shippers paid 21d. a last on tar, an impost of 2d. a wey on salt, and an impost of 2d. then 2½d. a chaldron on wheat, rye, malt and beans.

[41] *Ibid.*; Fraser, C.M., 'The early Hostmen of Newcastle upon Tyne', *AA*, 5th series, vol.12 (1984), pp.171-8. A deposition by John Robson, tailor, given in the case in Star Chamber in 1515, refers to the 'craft' of Hostmen. He had been required to pay 6s. 8d. to acquire its membership (Leadam, pp.88-9 and note 17).
[42] Mollat, M., *Le Commerce Maritime Normand* (Paris, 1952), p.424.
[43] Fraser, *Chamberlains' Accounts*, pp.262-6.

30 The annual Ascension Day celebration of Newcastle's monopoly on the Tyne in the early 19th century by J.W. Carmichael.

Freemen paid at a flat rate of 2d. on each type of commodity imported, except for barley and wheat, which paid a toll of 1d. a chaldron.[44]

Owners of 'unfree' ships were less happy. In 1524 the shipmasters of Aldeburgh – not in the charmed circle – were complaining about the Newcastle tolls. They grumbled that every ship or boat not free of the town had to pay an impost of 20d., with a further impost of 12d. if it discharged ballast, on which a further toll of 3d. a ton was charged. The outgoing cargo was charged at the rate of 2d. a chaldron on coal and 3d. a chaldron on grindstones. The tolls were bad enough but the ballast charges were outrageous. The full range of incoming cargoes cannot be quantified because freemen were exempt from toll, but ships were coming to the Tyne with surplus capacity and thus in ballast. The main object of the visit was to load coal. The laws of Newcastle required ships to discharge at Newcastle, nine miles up river. The ballast had to be discharged carefully to prevent it slipping into the river and so choking the channel. Ballast shores along the river bank were controlled by Newcastle

44 *Ibid.*, pp.xiii-xvi, xxiii, 248-51.

freemen. The chamberlains' accounts note regular payment to a clerk for keeping the ballast shore.[45]

From 1508 a new light is shed on town affairs with the survival of the chamberlains accounts, still recording by the day their expenditure on goods and services and receipts from tolls. There was a directly paid work-force of paviors, masons, sawyers and the like kept busy cleaning the streets and repairing houses. The town was responsible for maintenance of at least the clock and bell at St Nicholas' Church, which summoned the burgesses to formal business meetings and announced the various fairs. Costs arose from the town's coal-pits on the Town Moor. There were town charities, including gifts in money and coal to the various alms houses. There was official hospitality, with gifts of wine to distinguished visitors to the town. A town bull was provided, presumably for the benefit of the freemen's cows.[46] Master Hugh, the schoolmaster on 28 June 1510, was paid 43s. 4d. for a year's wages. The chief officers, mayor, sheriff and recorder, drew substantial fees and commensurate expenses. The mayor in 1509 received £23, and £25 in 1510; the sheriff in 1509 received £24 15s., and the recorder received £13. When in October 1509 the Mayor and Christopher Brigham went to London with the town farm their expenses amounted to £37 5s. 10d. Also charged to the town in January 1509 was the cost of new regalia: 27 grey skins for the mayor's 'hat', 9s; the furrier's services, 2s. 8d.; a belt for the mayor's sword, 12d.; canvas for the mayor's 'hat', 3d.; its sewing, 6d.; a 'wire' for the hat, 2s.; and a velvet belt for the scabbard, 12d. The making and silver-gilding of a buckle and pendant for the sword cost 9s. Even the town minstrel had a silver collar which weighed 16 ounces and cost 10s. 8d.[47]

The mayor of Newcastle symbolised the importance of the town in a national setting. In 1391 Richard II had granted the mayor the privilege of a sword of honour to be carried before him. Nine years later his successor, Henry IV, in his anxiety to attach the town's allegiance to him, granted it county status. This was supplemented in 1403 with remission of any outstanding fines in view of losses from the Scots, falling bridges occasioned by sudden floods, and expenses incurred in keeping armed ships victualled at sea and supporting a nightly watch on the town walls with 100 men. The mayor also had admiralty jurisdiction over the river.[48]

[45] Welford, *Newcastle and Gateshead*, vol.2, pp.85-6.
[46] Fraser, *Chamberlains' Accounts*, pp.129, 134, 137, 140, 154, 164, 171, 185, 214-15, 238.
[47] *Ibid.*, pp.56, 102, 124, 266.
[48] Welford, *Newcastle and Gateshead*, vol.1, pp.212-13, 224-9.

Shipping

Information about the actual ships and where they were built is sketchy. In 1294 Edward I commissioned galleys from various ports around England. The accounts for building the Newcastle galley survive. The keel measured 135 feet and the vessel was to be propelled by 60 oars, assisted by a sail. The timber cost £50 8s. 4d., the nails and ironwork cost £22 16s. 7½d., pitch, tar and caulking material cost £11 2s., and the carpenters' wages amounted to £66 4s. 1¾d. Work lasted for 41 weeks and an average of 21 men were employed, including a master shipwright and his assistant, carpenters, hammer-men, 'holders-up', painters, a squad for launching the ship, berthing and rigging, smiths, sawyers and a watchman. General excavations of the Quayside area preparatory to building the new Law Courts suggest that the building yard lay beside the Pandon burn. No other accounts for shipbuilding on the Tyne survive for the medieval period.[49]

In general the ships plying from Newcastle were of modest tonnage – measured by capacity for tuns of wine. In 1324 Edward II required the mayor and bailiffs to send information about ships in the port of more than 100 tons' burden, and they returned the names of six ships and their owners. Only two were of the prescribed size. One was of only 50 tons. Merchants generally spread their cargoes over several ships to minimise losses at sea. Newcastle ships were small but sturdy, suitable for carriage of coal.[50] Little is known of the ship masters. One of the few was Lewis Southern, who appears as master of the *Mary Harden* of Newcastle in June 1489. In October 1499 he was master of the *James* of Newcastle in which he carried 1¾ sacks of wool under his own name and was described against the entry as a Merchant Adventurer. On 12 December 1505 he imported seven tuns one pipe of Gascon wine in the *Trinity* of Newcastle. On 17 April 1506 he entered the Tyne as master of the *Elizabeth* of Newcastle with a cargo of Gascon wine and a personal shipment of seven tuns one pipe. The following day he shipped 360 shorlings and morlings in the *Trinity* of Newcastle. The majority of ships recorded that year were foreign-registered, coming for coal, although Bertram Yonghusband shipped two fothers of lead on 17 July. Southern recurs on 3 December 1508 importing one hogshead of unsweet wine in the *Trinity* of Newcastle, and again on 9 January 1509 he shipped three hogsheads in a different *Trinity*. (At least the master had changed.) The same day he shipped eight tuns in the *Elizabeth* of Newcastle. On the outward voyage on

---

[49] Whitwell, R.J. and Johnson, C., 'The Newcastle Galley A.D. 1294', *AA*, 4th series, vol.2 (1926), pp.142-93.
[50] TNA, SC.2 (Ancient Correspondence) XXXIV, p.140; Wade, J.F., 'The Overseas Trade of Newcastle', *Northern History*, vol.30 (1994), pp.35-6.

24 April, Southern exported 100 shorlings. He also paid on 20 chaldrons of coal and 10 chaldrons of millstones. Southern appears again on 30 November 1513 when he shipped four sarplers of wool, 10 chaldrons of coal, and a quantity of hides in the *Trinity* of Newcastle. When the master, John Watson, returned to Newcastle on 6 March 1514, his ship was named, perhaps significantly, the *Trinity Lewes* and Southern had a cargo of eight tuns of wine and a butt of rumney. It is fitting that the chamberlains' accounts for 10 July 1509 note payment of £6 to Southern for a tun and a hogshead of wine 'to the town'. These accounts have references aplenty to him as a Hostman, handling coastwise shipments from Hull to Hythe and across the Channel at Calais and Dieppe.[51]

In keeping with this upturn in shipping trade a guild of masters and mariners had been established in Newcastle before 1500. Its first known activity was the founding of a chantry dedicated to the Trinity in All Saints' Church. In 1506 a site was acquired in Broad Chare off the quayside for a hall, chapel and alms house for its poor brethren and in 1536 Henry VIII formally incorporated the guild, to be governed by a master and four wardens. It was made responsible for the maintenance of the buoys in the haven and river of Tyne and given exclusive rights of pilotage. The guild was to build two lighthouses, one at the entrance to the haven and another on the hill adjoining, and maintain a light at night. To meet the costs they were authorised to levy 4d. from each foreign ship and 2d. from each English ship using the port.[52]

Newcastle maintained its ranking among the wealthiest towns in England throughout the Middle Ages, despite its proximity to the Scottish border – hence its massive walls. It was a superb centre for communications between east and west of North England which it combined with the bridge-crossing of the Tyne carrying traffic from north and south. The river being navigable enabled the town to enjoy the economies of water transport. In short, it was the regional centre for trade in wool, corn and coal, and its port facilities enabled its merchants to reach down the east coast and across to the Baltic and the ports of the Netherlands and France, warfare permitting. Its potential for tax revenue ensured royal favour, to the detriment of local rivals. The omens were bright for the future.

[51]   TNA, E.122/108/13 mm 2, 6d: 109/1 mm 3, 5. Among the depositions made in Star Chamber in 1515 is one from Southern. He said that he was about sixty years old and in 1403 had paid 26s. 8d. for admission to the craft of boothman (Leadham, *Select Cases*, p.87). Scrutiny of the admissions books for the Merchant Adventurers leads to a suspicion that the nominated speciality of wool merchant, mercer or boothman was notional rather than real. In the case of Southern his incoming cargos tended to be wine rather than corn.
[52]   Brand, *Newcastle*, vol.2, p.324; Welford, *Newcastle and Gateshead*, vol.2, pp.21-2, 77-80, 120, 151-7.

4

The Church and Religion in Newcastle, 1080-1540

ANTHONY GOODMAN

Introduction

The name, Newcastle upon Tyne, neatly conjoins the strategic purpose of its function and its possession of a prime communications facility, which were to be essential in making it into the most commercially successful English new town of the Middle Ages. For Newcastle cannot trace its roots, or the flowering of its fame and prestige, to a holy presence or aura – to origins as the suburban adjunct either of a powerful and rich monastic house, or the seat of a bishopric, or of a shrine housing a major relic. The secular character of much of the patronage it received is symbolised in the surviving sculpture of the royal coat of arms, which was placed in the 14th century over one of its principal gates. Its ecclesiastical institutions did not glimmer with anciently hoarded numinous power. They were newly minted during the course of the Middle Ages. Though their foundation and good maintenance required clerical authority and input, they tended to be strongly moulded by secular society and to cater for its daily humdrum needs. In the 200 years or so after the foundation of the castle, kings and nobles were conspicuous, and probably often dominant, among secular founders and patrons of religious institutions in the town. In the later Middle Ages, shifts in economic and social power brought to the fore as their equivalents rich members of a mercantile elite. They displayed their own preferences in devotion. Some of them were prompted to take initiatives which stood on clerical toes. Others, notably Roger Thornton and Robert Rodes, left their handiwork writ large in ecclesiastical architecture and the furnishing of churches.

There are religious parallels with the region in classical times. The existence of at least three temples of Mithras associated with Hadrian's Wall reflects the presence of cosmopolitan elements in a society remote from the centres of civilisation in the Roman Empire. However, some surviving inscriptions show the continued liveliness of pre-Roman cults in the Wall settlements. In medieval Newcastle, which at least one distinguished traveller considered as an outpost against barbarism, there were also culturally diverse influences at work. We need to consider the interplay of cosmopolitan innovation and regional traditionalism in Newcastle's religion; and also how dynamic the influence of the town was in the ecclesiastical and religious life of the North East.

It is difficult to make comprehensive judgements on how well the clergy sustained their offices, fulfilling the pristine, fundamental objectives of their ministries, especially in changing circumstances, such as occurred in periods of deteriorating finances, or when religious mentalities were generally in flux. Our information about the Church in Newcastle tends to be more sparse and random for the early Middle Ages than for the 14th and 15th centuries. It is easier to take a more roseate view of the former period, especially because it was *par excellence* the age of soaring religious aspirations and new foundations. One is inclined to believe that first flushes of zeal often overcame teething troubles, such as resulted from mundane practicalities. For instance, some friaries in Newcastle either experienced problems in protecting their water supplies, or endured encroachments from the construction of the town wall. However, the demise of the short-lived house of the Friars of the Sack provided a cautionary tale of the failure of good intentions.

We are better informed about problems and shortcomings in the later Middle Ages, such as disputes over the distribution and collection of parochial revenues, the alleged backslidings of secular priests, tensions between the seculars and regulars, and infighting among the nuns of St Bartholomews's Priory. The economic and social factors which caused or exacerbated problems are more fully apparent; notably falls in income from urban rents and estates, and the often interconnected outbreaks of plague. Yet perhaps we should see these times of trouble, when the record spotlight so often illuminates institutional malfunctions and the clergy's failings, against a background in which shoots of reform and renewal appear. They constituted a largely bourgeois reformation, with the foundation of chantries and charitable institutions, and the embracing of christocentric cults which were strongly connected to the *devotio moderna*.

Clergymen indeed played roles in developing and channelling lay religious impulses. Newcastle friars seem to have been efficacious in this respect down to the Reformation. A couple of Dominican friars who were would-be reformers, albeit of different stripes, stand out. A Lollard preacher briefly inspired cells of clergy and laity. Towards the end of our period, the Franciscan Observants increased devotion among the laity. Today we have prominent reminders of the piety of later medieval Newcastle: the predominantly rebuilt parish churches. The principal monument of the soaring aspirations of its mercantile elite is the great tower of St Nicholas', comparable in its spiritual significance to other dominating urban rebuildings of churches of the period, such as the dome of the Duomo in Florence.

Ecclesiastical Authority and Parochial Organisation

The first glimmer of documentary light on the Church in medieval Newcastle is shed by the account by Symeon of Durham (*fl. c.*1090 – *c.*1178) of how in 1073 Aldwin, Prior of Winchcombe (Glos), and two monks from Evesham, set out on a pilgrimage to Northumbria. Aldwin and his companions had been inspired to do so by reading Bede's *Historia Ecclesiastica*. They joined Aldwin in his aim to lead a life of poverty and contemplation amidst hallowed Northumbrian settings. They were given land by Bishop Walcher of Durham on the north bank of the River Tyne, in the earldom of Northumbria, at *Muncaceastre* (Monkchester), a place which Symeon identified with Newcastle. The name 'Monkchester' suggests that this was on the site of an earlier monastery within remains of a Roman fort; presumably one which guarded the Tyne crossing. However, the newcomers were disappointed that they could find no vestige of an ancient monastic settlement there. The Bishop persuaded them to move, granting them St Paul's Church, Jarrow, substantially the structure known to Bede. Another possible reason for their abandonment of Monkchester was that it may have been, for the monks' purposes, too near to a busy secular settlement, such as one might expect to have existed close by the ancient thoroughfare carried across the Tyne by the *Pons Aelius*.[1]

Robert Curthose's building of the new castle in 1080 provided an impulse for ecclesiastical development in the vicinity. St Nicholas', which was to be the sole church with full parochial rights in medieval Newcastle, is first mentioned in 1094.[2] It lay between the castle gates and the main urban markets, and it may have developed to serve artisans and traders who clustered around there to cater for the castle folk.[3] The church belonged to the king, for in 1125 Henry I granted it to

---

[1]   Arnold, T. (ed.), 'Historia Ecclesiae Dunelmensis', *Simeonis Monachi Opera Omnia*, Rolls series, vol.2 (1882), pp.108-10; 'Historia Regum', *ibid.*, p.201; Aird, William M., *St Cuthbert and the Normans. The Church of Durham, 1071-1155* (1998), 101, 199n, 237n, 260, 273. I owe thanks to Dr Aird and Dr Marilyn Dunn for their advice on the background to this mission, and to Professor Tony Pollard for much helpful advice on a variety of other issues. I am grateful for Dr Harry Schnitker's advice too.

[2]   Quiney, Anthony, 'Newcastle Cathedral', *The Archaeological Journal*, vol.13 (1976), p.245.

[3]   Fullett, Edmond, and McCombie, Frances, 'Excavations in the Cloth Market, Newcastle upon Tyne, 1979', *AA*, 5th series, vol.8 (1980), pp.127-9.

31   St Nicholas' Church (now Cathedral),
a detail from James Corbridge's map of
Newcastle.

the Church of St Mary of Carlisle and its canons.[4] In 1194-5 Bishop Hugh Puiset of Durham made an important settlement of the priory's and the vicar of Newcastle's respective financial rights in the church. The former was to receive the great tithes (of sheaves and crops), and the latter, with the consent of the prior as rector, all the other revenues. However, by the mid-13th century the bishops of Carlisle established a right to a portion of the priory's revenues from the church. According to the general valuation of benefices of 1291, the great tithes were then divided equally between the bishop and the cathedral priory. They shared the bulk of the annual income from what was a very wealthy parish Their portions were calculated at £38 13s. 4d. each, with the bishop also receiving an additional pension of 13 marks from the vicar. The vicar's income was calculated at the substantial sum of £20.[5] However, a valuation of 1318 shows a big decline in parochial income, especially of that from the great tithes: only £10 was ascribed to the vicar, but merely £5 each to the bishop and prior.[6] Perhaps revenue from crops had declined because Northumberland had suffered from harvest failures or Scottish ravages. On the other hand, the vicar's portion may have been better sustained from the dues owed by leading burgesses, who were protected by the formidable new town walls, and enriched by supplying the king's armies, and by overseas trade. Some of the burgesses were notable in the period for their endowments of friaries in the town, and of chantries in its secular churches. The vicar's income was, it seems, relatively substantial later on in the century: in 1381 the vicar, Matthew de Bolton, was assessed for subsidy at 13s. 4d. – more than any other vicar in the Archdeaconry of Northumberland.[7]

    ⁴ Johnson, C. and Cronne, H.A. (ed.), *Regesta Regum Anglo-Normannorum 1066-1154*, vol.2, *Regesta Henrici Primi* (1956), no.1431.
    ⁵ Snape, M.G. (ed.), *English Episcopal Acta, 25, Durham 1196-1237*, vol.1, nos 105-6; Brand, *Newcastle*, vol.1, pp.238-9, 242-3. The Prior of Tynemouth had a portion of the parochial revenue, then £8. Cf the assessments made in 1254, in Lunt, W.E., *The Valuation of Norwich* (1926), p.201.
    ⁶ Brand, *Newcastle*, vol.1, p.243. The Prior of Tynemouth's share was then reduced to £2.
    ⁷ TNA, Exchequer T.R., E359/4, clerical subsidy.

Tensions arose over parochial revenues. In 1341 Bishop Kirkby of Carlisle leased the tithes of his churches in Northumberland for two years to the rector of Rothbury (Northumberland) and Robert de Penereth, burgess of Newcastle, in return for a loan. This particular alienation does not seem to have been licensed by Bishop Bury of Durham, for Kirkby indemnified the lessees against action by his fellow bishop or other interested parties.[8] In 1376 Bishop Hatfield of Durham declared that the pensions due from the prior and convent of Carlisle to St Nicholas' and its (separate) chapels were in arrears. The Bishop had therefore sequestrated Carlisle Priory's portion, and now threatened an interdict if payment was not forthcoming. The prior and convent had for a long time let their revenues from the church at farm to lay persons without special licence, Hatfield declared. In 1380 he once again alluded to non-payment of such pensions by the prior and convent. He denounced their farming of St Nicholas' revenues to laymen in strong terms, and threatened excommunication and interdict.[9] Perhaps these disputes strengthened the laity's natural tendency to evade the payment of tithes. In 1382 Bishop Fordham of Durham, as a result of a complaint by Bishop Appleby of Carlisle, and by its prior, ordered the vicar of St Nicholas' to excommunicate all those who had obstructed the collection of tithes in the parish.[10] It may have become a long-standing grievance among poorly endowed Carlisle prelates that their share of the profits from the church had fallen. In 1402 the Abbot of St Mary's Abbey, York, was commissioned by Pope Boniface IX to enquire into the complaint of Bishop Strickland of Carlisle, and the Prior and Chapter of Carlisle Cathedral, that the value of the great tithe allotted to them (worth, they said, more than 140 marks p.a. when the original division of revenues was made) had so diminished, as a result of 'wars and other evil dispositions of those parts', that at present it did not exceed 50 marks. On the other hand, they claimed, the value of the vicar's allotment of profits had risen from at most 100 to over 200 marks. They wanted the old balance to be restored.[11]

The bishops and canons of Carlisle had to be on the watch to make sure that their authority in Newcastle was not ignored and flouted in a variety of ways. In 1368 Thomas de Salkeld, the proctor of Bishop Appleby of Carlisle and of the prior and convent there, found Robert de Merlay, chaplain, sitting near partially completed building works at St Nicholas', which the proctor was convinced the

[8]   Storey, Robin L. (ed.), *The Register of John Kirkby Bishop of Carlisle, 1332-1352 and the Register of John Ross Bishop of Carlisle 1325-32*, Canterbury and York Society, 81 vol.2 (Woodbridge, 1995), no. 587.
[9]   DCM, DPK, fos 76, 114v-115r. Hereafter Reg. Hatfield.
[10] Storey, R.L. (ed.), *The Register of Thomas Appleby Bishop of Carlisle, 1363-1395*, Canterbury and York Society, 96 (Woodbridge, 2006), p.94.
[11] Bliss, W.H. and Twemlow, J.A. (eds), *Calendar of Papal Registers. Papal Letters*, vol.5, 1396-1404 (1904), pp.513-14.

suspiciously evasive chaplain was involved in. He forbade him from proceeding with the demolition of the adjoining choir. The same day the proctor met two burgesses on Sandhill, Robert Angreton and John del Chambre, whom he considered were encouraging the building works: he repeated his prohibition to them. It would seem that the vicar and some rich parishioners, intent on modernising the church, were colluding to bypass the rights of the patrons.[12] They were apparently ignored in the case of a later presentation to the vicarage. Pope Boniface IX authorised the Prior of Bridlington to execute an exchange of benefices, as desired by the vicar of St Nicholas', Robert Thirsk. Bishop Strickland seems to have petitioned that the resulting collation to the church was invalid, on the grounds that he and other interested parties had not given consent. In 1405 Innocent VII upheld the validity of his predecessor's action.[13]

The sometimes cavalier behaviour of later medieval vicars of Newcastle towards their patrons was probably emboldened by the singular authority which they wielded over an important town, an authority occasionally supplemented and extended geographically by *ad hoc* commissions and other offices to which bishops of Durham appointed them.[14] The church of St Nicholas was, indeed, well known in Northumberland, for it was a convenient venue for the discharge of some of Northumberland's ecclesiastical business and for the conduct of some layfolks' secular affairs as well. It provided a widely accessible and spacious as well as hallowed setting for various sorts of settlement. There were numerous chaplains attached to it who might prove useful in discharging such matters, and there was plenty of nearby accommodation. So in 1316 an inquisition was held there as to the rights of presentation to Edlingham church (Northumberland).[15] In 1376-7 ordinations were carried out by suffragan bishops.[16] In 1430 a commission met in the church to enquire as to whether the vicarage of Woodhorn (Northumberland) was vacant. A chaplain of St Nicholas', John Coke, was one of the jurors.[17]

---

[12] Welford, *Newcastle and Gateshead*, vol.1, pp.173-5. Robert Angreton was elected mayor in 1363 and 1364, and in the years from 1369 to 1374 (*ibid.*, p.427). John del Chambre was elected mayor in 1361 and 1371 (Hunter Blair, C.H., *The Mayors and Lord Mayors of Newcastle upon Tyne and the Sheriffs of the County of Newcastle upon Tyne 1399-1940* (Newcastle, 1940), pp.6, 7.

[13] Twemlow (ed.), *Calendar of Papal Registers. Papal Letters*, vol.6, 1404-1415 (1904), pp.25-6.

[14] Example in Storey, R.L., *Thomas Langley and the Bishopric of Durham, 1406-1437* (Oxford, 1961), p.171. Professor Storey noted that the vicar was Dean of one of the three rural Deaneries of Northumberland.

[15] Welford, *Gateshead and Newcastle*, vol.1, p.39.

[16] Reg. Hatfield, fos 76-7.

[17] Storey, R.L. (ed.), *The Register of Thomas Langley, Bishop of Durham 1406-1437*, SS, 6 vols (1956-70), vol.3, p.80. For an example of settlement of secular disputes in St Nicholas', see below, p.109. Some diocesan business was conducted in other ecclesiastical premises in Newcastle. In 1417 an instrument recording the vicar of Mitford's appointment of proctors to resign his cure was exhibited in the Dominican priory in Newcastle, with the Prior and a *lector* of the house as witnesses (Storey, *Reg. Langley*, vol.5, pp.100-1). In 1427 an enquiry about the status of the vicarage of Alwinton (Northumberland) was held in St John's Church (*ibid.*, vol.6, pp.2-3).

As elsewhere, notably in urban parish churches, in the later Middle Ages, the foundation of perpetual chantries by the rich became popular as a means to minimise their pains in Purgatory. Such foundations had notable effects on the institutional, devotional and architectural development of St Nicholas' and the town's principal chapels. Most of the licensed chantries received endowments in order to provide for one established cantarist. Nearly all of them were set up by, or on behalf of, wealthy individual burgesses (eligible for high urban office), sometimes conjointly with their wives. The endowments usually consisted of tenements and/or rents within the town. In the early 14th century, anticipated annual incomes of £5 and six marks from endowments were not uncommon, providing better livings than those enjoyed by many stipendiary priests.[18] With exceptional generosity, Richard de Emeldon (frequently elected mayor) in 1332 granted town rents totalling £10 p.a. for the maintenance of two chaplains at St John the Baptist's altar in St Nicholas' Church. By contrast, some original endowments turned out to be inadequate. The 20s. which the burgess Laurence de Durham provided in 1327 at St Katherine's altar in the same church proved so: in 1379 it was topped up with an additional 20s. in rent.[19]

One principal source of knowledge for the institution of perpetual chantries consists of the royal licences for alienation of property in mortmain enrolled on the Patent Rolls. Professor Krieder has warned that these do not prove that intended foundations were implemented, and, besides, many unlicensed foundations were made. Especially in the North, there were numbers of unlicensed foundations dating from the first half of the 16th century. However, there is a consensus that the tallies of licences do reflect that the 14th century, especially in its early decades, was the heyday of foundations.[20] This is certainly the impression given by the sequence of 20 or so licences enrolled for Newcastle on the Patent Rolls. The chantry surveyors of 1546 listed 24 functioning chantries, some of them particularised as of old foundation. Nine of them were in St Nicholas', a large number for any parish church.[21]

[18] For instance, Hugh de Angreton had a royal licence to endow a chantry in St Nicholas' with a rent of 6 marks in 1333, and John Shapacope one there, at the altar of St Thomas the Martyr, with £5 rent in 1338 (CPR, 1330-1334, 430; CPR, 1338-1340, 116).

[19] CPR, 1327-1330, 109; CPR, 1330-1334, 264; CPR, 1377-1381, 347; Welford, Newcastle and Gateshead, vol.1, pp.421-4. In York only a minority of founders made provision with the expectation that it would provide an income for the cantarist above the statutory minimum of five or six marks (Dobson, R.B., 'The Foundation of Perpetual Chantries by the Citizens of York', in Cumming, G.J. (ed.), Studies in Church History, vol.4 (1967), pp.30-1).

[20] Krieder, Alan, English Chantries. The Road to the Dissolution (Cambridge, MA, 1979), pp.72-3, 89-90; Dobson, 'Foundation of Perpetual Chantries', pp.26-7; Rosenthal, Joel T., The Purchase of Paradise. Gift Giving and the Aristocracy, 1307-1485 (1972), pp.33-4.

[21] Valor Ecclesiasticus, vol.5, pp.27-8 (Deanery of Newcastle).

According to Krieder, between the compilation of the *Valor Ecclesiasticus* (1535) and the Act of 1545, which abolished chantries and confiscated their possessions, there appears to have been a general increase in their private abolition.[22] In Newcastle the chantry of Our Lady, founded on leading citizen George Carr's behalf in St Nicholas' by his executors in 1524, was terminated by Thomas Carr in 1536: it then had an income of £5 6s. 8d. It had been funded, unusually, by annual charges on the family's estates in Yorkshire and the County Palatine.[23] Comparisons of the incomes from tenements and rents for other Newcastle chantries recorded in 1535 and after the 1545 Act suggest that their cantarists' annuities had generally risen at face value over the period, if not usually by much. The Thornton Chantry at St Peter's altar in All Saints' Church (founded by Roger Thornton about a century before) had an income of £6, according to these surveys, which provided its cantarist with £5 8s. p.a. in 1548. Four other cantarists in the town received over £5 then, better renumeration than that of many curates. Seven cantarists in St Nicholas' received over £4, and five between £3 and £4; only one fell short of £3. Based on the dissolution survey, the median for cantarists' incomes in this church was £4 9s. 7d., just over 2s. more than the median for those in All Saints' Church. The medians for the few cantarists in the churches of St John the Baptist and St Andrew were lower, respectively just over £3 14s. and £3 2s. On the whole, on the eve of dissolution, Newcastle chantries seem to have maintained an adequate financial basis. The survival of most of them since the survey of 1535 suggests that conservatism in religion was strong in the city.[24]

Churches and chapels provided other pathways to seek to alleviate the pains of Purgatory, some open to the less well-off. Indulgences might be offered to those who contributed to the costs of improving church buildings and furnishings. Especially in the later Middle Ages, when literacy was more widespread, wealthy donors sometimes solicited suffrages by having the works they had paid for in churches identified not just by their heraldic devices, but by name tags requesting prayers. St Nicholas' provides examples. It had already been rebuilt on a more impressive scale in the second half of the 12th century, but it was damaged by a fire in 1216. The church has few visible early features: it was thoroughly reconstructed in the 14th and 15th centuries. According to a mandate of Bishop Hatfield (1359), the greater part of the rebuilding was then completed. He granted an indulgence of 40 days for those who offered at Mass there on particular feast days, in order

[22] Krieder, *Chantries*, pp.5, 134, 136. Cf Dobson, 'Foundation of Perpetual Chantries', p.23.
[23] Brand, *Newcastle*, vol.1, pp.258-9.
[24] *Valor Ecclesiasticus*, vol.5, pp.27-8; Brand, *Newcastle*, vol.1, pp.106-9 (St John's Church), pp.181-2 (St Andrew's), pp.252-9 (St Nicholas'), pp.361-7 (All Saints').

32   The south transept of St Nicholas' Church, by T.M. Richardson, snr.

to contribute towards the fabric and furnishings.[25] However, though the structure was manifestly transformed by 1400, much work remained to be done, especially in raising the new tower. In 1426 the Coopers' Guild diverted a portion of their fines in aid of 'kyrke warke'.[26] In 1429 Roger Thornton, whom John Leland was to describe as 'the richest merchant ever to live in Newcastle', bequeathed as much as 40 marks for repairs and fittings. He or his executors apparently paid for the cost of glazing the east window. An inscription in it requested prayers for him and his children.[27] In 1435 Bishop Langley provided another indulgence of 40 days for parishioners and others from the diocese who made donations or bequests for the fabric and furnishings.[28] On the tower vault was painted the inscription, 'Orate pro anima Roberti Rodes': Rodes was an outstanding benefactor of Newcastle churches.[29] The son of a mayor of Newcastle, Rodes (d.1474), was a lawyer who was mayor himself in 1429-31, and sat for the city in five Parliaments between 1427 and 1441. However, his principal career was as a leading administrator in the service of Durham Cathedral Priory.[30] His outstanding gifts for the fabric of St Nicholas' and the city's other churches suggest a vein of piety which went deeper than conventional expectations of the efficacy of indulgences, and of the prayers of passers-by. Like some munificent *signori* in Italian communes, he helped to transform his native city's church interiors, and to redefine its skyline for centuries to come. The fine marble font in St Nicholas' is prominently decorated with his arms and those of his kin. Some other later medieval furnishings remain in the church – the stylish wooden font cover (similar to the one in St Andrew's Church), and the brass eagle lectern, all dating from *c.*1500.[31]

There are no tomb effigies or brasses remaining *in situ* which commemorate medieval burgesses in St Nicholas', though the effigy of the wife of George Carr (elected mayor nine times between 1484 and 1502) survived from their lost canopied tomb.[32] Peter Marshal, former squire of Edward I, was buried there

---

[25]   Reg. Hatfield, fos.155-6.

[26]   Brand, *Newcastle*, vol.1, p.246. For stages in the rebuilding, Quiney, 'Newcastle Cathedral', pp.245-7; Pevsner, Nikolaus, *The Buildings of England. Northumberland* (Harmondsworth, 1957), pp.224-8.

[27]   Storey, *Reg. Langley*, vol.3, pp.64-7; Chandler, John (ed.), *John Leland's Itinerary* (Stroud, 1993), p.140; Rawcliffe, Carole, 'Thornton, Roger', in *Hist. Parl., 1386-1421*, vol.4 (1992), pp.596-8; Brand, *Newcastle*, vol.1, pp.267-8.

[28]   Storey, *Reg. Langley*, vol.4, p.156.

[29]   Hunter Blair, C. (ed.), *Northumbrian Monuments* (Newcastle, 1924), p.83.

[30]   Wedgwood, J.C. and Holt, A.D., *Biographies of the Members of the House of Commons 1439-1509* (1936), p.720; Dobson, R.B., *Durham Cathedral Priory 1400-1450* (Cambridge, 1973), pp.44-5, 129-31.

[31]   Hunter Blair, *Northumbrian Monuments*, pp.83-4; Pevsner, *Northumberland*, pp.226-7. Cf Bond, Francis, *Fonts and Font Covers* (1908).

[32]   Bourne, Henry, *Newcastle*, p.63. Cecilia de Hamelden (possibly of the burgess family of Emeldon) willed to be buried in the church in 1408 (Storey, *Reg. Langley*, vol.1, pp.90-1), and so did William Eslington, burgess in 1416 (*ibid.*, 146). Former tomb inscriptions to Christopher Brygham and Robert Brandling (d.1511) and their wives, recorded by Sir William Dugdale, proclaimed them to have been Merchant Adventurers and former mayors of the town. Brygham was mayor in 1504-5 (Hunter Blair, *Northumbrian Monuments*, pp.39-40, 59).

in 1322.[33] A knightly stone effigy remains, with a style of arms of the early 14th century. As we have seen, in the 14th century the church was the most favoured in the town by burgesses wishing to found chantries. The surveyors at their dissolution listed altars there dedicated to St John the Baptist and St John the Apostle, St Peter and St Paul, St Thomas (of Canterbury), St Cuthbert, St Katherine, Our Lady, St Margaret and St Loy (Eligius). The last was patron of the Gild of Smiths, which may have helped to maintain this altar, and the one dedicated to the saint in All Saints' Church. There was also another altar of Our Lady in St Thomas's chapel. The chapels were all well furnished then, especially in comparison with some of the rural ones in Northumberland.[34]

Special accommodation for some cantarists was provided in the 14th century. In 1332 Richard de Emeldon received a licence to alienate land in mortmain, in order to build a dwelling on an empty plot in the town for the chaplain who was to serve at the chantry which he was founding in St Nicholas'.[35] The following year John de Denton was likewise authorised to provide a plot in the church's cemetery for the cantarist in his chantry there.[36] Peter Angrym's case was another in point. In 1380 he was appointed by the Crown as cantarist at the chantry founded there in 1323 by the burgess Nicholas de Ellerker. He had previously been appointed to it, it was said, by Nicholas's son John, but on his death the advowson had reverted to the Crown. At his own cost, Angrym had a chamber built for himself, 20 feet in length, on waste ground belonging to the Crown, next to St Nicholas' cemetery – without seeking permission. In response to his petition, in 1389 the Crown granted him the dwelling without rent. His previous chequered career as a cantarist there illustrates how laymen might flout ecclesiastical authority in making appointments to chantries. In 1378 he had been instituted by Bishop Hatfield to St Katherine's altar – which he had, indeed, long served, but solely on presentation by the mayor, bailiffs and other laymen. The following year Angrym complained to the Bishop that, as a consequence of this dispensation, Adam York, Mayor, and others had expelled him from the chantry, and installed John Eland in his place.[37]

---

[33]   Welford, *Newcastle and Gateshead*, vol.1, p.55. There were coats of arms in stained glass of some leading noble families of the North East – Percy, Neville, Montague, Grey of Heton (Hunter Blair, *Northumbrian Monuments*, pp.75-6).

[34]   *The Inventories of Church Goods in the counties of York, Durham and Northumberland*, SS, vol.97 (1896), pp.159-62; Anderson, J. (ed.), *Newcastle upon Tyne*, Records of Early English Drama (Manchester, 1982), p.4. St Loy was generally the patron saint of metalworkers and smiths. In England in the 1530s there were references to him as the protector of blacksmiths and carters, and of horses (Duffy, Eamon, *The Stripping of the Altars. Traditional Religion in England 1400-1580* (Cambridge, 1992), pp.162, 405).

[35]   *CPR, 1330-1334*, 267.

[36]   *Ibid.*, p.461. Denton was elected mayor in 1333 and 1336 (Hunter Blair, *Mayors and Lord Mayors*, pp.4, 5).

[37]   *CPR, 1377-1381*, p.407; *CPR, 1385-1389*, p.9; Fraser, Constance M. (ed.), *Ancient Petitions relating to Northumberland*, SS, vol.176 (1981), pp.12-13; Hatfield Reg., fos. 76r and v, 168v. York was a bailiff in 1379 (Welford, *Newcastle and Gateshead*, vol.1, p.428).

Besides chaplains with relatively secure tenure as incumbent chantry priests, there were others who fulfilled this and other ministries on a more precarious or occasional basis. In 1336, at the request of Richard de Emeldon's executors, Bishop Richard de Bury laid down ordinances for his exceptionally well-endowed chantry in St Nicholas'. Its keeper, a priest with life tenure, was to be assisted by a second priest who lacked such security and whose wages he paid. The keeper would make future appointments of his assistant, and have power of dismissal.[38] The conduct of cantarists – especially, one suspects, those without tenure – could be unruly. A mandate of Bishop Hatfield (1376) addressed to the vicar of St Nicholas' and the parish priest there suggests that chantry chaplains were causing scandal in the town. They were alleged to be neglectful, and inclined to wander around *per patriam*, exposing themselves to temptations, and contrary to the intentions of the founders of chantries. A date was set for the summons to St Nicholas' of the beneficed chantry chaplains, who were to bring their letters of institution and chantry ordinances: other chantry chaplains were to provide their authorisation. Ten jurors from the town were to give evidence of derelictions.[39]

Some unbeneficed priests made a living by assisting curates, by performing random obits, and celebrating feast days for the misteries, of which 12 were in existence by 1342.[40] Some may have performed liturgies in the private chapels which it was fashionable for wealthy inhabitants to set up in their houses in the 15th century.[41] It is possible that the numbers of chaplains in Newcastle had dipped as a result of the severe outbreak of plague in Northumberland in 1379. On 4 May 1380 the Crown responded to a petition from the townsmen for assistance, alleging that 6,054 inhabitants had died of pestilence in the present year. It had apparently been virulent among the 'Northumbrians' (*Northumbrensium*) since the previous summer. Its rural spread, and the coincidental ravages of a Scottish raiding force in Northumberland, probably inhibited escape from it in Newcastle.[42] However, plague provided work for chaplains. In 1381 there were no less than 63 chaplains in the Deanery of Newcastle assessed for subsidy.[43]

---

[38]   *CPR, 1334-1348*, 262.

[39]   Reg. Hatfield, fo.115r.

[40]   Welford, *Newcastle and Gateshead*, vol.1, pp.114-15.

[41]   See below, p.105.

[42]   *CPR, 1377-1381*, p.510; Thompson, E.M. (ed.), *Chronicon Angliae*, Rolls series (1874), pp.239-40; Macdonald, Alastair J., *Border Bloodshed. Scotland and England at War, 1369-1403* (East Linton, 2000), p.60. The figure for mortality appears to be greatly inflated. Cf population totals projected on the basis of the 1377 poll tax returns: Butcher, A.F., 'Rent, Population and Economic Change in Late-Medieval Newcastle', *Northern History*, vol.14 (1978), p.74; Palliser, David M., 'Urban Decay Revisited', in Thompson, John A.F. (ed.), *Towns and Townspeople in the Fifteenth Century* (1988), p.9.

[43]   TNA, Exchequer T.R., E359/4, clerical subsidy.

In 1417 Bishop Langley believed that there were a large number of chaplains in the city chanting for souls, one of whom might be found to serve as a country parish priest at Wearmouth.[44] Some religious and social coherence may have been given to the city's secular priests by their guild of Corpus Christi, the first reference to which appears in 1508.[45]

Newcastle had three major chapels which acquired some parochial rights. All Saints' (or All Hallows'), St Andrew's and St John the Baptist's were all exercising burial rights by the 14th century, and baptismal rights by the 15th. The churches had or have Romanesque features, indicating that they were functioning by the end of the 12th century. All Saints' served the area of crowded streets and quays to the east of Tynebridge. St Andrew's was off one of the principal thoroughfares, Westgate, and St John's was by the north-west gate (Newgate). All Saints' was entirely rebuilt in the 18th century. The west front of the previous church had kept its 'Norman' arch, but this church had been extensively reconstructed during the Middle Ages. In his will of 1349, John Cragg of Newcastle directed that

33 The font in St Nicholas' Cathedral.

he was to be buried beneath the new chancel.[46] Robert Rodes' request for prayers was carved 'under the belfry of the steeple', and his coat of arms on a corbel at the east end – suggesting that he had a large part in funding the rebuilding.[47]

44 Storey, *Reg. Langley*, vol.5, p.109.
45 Anderson, *Newcastle upon Tyne*, pp.xi, 15.
46 Welford, *Newcastle and Gateshead*, vol.1, p.34. For the parish and chapelry boundaries see above, p.39, Fig. 24.
47 Bourne, *Newcastle*, p.89.

The late medieval font survives; in the secularly grandiose fashion for Newcastle fonts of the period, it has seven coats of arms on its side panels. They are of local landed and burgess families, including George Lord Lumley (d.1507) and his wife, who was of the Thornton family.[48]

All Saints' had some wealthy parishioners, numbers of whom, especially in the first decades of the 14th century, set up chantries at its altars. In 1415 the Mayor, Robert Hibburn, willed to be buried there, near the altar of St John the Evangelist.[49] Roger Thornton, making his will in his house nearby, in Broad Chare, not long before he died, willed to be

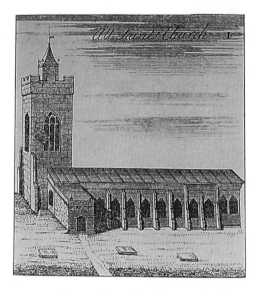

34 All Saints' (or All Hallows') Church, a detail from Corbridge's map.

buried in this church too, beside his wife Agnes (d.1411). He left the large sum of £100 for his exequies, and provided for as many as 30 priests to say Masses for his soul for two years, and for four priests to do so for a time thereafter (besides those celebrating at the chantries he had founded). He was determined to leave his stamp on All Saints'. He left £20 for its fabric and furnishings, and £10 to furnish his chantry of St Peter there. His children were depicted in stained glass in a window above the south door which led into the choir. A notable survival from medieval All Saints' is the monumental brass which was on top of the conspicuous, raised tomb of Agnes and Roger to the south of the High Altar.[50] The brass is an import from the Low Countries. In scale, execution and detail, it is one of the finest remaining brasses in England.

The text of Thornton's ordinance endowing his chantry at St Peter's altar survives, dated 25 November 1425. It was to have one chaplain, who was to celebrate daily for the souls of Thornton, his late wife, their ancestors and children, and for the welfare of all who supported the chantry and the chaplain in any way. Thornton appointed William Harwode as chaplain and custodian,

[48] Hunter Blair, *Northumbrian Monuments*, pp.89-90. The font is now in Kirkharle Church, Northumberland (Pevsner, *Northumberland*, pp.230-1).
[49] Storey, *Reg. Langley*, vol.2, pp.74-6.
[50] *Ibid.*, vol.3, pp.64-7; Hunter Blair, *Northumbrian Monuments*, pp.84-5; Noble, Claire (ed.), *Calendar of Inquisitions Post Mortem*, vol.23 (2004), no.377; Bourne, *Newcastle*, pp.89, 95-6.

35 St Andrew's Church, a detail from Corbridge's map.

and granted him and his successors various properties in the city. The incumbent was to observe detailed conditions whilst in office, subject to judgement, and possible expulsion and replacement by the founder or his heirs and assigns. No chaplain was to hold any other clerical office. (Cantarists widely served more than one chantry.) If the heirs and assigns were negligent in filling a vacancy in the chantry, Thornton was insistent that this responsibility devolved upon secular, not on ecclesiastical authorities: it was vested in the mayor, sheriff and aldermen of the city, and in the event of their disagreement, solely in the mayor.[51] Thornton's concern to make adequate provision and firm regulations for the chantry may have been sharpened by difficulties faced by another chantry in the same church. There were to be three successive appointments to the chantry of St Thomas there in 1426-7, and no less than six between 1431 and 1441.[52] St Peter's was one of the seven altars surveyed in the church at their dissolution. Most of them had similar dedications to those of chantries in St Nicholas': to Our Lady, St Anne, St John the Evangelist, St Peter, St Katherine, St Thomas of Canterbury and St Loy.[53]

St Andrew's Church exhibits early features more notably than can be seen in the other principal Newcastle churches, on a large scale – perhaps their survival in the tower and nave signifies that the wealth of the parish declined in the later Middle Ages. The lower stage of the tower, the nave arcades and the dominating chancel arch date mainly from the 12th century, but there was to be extensive remodelling, especially in the following two centuries, the east

---

[51] Lumley Archive, Sandbeck Park, Catalogue no.4364 MTD/E2/1: Foundation Charter of St Peter's Chantry in All Saints' Chapel, Newcastle. I owe thanks to the Trustees of the Earl of Scarbrough's 1979 Settlement for permission to cite this document, and to Mrs Alice Rodgers, Archivist at Sandbeck Park, for supplying me with a copy and transcript. St Peter heads the figures of the Apostles depicted on Thornton's right hand on his brass.

[52] *CPR, 1422-1429*, 341, 411, 445; *CPR, 1429-1436*, 248, 344, 540; *CPR, 1436-1441*, 93, 547.

[53] *Inventories of Church Goods*, p.162; Brand, *Newcastle*, vol.1, pp.359-61.

end in particular being transformed.[54] In 1376 Bishop Hatfield accepted a plea that the church needed chantry priests, that it lacked liturgical furnishings (*ornamentis*), and needed repairs. He permitted the erection of a building in the cemetery, rents from which were to be used in aid of the church.[55] Only two chantries were listed at St Andrew's at the dissolution, those of Our Lady and Holy Trinity. There has been at least one other chantry, that of St Thomas of Canterbury, situated to the north of the chancel.[56] Holy Trinity Chapel had attracted the patronage of a notable knight from Northumberland, of distinguished Scottish lineage, Sir Aymer de Atholl (d.1402), younger son of David Earl of Atholl (d.1336-7). Aymer married into the Northumberland family of Eure, and he played leading roles in the county's administration. His wife Mary's remains lay buried in the church in 1392, the year in which he procured an indulgence of 40 days for those who contributed towards repairing it and its furnishings, and who prayed for the couple's souls before the chapel's image of Holy Trinity.[57]

The early origins of St John's Church are evident from the remnant of a Romanesque window in the chancel. However, as at St Nicholas', its parishioners and benefactors rebuilt the rest of the church in the later Middle Ages. In 1363 a large group, including some of the wealthiest men in town, received a licence, for the payment of as much as £80, to form a fraternity in honour of the Nativity and Resurrection, and of the Virgin Mary. A chantry with as many as three chaplains was to be founded in St John's. Twenty-one burgesses were among those involved, headed by Robert Angreton, John del Chambre (prime movers in the rebuilding of St Nicholas' in 1368), John de Emeldon and Robert de Penereth (former lessee of the town's tithes). However, some folk, particularly of lesser standing, believed that the guild had secular objectives inimical to their interests. The Crown appointed the mayor and county escheator to hold an enquiry as to whether, as alleged, the guild would damage the Crown's and the urban government's and community's interests. The inquest found in the affirmative. In 1364 the king revoked the guild's ordinances, though the chantry was allowed to continue. Some members of the guild were defiant, forming armed assemblies in order to coerce the 'mean people' to consent to the guild ordinance.

[54] Pevsner, *Northumberland*, pp.229-30. Robert Rodes's arms appeared carved on the boss of the tower vault (Hunter Blair, *Northumbrian Monuments*, p.143).

[55] Reg. Hatfield, fos 115.

[56] *Inventories of Church Goods*, p.163; Brand, *Newcastle*, vol.1, pp.80-1.

[57] Balfour Paul, James (ed.), *The Scots Peerage*, vol.1 (Edinburgh, 1904), pp.428-30; Oliver, A.M. (ed.), *Northumberland and Durham Deeds from the Dodsworth MSS. in Bodley's Library, Oxford* (Newcastle, 1929), pp.130-1; *Northumbrian Monuments*, pp.136-7; Welford, *Newcastle and Gateshead*, vol.1, p.215. The indents for the Atholls' large monumental brass can be seen in the pavement, in front of the Holy Trinity altar. For part of the inscription formerly on it, Brand, *Newcastle*, vol.1, p.189.

36 St John's Church, a detail from Corbridge's map.

Stern measures were ordered by the Crown against the disobedient. The mayor and townsmen petitioned the Crown for the repeal of the licence for confraternity to be affirmed in Parliament, since, despite the fact that it had been annulled by king and council, some of the fraternity 'by false suggestion' were attempting to revive it. The prohibition of the fraternity, but not the chantry, was confirmed in Parliament in 1365.[58]

The benevolence of wealthy petitioners to St John's in the 14th century is attested by the building of the nave arcade and the north transept. A south aisle was added c.1370. Perhaps this was intended for the chantry of the aborted guild. Subsequently St John's may have had an illustrious benefactor. The coat of arms of Henry Percy, 1st Earl of Northumberland (d.1408) was prominently displayed in the east window of the chancel. The church's position near Westgate Street is likely to have attracted offerings from those travelling to and from the more hazardous northern parts, as Percy often did. Robert Rodes made notable gifts to the church: the south transept may been added through his benefaction, and he was probably responsible, too, for the building of the tower as it stands: his arms encircled by a request for prayers are on the central boss in its vault. Like St Andrew's, St John's had chantries of the Trinity, Our Lady and St Thomas at the dissolution.[59]

Religious Communities, other Chapels and Charitable Foundations

There was only one monastic house in Newcastle, the Benedictine convent of St Bartholomew, whose grounds were bounded by High Friar Chare, Pilgrim Street and Newgate Street. It was founded in the 12th century and in its early

[58] *CPR, 1364-1367*, 20, 74; *Ancient Petitions*, pp.250-1. Robert Angreton was mayor 1363-4, and Richard Stanhope was mayor 1364-5 (Hunter Blair, *Mayors and Lord Mayor*, pp.6, 7).
[59] Pevsner, *Northumberland*, pp.231-2; Brand, *Newcastle*, vol.1, pp.106-9; *Inventories of Church Goods*, p.162; *Northumbrian Monuments*, p.143.

days enjoyed Scottish royal patronage, during the time when David I had controlled the region. In a charter of his son Henry, Earl of Northumberland (datable 1141-51), the earl granted the convent possession of his Newcastle burgess, Aslach, all the latter's property in and out of the borough, and some of the earl's demesne land as well. He confirmed the nuns' existing possessions, and took the house under his protection.[60] In that and the following century the nuns received grants of land or rent in the countryside from ecclesiastics and lay persons. In 1235 Richard Poore, Bishop of Durham, 'having compassion on the poverty of the nuns', granted them an annuity of 10 marks from the revenues of Washington Church (Co. Durham). Such grants suggest, as does Henry III's generous gift to the nuns of £10 in 1252, that they retained a good repute for long after their foundation.[61] However, there were to be episodes of dissension in the convent in the later 14th century. In 1365 Bishop Hatfield appointed a commission to visit St Bartholomew's, empowered to punish and reform any wrongdoings by the nuns. The visitors apparently found a dismal situation: the Bishop appointed Hugh Arnecliffe, priest at St Nicholas', as the convent's custodian. The Bishop wrote that he was moved by the nuns' miserable spiritual and temporal state, for they were in poverty and distress. In 1367 the prominent burgess Robert Angreton was alleged to be planning to destroy the nuns, and to have oppressed their servants and poor tenants in the town and elsewhere in Northumberland, and to have so intimidated the Prioress and nuns that they had fled and did not dare to return and maintain services. Angreton's actions may have been connected with the internal problems of the convent. A few months later Hatfield commissioned Arnecliffe to inquire whether Amice Belford was lawfully the Prioress. Shortly afterwards he ordered Amice to receive back two nuns, Emma Hill and Joan Farley, whom she had expelled, and to treat them properly. However, she was found to be an intruder in office: Hatfield deposed her. Amice remained defiant, forcing Katherine, now elected Prioress, to appeal for the intervention of the lay power. Amice and her supporters, she alleged, had made off with the convent's common seal, all its muniments, and some of its other possessions. She travelled around, living off the convent's rents and goods, and leaving the sisters in poverty. Leading Northumberland gentry, including Aymer de Atholl, were appointed to enquire into this.[62]

[60]   Barrow, G.W.S. (ed.), *The Acts of Malcolm IV King of Scots 1153-1165* (Edinburgh, 1960), pp.152-3.
[61]   *English Episcopal Acta*, 24, vol.1., no.103; *ibid.*, vol.2, nos 231, 331; *Calendar of the Liberate Rolls. Henry III, vol.4, A.D. 1251-1260* (1959), no.14. For grants to the convent, see also Brand, *Newcastle*, vol.1, pp.205-6, 208-10, 212, 215. For examples of leases of property held in Newcastle by the prioresses and convent, 1230-50 and 1292-3, Oliver, *Northumberland and Durham Deeds*, pp.135-6.
[62]   Welford, *Newcastle and Gateshead*, vol.1, pp.166-7, 170; *CPR, 1367-70*, 50.

In the following decade Hatfield had to deal with problems among the nuns again. The convent, he declared in 1376, was in need of reformation; the church had been polluted by the shedding of human blood. He ordered a visitation to be held. An individual case suggests dissension among the nuns. One of them, Idonea Stamford, petitioned that she had absented herself from the convent, but that when she wished to be re-admitted the community had refused. Hatfield thought that her withdrawal had been on reasonable grounds, and ordered them to receive her back.[63] The apparent dearth of bequests to the house in the later Middle Ages suggests that its religious standing may have remained low. The nuns' problems may have been compounded because surrounding commercial premises produced pollution, and their buildings needed repair. In 1427 Elizabeth Falowfeld was given permission to transfer to another convent, on the grounds of the 'inclemency of the air' near St Bartholomew's and her own poor health. Roger Thornton left the nuns a stock of lead in his will, with which to repair the fabric of their house, as, indeed, he did to some other ecclesiastical institutions in the city.[64] In the mid-15th century Bishop Robert Neville of Durham attempted to help with the convent's financial problem. The nuns claimed that it had been sufficiently endowed at the time of foundation, but that since then revenue had dwindled. The outbreak of fires had diminished their resources. Neville's attempts to alleviate this by granting them successive pensions of £10 and 10 marks from parishes in County Durham had failed to produce the anticipated boost, so he arranged for them to receive the appropriation of the Chapel of St Edmund in Gateshead.[65] Yet valuations of the convent's annual income in 1535 were in the region of £36-7, and at its dissolution in 1540 it sustained a prioress and nine nuns.[66]

Newcastle had a full complement of friaries. A Franciscan house was founded in 1237, and the Dominicans followed fast behind, by 1239. The Carmelites were granted a plot by a local landowner, John de Byker, in 1262.[67] Newcastle had one of the 18 known English houses of the 'Brethren of the Penance of Jesus Christ'. They first appeared in Provence in the 1240s, and Henry III granted them his protection in 1256. They were commonly known as 'friars of the Sack', because they wore humble raiment like penitents. In 1266 Henry III, at the instance of Robert de Bruce (probably the grandfather of Robert I of Scotland), granted them

[63]   Hatfield Reg, fos. 117v, 127r and v.
[64]   Tremlow, *Calendar of Papal Registers. Papal Letters*, vol.7, p.362; Storey, *Reg. Langley*, vol.3, pp.64-7.
[65]   Twemlow, *Calendar of Papal Registers. Papal Letters*, vol.11, 1455-1464 (1921), pp.373-4.
[66]   Brand, *Newcastle*, vol.1, p.230.
[67]   Knowles, David, *The Religious Houses of Medieval England* (Oxford, 1940), pp.105, 110; Harbottle, Barbara, 'Excavations at the Carmelite Friary, Newcastle upon Tyne, 1965 and 1967', *AA*, 4th series, vol.46 (1968), p.169.

37   The remains of the Augustinian Friary still standing in the early 19th century.

land for the enlargement of their close in Newcastle.[68] The order was disbanded at the Council of Lyons (1274), but apparently some of the friars continued to occupy the Newcastle house for decades (as happened in some of their other houses). In 1306 Brother Walter de Carleton was said to have been the solitary friar living there for the past seven years.[69] The Augustinian friars were established in the town around 1290.[70] In 1498 there was a transformation of the Franciscan house: it was changed from being a Conventual to an Observant convent. The Observants, who followed a stricter interpretation of the Rule of St Francis, had been allowed to develop a separate provincial organisation. Henry VII, acting

[68]   *CCR., 1266-1272*, p.10; Andrews, Frances, *The Other Friars* (2006), pp.175-83, 201.
[69]   Bliss, W.H. (ed.), *Calendar of Papal Registers. Petitions to the Pope*, vol.1, 1342-1419 (1896), p.20; Andrews, *Other Friars*, pp.207-22.
[70]   Knowles, *Religious Houses*, p.115.

promptly on a bull of Pope Alexander VI permitting such a reform, transferred the houses at Canterbury and Newcastle to the Observance.[71]

Newcastle's friars probably had a wide influence in North East England, only if because there were few other friaries in the region. There were Franciscans only in Durham and Hartlepool, Dominicans in Jarrow, Hartlepool and Bamburgh, and Carmelites at Hulne by Alnwick. There was no other Augustinian Friary in the diocese. It was not unusual in the later Middle Ages for gentlefolk and higher clergy to make bequests (usually monetary), in expectation of prayers for their souls, to the houses of the 'four Orders' (Franciscans, Dominicans, Carmelites and Augustinians) in one or more towns. Newcastle was no exception. Such bequests are found in the wills of some denizens: John Cragg (1349), Nicholas Coke (1369), Cecilia de Hamelden (1408), the burgesses William de Eslington (1415) and Roger Thornton (1429).[72] They are also found in those of outsiders, gentlefolk and beneficed clergy mostly hailing from the North East (also usually making bequests to friaries elsewhere): William de Neuport, rector of Wearmouth (1366); William Meneville, landowner in Easington, County Durham (1372); John Ogle (1372); William Bowland, rector of St Nicholas', Durham (1380); John Roddam of Roddam (Northumberland) (1390); Richard Lord Scrope of Bolton (Yorks.) (1400); Sir Robert Ogle, leading Northumberland landowner (1410); Lady Maud Bowes, of Barnard Castle (1421); Master Thomas Hebden, dean of Auckland (1435); John Palman, *alias* Coke, of Auckland (who, instead of money, left altar cloths to the friaries), and Sir Thomas Fulthorpe, of a leading family in County Durham (1456).[73] Some donors picked out or were more generous to particular Newcastle houses. For instance, Henry Lord Percy singled out the Dominicans and Franciscans (1349). In 1378 the Prior of the Dominicans was licensed by Bishop Hatfield to confess and minister to Margaret, widow of Sir John Eure, as long as she stayed in the friary. She willed to be buried in the choir of the church. She made monetary bequests to the house and some of its individual friars, and appointed the Prior, William Laton, to head her executors. Another widow, Lady Isabella de Wyleby, of Derbyshire provenance, in the will she made at Raby Castle (County Durham)

[71] Knowles, D., *The Religious Orders in England, vol.3, The Tudor Age* (Cambridge, 1959), pp.10-13; Howlett, Richard (ed.), *Monumenta Franciscana*, vol.2, Rolls series (1882), p.182.

[72] Welford, *Newcastle and Gateshead*, vol.1, p.134 (Cragg), p.176 (Coke); Storey, *Reg. Langley*, vol. I, p.90 (Hamelden); *Wills and Inventories*, vol.1, pt 1, SS (1835), pp.59-60 (Eslington); Storey, *Reg. Langley*, vol.3, pp.64-7 (Thornton).

[73] *Testamenta Eboracensia*, vol.1, pt 1, SS (1836), pp.80-2 (Neuport); Welford, *Newcastle and Gateshead*, vol.1, p.181 (Meneville), p.182 (J. Ogle), pp.108-10 (Bowland), pp.137-8 (Roddam); Nicolas, Nicholas H., *The Controversy between Sir Richard Scrope and Sir Robert Grosvenor in the Court of Chivalry*, vol.2 (1832), pp.30-2 (Scrope); Storey, *Reg. Langley*, vol.1, pp.18-20 (R. Ogle), vol.2, pp.195-7 (Bowes); *Wills and Inventories*, vol.1, pt 1, pp.82-4 (Hebbeden), pp.86-7 (Palman); *Testamenta Eboracensia*, vol.1, pt 2, SS (1855), p.203 (Fulthorpe). Hebden, from a local knightly family, had been spiritual chancellor of the bishopric of Durham (Storey, *Thomas Langley*, pp.5, 169, 186).

in 1415, left sums to a Newcastle Augustinian, Master John Bawmburgh, and to his house. Robert Conyers of Sockburn (County Durham) singled out the Augustinians (1431), John Trollope, esquire, of Thornlaw (Northumberland), the Franciscans (1471), William Lambert, vicar of Gainford and Master of the Staindrop collegiate church (below Raby Castle), the Augustinians (1480).[74]

The Franciscan Observants of Newcastle seem to have had a widespread northern reputation for holiness in the early 16th century. Sir Ralph Bigod of Settrington in Yorkshire (d.1515) left sums of 6s. 8d. widely to houses of the four orders in the County Palatine and Yorkshire, for intercessions for his and his family's souls, but he only left that amount to be repeated for seven years to the Newcastle Observants. Another John Trollope, following a family tradition of Franciscan patronage, made a bequest to them in 1521. Thomas Boynton left them a fat ox in 1523. Thomas Wentworth, esquire, of Elmshall (Yorks.), in his will proved in 1524, set aside £100, from which his executors were to dispense sums for the repair of their churches and houses at Newark and Newcastle. William Bulmer, of Brotton (Yorks.), willed the Newcastle Observants wheat and a cow in the same year. In 1530 they were the only friars in Newcastle who received a bequest from John Ledum of Whitby.[75] In the light of such tokens of pious respect, it is not surprising that the Newcastle convent was briefly restored during the Pilgrimage of Grace (1536). The Mayor, Robert Brandling, writing to William Blytheman, one of the commissioners for the dissolution of monasteries, denounced 'our ungodly dissembling knaves the Friars Observant', whose re-entry into their house had to be endured, 'for [the sake of] Sir Thomas Hilton [sheriff of County Durham] and others who have quarrelled with us and, as you know, they were favoured by my cousin Anderson and others'. Clearly the Observants had strong local support: Brandling justified his acquiescence on the grounds that he wished to avoid strife in a town whose continued loyalty was crucial to contain disaffection in the region.[76]

Out-of-town bequests sometimes reflected the Newcastle origins of the donor, or of members of the donor's family. Agnes Bedford, a widow domiciled in Hull, was probably a case in point. She made provision for obits

[74] *Testamenta Eboracensia*, vol.1, pt 1, pp.57-61 (Percy); Welford, *Newcastle and Gateshead*, vol.1, p.191 (Eure); *Testamenta Eboracensia*, vol.1, pt 1, pp.381-3 (Wileby); Storey, *Reg. Langley*, vol.4, p.4 (Conyers); *Wills and Inventories*, vol.1, pt 1, pp.97-8 (Trollope); *Testamenta Eboracensia*, vol.3, SS (1864), pp.254-6 (Lambert). Sir John Eure had died in 1367, when his lands in Northumberland were already demised to his son Robert (*Calendar of Inquisitions Post Mortem*, vol.11 [1938], no.138).

[75] *Wills and Inventories*, vol.1, pt 1, pp.105-6 (Trollope); *Testamenta Eboracensia*, vol.5, SS (1884), pp.55-7 (Bigod), pp.110-12 (Boynton), pp.144-6 (Wentworth), pp.89-91 (Bulmer), pp.300-2 (Ledum).

[76] Gairdner, James (ed.), *Letters and Papers, Foreign and Domestic, of the reign of Henry VIII*, vol.11 (1888), no.1372.

for two of her husbands in the Franciscan house at Newcastle in 1459.[77] Some connections with the orders were doubtless made by Northumbrian gentlefolk on visits to town, others by visitors from further afield during their passage through it. The sojourns of kings, nobles and their retinues there, especially during the Scottish Wars of Independence, though sometimes intrusive and destructive, could provide paths to seek pious favours from the great. William Roos, Lord of Helmsley (Yorks.), granted a property in the town to the Augustinians: the grant was confirmed by the Crown in 1317. The following year Edward II granted the Dominicans property forfeited by Sir Gilbert de Middleton adjacent to their premises.[78] Friars are likely to have made connections with gentlefolk on their circuits. In 1367 Bishop Hatfield licensed Richard de Tynemouth, Augustinian friar from Newcastle, to act as penitentiary for several months in Northumberland parishes, Haltwhistle, Simonburn, Elsdon and Tynemouth. A few examples of spiritual connections made with friaries survive. In 1426 John Fenwicke and his wife Elizabeth Halle were granted an indulgence by the Minister of the Franciscans.[79] In 1474 Brother John, Custodian of the Carmelite house, issued a letter of confraternity to John Swinburne and his wife.[80]

The Franciscans may have attracted offerings from travellers because their house was near the upper end of Pilgrim Street, a main thoroughfare for those passing to and from the North through Pilgrim Gate. The friary, according to 16th-century testimony, possessed some notable relics of St Francis: his sandals, cord and breeches.[81] Possibly as a result of population density, or the pollution of watercourses, the Franciscans in the 1340s faced neighbours' hostility over their water monopoly. According to the terms of a commission of enquiry (1345), weightily composed of gentlefolk, they had long had royal licence for sole use of 'Sevenwelhedes'. However, a group including William de Acton and Robert Angreton (both to be influential burgesses), two chaplains, a shoemaker, a smith and a tailor, were said by the friars to have broken the cover on the wellhead and pierced the pipes of the conduit, diverting the water to their own uses.[82]

[77] *Testamenta Eboracensia*, vol.1, pt 2, pp.234-7.
[78] *CPR, 1317-1321*, pp.32, 112. The Roos grant may have been in return for Masses for the soul of the William Roos, who had died the previous year and who in the early 1300s who had been heavily involved in the defence of Northumberland against the Scots (*Complete Peerage*, vol.11, pp.96-9).
[79] Oliver, *Northumberland and Durham Deeds*, p.117.
[80] NCRO, Swinburne of Capheaton MSS, ZSW/1/74. Lady de Cossele, whose executors were John and William de Swinburne, had made bequests to the Carmelite Order and its Newcastle house, which they were administering in 1361 (ZSW/1/76).
[81] Fraser, R., 'St Mary's Well, Jesmond, Newcastle upon Tyne', *AA*, 5th series, vol.2 (1985), p.93, n.19. The source is John Bale.
[82] *CPR, 1343-1345*, 496.

The BLACK FRIARS, *at* NEWCASTLE, *in* Northumberland.

Hawkins sculp.

Published according to Act of Parliament by Alex.Hogg N:16 Paternoster Row.

38 Eighteenth-century view of the Dominican Friary.

The Dominican house was on the northern edge of town (near the Newgate). It may betoken an increase in the number of brethren (or increased pressure of population in the area) that, according to a royal inquisition of 1263, they had arranged for water to be piped to the friary from a well outside their premises.[83] A problem arose for them (as was to happen for some other religious houses on the outskirts of the town) from the construction of the town walls. The years 1265-1318, according to Hilary Turner, defined the period of greatest activity on the works. The walls ran through the urban chapelries, leaving parts of them outside the defences. The section within a stone's throw of the Dominicans' house cut them off from their garden. In 1280 Edward I licensed them to have a narrow postern made in the wall, so as to reach it. Also, he granted them a

[83] *CPR, 1258-1266,* 298.

street adjacent to their house.[84] The making of a ditch outside the town wall presented the friars with another obstacle. In 1312 they had royal permission to erect a swing bridge over the ditch, at their postern. As we have seen, Edward II shared his father's concern to improve their facilities.[85] Theirs is the only friary of which large parts still stand. The impressive conventual buildings (much altered) are ranged around three sides of a large quadrangle. The cloisters have disappeared, and there are only a few traces of the large church which filled the north side of the quadrangle, from the east side of which the choir projected outwards. Its east window had striking tracery in the 'Decorated' style of the first half of the 14th century. The nave was aisled (unlike the choir), convenient to accommodate lay folk eager to hear sermons.[86] The facilities at the Blackfriars helped to make it a suitable venue for visits by kings and nobles. In 1334, in its church, Edward Balliol did homage to Edward III for the kingdom of Scotland.[87] A lay presence was not always congenial. The friars asked the king's permission to have new gates made in 1341 because, when John de Warenne, Earl of Surrey, was staying in their house, they had been broken down during a fight between his men and some townsmen.[88]

A *cause célèbre* in the 1380s, centring round the preaching of a Dominican of Newcastle, exemplifies the disputes that could flare up between conventual and secular clergy, especially over penitential and other spiritual ministrations, and the financial rights which flowed from them. Tensions may have been fuelled because in England some of the leading theological protagonists among the seculars and religious had been bitterly at odds in recent decades. A Newcastle Dominican, Richard Helmslay, launched a series of attacks in his sermons, preached in the friary and elsewhere in the town, against the privileges and standards of parish priests. He was in good standing with Bishop Hatfield, who seems to have been well disposed to some Newcastle friars. The bishop licensed him to hear confessions in the Archdeaconry of Northumberland in January 1379, a licence renewed the following December. Helmslay's controversial sermons were delivered between January and March 1379, and

[84]   Turner, Hilary L., *Town Defences in England and Wales* (1970), pp.104-9; Dodds, Madeleine Hope, *NCH*, vol.13 (1930), pp.211, 257, 289; *CPR, 1272-1281*, 397.
[85]   *CPR, 1307-1313*, p.333. In 1329 John Barron of Newcastle granted property to the Dominicans adjacent to their own (*CPR, 1327-1330*, 392).
[86]   Harbottle, B., 'The Black Friars, Newcastle upon Tyne', *The Archaeological Journal*, vol.13 (1976), pp.242-4. The east end of the church is illustrated in a print of 1773 (see above, Fig. 38). There survives from the Blackfriars Church the lower half of a grave slab, probably of Tournai marble, with the indent for a civilian male figure under a canopy, dating from the 1320s or '30s (Badham, Sally F., 'A Fourteenth Century Composite Slab from Newcastle Blackfriars', *Transactions of the Monumental Brass Society*, vol.14 (1986), pp.44-9).
[87]   Brand, *Newcastle*, vol.1, p.127.
[88]   *Ancient Petitions*, pp.26-7; *CPR, 1340-1343*, 352. In 1397 the English Province of the order held their chapter in the house (*Calendar of Papal Registers. Papal Letters*, vol.5, p.151).

February and May 1380. In particular, he denounced Matthew de Bolton, the elderly, pugnacious vicar of Newcastle. An issue provoking Helmslay, Dr H.L. Spencer has shown, was the dispute arising from the will of Lady Eure, who, as we have seen, had resided in the friary in her widowhood. The friars failed to hand over a quarter of the worth of the bequests which they had received from her to Bolton as her parish priest, though they were technically obliged to do so. In defiance, Helmslay riposted on a broad front. Among the scandalous or controversial opinions which he expressed were that parishioners were not obliged to offer candles in their parish church on Candlemas Day; women were not obliged to be churched and make offerings after childbirth; friary churches were as much mother churches as parish churches were, and should be accorded the same honour; bequests which parishioners made out of devotion to their parish church ought rather to go to friaries. He also accused secular clergy of having criminal tendencies, and 80 curates in the diocese of Durham of being illiterate. His listeners, he said, should hold threats of summons before the bishop's consistory court in contempt. They were not obliged to pay mortuary dues to their curate.[89]

These propositions were among the charges made against Helmslay when he was examined in Rome in 1385, on Bishop Hatfield's delation. He was found guilty of holding unorthodox opinions, and obliged to recant there, and to promise to retract them publicly in St Nicholas' and elsewhere in the diocese of Durham. There was an even more startling opinion which he repudiated. The 21st decree of the Third Lateran Council (1215), *Omnis utrique*, laid down that everyone of both sexes (*utriusque sexus*) was obliged to confess to the curate once a year. Helmslay's interpretation of this was that only those who had the physical characteristics of both sexes were obliged to make confession to a curate. This opinion caused hilarity throughout the papal curia, where he was nicknamed Richard 'of Both Sexes'. Could he have been serious? Maybe he had indulged in a bit of facetious word-play, which had been seized on by his opponents to discredit him. Apart from this episode, he appears to have been well informed, and to have continued to be respected, resuming a not undistinguished clerical career in Newcastle after his imbroglio.[90]

What had been the local background to the controversy? Maybe the problems with Carlisle Cathedral Priory over parochial revenue had adversely affected the remuneration and the performance of duties by the chaplains (*stipendarii*),

[89] Hatfield Reg., fos.150v, 168r; Spencer, H.L., 'Friar Richard "Of Both Sexes"', in Barr, Helen and Hutchison, Ann M. (ed.), *Text and Controversy from Wyclif to Bale. Essays in Honour of Anne Hudson* (2005), pp.13-31.
[90] *Ibid.* Matthew de Bolton had probably died by September 1383, when Master Henry Hedlam was vicar of Newcastle (*CPR, 1381-1385*, 455).

39 Blackfriars: the impressive exterior Dominican friary's refectory today.

on whom the tasks of maintaining parochial worship in the principal secular churches mainly fell. Perhaps disputes over mortuaries and bequests between the parish and the convent had multiplied too as a result of an unusual degree of mortality, consequent on the dire outbreak of plague mentioned above.[91] On 27 March 1380, Bishop Hatfield licensed the Dominicans to say Masses in St Nicholas' Church and its separate (parochial) chapels, for the living and dead, especially if a parishioner had requested them to perform the office in his or her last will, or bequeathed them a mortuary of sixpence. The vicar of Newcastle's permission for them to say Mass in these churches was to be sought, but they might proceed without it. They were to conduct services in a way which did not prejudice the rights of the secular clergy. The parish priests and secular chaplains who served in the churches were not to make the friars' ministrations an excuse to evade their own usual liturgical duties.[92] Perhaps in the febrile atmosphere of fear of the plague, and with Helmslay's denunciations of the seculars ringing

[91] For the outbreak of plague, see above, p.76.
[92] Hatfield Reg., fo.172v.

in their ears, a larger number of lay persons than usual were turning to the Dominicans for spiritual consolation, and the Bishop sought to ease terrified folk by allowing the friars an unusually wide licence, as an emergency measure. A few years before, in 1376, the Bishop had licensed another Newcastle Dominican, Robert Heron, to hear confessions and to give absolution, even in reserved cases. His mission was confined to a limited number of burgesses and common folk – perhaps because Hatfield considered that the parochial system needed supplementing but did not wish to offend seculars unduly. The number of people that Heron was to confess was set at 40; none of them were to be lords, ladies or knights.[93] In 1379 Hatfield was prepared to be less restrictive with Helmslay, as we have seen. The friar apparently misjudged the Bishop's degree of tolerance for his order's wish-list, overstepping the mark by proposing drastic and impractical solutions to some of the traditional grievances of his order and house. Clearly – whatever the explanation of his hermaphroditic gaffe – he was respected. That probably increased the pressure on the Bishop from secular clergy to take firm action to silence his broadcasting of opinions which drastically threatened the institutional status quo. Moreover, there was a growing climate of nervousness in England about proposals for radical religious change, consequent on fears of the contagion of Wycliffite heterodoxy.

Near another of the town's boundaries, on the eastern side, the Carmelite house had been founded, to the south-east at Wall Knoll. The brethren there had had problems over their water supply in the 1270s. The grant to the friars by Edward I of Crossewell Spring provoked an outcry. In 1278 the commons of the town petitioned the King against the grant, stating that the spring's sweet water was necessary for dyers, fullers and other craftsmen, as well as for cooking and brewing. Since the Tyne was polluted, sailors and foreign merchants relied on the well, too.[94] A local landowner, Philip de Crauden, was more sympathetic to the friars' needs, granting them (before 1285) land adjacent to their house, to improve its cramped setting.[95] However, the integrity of their site was threatened by the construction of the town wall. A mandate of Edward I (1300) ordered the friars' removal in order to extend the line of the wall, which it was intended should go through the middle of their cloister, adjoining the front of their church. The church itself was to be demolished to make way for a wall tower. To Edward's exasperation, the urban authorities failed to provide the friars

---

[93] *Ibid.*, fo.82.

[94] *Ancient Petitions*, pp.10-11. In 1351 Peter Graper, burgess, granted the well to the Augustinian friars at a nominal rent (Oliver, *Northumberland and Durham Deeds*, p.83). Perhaps use of it had diminished in the wake of the plague. Graper was elected mayor six times between 1347 and 1354 (Welford, *Newcastle and Gateshead*, vol.1, p.426).

[95] *Ancient Petitions*, p.5.

with a suitable alternative site within the town walls, as he frequently enjoined them to do. The friars remained in uncomfortable occupation after the wall was built, its course modified so that it had not necessitated the destruction of the church, but went close to it. A possible solution to the friars' problem was their removal to the convent of the abolished Friars of the Sack, which was on the edge of the opposite side of town, west of the castle. In 1286 John de Vescy, Lord of Alnwick, had his eye on the site for a new pious development. He received papal permission to purchase this convent, with the intention of founding a house of Minoresses there. A well-travelled crusader and pilgrim, he clearly considered that a more austere alternative to St Bartholomew's Priory was desirable for local girls. However, he had died in 1289, his intention unfulfilled. In 1300, the mayor, bailiffs and commons petitioned Edward I for the hand over of the Sack convent to the Carmelites. In 1306 a papal grant of the house, chapel, ornaments and other former Sack possessions was made to them, on their plea that, for the defence of the town against the Scots, their own house had been taken from them by the mayor and bailiffs, and pulled down. The Crown gave its authority for the transfer the following year.[96] Yet a bad collective memory of the brethren was to be dismally reawakened: they were to be incommoded in their new home by the construction of another section of the walls. Their petition to the Crown, probably dated 1333, made together with the Augustinian brethren of St Mary's Hospital, Westgate, and various laymen, claimed compensation for encroachments on their properties by the town wall and ditch.[97]

Barbara Harbottle's conclusions from the excavation of the new Carmelite site were that its claustral buildings were ranged round three sides of a cloister, on the south side of the church. That perhaps dated from the late 13th century (in which case it is most likely to have been the Sack Friars' church). The Carmelites must have built new accommodation, for the other works dated from the 14th century. An inventory made in 1538 of the convent's mostly frugal possessions gives some indications about the church's interior. The High Altar was backed by an impressive alabaster reredos, above which was a wooden canopy. There were gravestones with monumental brasses on them in the choir — so it was a

[96] *Calendar of Chancery Warrants preserved in the P.R.O. A.D. 1244-1306* (1927), pp.243-4 (1304, 1300), p.263 (1307); Bliss, W.H. (ed.), *Calendar of Papal Registers. Papal Letters*, vol.1, 1198-1304 (1893), p.490. *Complete Peerage*, vol.12, pt 2, pp.278-80; *Ancient Petitions*, pp.19-20; Bliss, W.H. (ed.), *Calendar of Papal Registers. Papal Letters*, vol.2, 1305-1342 (1895), p.20; Harbottle, B., 'Excavations at the Carmelite Friary, Newcastle upon Tyne, 1965 and 1967', *AA*, 4th series, vol.46 (1968), pp.163-223.

[97] Harbottle, 'Excavations', p.197; *Ancient Petitions*, pp.197-8. Adam Page of Newcastle may have had the Carmelites' loss of land in mind when he received a licence in 1336 to grant them a garden to enlarge their dwelling-place (*CPR, 1334-1338*, 386).

burial place for patrons. There were three other altars in the church, the most impressive in the Lady Chapel, which was furnished with two alabaster tableaux and its own organ.[98]

The convent had been involved in an episode in 1425 concerning a controversial opinion to which the Dominican Helmslay had once subscribed. That suggests the continuance, or recurrence, of tensions between some of the seculars and the religious in the city over offerings. At Auckland, Master William Glym, vicar of Newcastle, presented articles condemnatory of the teaching of William Boston, Prior of the Carmelites. He had expressed the opinion that there was no need for people to make offerings of candles in their parish churches at the Purification (Candlemas). Boston was unable to defend his assertion adequately, and made his submission.[99]

The Augustinians seem not to have run into eventual troubles either over the location of their premises or their access to water. Their convent was in a less congested area of town, to the east of the lower end of Pilgrim Street. It, too, was near the town wall, but may have been erected only after the wall's line had been determined, or after it had been built. The original plot may have been small, for the burgess John de Denton and the chaplain Adam Colewell were licensed respectively in 1323 and 1331 to grant the friars plots of adjacent land.[100] As we have seen, the Yorkshire landowner Lord Roos had granted them property in the town in 1317. A survival from the claustral buildings may be the rectangular medieval tower to which the 17th-century Holy Jesus Hospital is attached.[101]

The Augustinians long continued to win favour and to attract patronage. Bishop Hatfield entrusted spiritual duties to a brother of the house, in the same way as he was to do with the Dominican Helmslay: in March 1378 he licensed Thomas Hawkisgarth to hear confessions in the Archdeaconry of Northumberland, a licence renewed for a year in January 1379.[102] The friars sought the patronage of John of Gaunt, Duke of Lancaster (Richard II's uncle), probably when he was Lieutenant of the Marches (1379-83). He was well known as a patron of the mendicant orders, and was not averse to lay interventions in ecclesiastical affairs. The Augustinians were embroiled with the vicar of

---

[98] Harbottle, 'Excavations', pp.197-201; St John Hope, W., 'Inventory of the parish church of St Mary, Scarborough, 1434; and that of the White Friars or Carmelites of Newcastle-upon-Tyne, 1538', *Archaeologia*, 2nd series, pt 1, vol.51 (1888), pp.69-72.

[99] Storey, *Reg. Langley*, vol.3, pp.27-8; Storey, *Thomas Langley*, p.206.

[100] Welford, *Newcastle and Gateshead*, vol.1, pp.59, 76.

[101] Perhaps this was the prior's lodging or for guest accommodation.

[102] Hatfield Reg., fos. 132v, 151v. Cf the privilege granted by Hatfield to Richard de Tynemouth, above, p.87.

40   The tower of the Augustinan (Austin) Friary today.

Newcastle, Matthew de Bolton, Helmslay's opponent. They requested Gaunt to procure for them a Privy Seal letter inhibiting Bolton from proceeding in a suit against them, contrary, they said, to the Order's papal privilege – until evidence about their immunity could be obtained from the Roman curia. The endorsement of the petition shows that Gaunt took the issue seriously, and was prepared to enlist high-powered consideration of the friars' grievance (albeit pointedly ignoring provincial and diocesan jurisdictions). The case was to be considered by the Archbishop of Canterbury, the Bishop of Salisbury (Ralph Erghum, the Duke's former chancellor), and a doctor of the Church chosen by each of the parties.[103]

As we shall see, Walter Skirlaw, Bishop of Durham from 1388 to 1406, seems to have shared with Hatfield and Gaunt a good opinion of the house. He reposed particular trust in the theological expertise and sound sense of an unnamed Newcastle Augustinian, who was of his counsel in 1402-3. In 1428 and 1431 Bishop Langley stayed in the friary, and in the latter year licensed one of the brethren, Thomas Tatkastre, to hear confessions and to preach in the diocese.[104] In 1503 the friars were singled out for an honour which implies that they were considered discreet and proper, and their house well appointed. Henry VII's daughter Margaret, on her stately progress northwards to marry James IV of Scotland, was lodged with them. On her arrival at the city, she was greeted on Tynebridge by a procession headed, in front of the civic dignitaries, by 'the College of the said town' (perhaps the priests attached to St Nicholas' and its principal chapels) and the Carmelites and Franciscans, whose crosses she kissed. She was 'brought & conveyd to the freres austyns where she was lodged. And honestly Receyved by thos Revested with the crosse ... and she was broght [hyre] to hyre lodgyng euery men hym [owt] drew to hys awn'.[105] In 1540 the conventual buildings of the dissolved house were so convenient that they were earmarked for the use of the Council of the North.[106]

In the later 14th century, Newcastle acquired a new religious house belonging to an international order, one which had organisational similarities

[103] *Ancient Petitions*, pp.130-2; Goodman, A., *John of Gaunt* (Harlow, 1992), pp.7, 250. Appointments from the southern province may have been canvassed because ones from the northern province might have been considered obtrusive by the friars.

[104] Storey, *Thomas Langley*, p.206; Storey, *Reg. Langley*, vol.4, p.22.

[105] Anderson, *Newcastle upon Tyne*, pp.9-10. Presumably the Princess stayed in the friary for two nights. John Young's account of her progress does not make clear whether the church in which she celebrated the Feast of St James the day after her arrival was St Nicholas' or the conventual church.

[106] Brand, *Newcastle*, vol.1, p.349 and n. At the surrender of the friaries in 1539, the Franciscans (the Prior, eight friars and two novices) were said to have a tiny regular income (5s.); the Dominicans (Prior and 12 friars) had £2 9s. 4d; the Carmelites (Prior, seven friars, two novices) £9 7s. 4d. The Augustinians had a Prior, seven friars and three novices (*ibid.*, vol.1, pp.63, 336, 337n, 348, 406). For their income, *ibid.*, 349n.

to the orders of friars, but eschewed the practice of mendicancy. These were the Trinitarians, who followed the Rule of St Augustine. Their order predated the foundation of the friars: it existed by the end of the 12th century. They concentrated on raising money to ransom Christians captured by infidels. Some of their houses in northern Europe were developed as hospitals for returned captives, and then for patients generally.[107] In 1360 William de Acton (burgess in Parliament for Newcastle in 1365 and 1366), received a royal licence to purchase from the Carmelites their old site at Wall Knoll, and to found there a hospital in honour of the Holy Trinity to house its brethren, and the poor and infirm, and to endow it with other property in the town, including two cellars and a rent. It was to be dedicated to St Michael. Its first Master may have been a certain William de Wakefield, a brother of the Trinitarian house at Berwick upon Tweed. The Hospital 'of Holy Trinity of Redemption of Captives of le Wall knoll' had him as Master in 1369, when John de Bentele, chaplain was licensed to grant land and rent in the town to the house, in order support a chantry chaplain in St Nicholas'.[108] The Trinitarians needed aid in the 15th century. Bishop Langley granted them an indulgence, ordering ecclesiastical officials to receive their collectors. In 1460 their resources were being strained by the poor and infirm who flocked to seek succour from them. The Master, John Beverley (*Beberlai*), was granted a dispensation to retain a secular benefice for life, the better to maintain his state and the 'hospitality' of the house.[109] They were in good spiritual standing with a leading Northumberland family in 1480: Sir Ralph Widdrington and his wife Felicia then received a letter of confraternity from the Master, Richard.[110] The house was surrendered to the royal commissioners in 1539.[111]

Newcastle developed the full spread of urban devotional phenomena – minor chapels, *reclusoria*, alms houses and hospitals. Some of them or their denizens are mentioned among the many north-east ecclesiastical institutions

---

[107] Knowles, *Religious Orders*, vol.1, pp.201-2.

[108] *CPR, 1358-1361*, p.339; Chandler, *Leland's Itinerary*, p.346; *CPR, 1367-70*, 333. On 3 March 1360 Bishop Hatfield licensed Acton to have Mass celebrated within the chapel of the Hospital of Holy Trinity, founded by him for poor and infirm brethren and other suitable chaplains (Hatfield Reg., fo. 40r.) Acton was elected mayor in 1366, 1367 and 1368 (Hebden, Percy, *Northumberland Families*, vol. 1 (1968), pp.30-4; Welford, *Newcastle and Gateshead*, vol.1, p.427). Laurence Acton, either his brother or his nephew, was later to be associated with the Master of the house, John de Lilleburn (*CPR, 1381-1385*, 283).

[109] Storey, *Reg. Langley*, vol.4, p.195; *Calendar of Papal Registers. Papal Letters*, vol.11, p.586. In 1396 two chaplains, John Gaudes and Robert de Alnewyk, had granted a messuage and its appurtenances to the Trinitarians in aid of maintenance (*CPR, 1396-1399*, 5).

[110] Oliver, *Northumberland and Durham Deeds*, p.240.

[111] For a rental from the period of the dissolution see Brand, *Newcastle*, vol.1, p.407 and n.

41   The vaults of St Thomas' Chapel on the bridge.

to which Roger Thornton made bequests. Besides parochial churches and religious houses, his intended recipients in the city of quantities of lead (a principal commodity in which he dealt) included the chapel of St Thomas on Tynebridge, 'Westspitall', the 'lepremen', the Maison Dieu of St Katherine 'of my foundation', and every alms house of the bedridden. He particularly valued the prayers of the 'recluse of Newcastle'.[112] Thornton does not mention one of the most ancient minor chapels in the city, one which was outside civic jurisdiction. The fine Romanesque chapel in the castle keep is the only ecclesiastical building of its period which survives intact and unaltered. Its arches and ribs are lavishly decorated with dog-tooth carving.[113] A chaplain was appointed by the Crown to celebrate for the souls of the king's progenitors; he received his annual wages from the sheriff of Northumberland's receipts. In 1383 it came to light that the chapel had not been well served and supervised: its furnishings had disappeared, and a commission was appointed to enquire into the allegation that they had been carried off by the chaplains.[114]

Among the town's chapels, the one on Tynebridge was surely the most famous. The stone bridge over the Tyne was built to replace one destroyed in a fire in 1248. Its bridge chapel was a distinctive, but not unique feature, doubtless familiar to and reverenced by generations of travellers as well as townsfolk. It attracted local benefactors. William Heron was licensed to endow a chantry of St Anne there in 1329 with rent from adjacent Sandhill; Cecilia de Hamelden (of the parish of St Nicholas) made a bequest (1408); St Thomas's altar had a customary rent charge from the Percy family's nearby

[112]   Storey, *Reg. Langley*, vol.3, pp.64-7.
[113]   Pevsner, *Northumberland*, p.236.
[114]   *CPR, 1367-1370*, 47; *CPR, 1377-1381*, 54, 132, 195, 357; *CPR, 1381-1385*, 203; *CPR, 1452-1461*, 51, 634.

property in 1445, and there were two altars of Our Lady, one of them founded by George Carr.[115]

The way in which Thornton mentions a recluse in his will suggests that there was only one in Newcastle in 1429; or one so outstanding that he was known as *the* recluse. If there was just one, that would have contrasted with the numbers of them to be found, for instance, in York or Norwich in the 15th century, where some of them (most notably, Dame Julian at Norwich) practised and fostered contemplative devotion. However, Newcastle had a long eremitical tradition, despite Aldwin's rejection of a site in the area as unsuitable. In 1260 the Crown confirmed a grant by the Bishop and Prior of Carlisle, with the assent of the mayor and burgesses of Newcastle, of a 'place of inclusion' to Christina Umfred for life. This was in the churchyard of St John's. The present two-storied vestry of the church is a former anchorhold, but its medieval features are now obscured, apart from the cruciform aperture in the interior north wall of the chancel, through which the anchorite or anchoress could view the High Altar and receive the Sacrament.[116] In 1408 Cecilia de Hamelden left eight marks to the 'anchorites of the town' to celebrate for her for one year. At least two religious houses are likely to have had anchorholds in the period. In 1378 Bishop Hatfield had licensed Margaret Yorke, recluse in St Bartholomew's Convent, to have her own confessor.[117] In his will of 1415, Henry Lord Scrope of Masham (Yorks.) made a bequest to the Dominican recluse in Newcastle. Scrope was a patron of anchorites and disciple meditative devotion: this particular beneficiary may have been John Lacy, who, in books which he possessed *c.*1420 and *c.*1434, described himself as an anchorite.[118]

Newcastle had old-established hospitals and alms houses, which were to be augmented by Acton's and Thornton's foundations in the later Middle Ages. The 'Westspitall' mentioned by Thornton in his will was the Hospital of St Mary the Virgin, in Westgate, within the walls. By his time it was an ancient foundation. The 18th-century antiquary John Brand identified as its foundation charter a grant dating from Henry II's reign (1154-89) by Aselack of 'Killinghowe' (Kelloe, County Durham?) of land in Newcastle, for two members of an order (*fratres regulares*) and a chaplain to serve God and the

---

[115]   Welford, *Newcastle and Gateshead*, vol.1, p.72; Bourne, *Newcastle*, p.130; Brand, *Newcastle*, vol.1, p.32; Storey, *Reg. Langley*, vol.1, p.90 (Hamelden). In 1425 it was decided that arbitrators in a dispute between Sir William Elmeden and Robert Ogle should make their award in the chapel (*CPR, 1422-1429*, 210).

[116]   *CPR, 1258-1266*, 118; Clay, R.M., 'Some Northern Anchorites', *AA*, 4th series, vol.33, p.205.

[117]   Hatfield Register, fo.5v.

[118]   Bodleian Library, Oxford, MS. Rawlinson C258, fo.86r; St John's College, Oxford, MS.94, fo.101b; Clay, 'Some Northern Anchorites', p.210. For a treatise by Lacy, printed from the St John's College MS, see below, pp.111-12. For Scrope's will, Nicolas, *Scrope and Grosvenor Controversy*, vol. 2, pp.142-7.

poor. They were to lodge poor people, destitute clerks and pilgrims.[119] The house attracted bequests. For instance, in 1304 John de Lisle (*de Insula*) was licensed to alienate properties in the town to the Master and brethren, including four shops.[120] In 1295 the Master seems to have found no difficulty in paying subsidy for the house, but revenue was adversely affected by the effects of the Scottish Wars of Independence. In 1333 the Crown licensed the house to acquire revenue up to the yearly value of 100s., in order to compensate for destruction by Scottish forays. This opened the way for the donation of rents worth six marks p.a. in the town by the rich and pious burgess Nicholas de Ellerker. Nevertheless, the brethren were described as poor and in debt two years later, when the bulk of a sum which they had paid for a licence to acquire property was remitted.[121] They had a sufficiently large hall in 1342 to accommodate a meeting of the burgess community.[122] In 1398 the brethren were following the Rule of St Augustine, as hospital staff often did, and as they had probably customarily done. One of the brothers, William de Karliole, then received a papal dispensation to hold an additional benefice without cure of souls. As Professor Robin Storey showed, Bishop Langley's commissioners found Karliole's absenteeism as Master in 1415 unacceptable, and two years later, when commissions appointed by Langley confirmed the run-down and neglectful state of the hospital, his resignation was required.[123] In the later 15th century the hospital seems to have had a worthy repute among some relatives of the knightly Northumberland family of Swinburne; it had enjoyed Swinburne patronage in the later 14th century. In her will of 1502, Lady Elizabeth Swinburne alluded to her mother's place of burial in its chapel. Elizabeth left the chapel a covered silver piece of plate for use as a pyx, to hold the Blessed Sacrament, and another piece of silverware to be used to fashion a Crown for the statue of the Blessed Virgin, before whose altar her mother's remains lay. Elizabeth had high standards of piety, for she

[119]   Brand, *Newcastle*, vol.1, p.67; *CPR, 1348-1350*, 490. David I of Scotland (reigned 1124-53) had granted the 'hospitalarii' of Newcastle land in the town (Barrow, *Acts of Malcolm IV*, p.171). The brethren of the hospital received a royal confirmation of their lands and holdings, *c.*1174 x 3 March 1195. Richard *capellanus* of Newcastle was among the witnesses (*English Episcopal Acta*, 24, vol. 1, no.105). In 1252 Henry III confirmed the Master and brethren of the Hospital of St Mary in their possessions (*CChR, 1225-1257*, 40).

[120]   *CPR, 1301-1307*, p.223. Cf Brand, *Newcastle*, vol.1, pp.69-71

[121]   *CPR, 1292-1301*, 215; *CPR, 1330-1334*, 459, 488; *CPR, 1334-1338*, 182. In 1380 they had the patronage of a principal landowner in County Durham, William Lord Hilton, and of Thomas, son of the Northumberland knight Sir Robert Swinburne. They were storing muniments in 'le Westp ...', which were stolen (Hatfield Reg., fo. 179v.).

[122]   *CPR, 1340-1343*, 575.

[123]   Orme, Nicholas and Webster, Margaret, *The English Hospital 1070-1570* (New Haven, 1995), p.70; *Calendar of Papal Registers. Papal Letters*, vol.5, p.159; Storey, *Langley*, pp.190-1. The clear annual income of the hospital's estate at the dissolution was found to be as much as £29 9s.; the Master (then non-resident) received a stipend of £5 (Brand, *Newcastle*, vol.1, p.278 and n).

wanted her mother, herself and her sister to be remembered in perpetuity in the prayers of the Carthusian monks of Mount Grace in Yorkshire (also patronised by the merchant Roger Thornton). Mount Grace was to maintain until its dissolution an exemplary reputation for spirituality, and for expertise in contemplative devotion.[124]

Among other alms houses were St John's (the Spital), and the leper hospital of St Mary Magdalene. The latter was outside Newgate, one of the two northern gates leading out of town. It may have been the leper hospital referred to in 1252.[125] In 1291 the Master and brethren were licensed to hold a house in town left to them in his will by John Hertelawe.[126] Perhaps it was a token of indigence that in 1378 Bishop Hatfield awarded an indulgence of 40 days to those who contributed to the costs of the fabric of the hospital or its repair, or to the maintenance of its poor, feeble and infirm folk. In 1390 and 1399 the Warden, John Refham, combined his office with that of Archdeacon of Northumberland.[127] By 1546 St Mary Magdalene's catered for poor folk who had fallen sick of pestilence, on the grounds that leprosy had abated.[128]

The Maison Dieu founded by Roger Thornton, with its chapel of St Katherine, had a prime position, closely associated with the Guildhall, in the grandest part of the city, on Sandhill. It was just to the east of Tynebridge, on the river side of the street. In 1403 Thornton acquired a licence to grant the plot, 100 feet long and 80 feet wide, to the mayor, sheriff and aldermen for a Maison Dieu which he intended to build.[129] The licence which he acquired in 1412 shows how his plans had matured. The hospital was by then apparently built. A chaplain was to celebrate daily for members of his family. The beneficiaries were to be a select group. Nine poor men and four poor women known as the brethren and sisters of St Katherine's Hospital, otherwise known as Thornton's Hospital, were to be accommodated. Thornton's preoccupation with prayers for his family, in contrast to the greater concern which he had shown for the spiritual welfare of the community in 1403, may have been prompted by the death of his wife in 1411. The dedication to St Katherine perhaps reflected the fact that Agnes had died on her vigil and a hope that

---

[124] *Testamenta Eboracensia*, vol.4, SS (1869), p.108. For earlier Swinburne patronage of the 'Westspitall', see above, n121.

[125] *CPR, 1247-1258*, 123. For the location of the hospital, *Calendar of Inquisitions Post Mortem*, vol.23, no.193.

[126] *CPR, 1281-1292*, 215.

[127] Hatfield Reg., fo.26v.; *CPR, 1385-1389*, 229; *CPR, 1399-1401*, 27.

[128] Brand, *Newcastle*, vol.1, p.427. The clear income of the hospital was said at the dissolution to be £8 18s. 10d.: the Master was then non-resident (*ibid.*, pp.428-9).

[129] *CPR, 1401-1405*, 207. For the location of the Maison Dieu see Chandler, *Leland's Itinerary*, p.340; Bourne, *Newcastle*, pp.123-4.

the saint would intercede for Agnes's soul.[130] The saint was prominently represented on the Thorntons' monumental brass.

Thornton was particularly concerned to provide both adequate and incremental funding for his foundation, and to limit its benevolence to a few recipients – perhaps with the toils of some other established hospitals in mind. He was licensed in 1412 to endow the Warden and Maison Dieu with a property, in aid of the community's maintenance; he, his heirs or executors could acquire further property to the value of £10 a year. The prospective additions were also intended to help to fund the chaplain of the chantry which he was founding at St Peter's altar in All Saints' Church. In 1424 he considered that 10 messuages and 10 tofts acquired in the city, producing £7 p.a., were adequate for these purposes.[131] The association of the Thornton family with the Maison Dieu appears in the later 15th century. In 1479 and 1482 another Roger Thornton received leases of the parochial revenues of nearby Long Benton (Northumberland). They were dated at St Katherine's Hospital, and its Master was associated with them. Perhaps Thornton made them for the hospital's benefit.[132]

Religious Culture

Newcastle had a relatively homogeneous religious culture. The simplicity of its ecclesiastical structure provided a benign context for co-operation between the town's clergy and layfolk in matters of worship. There were no powerful, watchfully maintained ecclesiastical liberties, prone to produce jurisdictional friction with urban government, like those of St Mary's Abbey in York or the Cathedral Priory at Norwich. Clerics and layfolk in Newcastle in the 14th and 15th centuries seem to have been generally at one in inclination to marginalise the rights of patronage exercised there jointly by the bishops and priors of Carlisle. In contrast to some other leading English towns, Newcastle had failed to develop a multiplicity of independent parishes. Before 1300 London had 126 parish churches, Lincoln, 43 and Canterbury, 22. In the 1520s Norwich had at least 46, and York and its suburbs at the end of the 15th century had forty.[133] Even Carlisle, insignificant in size and wealth compared to Newcastle,

[130]   *CPR, 1408-1415*, 412; Bourne, *Newcastle*, p.95.
[131]   *CPR, 1422-1429*, 213.
[132]   Balliol College, Oxford, Long Benton Deeds, E1, nos 52, 54. For Henrician valuations of the Maison Dieu's income see Brand, *Newcastle*, vol.1, pp.27-8.
[133]   Reynolds, Susan, *An Introduction to the History of English Medieval Towns* (Oxford, 1977), p.84; Tanner, Norman P., *The Church in Late Medieval Norwich 1370-1532* (Toronto, 1984), pp.2-3; Palliser, D.M., *Tudor York* (Oxford, 1979), p.226. York's population in 1377 has been calculated at 14,500, Norwich at 8,500, Lincoln at 7,000, Canterbury at 5,100 and Newcastle at 5,300 (Palliser, 'Urban Decay Revisited', p.9). See also above, p.76 and n.42.

had two. Towns which had been major urban centres in the late Anglo-Saxon period tended to have a large number of parishes, which had evolved from private chapelries before the elaboration of parochial rights inhibited further fragmentation. The authority exercised by the vicars of St Nicholas' over the whole of the town could be a powerful unifying force, especially as the bishops of Durham upheld and reinforced it.

The duplication of dedications at the altars of the principal secular churches suggests the solidarity and compatibility of separate parochial communities in the principal chapels as well as that of the parish church.[134] It is paradigmatic of the inclusive piety of the Newcastle elite in the 15th century that its two leading benefactors of ecclesiastical institutions, Roger Thornton and Robert Rodes, were patrons of both its parish church and its major chapels. Thornton made bequests to all of them, and maintained altars in St Nicholas' and All Saints': presumably he habitually worshipped in All Saints'. Rodes was apparently responsible for substantially modifying and enhancing the structures of both St Nicholas' and St John's (and possibly that of All Saints', too). Thornton also made widespread bequests to religious houses in Northumberland and County Durham, reflecting the geographical scope of his commercial activities as well as illustrating one way in which the trade of Newcastle helped to foster a hinterland of religious links. However, the town's mercantile elite had long tended to concentrate their pious activities in the town. Throughout the Middle Ages, and especially in the later period, they were a force in shaping the character of its religion. In the 12th and 13th centuries they helped to endow its varied religious institutions. Since the numbers of parishioners were large, they may have strongly influenced the character of worship in its four principal secular churches. Besides, a leading burgess such as Robert Angreton in the 1360s might put his knife into different ecclesiastical pies; he was one of the instigators of a new religious guild, he was involved controversially in the convent's affairs, and was suspected of plotting to rebuild the chancel of the parish church. Rich burgesses provided endowments for their churches' altars and set up perpetual chantries, especially (as elsewhere) in the early 14th century. Their chantries sustained the traditional cults to which existing altars were dedicated, underpinning a devotional continuity, a force against change. At various times in the 14th and 15th centuries, some religious institutions found their current incomes inadequate, but, though Acton and Thornton provided rents for their new charitable foundations, burgesses were now disinclined to alienate properties in order to prop up struggling older ones.

---

[134] I owe thanks for this point to Professor Pollard.

42 The Thornton
Brass, originally
in All Saints', now
in St Nicholas'
Cathedral.

They were prepared, however, to make monetary gifts and bequests for the fabric and furnishings of the churches in which they customarily worshipped, especially the parish church. The orders of friars, as was the case more generally, continued to receive support, but now mainly in the form of small donations in coin or kind. Clearly friars continued to interact positively with lay piety in Newcastle, an engagement which was probably enhanced because, as we can reasonably assume, they heavily outnumbered the town's curates.

In the later Middle Ages, the burgesses' inclination to mould public religion is manifest. It was matched by their urge to privatise some aspects of it, seen in their chantry foundations, in whose regulation they sometimes intended the town government or their heirs to have a patronal stake. It is also seen in their petitions for individual privileges. John Warton (1407), William de Langton, mayor, William Eslington, burgess (both 1410), and Thomas Thyrden, merchant, and Agnes his wife (1435), were licensed to have private chapels in their houses.[135] Some received other papal privileges for their family worship; in 1430 William Belle, styled nobleman and burgess, and Margaret his wife, were licensed to have a portable altar, and to choose a confessor with power to give them plenary remission at the hour of death. John Rodes, similarly styled, and Isabel his wife, were licensed to have a portable altar soon afterwards. Perhaps they were intending to travel abroad. Foreign merchants in Bruges were often domiciled there with their wives. They may have been planning to make distant pilgrimages, and wanted to be assured that they could worship on shipboard or in isolated places.[136]

The cults long favoured in their churches by the townsfolk were, for the most part, ones popular in other parts of England – that of St Thomas of Canterbury notable among them. The cosmopolitan nature of the town's piety in part resulted from its strong commercial links with the ports of eastern England, with London, and the Low Countries. This cosmopolitanism is reflected in the lavish iconography of the monumental brass of Roger and Agnes Thornton, which perhaps provides a window on their individual world of the supernatural. Above them are figures symbolic of Heaven, with, centrally, the Blessed Virgin and Child. At the four corners of the brass are symbols of the Evangelists. To the right of Roger's figure, in descending order, are ones of six Apostles, with St Peter (to whom Thornton dedicated his chantry in All Saints') at the top. To the left of his wife, there are matching

<hr>

[135] Storey, *Reg. Langley*, vol.1 (Warton); pp.111-12 (Langton, Eslington); vol.4, p.150 (Thyrden). In 1361 Simon Spalding, Prior of the Newcastle Carmelites, had been absolved for celebrating Mass without licence in a chamber in the house of Thomas Holt of Newcastle (Hatfield Reg., fo.40r.)

[136] Twemlow, J.A. (ed.), *Calendar of Papal Registers. Papal Letters*, vol.9, 1431-1437 (1912), pp.185, 187, 188.

figures, St Paul above five Apostles. Between them, with St John the Baptist at the top and St Lawrence at the bottom, are four female saints – in descending order, Katherine, Barbara, Agnes and Mary Magdalene. The cults include strong international ones, but no local ones. The emphasis is on the authority of the New Testament; female martyrs whose cults were generally popular are prominent too. We may attribute to the couple a well-informed 'modern' piety. Perhaps it was influenced by the discourse of 'the recluse of Newcastle', one of the priests whom the dying Thornton specially trusted to aid his soul, and who is likely to have been the Dominican John Lacy.

The leading regional cult, that of St Cuthbert, is likely to have flourished in Newcastle; there was his altar in St Nicholas' Church. Thornton bequeathed 100 fothers of lead for work on the tower of Durham Cathedral, whereas he gave only 18 in total to the chapels and religious institutions of Newcastle. Robert Rodes, great servant of Durham Priory, founded a chantry in the Cathedral.[137] Newcastle had nothing to compete with the shrine of St Cuthbert: unlike most English cities, it apparently lacked either a major relic of Christ or the Blessed Virgin Mary, or any impressive bodily remains of a saint. However, passing pilgrims are likely to have worshipped in the Franciscan Friary, reverencing the relics of St Francis there. The image of the Holy Trinity in St Andrew's Church and the statue of Our Lady in the Hospital of St Mary, Westgate, may have been objects of their devotion, too. Local folk had the incentive to visit some Newcastle churches when an indulgence for doing so was on offer.

As we have seen, in the 12th century the Hospital of St Mary, Westgate, was intended in part to accommodate pilgrims. Probably many of them were going to and from St Cuthbert. The name of Pilgrim Street may commemorate a hospice there used for the same purpose. 'Vicus peregrinorum' is mentioned in a document dating from the 1250s/60s, but that may refer, Frances McCombie has argued, to travellers in general.[138] Durham-bound pilgrims probably declined in numbers in the later Middle Ages. Dr Ben Nilson has noted falls in offerings at the shrine from the 1380s onwards.[139] Perhaps, in an age when intense spiritual relationships with Christ and the Blessed Virgin were being experienced and widely broadcast, their many cults were exercising a greater pull than some traditional saintly ones were. Moreover, numbers of Scottish pilgrims are likely to have declined as a result of Anglo-Scottish

[137]   Storey, *Reg. Langley*, vol.3, p.164; Dobson, *Durham Cathedral Priory*, pp.44-5.
[138]   McCombie, F., 'The possible site of a Pilgrim's Inn, Newcastle upon Tyne, *AA*, 5th series, vol.24 (2005), pp.83-5.
[139]   Nilson, Ben, *Cathedral Shrines of Medieval England* (Woodbridge, 1998), pp.161-2.

wars and border insecurities, and of the growing popularity in Scotland of its native saints.[140]

There was a chapel dedicated to the Blessed Virgin Mary at Jesmond, outside the town walls, but within the urban parish, in the chapelry of St Andrew. It was mentioned in 1279. In 1428 a papal grant was made, for a period of 10 years, of relaxation from 40 days of enjoined penance to those who visited the chapel, and gave alms to it for its repair; the buildings were said to be very ruinous. The pope declared that multitudes resorted there on account of the miracles wrought through the merits of the Blessed Virgin. There is a well near the ruins of the chapel which was associated with the healing. We may surmise, from this indulgence, that the shrine had recently acquired a miracle-working reputation locally. The town's population was especially anxious about disease in an era of epidemics. A few years later its Dominican recluse, John Lacy, wrote about popular fears of the pestilence there, and the tendency for inhabitants to take flight, which he in a vein of Christian resignation advised against.[141]

Despite the fact that Newcastle lacked the draw of a major shrine, or of a famous abbey, its notable religious culture had a strong influence in its hinterlands, and was in itself invigorated by patronage from noble and gentle families of the North East. Leading burgesses continued to have traditionally strong ties with county elites, variously familial, commercial and concerned with rural or urban property-holding. Roger Thornton purchased the manor of Whitton in Northumberland, and built a tower-house there, as befitted a border lord rather than a great merchant. Landowners invested in urban rents. Some stayed in the accommodation which they had rented or purchased in Newcastle, either because it was a convenient place to conduct business, or had attractions in its markets and taverns, as well as its ecclesiastical institutions, the like of which were not to be found in such profusion, and in such security from attack, anywhere else in Northumberland. Moreover, one regionally unmatched religious draw which developed in the 14th century was the specially elaborate celebration in Newcastle of Corpus Christi, the feast proclaimed in the mid-13th century, which became popular throughout western Christendom. As in some other English towns, a cycle of miracle plays came to be put on by the

[140] St Cuthbert, whose cult historically flourished on both sides of the Borders, was being invoked in North-East England in the later Middle Ages as defender against the Scots (Dobson, Barrie, 'The Church of Durham and the Scottish Borders, 1378-88', in Goodman, Anthony and Tuck, Anthony (eds), *War and Border Societies in the Middle Ages* (1992), pp.124-54).

[141] Twemlow, J.A. (ed.), *Cal. Papal Registers. Papal Letters*, vol.8 (1909), p.22; Dodds, *NCH*, vol.13, pp.298-9, 302-4; Royster, James Finch (ed.), *A Middle English Treatise of the Ten Commandments. Studies in Philology*, vol.6 (1910), p.16. The chantry surveyors appointed after the 1546 Act reported that the chaplain was not resident, and that no liturgies were celebrated in the chapel. It had no plate or goods, and the lands attached to it had been sold since 1537 (*NCH*, vol.13, p.307).

craft guilds to mark it. The first mention of a play associated with Corpus Christi in Newcastle occurs in 1427 and it was staged by the Coopers' Guild. The full cycle was presented at various stations on the feast day itself, separate from the solemn procession with the Host which set out from St Nicholas'.[142] Landowners who dated property transactions at Newcastle on such a hallowed feast day may have been there, up from the country, because the celebrations were so much more awesome than those on their native heath. On Corpus Christi 1411 Sir John Widdrington made an agreement with the Lilburne family for an assignment of dower to his widowed daughter Agnes de Lilburne. The parties swore before witnesses in the royal castle to keep the covenants.[143] Newcastle probably acquired a colourful and joyful religious attraction in the 15th century, when such celebrations became common in England: a play or pageant of St George and the Dragon. In 1510 civic payments were made for the provision of a dragon in Newcastle.[144]

Lady Eure's attachment to the Dominicans, Sir Aymer and Mary de Atholl's to the image of the Holy Trinity in All Saints', and their burials in the respective churches, suggest that the town may have already had resident country ladies and gentleman, a phenomenon found in leading English towns especially from the 15th century onwards. Great lords might be found in residence there, too. The sick and the frail valued its shelter and amenities, especially when the Scots were threatening. In 1388 a Scottish army ravaged John Lord Neville's estates in County Durham. A few weeks afterwards, the ageing lord was lying in Newcastle, mortally sick.[145] In the 15th century the earls of Northumberland had their inn on the riverside of the Close, the fashionable street running westwards from Sandhill. The family had some devotional associations with churches in the town – the 1st Earl, as we have seen, with St John's Church. Formerly there was a devotional painting on wood in St Nicholas', with solicitations for prayers for the soul of the 4th Earl (d.1489).[146]

---

[142]   Anderson, *Newcastle upon Tyne*, pp.xi-xv; Lancashire, Ian, *Dramatic Texts and Records of Britain. A Chronological Topography to 1558* (Cambridge, 1984), pp.229-32.

[143]   Oliver, *Northumberland and Durham Deeds*, pp.236-7.

[144]   Fraser, C.M. (ed.), *The Accounts of the Chamberlains of Newcastle upon Tyne 1508-1511*, Society of Antiquaries of Newcastle upon Tyne, record series, 3 (1987), p.xxvii.

[145]   Madox, Thomas, *Formulare Anglicanum* (1702), pp.327-9. An inquisition after Atholl's death found that he possessed no property in the city – but clearly it was anticipated that he might have had some (Kirby, J.L. (ed.), *Calendar of Inquisitions Post Mortem, vol. 18, 1-6 Henry IV, 1399-1405* (1987), no.582). In 1428 Edward Bertram esquire and his wife Elizabeth were licensed to have an oratory in their house in Newcastle (Storey, *Reg. Langley*, vol.3, p.94). Son of Sir John Bertram of Bothal, he was sheriff of Newcastle, 1423-4 (Hunter Blair, *Mayors and Lord Mayors*, p.15).

[146]   Brand, *Newcastle*, vol.1, pp.276-7. The 5th Earl of Northumberland gave a banquet for lords and gentlemen in Newcastle when Princess Margaret was lodged there in 1503, but it is not clear where it was held (Anderson, *Early English Drama*, pp.9-10).

A gathering of gentlefolk in town in 1402 was recalled by witnesses to the proof of age of John Mitford, esquire. His mother may have been moved there from the family home at Mitford for her lying in, and kinsfolk also from Northumberland may have gathered there for the birth, because a Scottish invasion was imminently expected. Witnesses recollected a happy gathering for the baptism in a bustling St Nicholas'. Thomas Fox, skinner, said that Sir Robert Lisle, the infant's maternal grandfather, purchased an expensive fur in which the infant was wrapped on the way to church (it was April). The other grandfather, Sir John Mitford, on arrival at the churchyard kissed and blessed him. He took him to the font into which the officiating priest, Thomas Galen, accidentally dropped him. The godfather, Sir John Widrington, exclaimed, 'Prest, prest, fond be thi hened.' A witness afterwards met 'many men and women coming joyfully from the church, and among them a woman carrying John'. Another witness met Sir Henry Percy coming out, who enquired who the infant was. Other business, sacred and secular, went on in the church that day. Robert Kirkeby, chaplain, chatted after celebrating the Mass of St Mary at the altar of the Holy Trinity. Sir John Widrington and Sir Robert Lisle negotiated a settlement of their disputes.[147] One reason for the city's attractiveness for country gentlefolk may be reflected in the observations (barbed and prejudiced as they may have been) of Aeneas Sylvius Piccolomini, who recalled that, after travelling from the Borders in 1435, he 'came to Newcastle, which is said to have been built by Caesar. There for the first time he seemed to see a familiar world and a habitable country; for Scotland and the part of England nearest it are utterly unlike the country we inhabit'.[148]

It was from the 'habitable' lands to the south (and perhaps, too, from the east across the North Sea) that, as we have seen, new religious impulses came to Newcastle, some with lasting effectiveness – for instance, with the foundation of friaries, and the spread of the cults of St Thomas of Canterbury and of Corpus Christi. Alien merchants at host in the town in the later Middle Ages would have found that devotion to cults familiar to them (such as those of St Eloy and of female martyrs) often outshone regional and local ones there. However, evidence for the impact of some late medieval religious movements is patchy. There is a dearth of evidence about any influence exercised by contemplative devotion. Lady de Wyleby, a member of Joan Neville, Countess

---

[147] *Calendar of Inquisitions Post Mortem*, vol.23, no.358; Macdonald, *Border Bloodshed*, p.152. Besides Sir John Mitford (d.1409) of Molesden in Mitford, Sir Robert Lisle (c.1355-1425) of Woodburn and Sir John Widdrington (1377-1444) of Widdrington and Shotton were Northumberland landowners, all of them elected for the shire in Parliament (*Hist. Parl., 1386-1431*, vol.3, pp.744-9, 610-12, 853-6).

[148] Gragg, Florence A. (trans.), Gabel, Leonora. C. (ed.), *Memoirs of a Renaissance Pope. The Commentaries of Pius II* (1960), pp.35-6.

43 The cult of St Mary celebrated in a glass roundel in St Nicholas' Cathedral.

of Westmorland's household at Raby Castle in 1415, was close to the Countess and two of her daughters. The Countess had received sympathetically the Norfolk mystic Margery Kempe, probably at one of her Yorkshire castles in 1413: another of her daughters, wife of the Northumberland landowner Lord Greystoke (into whose family Roger Thornton's son Roger married), was alleged some years later to have been under Margery's religious influence. The evidence of the Countess's patronage of Margery suggests that she was strongly interested in contemplative devotion. If that interest was shared by Lady de Wyleby, the latter may have received instruction and counsel about the devotion from the Newcastle Dominican whom she patronised, Master Thomas Bawmburgh.[149]

We are on firmer ground about religious impulses and attitudes in this period when considering the ministry of the Dominican recluse John Lacy, and the theological and devotional works which he knew and possessed. They give us insights into the ways in which a friar who gained widespread respect envisaged the problems of the laity, high and low born. They reveal the intellectual background of a brother from a convent which, towards the end of the 14th century, was one

[149] *Testamenta Eboracensia*, vol.1, pt 1, pp.381-3; Windeatt, Barry (ed.), *The Book of Margery Kempe* (2000), pp.265-6; Goodman, A., *'My most illustrious mother, the lady Katherine': Katherine Swynford and her daughter Joan* (Lincoln Cathedral Publications, 2008, pp.13-15).

of seven in the order in England where the higher study of theology seems to have been pursued.[150] Lacy possessed a copy of the first version of the Wycliffite New Testament – neatly written, well kept, with annotation marks and a few unexceptionable glosses.[151] However, Lacy was solidly orthodox. In the collection which he penned of extracts from mainly patristic texts, and some short works in English, there are included *Horae Beatae Mariae Virginis* and an English hymn to the Virgin. In his own brief treatise on the Ten Commandments, included in the collection, a treatise which he wrote mainly in English, his theology was orthodox. A miracle of Our Lady is recounted.[152]

Lacy's collection starts with a request for prayers for him, dated 1434, and a statement that he gave it to Roger Stonysdale, chaplain at St Nicholas', and that it was to be passed on to a succession of chaplains there. So we have here an instance of eminently practical pastoral help being given by a friar to edify and assist seculars. Perhaps Lacy anticipated that the Latinity of some of the chaplains was likely to be limited. For his method was to provide short extracts from the Bible and Church Fathers (mainly St Jerome, St Gregory and, above all, St Augustine) in Latin, followed by an English translation or paraphrase. Possessing, as he did, a heretical English translation of the New Testament, he was sensitive lest Lollard tendencies be attributed to him, if some of his Biblical extracts in English were culled and distributed separately. He instructed 'that neuer man ne woman lete departe the engeliche from the latyn, for diuers causes that ben good and lawful to my felynge'.[153]

Exhortations in the treatise directed at sinners in general, and at some specific sins, suggest that it was meant to be read to or by laymen and laywomen as well as being studied as a practical manual by curates. Lacy aimed to bring all of them into closer contact with sacred literature, and to relate its import directly to forbidden customs and practices common among the laity in Newcastle. In his denunciation of sorcery, he exclaimed, 'Now ye wemen takethe ye heed.' Many of you, he said, in superstitious wise lay your new born babies in a sieve (*syf*), and put out bread and cheese, or else a 'preuvy clooth' belonging to the father, to divert evil spirits.[154] Lacy was concerned, too, about profanity, such as was used in common speech in buying and selling. He said that the common people, men

[150]   Orme, Nicholas, *English Schools in the Middle Ages* (1973), p.230.
[151]   Bodleian Library, Oxford, MS Rawlinson, C258; Deanesley, Margaret, *The Lollard Bible and other medieval biblical versions* (Cambridge, 1920), p.333.
[152]   *Ten Commandments*, pp.6, 18-19.
[153]   *Ibid.*, p.9. Lacy also has a citation from the work of the Dominican theologian Robert Kilwardby (d.1279), whom he described as a 'gret clerke' (*ibid.*, pp.20-1).
[154]   *Ibid.*, p.4. I owe thanks to Mr James Gibson, Verger at St John the Baptist's Church, Newcastle, and Mr George Proctor and Mrs Eleanor Proctor, Church Wardens there, for their recollections of how, at christenings in the locality, presents would be brought of cheese and bread or cake, wrapped in a cloth.

and women, young and old, swore at one another so habitually that they were unconscious of offending God. Lacy focused on a contemporary preoccupation, reflected in sermons and iconography, that swearing by parts of Christ's body sinfully dismembered Him.[155] Lacy is engaged with the hustling, trafficking urban environment: he has a good deal of advice about what is lawful behaviour in commercial and property transactions.[156] His knowledge of and involvement with everyday living in market, inn and, indeed, bedchamber, illustrate how an urban recluse was not necessarily isolated from secular society, but might be positively immersed in its affairs, and an influence on clerical and lay attitudes and conduct at large. Lacy's treatise may have reflected a thirst for practical exposition of Scriptures among layfolk as well as chaplains, for which he was accustomed to catering in individual discourse through the window of his cell.

Among the new impulses which reached Newcastle was Lollardy. Richard Wyche, a priest probably from the diocese of Hereford, was arrested and appeared for examination before Bishop Skirlaw of Durham in 1402, accused of preaching without a licence in the diocese, and of being a Lollard, holding heretical views such as about the nature of the accidents in the Eucharist. Wyche, while in prison after his condemnation, wrote a letter to a local sympathiser, in which he gave a detailed account of his examination, held both in formal sessions and more privately in his cell. One of those who tried to win him over by promises of spiritual help as well as in debate, was an Augustinian from Newcastle, who was one of the Bishop's counsellors. Wyche stood firm, after months of pressure, in his refusal to swear to the declaration of faith put to him. In March 1403 he was declared a heretic and excommunicated. After several years in the bishop's prison he made a full recantation and submitted himself to correction by Skirlaw or his commissary.

During Wyche's examinations, the Bishop had remarked to him, he wrote, that a certain 'Jacobus' and himself had subverted people in Northumberland (*populum in Northumbria*). We cannot be sure that he founded this Lollard cell in Newcastle, but his success as a proselytiser in the region is credible, despite the facts that he was a stranger, a southerner, and that his dialect is unlikely to have been familiar to most people thereabouts. For he had charisma: when he was executed as a heretic in London in 1440, he was popularly accounted there as a saint and a martyr. According to his letter (singularly devoid of animus against the Bishop and other interlocutors), he had heard that the Bishop's Chancellor had conducted a search for Lollards in Newcastle, in which he netted a certain

---

[155] *Ibid.*, pp.17–20; Duffy, *Stripping of the Altars*, pp.72–3.
[156] *Ten Commandments*, pp.29, 30, 34.

Robert, *magister Lollardorum*, whom Wyche identified as 'Robert Herl my brother'. He asked his correspondent to contact various laymen for him, presumably resident in the city, and 'a priest staying near the church of St Andrew whom I believe is called Henry de Topcliffe'. Most notably, Wyche posited that he had a close friendship with the Master of the Trinitarian house at Wall Knoll, a priest whose virtues he held in high esteem.[157] Besides the intrinsic religious appeal of his message, Wyche's rejection of the mendicancy of the friars may have had a particular appeal to secular priests. However, Skirlaw's decisive action against Lollards appears to have stamped out an embryonic network of them. Indeed, Wyche's capitulation, after his heroic resistance, would have been disheartening for any obdurate disciples. Though we must be wary in view of gaps in documentation, later Lollardy and early Protestantism appear not to have made progress in Newcastle. One reason may have been the liveliness of traditional beliefs and practices there, articulated by a close-knit elite which informally had a good deal of control over ecclesiastical institutions, as founders and patrons. In Newcastle's hinterlands, ecclesiastical and, in some parts, secular authority was exercised by a single bishopric, whose jurisdiction was therefore hard to escape. So, in the city, was that of its solitary vicar. Southern strangers like Wyche, who attempted to proselytise society, may have been more conspicuous than in, say, London or Bristol, Towers of Babel and jurisdictional patchworks by comparison.

Since Henry Bourne and John Brand wrote well-documented chapters in their tomes on Newcastle in the 18th century, the medieval Church there, as a discrete subject, has been neglected, despite much revealing work on the archaeology, architecture and history of some of its institutions. The subject has been overshadowed in modern historiography by Durham Cathedral Priory and bishopric, graced by superb architectural remains, illuminated by often abundant literary and documentary evidence, and possessing great significance for regional and, in some respects, national history. The frequent modern interpretation of the significance of Pilgrim Street in Newcastle accords well with this balance of interest: for the supposed pilgrims, it implies, Newcastle was merely a staging post on the way to higher things. Indeed, in the eyes of its medieval inhabitants as well as of outsiders, Newcastle could not compete with the spiritual riches of

---

[157] Matthew, G.D. (ed.), 'The Trial of Richard Wyche', *EHR.*, vol.5 (1890), pp.530-44; Shirley, Walter W. (ed.), *Fasciculi Zizaniorum*, rolls series (1858), Appendix VI, pp.501-5; Snape, M.G., 'Some evidence of Lollard activity in the diocese of Durham in the early Fifteenth Century', *AA*, 4th series, vol.39 (1961), pp.355-61; Thomson, J.A.F., *The Later Lollards 1414-1520* (Oxford, 1965), pp.148-50; idem, 'Wyche, Richard (d.1440)', *ODNB*, vol.60, pp.606-7. In the period of the Wyche affair, three other priests in the diocese were denounced to Skirlaw as heretics and summoned to appear before him (Snape, 'Some evidence', pp.356-7).

Durham. Yet in the splendour of its churches, in the devotion they attracted, and in the numbers and high profile of its religious and seculars, Newcastle ranked with other major English cities. It ranked, too, with Durham, though so different in character, as one of the two principal ecclesiastical and religious centres of the northernmost parts of England. Beyond York and Chester there seems to have been no rival in scale and magnificence to its Corpus Christi celebrations. Wyche's attention to the conversion of Newcastle suggests that he perceived that the town was in fact a lamp that might illuminate the far North.

5

Newcastle, Northumberland and the Crown in the Later Middle Ages

ANTHONY TUCK

At the beginning of the 15th century the town of Newcastle underwent a significant and permanent change in its relationship with the county of Northumberland. On 23 May 1400 Henry IV granted a charter to the town whereby it was separated from the county of Northumberland and became a county of itself, to be know as 'comitatus ville Novi Castri super Tynam' (the county of the town of Newcastle upon Tyne).[1] Under this charter the county of Newcastle was to have its own sheriff chosen annually by 24 of the most 'suitable, discreet, honourable and honest' burgesses of the town. The sheriff replaced the bailiffs who had hitherto held office in the town. He was empowered to hold a county court, and the burgesses were authorised to choose six aldermen who, along with the mayor, would act as justices of the peace. However, even though Henry IV's charter created for the first time a clear jurisdictional separation between county and town, it was in some senses merely the culmination of a long process of separation, and of the development of a sense of civic pride and distinctiveness. In 1333, for instance, the mayor of Newcastle was granted power to act as escheator for the town, and the election of the town's bailiffs, who were to be superseded by the sheriff under the 1400 charter, had for long been largely a matter for the guild merchant of the town.[2] In 1391 Richard II granted the Mayor (William Bishopdale) and his successors in office the right to have a ceremonial sword carried before him when he processed through the town on mayoral business.[3] The achievement of county status in 1400 thus seems to have expressed civic pride as much as a fundamental change in the government of the town.

Newcastle was not alone in seeking to enhance its pride and sense of separateness by obtaining county status. Bristol was the first town in England

[1] *CChR, 1341-1417*, 397-8; the full text of the charter is printed in Brand, *Newcastle*, vol.2, pp.169-71.
[2] *Hist. Parl, 1386-1421*, vol.1, p.546.
[3] Brand, *Newcastle*, vol.2,. pp.167-8.

to do so. A charter of 1373 separated
it from Gloucestershire and permitted
the mayor, as in Newcastle, to have a
ceremonial sword carried before him.
The burgesses of Bristol regarded the
1373 charter as a major landmark in
the development of their corporate
identity, and they had an elaborately
sculpted cross erected in the centre
of the town to commemorate the
event.[4] (It is now at Stourhead Park
in Wiltshire.) Bristol was followed by
York in 1396, and here, too, the mayor
was to be the escheator and was to
have a sword carried before him on ceremonial occasions.[5]

44   The civic regalia, a detail from Buck's
18th-century view of Newcastle.

In the years after 1400 several other towns achieved county status: Dublin in
1403, when Henry IV gave the Corporation a civic sword, which still survives;
Norwich in 1404, and Lincoln in 1410. These were followed by Hull in 1440;
Southampton in 1447; Nottingham in 1449 and Coventry in 1451. Henry VI's
grants to Southampton and Coventry followed royal visits, but taken together the
number of grants in this short period may reflect general royal policy towards
important towns. Canterbury received its charter 1461, and this was in all probability
a reward for its support of the Yorkist cause in 1460.[6] The importance which these
towns evidently attached to the right of the mayor to have a civic sword carried
before him suggests that ceremony was as important to the burgesses of the newly
created counties as jurisdictional separation from their surrounding counties.

Thus Newcastle was, perhaps, doing no more than keeping up with other
large and prosperous towns in seeking county status. Yet the date on which
Newcastle's charter was granted almost certainly means that it has a wider
political significance than the mere enhancing of the town's sense of pride
and separateness. Henry IV had been on the throne, somewhat insecurely, for
only eight months, and one of the most important of the nobles who had

⁴   *CChR.* 1341-1417, p.228; Seyer, S., *The Charters and Letters Patent granted by the Kings and Queens of England to the town and city of Bristol* (Bristol, 1812), p.39.

⁵   Harvey, J.H., 'Richard II and York', in Du Boulay, F.R.H. and Barron, Caroline (eds), *The Reign of Richard II: Essays in Honour of May McKisack* (London, 1971), p.206.

⁶   *CChR.* 1341-1417, pp.421-3, 442; CChR. 1427-1516, pp.8-11, 138-41; Hill, J.W.F., *Medieval Lincoln* (Cambridge, 1948), pp.270-1; *Victoria County History of Warwickshire*, vol.2 (London, 1908), p.437; vol.8 (London, 1969), p.3; Wolffe, B.P., *Henry VI* (London, 1981), pp.365-6, 368-9; Ross, C.D., *Edward IV* (London, 1974), pp.25-6. The whole subject is not well researched.

helped him to the throne was Henry Percy, Earl of Northumberland. Percy, of course, was the leading landowner in Northumberland, with extensive estates in the Tyne valley west of Newcastle as well as further north in the county.[7] In Henry IV's grant of county status to Norwich a few years later Sir Thomas Erpingham seems to have acted as an intermediary, but it is not clear that there was a similar Lancastrian retainer close to the court who performed a similar function for Newcastle. It is tempting, therefore, to suppose that Percy used his influence at court to obtain the charter for Newcastle, thereby securing his influence in the town. Yet Percy's influence in the affairs of Newcastle, both before and after the grant of the charter, is not easy to discern. Few if any of the leading merchants seem to have been his retainers, and indeed he depended in part on their shipping and their goodwill to supply the garrison of Berwick as long as he or Hotspur held office as warden of the east march and captain of Berwick.[8]

Bourne maintained that the burgesses of Newcastle themselves petitioned the Crown for the town to be 'entirely separated' from the county.[9] This may well be true: the advantages for the burgesses were obvious. It is equally likely, however, that Henry IV was looking to secure the support of the mercantile community of Newcastle. Recent work on (King's) Lynn in the early 15th century has demonstrated how Lancastrian patronage benefited both Crown and town, not least because Henry IV's good relations with Prussia might prove an asset to the Lynn merchants in their trade with the Baltic.[10] The same might well have been true in Newcastle, where many merchants were similarly engaged in the Baltic trade. Towns were also an important source of finance for the Crown, and Henry IV's grant of county status to Norwich in 1404 may have been a reward for the loan of 1,000 marks which the burgesses made to the King in 1402 for his expenses in dealing with the rebellion in Wales. It may also have been intended to ensure the support of the town in the event of renewed opposition from the Despensers, an important issue in Henry's relations with Lynn.[11]

We do not know on what scale Newcastle merchants made loans to the Crown in Henry IV's reign, or whether the merchants made loans as a

[7] By 1399 the Percys held Newburn, Corbridge, and the former Umfraville barony of Prudhoe in the south of the county. See, in general, Bean, J.M.W., *The Estates of the Percy Family, 1416-1537* (Oxford, 1958), and Lomas, Richard, *A Power in the Land: the Percys* (East Linton, 1999), esp. chapters 5 and 6.

[8] *Rot. Scot.*, p.151. See also below pp.123-4.

[9] Bourne, *Newcastle*, p.205.

[10] Parker, Kate, 'Politics and Patronage in Lynn, 1399-1416', in Dodd, Gwilym and Biggs, Douglas (eds), *The Reign of Henry IV: Rebellion and Survival, 1403-1413* (York, 2008), pp.210-27, esp. p.213; Frost, Ruth, 'The Urban Elite' in Rawcliffe, Carole and Wilson, Richard (eds), *Medieval Norwich* (London, 2004), p.248.

[11] Frost, 'Urban Elite', pp.246, 248; Parker, 'Lynn', pp.211-12, 216.

corporate body or as individuals. In 1404, for example, Roger Thornton lent the Crown £100 towards the cost of the war in Wales, and other merchants may have done likewise.[12] In one respect, however, Newcastle was unique amongst the mercantile communities of England, and that was in its coal trade, especially with London. The trade was, of course, neither as developed nor as organised as it was to be after *c*.1550, but nevertheless exports from the Tyne seemed to have increased during the half century from *c*.1370 to an extent that might justify the suggestion that there was a minor boom, followed by a decline after *c*.1420.[13]

Although coal was exported overseas, particularly to the Baltic, London was the principal destination. Its use, however, was not primarily domestic. Wood continued to be the main fuel for domestic heating and cooking, but coal became increasingly important in certain industrial processes, notably lime-burning.[14] Coal was bought by the Crown for building works at royal castles throughout the 14th century. In 1364, for example, Edward III ordered the sheriff of Northumberland to purchase 576 chaldrons (probably *c*.700 tons) of coal from Winlaton mine for building work at Windsor Castle; and purchases were also made for work at the Tower of London and at Berwick Castle.[15] The king's works required a steady supply of coal shipped from the Tyne by Newcastle merchants, and he thus had an obvious interest in keeping on good terms with the merchants of Newcastle.[16]

The most prominent of the Newcastle merchants in the late 14th and early 15th centuries was Roger Thornton. His origins are obscure, though tradition has it that he came from somewhere to the west of Newcastle. He made money initially out of exporting wool, cloth and hides, but by the beginning of the 15th century he was regularly shipping coal and lead both to London and overseas. So important were his trading links with London that he acquired several properties there including, appropriately, a messuage in Seacoal Lane.[17] Thornton's best interests were served by loyalty to the Crown rather than the Percys after 1403, and during the Scrope rebellion of 1405, in which the Earl of Northumberland played an important role, he secured the defences of Newcastle against any attempt by the Earl to take the town. He did so, apparently, at his

[12] *CPR, 1401-5*, p.416.
[13] Blake, J.B., 'The Medieval Coal Trade of North East England: some Fourteenth-Century Evidence', *Northern History*, 2 (1967), pp.1-26; Hatcher, J., *The History of the British Coal Industry*, vol.1 (Oxford, 1993), pp.72-7.
[14] Hatcher, *Coal Industry*, p.26; Barron, Caroline, *London in the later Middle Ages* (Oxford, 2004), p.264; Galloway, J., Keene, D. and Murphy, M., 'Fuelling the City: Production and Distribution of Firewood and Fuel in London's Region', *Economic History Review*, 49 (1996), pp.447-72.
[15] Hatcher, *Coal Industry*, p.26; Blake, 'Medieval Coal Trade', pp.3-4, 11-12.
[16] Blake, 'Medieval Coal Trade', p.4.
[17] *Hist. Parl., 1386-1421*, vol.4, pp.596-8.

To SIR JOHN CHRICHLOE TURNER KNᵀ the GRANTEE under the CROWN.
This View of the Old Caſtle of Newcaſtle upon Tyne
Engraved at his Eſpence is reſpectfully inſcribed by his very obliged & most obedᵗ humble Servᵗ
John Brand.

45 The castle, a royal enclave within the new county, by John Brand.

own expense, and after the earl's forfeiture he was rewarded with some of the Percy lands in Yorkshire.[18]

Whether or not the leading merchants of the town actively sought county status, they certainly benefited from it; and Henry IV could evidently rely on their loyalty during the Percy rebellions. However, the jurisdictional separation of town from county was not total. Although the charter of 1400 does not say so explicitly, the castle and its precincts remained under royal control, and appointments to the office of custodian remained in the hands of the Crown. In Henry VI's reign in particular, the post was given to trusted household officials. Assizes continued to be held in the town, and Parliamentary elections for the county of Northumberland took place there until 1420, after which they were

18 *Ibid.*, p.597.

held in Alnwick.[19] This in itself would bring members of the knightly class with estates in Northumberland to Newcastle to participate in the elections. It seems clear that the grant of county status to the town made virtually no difference to the links between the merchants of the town and the gentry families of Northumberland.

Nor, in all probability, did it greatly affect the relationship between the town and the Crown in commercial and military matters. In both these respects the town was of importance to the Crown, regardless of whether the town was or was not a county of itself. Newcastle was, of course, a head port for the collection of customs revenue, with responsibility for collection along the coast from Berwick upon Tweed to Scarborough. During the 14th century an elaborate bureaucratic structure developed for the administration of the customs, with officials responsible for collection, investigation, and indeed supervision of the other officials. Appointments to the positions of collector, controller, surveyor and searcher were made by the Crown, and although the Crown generally chose local men, the customs bureaucracy was essentially royal rather than local in its accountability.[20]

In this respect, of course, Newcastle's relationship with the Crown was no different from that of other major ports such as Hull, Southampton and Bristol. The town's military relationship with the Crown in the 14th and 15th centuries, however, was paralleled only by Carlisle and, perhaps, Berwick upon Tweed and Calais.[21] After Edward III's capture of Berwick in 1333, Newcastle was no longer in the front line of wars against Scotland, but it was still thought of as vulnerable. In 1383 Richard II wrote to John Neville of Raby stating that 'the town of Newcastle, facing the marches of Scotland, might be in great peril from the enemy in case of war, and ought to be made the great refuge of the kingdom for the king's faithful subjects in those parts'.[22] A similar observation was made by a jury in 1447, who stated that 'the ... town ... is as a shield of defence and safe refuge against the invasions and frequent incursions of the Scots'.[23] Only occasionally after 1333 was the town directly threatened, such as in 1346 with the Scottish invasion culminating in the battle of Neville's Cross, and in 1388, the battle of Otterburn. Yet the ever-present possibility of invasion

---

[19] *Ibid.*, vol.1, p.544.

[20] Gras, N.S.B., *The Early English Customs System* (Cambridge, Mass., 1918), esp. pp.94-100; Baker, R.L., 'The English Customs Service, 1307-1343: A Study of Medieval Administration', *Transactions of the American Philosophical Society*, new series, vol.51, part 6 (1961), esp. pp.5-12.

[21] Summerson, Henry, *Medieval Carlisle*, Cumberland and Westmorland Antiquarian and Archaeological Society, extra series, vol.25 (1983), 2 vols, esp. vol.2, chapter 6.

[22] Welford, *Newcastle and Gateshead*, p.200; *Rot. Scot.*, vol.2, p.55.

[23] Welford, *Newcastle and Gateshead*, p.316; Pollard, A.J., *North-Eastern England During the Wars of the Roses* (Oxford, 1990), p.15.

from the north meant that the defences of the town had to be maintained in good order, and this was evidently the real purpose of Richard II's letter in 1383, enjoining Neville to ensure that the walls were repaired and the townsmen arrayed and equipped with weapons. When English campaigns in Scotland were undertaken, however, as in 1385 and 1400, Newcastle was an important base for the mustering of troops and the assembly of supplies. This was its chief importance to the Crown in the 14th and 15th centuries.

However, after the Yorkist victory at Towton in March 1461 Queen Margaret sought refuge in Scotland and, as the price of Scottish support, agreed to surrender Berwick to James III. Berwick itself was not regained by the English until 1482, and despite Edward IV's assumption of the English throne in 1461 parts of Northumberland remained under Lancastrian control until the Yorkist victories at Hedgley Moor and Hexham in 1464. For a time, therefore, as Professor Pollard has pointed out, the river Tyne became 'the effective front line', though after the Yorkist capture of Alnwick and Dunstanburgh castles later in 1461 the threat to Newcastle itself was diminished.[24]

Thus throughout the 14th and 15th centuries, Northumberland, if not always Newcastle itself, was a frontier zone, and the office of warden of the marches evolved to control the military administration of the frontier. As the office developed in the 14th century, so it was assumed that the jurisdiction of the warden of the East March extended to Newcastle as well as Northumberland. This was not explicitly stated in statute until 1453, but in this respect, too, Newcastle came to differ from other major English ports.[25] In time of war the warden had wide powers to array men for the defence of the March, and in time of peace he was responsible for supervising truces between England and Scotland and punishing breaches of the truce. All officials within his jurisdiction were required to obey his mandates. In effect his jurisdiction overrode that of other local officials both in Newcastle and Northumberland in matters concerning war and the enforcement of truces.[26]

The militarisation of the northern frontier in the 14th and 15th centuries, and the demands of the Crown in times of war with Scotland, provided a framework for county and town life different from other parts of England except Carlisle and the West March. Yet the town and the county had links of a peaceful nature which continued whether or not there was war with Scotland. Again, Roger Thornton exemplifies how such links developed and were maintained, and if he

[24] Pollard, *North-Eastern England*, p.225; MacDougall, N., *James III* (Edinburgh, 1982), pp.57-8.
[25] Curry, Anne and Horrox, Rosemary (eds), *The Parliament Rolls of Medieval England 1275-1504, vol. XII, Henry VI, 1446-1460* (London, 2005), pp.311-12.
[26] See, for example, *Rot. Scot.*, vol.II, pp.145-8 and Summerson, *Medieval Carlisle*, vol.2, p.408.

46 Roger Thornton, detail from his brass.

is untypical it is by virtue of the scale rather than the nature of his activities in Newcastle and in Northumberland. After making his fortune by trade, he followed the well-trodden path of the successful merchant in late medieval England and invested his profits in land. In the latter part of Henry IV's reign he purchased lands around Netherwitton and also bought the manor of Byker. He acquired land in the bishopric of Durham, including Whickham and Gateshead, perhaps to safeguard his interest in the coal trade, and he also, as we have seen, bought property in London, perhaps the first Newcastle merchant to do so on a significant scale.[27] Like other successful merchants he enhanced his social prestige by making good marriages for his children. In 1429 his son and heir, also called Roger, married the daughter of John lord Greystoke. The lands of the Greystoke barony were widely scattered throughout the northern counties, though the *caput* of the barony was in Cumberland. In Northumberland the family's lands included several manors in the Coquet valley west of Rothbury, no great distance from Thornton's estate at Netherwitton.[28] Thornton's daughter Isabel also married into the community of Northumbrian gentry: her husband was the son of Sir John Middleton of Belsay.[29]

Roger Thornton the younger maintained his family's links with Newcastle. He was an alderman and a member of the Skinners Company, but it is

[27] *CIPM, 1427-1432,* p.195. Thornton's messuage in Seacoal Lane, London, was described as 'waste' at his death; he also held a messuage, four cottages and one small dwelling in Turnagain Lane, and three parts of a messuage in the parish of St Mary-le-Bow in London. His inquisition states that he held a messuage in Broad Chare, Newcastle, 'where he resided when he died'.

[28] Hedley, W. Percy, *Northumberland Families,* 2 vols (Newcastle upon Tyne, 1968, 1970), vol.1, p.233.

[29] *Hist. Parl., 1386-1421,* vol.4, p.597.

significant that he served as sheriff of Northumberland (in 1457) rather than of Newcastle, and he was appointed to various commissions to negotiate with the Scots in the 1460s.[30] He was both a merchant and a member of the gentry community of Northumberland, though unlike his father he apparently never served as MP for either the town or the county. He continued to develop the family landholdings, and it was perhaps his wealth as a merchant rather than his income from land that enabled him to make purchases of land in the bishopric of Durham.[31]

The careers of Roger Thornton, father and son, would not have appeared unusual in any other part of England in the later Middle Ages, except to the extent that their wealth was derived from the coal trade. But the militarisation of Northumberland society in the 14th and 15th centuries had a distinctive impact on the relationship between Newcastle and its hinterland to the north. Although Newcastle was unrivalled as a coal exporting port, it had to compete with Berwick upon Tweed in the export of wool and hides. The burgesses of Berwick argued tenaciously and successfully for their right, guaranteed by Edward III when he captured the town in 1333, to levy customs duties at the rate which prevailed in Scotland in the time of Alexander III. Berwick had, of course, been one of the leading ports in Scotland in the 13th century. As the duty on wool exported from English ports increased during the 14th century, Berwick enjoyed a substantial fiscal advantage, and there is evidence from the 1340s onwards for the smuggling of Northumbrian wool into Berwick for export there.[32] The Crown was the main loser, but so too were Newcastle merchants who might otherwise have shipped the wool overseas. They may have been behind the complaints in Parliament in 1379 and on other occasions that wool grown in Northumberland was being taken into Scotland for export, to the great loss of the Crown (and, to some extent, themselves).[33]

On the other hand, Berwick's role in the defence of the northern border also provided opportunities for Newcastle merchants, who were in a good position to supply the town with food and other necessities. In Edward III's campaign in Scotland in 1332-3, John of Denton supplied the English armies and the garrison of Berwick after its recapture in 1333.[34] William Bishopdale, who died

---

[30]   *Rot. Scot.*, vol.2, pp.392, 410, 414, 418, 420.
[31]   Hodgson, J., *A History of Northumberland in Three Parts*, 7 vols (Newcastle upon Tyne, 1827-58), part 2, vol.1, p.317.
[32]   For this see Tuck, Anthony, 'A medieval tax haven: Berwick upon Tweed and the English Crown 1333-1461', in Britnell, Richard and Hatcher, John (eds), *Progress and Problems in Medieval England* (Cambridge, 1996), pp.148-67.
[33]   *Ibid.*, p.160.
[34]   Fraser, C.M., 'The life and death of John of Denton', *AA*, 4th series, vol.37 (1954), pp.303-25.

in 1398, was a prominent merchant in Newcastle and also a member of the Earl of Northumberland's retinue at Berwick in 1395. He was probably engaged in supplying Berwick, for he was granted a licence by Richard II to equip some ships for the purpose of attacking enemy shipping in the North Sea.[35] Both Scottish and French ships attempted to cut the supply lines on which the Berwick garrison relied, particularly during the Anglo-Scottish war of 1384-9. Later, in 1404, Henry IV licensed George Dunbar, son of the (Scottish) Earl of March, who was now in the English allegiance, to take four ships from Newcastle with food and other necessities for the garrison of the 'fort called Colbrandespath'. This may be Cockburnspath Tower, which belonged to the earls of March; but it may on the other hand be Fast Castle, on the coast a few miles east of Cockburnspath, which had been in English hands since 1346 and which was difficult to supply except by sea.[36]

Another Newcastle merchant who, like William Bishopdale, served with the Berwick garrison was William Johnson. Johnson was mayor of Newcastle in 1398-9 and again in 1412-13, and sat as MP for the town in the Parliaments of 1407 and November 1414. He, too, may have been involved in the supply of food to the Berwick garrison, but he was a shipowner as well as a merchant, and when Henry IV invaded Scotland in 1400 he was ordered to recruit sailors for the King's service and to fit out two of his own ships for the King's use.[37] Like Roger Thornton, he used some of his mercantile wealth to purchase land. He bought property in Gateshead and Whickham, and after his first wife died he married Elizabeth Heton, daughter and co-heiress of Sir Henry Heton of Heton and Chillingham. By the time of his death in November 1399, Heton had held Chillingham, Tritlington and part of the manor of Hartley; Elizabeth's share of her father's inheritance was a part of the manors of Chillingham and Hartley. William Johnson died in 1420, and although he and Elizabeth had a son, John, he did not long survive his father. Elizabeth, who was only 29 in 1420, then married John Parke, and their son inherited his mother's share of the Heton estates.[38]

Sampson Hardyng, a Newcastle merchant who died c.1427, played an even more prominent part in the affairs of the county. His career was unusual, even perhaps unique, in at least two respects. He served as MP for both Northumberland and Newcastle: five times for the county, and four times for

[35]   *Hist. Parl., 1386-1421*, vol.2, pp.237-9.
[36]   *CPR, 1401-5*, p.428; *Royal Commission on the Ancient and Historical Monuments of Scotland: The County of Berwick* (Edinburgh, 1915), pp.xxi-xxii.
[37]   *Hist. Parl., 1386-1421*, pp.498-500; *CPR, 1399-1401*, p.351.
[38]   *CIPM*, 1399-1405, pp.2-3; *Hist. Parl., 1386-1421*, vol.3, pp.498-500.

the town in a long career in public life between 1382 and 1421. He also served as a justice of the peace for Northumberland in the 1380s and again from 1393 until his death. Carole Rawcliffe observed that amongst the merchants of Newcastle in the late 14th and early 15th centuries, 'Hardyng alone possessed sufficient stature to be returned as a shire knight', and the same no doubt applies to his appointments as justice of the peace. He probably also acted in effect as a justice of the peace in Newcastle after 1400.[39] As we have seen, the charter granting county status to the town specified that the mayor should appoint six aldermen to act in the town as justices of the peace. The Hardyng family owned some property in Beadnell, and by marriage he acquired an interest in lands at Crawcrook in the bishopric of Durham; but he does not seem to have built up a large landed estate.[40]

The history of families such as the Thorntons, the Hardyngs and the Johnsons demonstrates how mercantile capital was invested in land, even though the establishment of a dynasty depended as much on the ability to produce sons who survived as on wealth. Yet, just as successful Newcastle merchants invested their wealth in landed property, so there is evidence that Northumbrian gentry families sought to enhance their wealth and standing by engaging in trade in Newcastle. For younger sons of minor gentry families in particular, advancement depended upon a fortunate marriage, service with the king or the great nobles and the patronage that could be expected to follow such service, or, sometimes, the unexpected death of the eldest son. In the case of John Strother, for example, a series of unexpected deaths enabled him, late in life, to inherit lands under his uncle's entail.

The Strother family held lands around Kirknewton in Glendale, and Kirkwhelpington, Sweethope and Wallington in mid-Northumberland. They had had connections with Newcastle since the mid-14th century. The two younger sons of William Strother of Kirknewton had both been mayors of Newcastle, William II between 1355 and 1360, and Alan in 1375. William II was also MP for Newcastle in 1358 and 1360.[41] In the early 15th century Alan's younger son

[39] *Hist. Parl., 1386-1421*, vol.3, p.289.
[40] *Ibid.*, p.289.
[41] For a list of mayors of Newcastle (and of sheriffs after 1400) see Mackenzie, E., *A Descriptive and Historical Account of the Town and County of Newcastle upon Tyne* (Newcastle upon Tyne, 1827), pp.612-18; for members of Parliament for Newcastle before 1386 and between 1422 and 1439, see *The Names of Every member Returned to Serve in each Parliament from 1213 to the Present*, Part I (London, 1897); for those returned to serve for Northumberland between 1258 and 1399, see Blair, C.H. Hunter, 'Members of Parliament for Northumberland', *AA*, 4th series, vol.10 (1933), pp.140-77 and vol.11 (1934), pp.21-82; Walker, S., 'Profit and loss in the Hundred Years War: the subcontracts of Sir John Strother, 1374', *Bulletin of the Institute of Historical Research*, vol.58 (1985), pp.100-2; Hodgson, *Northumberland*, part II, vol.I, pp.254-5, but corrected by Carole Rawcliffe in *Hist. Parl., 1386-1421*, vol.4, p.519, note 2.

47 The Close, where gentry families had their town houses; a detail from Buck.

John, like younger sons of the family in an earlier generation, pursued a career as a merchant in Newcastle and served as MP for the town in 1417, 1419, and May 1421. He was also sheriff in 1416. But he retained his links with county gentry families, notably the Swinburnes of Capheaton, for whom he acted in an official capacity on several occasions.[42] By the accidents of death he was eventually to inherit extensive lands in Northumberland,[43] but the essential point is that for younger sons with no immediate expectation of landed wealth, a career in Newcastle offered opportunities for prosperity and advancement. If the Strother family is in any way typical, the boundary between the society of the town and that of the county seems to have been fluid and the interconnections extensive. A man might prosper as a merchant and still retain close links with the county gentry, and by the accidents of death and inheritance it was easy to move from town to county. The mercantile community of Newcastle was not a closed oligarchy, existing apart from the landed families of the town's hinterland.

Another family whose history illustrates the same fluidity even more clearly is the Actons. The Acton family had held land in and around Acton and Old Felton in mid-Northumberland since at least the early 13th century. In the reign of Edward II, Richard Acton had been a retainer of the earl of Lancaster, and

[42] *Hist. Parl., 1386-1421*, vol.4, pp.518-9.
[43] *Ibid.*

in 1313 he was pardoned for his part in the murder of Gaveston.[44] Like his Strother counterparts, he and his descendants made careers for themselves in Newcastle. His son Nicholas was MP for Newcastle in 1339, and Nicholas's cousin William was MP in 1346 and 1348 and also mayor in 1366. William's brother Laurence I, his son Laurence II and his grandson Laurence III continued the family tradition of representing the town in Parliament. Laurence III was also mayor of Newcastle in 1432 and 1437 and sheriff in 1421.[45] The family married into various Northumbrian gentry families such as the Widdringtons, the Musgraves and the Sturmys, while Laurence III married his daughter Elizabeth to Sir Ralph Percy (d. 1464), younger brother of Henry 3rd Earl of Northumberland and Hotspur's grandson.[46]

Marriage into the leading noble family of Northumberland was the culmination of the family's successful career both as landowners and merchants. In the course of the 14th century they acquired lands well beyond their original inheritance around Felton. In 1319 Richard Acton acquired Great Whittington near Corbridge from Sir John Halton, and he benefited from the forfeiture for treason of John Middleton in 1330, receiving from the Crown lands in West Swinburne. Marriage into the Musgrave family later in the century brought further lands in East and West Swinburne, and in 1380 Laurence Acton II purchased the manor of Hazon near Shilbottle.[47] By 1387 the family had built up a substantial inheritance around Newcastle, including property in the town itself and lands in Jesmond, Elswick, Blagdon and Cramlington. For more than a century the family was prominent in both the merchant society of Newcastle and the gentry community of Northumberland; but despite the distinguished marriage made by Laurence III's daughter Elizabeth, she had no male heir, and the male line of the family came to an end with her father.

The careers of the Strothers and the Actons suggest that there were few if any barriers to prospering both in town and in the country. Yet it is difficult to say how far this fluidity is characteristic of other parts of England, such as Hull and the East Riding or Bristol and Somerset and Gloucestershire. There were, however, certain circumstances which may have enhanced this fluidity in Northumberland. In most mercantile towns some younger sons from the surrounding countryside may have sought to make a career there. But the Actons who prospered in Newcastle were not just younger sons with the senior line remaining on their landed estates, and it may be that the disturbed conditions

44 *NCH*, vol.7, pp.366-9.
45 Hedley, *Northumberland Families*, vol.1, pp.30-4; *NCH*, vol.7, pp.366-9.
46 Hedley, *Northumberland Families*, vol.1, p.33.
47 *NCH*, vol.7, p.369.

in Northumberland, especially in the 14th century, made landed property a less reliable source of wealth, particularly for the lesser gentry, than it was in other parts of England, away from the threat of Scottish incursions.[48]

Amongst the more substantial gentry families, however, ties with the mercantile community of Newcastle do not seem to have been so close. Families such as the Delavals, the Ogles, the Claverings of Callaly and the Swinburnes of Capheaton were evidently less involved with the commercial life of the town than the families discussed above. None of them held office as mayor or (after 1400) sheriff of the town. Many of them served as MPs for Northumberland in the 14th and 15th centuries, but none of them was elected MP for Newcastle.[49] Like their counterparts in other parts of the country, they held office as justices of the peace and on the many commissions appointed by the Crown: but essentially within the county community rather than in the town.

Even here, however, there were some exceptions. Although the collectors and controllers of the customs in Newcastle in the late 14th and early 15th centuries were generally drawn from the mercantile community of the town (such as Sampson Hardyng, Robert Oliver and William Bishopdale),[50] some members of gentry families held these offices in the 1390s and during Henry IV's reign. Sir John Mitford, who died in July 1409, is a good example. He held lands in the Wansbeck Valley and in east Northumberland. He was escheator of Northumberland in 1401, sheriff in 1402-3 and MP for the county 13 times between 1372 and 1402. He also, however, held office as collector of the customs in Newcastle in the 1390s and again in the early years of Henry IV's reign. Carole Rawcliffe described him as 'one of the most diligent and successful administrators to represent Northumberland in the Middle Ages'.[51] Yet his administrative career extended to Newcastle as well as Northumberland. Indeed, the family's origins may have been mercantile. His father had been a burgess of the town and collector of customs there, and he himself retained commercial links with the town. He was responsible, for example, for shipping a cargo of coal from the town in 1394 which was confiscated at Great Yarmouth for no good reason.[52] Once again, it seems,

[48] For this see Tuck, J.A.,'Northumbrian Society in the Fourteenth Century', *Northern History*, vol.6 (1971), pp.22-39; Tuck, J.A., 'War and Society in the Medieval North' *Northern History*, vol.21 (1985), pp.33-52; McNamee, Colm, *The Wars of the Bruces: Scotland, England and Ireland, 1306-1328* (East Linton, 1997) esp. ch.3.
[49] *Hist. Parl., 1386-1421*, vol.1, p.539, 545, for members between 1386 and 1421; for members before and after those dates, see *Return of Every Member*, Part I, passim.
[50] *CFR, 1377-83*, p.300; 1383-91, pp.169, 226, 234.
[51] *Ibid.*, 1391-9, pp.55, 104, 189; 1399-1405, pp.91, 179, 207; *Hist. Parl. 1386-1421*, vol.3, p.744.
[52] Hodgson, *Northumberland*, part 2, vol. 1, pp.45, 50; *Hist. Parl., 1386-1421*, vol. 3, p. 745.

the boundaries between town and county were fluid, and even if Mitford performed his official duties in Newcastle by deputy, office holding in the town was open to gentry as well as mercantile families.

Participation in urban life, however, involved much more than mercantile activity and occasional office holding. Newcastle in the 14th and 15th centuries was an important social centre for the county gentry as well as the mercantile community. The town was a place where the gentry conducted some of their business. Numerous deeds were sealed at Newcastle in the course of the 14th century, and Newcastle merchants sometimes acted as sureties for transactions between gentry families. For example, in 1319 Sir William Swinburne and Roger de Horsley agreed a marriage settlement between Swinburne's son and Roger's daughter. Under the terms of the agreement, Swinburne deposited a bond for £500 with Richard de Emeldon, Mayor of Newcastle, 'until Sir William shall make a recognisance before the Justices of the Bench or in Chancery for the debt'.[53] They also acted as trustees or feoffees for gentry families. Sampson Hardyng, for instance, was appointed feoffee to both the Swinburne and Bertram families in the early 15th century.[54]

Religious houses in the town sometimes acted as places of deposit for goods, especially those bequeathed under the terms of a will. Thus in 1381, following the death of Alan de Strother, Sir William Swinburne and others had taken charge of some of his goods under a bond of £300 for their eventual return to Strother's widow. On 7 December 1381 it was agreed that if the goods were returned to the Hospital of St Mary Magdalene in Newcastle, the bond should be void.[55] The religious houses of the town also played an important part in the spiritual life of the county gentry. As elsewhere in England, the Friars were especially popular. In 1374, for example, the custodian of the Franciscans in Newcastle granted letter of fraternity to John Swinburne and his wife, ensuring prayers for their souls after their deaths.[56]

The Newcastle friaries were also the recipients of many bequests from the gentry of both Northumberland and Durham. For example, when William de Menville, a landowner in the bishopric drew up his will in 1371 he left a legacy of 50 marks to be divided equally between the four friaries in Newcastle and the Franciscans of Hartlepool.[57] John Ogle, another Durham landowner who was perhaps distantly related to the Northumberland family, left 20 marks

[53] National Register of Archives, Calendar of the Swinburne Manuscripts in the Northumberland Record Office, Part I, p.23, no. 1/61.

[54] *Hist. Parl., 1386-1421*, vol.3, p.289.

[55] Cal. Swinburne Mss. I, p.38, no. 1/107.

[56] *Ibid.*, no. 1/160.

[57] *Wills and Inventories of the Northern Counties of England: Part I*, SS, vol.2 (1835), pp.32-3.

48 An unidentified effigy of a knight buried at the Augustinian Friary.

49 A fragment of an effigy head.

in 1372 to the four friaries in equal portions.[58] This seems to have been a popular form of bequest, suggesting that the four orders in Newcastle (the Augustinians, Carmelites, Dominicans and Franciscans) enjoyed equal esteem amongst the gentry families. Margaret de Eure of Witton Castle, on the other hand, who seems to have lived in Newcastle towards the end of her life, asked to be buried in the Dominican Friary, and she left bequests of 12d. to each friar who was an ordained priest, but only 6d. to those who were not. The friars also received many more modest bequests, such as 7s. 4d. left to the Newcastle Carmelites in 1361 under the will of Lady de Cossele.[59]

Newcastle, and to a lesser extent Hartlepool for the Durham gentry, seems to have been the main focus for bequests to the friars. Alnwick had a Carmelite Friary and Bamburgh a house of Dominicans, while Berwick upon Tweed had five friaries – the Dominicans, Franciscans, Carmelites and Augustinian Friars, together with the Trinitarian friars whose object was the redemption of Christians enslaved by the Turks. Yet they do not figure so prominently in the wills of Northumbrian gentry families, and judging by the will of Thomas Riddell, a burgess of Berwick in the mid-14th century, the town retained its

58   *Ibid.*, pp.33-4.
59   *Ibid.*, pp.35-6; Cal. Swinburne Mss, I, 28, no. 1/176.

Scottish orientation, at least in spiritual matters, for some time after its capture by the English in 1333. In his will, dated 1358, he left bequests to religious foundations in Kelso and Roxburgh, but not to those in Berwick itself or in Northumberland.[60]

Roger Thornton, however, spread his bequests more widely. In his will, proved in 1430, he left money to the four mendicant orders in the town, but also to the nunnery of St Bartholomew, the chapel of St Thomas on the Tyne Bridge, to St Nicholas' Church, and to various alms houses. As befitted a wealthy man with interests in both Newcastle and Northumberland, he left bequests to the monks of Newminster and Tynemouth, but also to religious houses further afield, such as Whitby, Hartlepool and Yarm. His bequests were perhaps unusually extensive, and served to demonstrate both the wealth and the piety of one of the richest men of his time in the North East.[61]

Various members of Northumbrian gentry families owned property in Newcastle, sometimes on a substantial scale. Sir Thomas Grey of Heton and Wark, for example, who died in 1400, held nine tenements in the town, and received rents from several others. At the time of his death he held 46s. 8d. rent from a tenement in Pilgrim Street let to Sampson Hardyng, and lesser sums from five other tenements.[62] Presumably his property holdings in Newcastle were investments; most of them seem to have been let to tenants, and there is no evidence that he had a house reserved for his personal use. Others, however, did. Sir Bertram Monbourcher, for example, who died in 1388, owned several properties in Newcastle, including a messuage 'in which he dwelt'. He had a distinguished military career under Edward III, and served both as MP and on numerous commissions in Northumberland, where he had an estate at Horton. Gentry families such as the Hetons and the Middletons, and also the Scropes of Masham, also had property in Newcastle, though whether as investments or as town houses for their own use when visiting Newcastle is not clear from their inquisitions *post mortem*.[63]

Once again, however, war cannot be ignored, and some business to do with Anglo-Scottish relations took place in Newcastle at the behest of the Crown. In December 1337 Edward III ordered the Bishop of Durham and three others to hold a conference there to discuss the progress of the war in Scotland.[64] In

---

[60]   *Wills and Inventories*, p.28. Newcastle also had a small house of Trinitarian friars, founded in 1360 by William Acton and sometimes known as Acton's Hospital; Knowles, D. and Hadcock, R.N., *Medieval Religious Houses, England and Wales*, 2nd edn (London, 1971), p.206; Brand, *Newcastle*, vol.1, pp.401-2.

[61]   Welford, *Newcastle and Gateshead*, pp.281-4.

[62]   *CIPM, 1399-1405*, pp.139-40.

[63]   Ibid., *1384-92*, pp.225, 275; *1391-99*, pp.113, 326; *Hist. Parl., 1386-1421*, vol.3, pp.755-63.

[64]   Welford, *Newcastle and Gateshead*, p.99.

the 1350s Newcastle was the venue for negotiations between representatives of the two kingdoms about the ransom of David II and a peace treaty or lengthy truce.[65] Just over a century later, the truce agreed in June 1466 was ratified at Newcastle, and in the treaty between Edward IV and James III in 1474 which agreed the marriage of James's eldest son with Edward IV's daughter, Cecily, the refundable portion of Cecily's dowry was to be paid over to Edward IV at St Nicholas' Church in Newcastle if the marriage did not take place.[66]

Although Newcastle and its institutions thus played an important part in the social and religious life of the gentry of both Northumberland and Durham, and in the wider political life of the kingdom, the gentry tended to marry mainly within their own community. Although marriages between gentry and mercantile families certainly took place, they seem to have been the exception rather than the rule. Newcastle may have been a place in which to do business, and perhaps for younger sons to engage in trade, but marriages were usually arranged within the landowning community. In the course of the 14th and early 15th centuries, for example, the men of the Delaval family married into the families of Felton of Edlingham, the Widdringtons, Mitfords, Bolbecs and Greystoke. Their daughters (where we know of them) made marriages with the Selbys of Seghill, Manners of Etal, and Ogle. The same is true of the Claverings of Callaly, a cadet branch of the family which had held Warkworth from the 12th century until 1332. They married into families such as Riddell of Tilmouth, Heton of Chillingham and Raymes of Shortflatt. The Widdringtons of Widdrington, too, conform broadly to this pattern, with marriages to the Swinburnes, Riddells, Greys of Heton, and Monboucher. Yet here, too, there were exceptions. As discussed above, a younger son, Roger Widdrington, who died in 1372, married the daughter of Richard Acton of Newcastle.[67]

It was essentially an endogamous community, with links even to the gentry families of Durham and Cumberland limited in extent. However, their links upward in the social scale to the great magnates were extensive and persistent. Some members of the Strother family pursued a career in Newcastle, but another, Sir John Strother, sought service in the retinue of the earl of March. He was the cousin of the two Strothers, William and John, who had been mayors of Newcastle in the mid-14th century, but he was the representative of the senior line and thus heir to the landed property of the family in north Northumberland. His father, however, proved long-lived, and as Simon

---

[65] *Ibid.*, p.144; Penman, M., *David II, 1329-71* (East Linton, 2004), pp.166-81.
[66] *Rot. Scot.*, vol.II, p.448.
[67] This paragraph is based on an analysis of the genealogical tables in Hedley, *Northumberland Families*, vols 1 and 2.

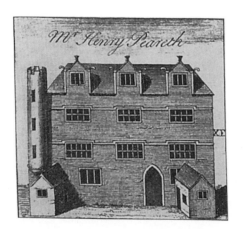

50 Mr Henry Peareth's house, on the
the Close in the 18th century, which may
originally have been the 'Erles Inne'. Detail
from Corbridge's map.

Walker pointed out, held most of the important appointments that came the way of the senior line of a gentry family. Sir John, therefore, entered upon a military career and engaged to serve with the Earl of March in Brittany in 1374 and 1375. Those who served under him came mainly from East Anglia: he showed no preference for men from Northumberland or Newcastle.[68]

The history of the Strother family in the late 14th and early 15th centuries clearly illustrates the range of opportunities open to a gentry family at that time: landowning, soldiering and mercantile activity in Newcastle. William Strother who was mayor of Newcastle in 1352 and 1355 even took advantage of the growing coal trade to acquire a mine. In September 1356 Thomas de Fenham granted Strother 'all the coal mines sunk within the grantor's land of Fenham, or which the grantee wishes to sink in the said land, in all parts where he pleases,' provided he did no damage to Thomas's crops and lands. It is not entirely clear how such damage could be avoided with the technology then available for extracting coal.[69] The family's career illustrates the fluidity of social boundaries in the late medieval north, and the way in which trade, and mining, played a part in the economic activities of gentry families.

The great magnate families of northern England, such as the Percys, Nevilles, and Scropes also had connections with Newcastle. However, there is no evidence that any of them engaged in trade on their own behalf. Their interest in the town was primarily social and professional, though they had town houses there for use when visiting Newcastle for business or for social activities. The Nevilles, for instance, had two messuages in Newcastle,[70] and it was no doubt in one of them, in October 1388, that John Lord Neville of Raby spent the last days of his life. On 13 October he drew up a codicil to his will in which he nominated his son Ralph as his principal executor, and

[68] Walker, 'Strother subcontracts', pp.104-5; see above, pp.125-6.
[69] Anderson, J. (ed.), *Calendar of Laing Charters, A.D. 854-1837* (Edinburgh, 1899), no.44.
[70] *CIPM, 1384-92*, p.279.

51   Westmorland Place, on the site of the Neville house in Westgate.

four days later he died. From Newcastle he was taken to Durham for burial in the Cathedral.[71]

It is, however, interesting that the Inquisition *post mortem* of Henry Percy of Alnwick, father of the 1st Earl of Northumberland, taken in 1368, makes no mention of any property in Newcastle. This is not, of course, conclusive evidence. It may, however, suggest that at that date, and despite the possession of extensive lands in Northumberland, the Percys saw themselves as a Yorkshire as much as a border family. However, by the 15th century the family had probably acquired some property in the town. After the 1st Earl's forfeiture in 1405 John, later Duke of Bedford, was granted Percy possessions in Newcastle which seem to have included 'The Erles Inne' in the Close, and the Inquisition *post mortem* of the 2nd Earl, who was killed at the first battle of St Albans in 1455, also listed a tenement in the Close in Newcastle, without giving it a name. But in York the 2nd Earl had a hospice known as 'Percy Inne' together with eight tenements,

[71]   *Wills and Inventories*, p.42; Raine, J.A. (ed.), *Historiae Dunelmensis Scriptores Tres*, SS, vol.9 (1839), p.137.

four messuages in Tadcaster and one messuage in Hull. The family's ties with Yorkshire were evidently still strong, though the IPM of the 3rd Earl, who was killed at Towton in 1461, mentions the property in the Close, but nothing in Yorkshire. In 1471 the 4th Earl granted the Close property to William Blaxton, who was mayor of Newcastle in that year.[72]

There is some evidence that the landed families of Northumberland were involved in, or at least derived income from, the mining of coal, which was presumably purchased and shipped by Newcastle coal merchants. On the manor of Hartley in the 14th century, for example, both the Delavals and the Middletons derived rents from coal mines on their lands. During the 15th century coal mines at Prudhoe and Ingoe, on the lands of the earls of Northumberland, were being exploited, but by lessees rather than the earls themselves.[73] For the most part, however, the coal seams that were being exploited in the late 14th and early 15th centuries were on land that belonged to the great ecclesiastical landowners, such as the bishop of Durham and the prior of Tynemouth, though here, too, the mines were generally leased. As early as 1292 Tynemouth Priory had an income of 61s. 3d. from their coal mines.[74] In the 14th century they leased out their mine at Wylam, and they had mines at Earsdon, Preston, Chirton, Cowpen and Monkseaton.[75] In Bedlingtonshire the monks of Newminster Abbey owned coal mines which they leased throughout the 14th and 15th centuries.[76] The profitability of these mines depended to a great extent on the lessees' connections with merchants and shippers in Newcastle, forming an economic nexus between town and rural hinterland which had few if any parallels in England at this time.

Thus the links between Newcastle and Northumberland in the later Middle Ages were complex, fluid and many-layered. In certain respects they were determined by those features which made Northumberland distinctive amongst English counties at that time: the insecurity and militarisation of society under the impact of the Scottish wars and the exploitation of coal, which was exported mainly through Newcastle. In other respects, the county presents a more familiar picture of successful merchants investing in landed property and accounting themselves gentlemen, while at the same time younger sons, who had to make

---

[72] *CPR*, 1405-8, p.50; *CIPM*, vol.12, p.221-32; *Calendarium Inquisitionum Post Mortem* (London, 1828), vol.4, pp.168, 267, 328; Blair, 'Members of Parliament, *AA*, vol.14, p.53; Tuck, J.A., 'The Percies and the Community of Northumberland in the Fourteenth Century', in Tuck, Anthony and Goodman, Anthony (eds), *War and Border Societies in the Middle Ages* (London, 1992), pp.178-91.

[73] *NCH*, vol.9, pp.100-12; vol.12, pp.163, 384.

[74] Brand, *Newcastle*, vol.2, p.591, citing Duke of Northumberland's Mss, Tynemouth Cartulary, fo. 54.

[75] *NCH* vol.7, p.17.

[76] Fowler, J.T. (ed), *Chartularium abbathinae de novo monasterio*, SS, vol.66 (1878) pp.45, 47.

their own way in the world might, in some instances, become involved in the mercantile life of the town. Most of the Northumbrian gentry seem to have held property in Newcastle, even if it was only a house where they might stay when visiting the town to transact business. The friaries of Newcastle, too, were important in the spiritual life of the gentry families, and, as we have seen, not just in terms of bequests in their wills. Yet at the same time the elites of town and county seem to have kept themselves apart in that most important of transactions, marriage. Urban and rural society remained distinctive, even if the links between the two were close, throughout the 14th and 15th centuries.

6

Medieval Gateshead

RICHARD BRITNELL

Introduction

Even in the absence of a borough or seaport at Newcastle in the early Middle Ages, the site of Gateshead was favoured by its situation at the southern end of a major Tyne crossing. The bridge that had given *Pons Aelius* its name was no longer usable by the time of the Norman Conquest,[1] but the former Roman road that had crossed it remained a recognised route north and south, and the river could be crossed by ferry. Bede's *Ecclesiastical History* records that in 653 there was a monastery located *ad Caprae Caput* ('at Goat's Head').[2] Place-name specialists agree that 'head' in this context means 'headland' or 'hill'.[3] A number of other English place-names are similarly formed from Old English *heafod* (head) with the name of an animal, but they are of no help in elucidating the precise interpretation of 'Goat's Head'.[4] According to the most recent guess, the headland or hill in question is where the church of St Mary now stands, and a goat (or goats) were once to be seen there.[5] This derivation from a natural feature, rather than from someone's settlement, suggests that the site was little occupied, but the name stuck even when it came to be more heavily populated. Symeon of Durham, in the early 12th century, represented the name, very much like Bede, as *ad Caput Capre*. The earliest known English form, *Gatesheuet*, is in a continuation of Symeon's work copied in the later 12th century.[6]

---

[1]   Oliver, A.M. (ed.), *Early Deeds Relating to Newcastle upon Tyne*, Surtees Society, vol.137 (1924), p.62.
[2]   Plummer, C. (ed.), *Venerabilis Baedae Opera Historica*, 2 vols (Oxford, 1896), vol. 1, p.170; Mackenzie, E., *A Descriptive and Historical Account of the Town and County of Newcastle upon Tyne, Including the Borough of Gateshead* (Newcastle upon Tyne, 1827), pp.51, 753.
[3]   Mills, A.D., *A Dictionary of English Place-Names*, revised edn (Oxford, 1995), p.141; Watts, V., *A Dictionary of County Durham Place-Names* (Nottingham, 2002), p.48.
[4]   Farcet, Cambridgeshire ('bull's head'), Hartshead, Lancashire ('stag's head'), Rampside, Cumbria ('ram's head'), Shepshed, Leicestershire ('sheep's head'), Swineshead, Bedfordshire ('pig's head'): Ekwall, *Concise Dictionary*, p.229.
[5]   Watts, V.E. (ed.), *The Cambridge Dictionary of English Place-Names* (Cambridge, 2004), p.247.
[6]   Rollason, D. (ed.), Symeon of Durham, *Libellus de Exordio atque Procursu istius hoc est Dunelmensis Ecclesie* (Oxford, 2000), pp.216, 308.

Gateshead stood at the north end of two landscape regions whose boundary is roughly defined by a line of major settlements stretching southwards to Chester-le-Street, Durham and Bishop Auckland. To the west and north of this line, settlement was predominantly scattered, the area of uncultivated land was particularly extensive and agriculture was heavily pastoral. Eastwards and southwards settlements were more likely to be nucleated and the proportion of arable was higher, though there was much moorland and waste even here until modern times.[7] Gateshead's territory belonged to the western rather than the eastern region. It was lightly settled before the 12th century, and there was extensive woodland and heath. To the east of the main highway lay the bishop's park, and beyond the Mereburn, that later separated the parishes of Gateshead and Felling, Heworth Wood or Chase stretched along the Tyne between Gateshead and Heworth.[8] In the early 13th century possession of Heworth Wood became a matter for dispute between the bishop and the monks of Durham, who had a forged charter of Henry I purporting to confirm their title. A witness who had long been a forester there, under Bishops Hugh du Puiset and Philip of Poitiers, attested in 1228 that the wood belonged to the manor of Gateshead and was a valuable asset. Bishop Richard Poore gave the wood to the monks in 1229, but the bishops maintained their park throughout the Middle Ages.[9] References to its boundaries in late medieval episcopal accounts refer to fences (*sepes*) in frequent need of maintenance.[10] There is no evidence that the park was used to protect deer or other game, though it contained pasture that could be used for the bishop's purposes or granted to others. In 1311, 16 foals belonging to the king were being kept there,[11] and in years when there were enough acorns to feed pigs the bishop received an income from *swyntake*, otherwise known as pannage.[12] The park could supply firewood,[13] and its timber was particularly valuable because, being so close to the river, it could be easily shipped. A record of 1514-15 refers to a 'wood staithe house' at Gateshead,

[7] Roberts, B.K., Dunsford, H. and Harris, S.J., 'Framing medieval landscapes: region and place in County Durham', in Liddy, C.D., and Britnell, R.H., *North-East England in the Later Middle Ages* (Woodbridge, 2005), pp.228, 232-5.

[8] Manders, F.W.D., *A History of Gateshead* (Gateshead, 1973), pp.2, 5.

[9] Scammell, G.V., *Hugh du Puiset, Bishop of Durham* (Cambridge, 1956), p.164; Offler, H.S. (ed.), *Durham Episcopal Charters, 1071-1152*, SS (1968), vol.179, p.62; Greenwell, W. (ed.), *Feodarium Prioratus Dunelmensis*, SS, vol.58 (1872), pp.234, 239. I am grateful to Linda Drury for sharing her knowledge of Gateshead Park, and for many of the following references to material concerning it.

[10] E.g. DUL, CCB B/31A, fos.39r, 72r, 127r.

[11] Hardy, T.D. (ed.), *Registrum Palatinum Dunelmense: the Register of Richard de Kellawe, Lord Palatine and Bishop of Durham, 1314-1316*, Rolls Series, no.62 (1873-8), vol.4, p.93.

[12] DUL, CCB B/83/1; B/31A, 220197, fo.75r.

[13] Hardy, *Registrum Palatinum*, vol.2, p.755.

52 The Gateshead end of the old bridge and the eastern end of Pipewellgate, a detail from Buck's view.

presumably on the banks of the Tyne and perhaps adjacent to the park.[14] The bishop's men used his timber from Gateshead mostly for estate purposes rather than as a source of cash.[15] It was taken to mend the Tyne bridge in 1480-1, and used to repair water mills at Whickham in the same year and at Bedlington in 1494-5.[16] Considerable quantities were shipped from the Tyne to the Tweed to strengthen the bishop's castle at Norham as a defence against the Scots in the years 1512-16.[17] Yet the potential commercial value of the bishop's timber throughout the Middle Ages is suggested by the felling and sale of 1,000 trees there in 1518-19.[18]

[14]   DUL, CCB B/31C/220204/4, fo.116r.
[15]   Brand, J., *Newcastle*, vol.1, pp.477-9; Surtees, R., *The History and Antiquities of the County Palatine of Durham*, 4 vols (London, 1816-40), vol.2, pp.107, 109; Raine, J. (ed.), *The Inventories and Account Rolls of the Benedictine Houses or Cells of Jarrow and Monk-Wearmouth in the County of Durham*, SS, vol.29 (1854), p.67.
[16]   DUL, B/75/5, 8.
[17]   DUL, CCB B/76/11, 12; B/76/15, fo.8r.
[18]   DUL, CCB B/76/19.

There are other references to woodland in the manor. In 1249 Nicholas de Farnham gave the chapel of St Nicholas the little wood called *Laddeley*, and the little wood of *Benchehelm*. The latter, containing 43 acres, lay between arable land belonging to the hospital of the Holy Trinity and the road leading to Farnacres 'in the direction of the meadow'.[19] Apart from woodland, the land around Gateshead contained extensive moors. Away from the river the main road southwards rose to about 500 feet above sea level on Gateshead Fell, which contained 1,300 acres in 1648.[20] At its highest point, by 1523, was the beacon that gave its name to Beacon Lough; it was part of a chain of beacons to communicate warning signals southwards when the Scots invaded.[21] Surtees describes the fell as 'formerly a wide spongy dark moor, extending from Wrecken Dyke on the South to the toll-bar on the North'.[22] It was used as rough pasture; in 1306 Bishop Anthony Bek gave Gilbert of Scarisbrick pasture rights 'in our woods of Birtley and Gateshead, and also in Gateshead Moor'.[23] The conclusion that much of the medieval parish was uncultivated in the 13th century and later is irresistible, and the area of woodland and heath must have been even greater before the agricultural expansion of the 12th and 13th centuries that we shall examine shortly.

The Origins of the Borough

At some point before the 12th century the lordship of Gateshead was acquired by the bishops of Durham, perhaps as a peripheral appendage of some major gift to St Cuthbert. It may have been part of a grant associated with the accession of Guthfrith I of Deira in 883, which seems to have included both a multiple estate centred on Chester-le-Street and the properties formerly belonging to the abbeys of Monkwearmouth and Jarrow. The Cuthbertine community settled in Chester-le-Street about the same time, which may explain why Gateshead remained one of a group of episcopal properties attached to Chester-le-Street for some administrative purposes.[24] Though of little commercial significance before the 12th century, its location at a river crossing increasingly contributed to its development as a central place. It has been surmised that Bottle Bank, the name of the steep slope on the main road down to the Tyne, is from the Old

[19]   Hoskin, P.M. (ed.), *English Episcopal Acta 29: Durham 1241-1283* (London, 2005), nos 16, 17, pp.16, 17.
[20]   Mackenzie, *Descriptive and Historical Account*, p.746.
[21]   DUL, CCB B/76/23.
[22]   Surtees, *History*, vol.2, p.107.
[23]   Fraser, C.M. (ed.), *Records of Anthony Bek, Bishop and Patriarch, 1283-1311*, SS, vol.162 (1953), no.118, pp.122-3.
[24]   South, T.J. (ed.), *Historia de Sancto Cuthberto* (Woodbridge, 2002), pp.52-3, 89; Rollason, *Symeon of Durham, Libellus*, pp.122-7; Lapsley, G.T., 'Boldon Book', in *Victoria County History of Durham*, vol.1 (London, 1905), pp.265-6; Offler, H.S., 'Re-reading Boldon Book', in idem, *North of the Tees: Studies in Medieval British History* (Aldershot, 1996), pp.4-5.

English *bothl* ('building') and recalls the site of an ancient hall.[25] A later bishop's residence of some kind was near the High Street, perhaps on the eastern side; an early 15th-century rental records a row of burgage tenements, apparently near Oakwellgate, beginning 'at the palace' (*ad la palace*).[26] The bishop's establishment served as a collection centre for produce renders from the bishop's estate north of the Tyne, and so presumably had storage facilities. Before the time of Bishop Walter of Kirkham (1249-60), tenants in Bedlingtonshire in Northumberland were responsible for carrying foodstuffs from Bedlington to Gateshead. Men of Whickham carried produce on from Gateshead to Durham, or alternatively northwards from Gateshead to Bedlington.[27] Because of its accessibility to both parties, Gateshead was also a convenient location for meetings between bishops of Durham and magnates of Northumbria.[28] It was chosen as the location for a large assembly on 14 May 1080, at which Bishop Walcher and his men met Northumbrian notables. We know of this meeting because it culminated not, as planned, in the reconciliation of a bitter feud, but in the assassination of the Bishop and members of his entourage.[29] There was another important meeting at Gateshead in August 1144 between William Cumin and David King of Scots.[30] In some respects Gateshead retained this importance as a meeting place in later centuries. In 1278-9 it was recorded as a custom that in order to claim his liberties the bishop, together with certain other local magnates, was obliged to meet the king's justices at Gateshead 'at a well called Chille' when they came northwards to hear pleas in Newcastle; this location was by the roadside to the south of the borough, on the edge of the fells at Sheriff Hill.[31]

There is little basis for speculating about the early settlement of Gateshead. The river crossing is likely to have attracted development on the south bank between the seventh century and the 12th, but of this we have no record. To judge from later evidence, there is unlikely to have been an agricultural population of any significance. The bishops had developed an arable demesne by the late 12th century, but for its cultivation had assigned to it labour services owed by

---

[25]   Aird, W.M., *St Cuthbert and the Normans: the Church of Durham, 1071-1153* (Woodbridge, 1998), p.264n. A burgage tenement in Gateshead 'in a streete theare called the Battell Banck' occurs in deeds of 1586 once in Gateshead Central Library, now returned to the depositor (former accession no.71/3/1 and 2). This is the earliest occurrence of the name I have found.

[26]   DUL, CCB B/21/38. Cf. Surtees, *History*, vol.2, p.105.

[27]   Greenwell, W. (ed.), *Boldon Buke*, SS, vol.25 (1852), pp.34, 39; Austin, D. (ed.), *Boldon Book* (Chichester, 1982), pp.30-1, 48-9; Offler, 'Re-reading Boldon Book', p.24.

[28]   Aird, *St Cuthbert and the Normans*, p.264n.

[29]   Rollason, Symeon of Durham, *Libellus*, p.216.

[30]   Arnold, T. (ed.), *Symeonis Monachi Opera Omnia*, 2 vols, Rolls Series, no.75 (1882-5), vol.1, p.159.

[31]   Page, W. (ed.), *Three Early Assize Rolls for the County of Northumberland, Saec. XIII*, SS, vol.88 (1891), pp.358-9; Brand, *Newcastle*, vol.1, 476n; Dodds, M.H., 'The history of Low Fell' (unpublished, 1966, Gateshead Central Library, L942.812), p.1; Mackenzie, *Descriptive and Historical Account*, p.746n.

the bondmen of Great Usworth.[32] The siting of a demesne at Gateshead, with no adequate labour force to support it, was no doubt another consequence of good communications, as well as a response to the growing population of nearby Newcastle; it was one of only about twelve demesnes on the episcopal estate in 1183. The arable area was nevertheless small. The bishop had only two plough teams there in 1183, when the core of his demesne was said to be a quarter of the arable of the whole manor. This implies that Gateshead as a whole had ploughed fields of little more than 960 acres, if each team worked a full ploughland, and if the ploughland here was one of 120 acres as at Chester-le-Street and Whickham.[33] The sown acreage would then have perhaps been only 480-640 acres, depending on the proportion of land fallowed each year, and this may be an overestimate if the demesne had less than two ploughlands, or if the ploughland was less than 120 acres.[34]

Even with six ploughlands in the hands of tenants, the arable fields would not have supported a large community, and there is no evidence of a village here of any size or antiquity. Gateshead lacked the customary features of manorial lordship. Unlike the older settlements on the bishop's estate such as Chester-le-Street or Whickham,[35] none of the land was divided into oxgangs, and the manor had no bond tenants. The bishop would have needed only a few men to work his demesne, especially given the labour input from Great Unsworth. There was a 'small church' at Gateshead in the later 11th century, in which Bishop Walcher was assassinated in 1080, but this was perhaps a chapel attached to the bishop's estate and does not imply a large village community.[36] It is impossible to say whether it was a successor to the earlier monastic church or whether it was an independent episcopal foundation. Whatever its origins, it eventually enabled Gateshead to become a parish in its own right rather than a chapelry attached to some other township. But parochial status is unlikely to have meant much before the founding of the borough, and precise parish boundaries were defined only gradually during the 12th and 13th centuries.[37]

The further development of Gateshead perhaps depended on the reconstruction of the Tyne bridge, at first only in wood, sometime between 1071 and about 1160,[38] though there is no means of knowing whether bridge or borough came first.

---

[32] Greenwell, *Boldon Buke*, pp.35-6.
[33] In these townships the oxgang, one eighth of a ploughland, was defined as containing 15 acres in *c*.1383: Greenwell, W. (ed.), *Bishop Hatfield's Survey*, SS, vol.32 (1857), pp.78, 94.
[34] Greenwell, *Boldon Buke*, p.2.
[35] *Ibid.*, pp.3, 33-4; Greenwell, *Bishop Hatfield's Survey*, pp.78, 94-5.
[36] Symeon of Durham describes the church where Walcher was killed as *ecclesiola*: Rollason, *Symeon of Durham, Libellus*, p.216.
[37] Manders, *History*, p.5.
[38] Oliver, *Early Deeds*, pp.62, 67.

53 A charter of the late 12th or early 13th century by which Nicholas, son of Thorold, of London (here called Thorald of Follingsby) granted land in Pipewellgate to Spakr son of Gamall Oter.

The earliest recorded urban development, though not necessarily the earliest in reality, was the creation of a new street running alongside the river. Between 1154 and about 1160 Hugh du Puiset, Bishop of Durham, sold a narrow strip of waste ground along the Tyne west from the bridge as far as Redheugh, to an entrepreneur called Thorald of London. Thorald and his father-in-law paid 20 marks (£13 6s. 8d.), and were in future to pay the bishop 1s. 7d. annually to hold the property 'in free borough'.[39] This was not a single burgage plot, but a tract of land on which Thorald developed the street later called Pipewellgate, named after its source of water. A well called Pipewell, and a stream called Pipewell running into the Tyne, are mentioned in charters of the late 13th century.[40] That

[39] Snape, M.G. (ed.), *English Episcopal Acta 24: Durham 1153-1195* (London, 2002), no.96, pp.83-4. For more about Thorald, see Offler (ed.), *Durham Episcopal Charters*, no.42, pp.167-70.
[40] DCM, 2.3.Spec. 21-2.

Thorald himself developed the land as burghal property is borne out by a later charter of his son, Nicholas, to one of his tenants with the Norse name Spakr son of Gamall Oter (Latinised as *Sparcus filius Gamelli Oter*). For 6d. a year, and no other rent or service, Spakr held a tenement in Gateshead that he is said to have developed from waste ground while Thorald was still alive. The property lay between land of Warnehald the moneyer and land of Adam the glovemaker.[41] This all suggests that, like the *locatores* who were simultaneously developing new towns in Germany, Thorald had created Pipewellgate as a new urban development, dividing it up into small plots side by side, subletting it to tenants with occupations in trade and manufacture, and retaining some rights as landlord.

Thorald's venture was perhaps from the beginning part of a broader episcopal project to develop Gateshead as a borough as a source of income. One of the bishops committed some of his land – whether cultivated or not we do not know – to accommodate small tenant properties, just as Thorald had done, but in greater numbers and on a busier site along the main road between Durham and Newcastle. We do not know when this project was begun, but it was certainly before 1183-4, when episcopal officers compiled the estate survey known as Boldon Book. Besides income from rural property and tenants in Gateshead, the bishop then received rents and other dues from a borough, mills, fisheries and ovens. There were about seventeen fish-weirs at Gateshead in the 12th century.[42] It seems likely that by this time the borough had been established for some time, and it is possible that its origins went back to the 1150s or earlier. It was leased for £40 in 1183, the same as Durham, and owed £10 for tallage in 1196, again the same as Durham.[43] A grant of liberties by Hugh du Puiset allowed burgesses of Gateshead the same rights in their tenements as the burgesses of Newcastle had in theirs, and confirmed their access to common pasture. It recognised their right to collect hay, rushes, bracken, peat, and thatch for their houses, and protected their right to travel with their goods within the bishop's territory. It also regulated their rights to collect timber and fuel in the bishop's woodland. This charter may belong to the early years of the borough's existence, but it can be dated only loosely to the years when du Puiset was bishop (1154-95), and is consequently of no help for dating its foundation.[44]

The church of St Mary, now Gateshead's visitors' centre, was perhaps established in the 12th century on a new site, integral to the plan of the borough.

---

[41]   DCM, 2.3.Spec. 48, printed as charter III in Surtees, *History*, vol.2, p.114.
[42]   Greenwell, *Boldon Buke*, p.2; Hardy, *Registrum Palatinum*, vol.3, p.40.
[43]   Scammell, *Hugh du Puiset*, pp.215-16.
[44]   Snape, *English Episcopal Acta 24*, no.59, pp.54-5. For further discussion, see Dodds, M.H., 'The bishops' boroughs', *AA*, 3rd series, vol.12 (1915), p.92.

54 St Mary's, Gateshead, with the Newcastle castle and St Nicholas' in the background to the left and the top of the tower of All Saints' to the right.

The earlier church is said to have been to the east of the present building, though on what authority is not clear.[45] The oldest surviving parts of the present building date from about 1200.[46] The church was allocated the great and small tithes of the parish.[47] In 1353 William Sire of Pipewellgate left £1 and a fine cloth to the altar of St Mary of Gateshead in lieu of tithes and other offerings.[48] The parson had 15 acres in the fields of Gateshead in *c*.1383, which appears to correspond to the 14 acres three roods two perches, in five parcels, with a parcel leased as a wayleave, which was the glebe before 1815.[49] The income of the church remained modest; in the late 13th and early 14th century it was valued at only £13 6s. 8d.[50] The names of rectors of Gateshead are known haphazardly from about 1240.[51]

Despite its expansion, Gateshead remained too small to attract a religious house, even of friars, but it had minor religious foundations. The hospital of

[45]   Mackenzie, *Description*, p.751 (for the location of the rectory, see p.753).
[46]   Pevsner, N., *County Durham*, 2nd edn, revised by E. Williamson (Harmondsworth, 1986), pp.282-3.
[47]   Surtees, *History*, vol.2, p.119.
[48]   DCM, 4.3.Spec.3.
[49]   Greenwell, *Bishop Hatfield's Survey*, p.89; Surtees, *History*, vol.2, p.119 and note v.
[50]   Brand, *Newcastle*, vol.1, p.488; W.E. Lunt (ed.), *Accounts Rendered by Papal Collectors in England, 1317-1378* (Philadelphia, 1968), p.10.
[51]   Boutflower, D.S., *Fasti Dunelmenses*, SS, vol.139 (1926), p.169.

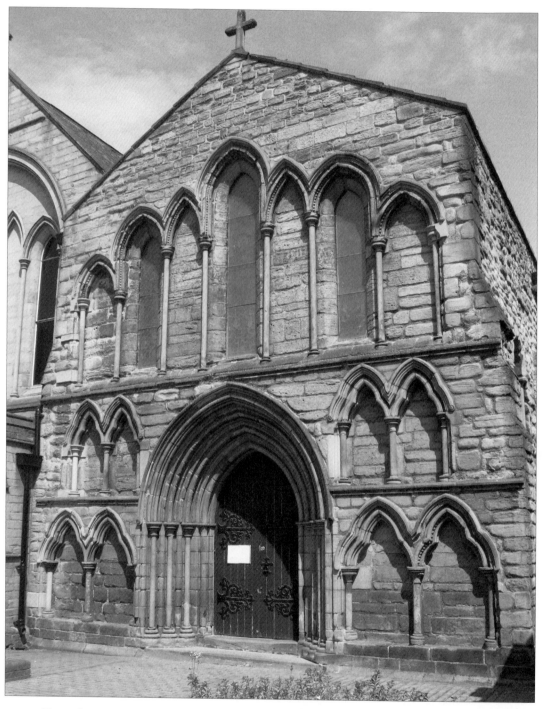

55 The 13th-century west front of St Edmund's hospital, Gateshead.

Holy Trinity, an alms house providing for a master and three poor brothers, is recorded in about 1200; it is unknown how much earlier it was founded. During the later 1240s Nicholas of Farnham, Bishop of Durham, integrated its endowment with his own foundation of the chapel or hospital dedicated to St Edmund the Confessor, whose relics had cured him. In January 1249 he established Gilbert the priest as master of the new hospital, and appointed three other priests to serve there. It was endowed with property in Ouston, Gateshead, Staindrop, Winston, Thimbleby, Crayke, Hardwick by Stockton, Stamfordham, and elsewhere. The duties of the clergy attached to the hospital were liturgical, and no specific provision was made for the needs of the poor or the sick.[52] This foundation, rather than the impoverished Trinity Hospital, must be the origins of the fine 13th-century chapel of St Edmund that stands on the east side of the High Street.[53] The hospital attracted some charitable donations from persons other than the bishop; in 1259-60, Martin of St Cross, the master of Sherburn hospital, bequeathed it ecclesiastical vestments and a cushion to support the gospels.[54]

No doubt the borough had a market from the beginning; it is first recorded in 1246.[55] An inquest held in Durham county court before Simon of Esh, the sheriff, in 1334 or shortly before, reported that the Gateshead market was held two days a week, on Tuesdays and Fridays 'up to the middle of the bridge'. These market days remained the same in the early 16th century, and trading at the southern end of the Tyne bridge is also recorded at this later date. From at least 1334 Gateshead also had an annual fair on 1 August, the feast of St Peter ad Vincula.[56] In the 16th century the market in grain and cattle was organised along the principal High Street, extending northwards from a market toll booth, said to have stood 'a little below the west end of Oakwellgate Chare', to a conduit whose location is unknown. A market cross that stood there had been removed before 1578, though some elderly witnesses remembered it.[57] Booths are recorded by a vennell leading to the church in a charter of 1296.[58] The

---

[52] Hoskin (ed.), *English Episcopal Acta 29*, nos 15-17, pp.13-18; Knowles, D., and Hadcock, R.N., *Medieval Religious Houses, England and Wales*, 2nd edn (London, 1971), p.360; Brand, *Newcastle*, vol.1, p.475. There has been some confusion between St Edmund, bishop and confessor, and St Edmund, king and martyr. The foundation charters record a dedication to the former.

[53] Pevsner, *County Durham*, revised Williamson, pp.283-4.

[54] Hoskin, *English Episcopal Acta 29*, no.111, p.98.

[55] Oliver, *Early Deeds*, p.202.

[56] DCM, Cartulary III, fo.3; Anon, 'The market and fair at Gateshead', *AA*, new series, vol.11 (1858), pp.227-9. The former record is dated by the reference to Simon of Esh, who occurs as sheriff in 1341-2 (DCM, 1.5.Pont.15), and the royal writ of 20 August, 8 Edward [III] that the bishop obtained following the inquest (Cartulary III, fo.3v).

[57] Anon, 'Market and fair', p.228; Mackenzie, *Descriptive and Historical Account*, p.750n. See also Surtees, *History*, vol.2, p.106.

[58] DCM, 3.3.Spec.35.

fullest list of goods sold there records beans and peas, salt, oatmeal, eggs, bread, butter and cheese. Convenient though the open market was, burgesses were not restricted to trading there; like those of other boroughs they claimed the right also to trade in their houses and shops.[59]

Gateshead in the Earlier Fourteenth Century

The complex structure of Gateshead, with its subordinate lordship of Pipewellgate, repeated on a smaller scale a feature of Durham, where the bishop's borough containing the market was surrounded by the three subordinate boroughs of Crossgate, Elvet and Gilesgate, the former two under the jurisdiction of the priory, and the last under that of Kepier Hospital.[60] Pipewellgate was not referred to as a separate borough, and was often described as 'in Gateshead', but sometimes it was said to be 'by Gateshead', emphasising its separate lordship.[61] Unlike Durham or Newcastle, Gateshead had no town walls.

It is not possible to follow step by step the growth of this compound borough during the 150 years or so following its foundation, but surviving charters record many details of the inhabited streets and lanes by the earlier 14th century. Pipewellgate stretched along the river westwards with tenements on both sides, but was severely constricted by the steepness of the bank on its southern side. In the 19th century it was described as 'a very narrow and dirty street', and its narrowness is confirmed by the earliest maps of Gateshead which show it as barely more than a long vennell.[62] Properties on the north side of Pipewellgate extended to the ebb water of the Tyne,[63] but were sometimes extended with staithes against the river on which were buildings and other constructions.[64] A late 13th-century charter records a property with stone steps leading from Pipewellgate to the river.[65] On the north side of Pipewellgate, properties ran steeply up against the bishop's demesne lands, which were bounded by a ditch.[66] On the other side of the main high road, east of the bridge, a similar development called Hillgate (*Hellgate*) stretched parallel with the river. Later maps

[59]   Anon, 'Market and fair', pp.227-9.
[60]   Bonney, M., *Lordship and the Urban Community: Durham and Its Overlords, 1250-1540* (Cambridge, 1990), pp.28-31.
[61]   E.g. 'Pipewelgate iuxta Gatesheued': DCM, 4.3.Spec.19 (1388).
[62]   Mackenzie, *Descriptive and Historical Account*, p.749.
[63]   DCM, 2.3.Spec.16, 2.3.Spec.21, 2.3.Spec.30, 2.3.Spec. 40, 2.3.Spec.41, 2.3.Spec.45a and b, 3.3.Spec.1-3, 3.3.Spec.6-8, 3.3.Spec.20, 3.3.Spec.23-4, 3.3.Spec.33, 4.3.Spec.1, 4.3.Spec.2.
[64]   DCM, 2.3.Spec.18, 2.3.Spec.28, 2.3.Spec.44, 2.3.Spec.29, 3.3.Spec.22, 4.3. Spec.2; 4.3.Spec.23.
[65]   DCM, 3.3.Spec.15.
[66]   DCM, 2.3.Spec.31, 3.3.Spec.15, 3.3.Spec.23, 3.3.Spec.33*, 4.3.Spec.22; Walton, J. (ed.), *The Greenwell Deeds Preserved in the Public Library, Newcastle upon Tyne* (Newcastle upon Tyne, 1927), no.216, pp.100-1.

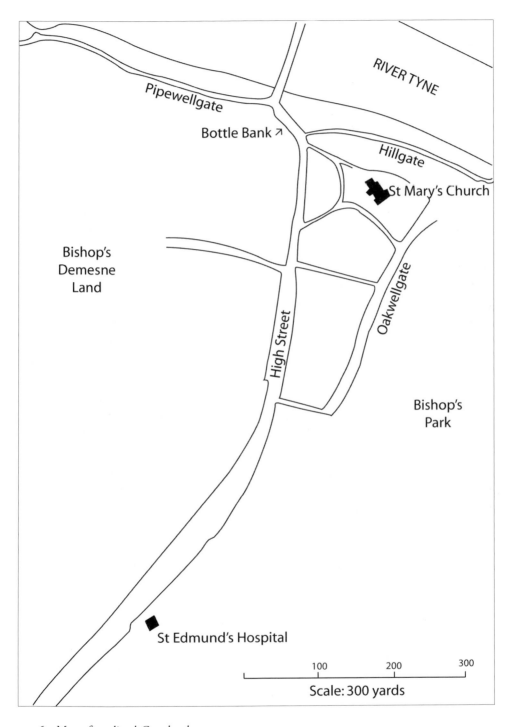

56 Map of medieval Gateshead.

show that, like Pipewellgate, it was narrower than the principal streets of the borough. Less is known about developments here for want of early charters. As along Pipewellgate, tenements to the north ran down to the banks of the river; Durham Priory had acquired one of these in 1354.[67] Along Gateshead's main road, burgage tenements rose up Bottle Bank into the High Street. In the 1420s there was an East Row and a West Row.[68] On the west side of Bottle Bank a narrow lane, known as the Narrow Chare or the Narrow Kirk Chare, led to the church of St Mary.[69] Oakwellgate, running south of the church and roughly parallel with the main street, occurs in charters of 1323 and 1342; it was named, like Pipewellgate, after a water source.[70] Other narrow lanes, Kirkgate Chare and Hillgate Chare, occur in 1323 as opposite boundaries of a borough property.[71] The site of St Helen's well and *Elyngate* are unknown; the latter ran in an east-west direction with episcopal demesne lands to the north.[72]

The medieval population of Gateshead probably peaked around 1290-1310, before the north-eastern economy was weakened by Scottish invasions, as well as by the famines of 1315-18 that affected most of Britain. How large that population was is impossible to say with any precision, but it probably reached a total of at least 300 families. An early 15th-century rental, unfortunately in poor condition, records about 260 burgage tenements (see Table 1), implying provision for a population of at least that number of burgess families and their servants, but it does not include those in the subordinate borough of Pipewellgate.[73] The earliest population estimate that is more than guesswork is one of 1,332 in 1548, based on the statement that the parish church then served 1,000 communicants.[74] The burgages were charged with rents called 'landmale', a term equivalent to the more common 'landgable' due to landlords in other boroughs.[75] These rents were exceptionally low. The 159 landmale payments from burgage tenements that are still legible in the rental range between ½d. and 7½d., but the mode was 1½d.,

[67] DCM, 4.3.Spec.7-8; Greenwell, *Feodarium*, 8 and 8n.
[68] DCM, 2.3.Spec.64; DUL, CCB B/31A, fo. 161v; Greenwell, *Feodarium*, p.7.
[69] DCM, 3.3.Spec.35, items 5-8. This was in 1339; it was later called Netherkirkchare: DCM, 3.3.Spec.35, items 11-13.
[70] Oliver, *Early Deeds*, nos 147, 167, pp.98, 109; Surtees, *History*, vol.2, p.105.
[71] Welford, R., 'Local muniments', *AA*, 3rd series, vol.5 (1909), p.124.
[72] Surtees, *History*, vol.2, p.106; Oliver, *Early Deeds*, no.172, p.111.
[73] DUL, CCB B/21/38. A principal property owner in the rental was John de Dolphanby, probably the man of that name who acquired property in Gateshead between 1399 and 1421 but was dead in April 1423: DCM, 3.3.Spec.35, 4.3.Spec.22; Welford, 'Local Muniments', p.125; Greenwell, *Feodarium*, p.4; Surtees, *History*, vol.2, p.117. Another property owner in the rental was William Gategang, who was dead in 1431, and whose heir was John Gildford: DCM, 2.3.Spec. 53, 54; Surtees, *History*, vol.2, p.116.
[74] Manders, *History*, p.342. I have modified Manders' figure in accordance with the proportion of non-communicants recommended by Wrigley, E.A., and Schofield, R.S., *The Population History of England 1541-1871: A Reconstruction*, new edn (Cambridge, 1989), p.565-6.
[75] Hemmeon, M. de W., *Burgage Tenure in Medieval England* (Cambridge, Mass., 1914), pp.64-74.

[*East Side*]	
[East Row?]	about 25 burgages
Helgate	10 burgages, 2 shops
Kyrchar	25 burgages (one of them 'beside the oven'), Rughedland
Akwelgate	16 burgages (one of them 'beside Akwell')
beginning at the Palace[a]	40 burgages, 3 lands (one with a garden attached), 2 forges on Smethyrawe, 1 field
Pelet char	23 burgages (3 of them lying 'together with 9 selions')
[*West Side*]	
[West Row?]	35-38 burgages, a parcel of land called Cabyndyke, Abraamcroft (3 acres), Peletland, a land once William the chaplain's, Tunokland, a land once Walter of Hesildon's, a land once Semanson's, another land
Waldenchar	50 burgages, William Gategang's hall
Colyarchar	11 burgages, 1 house (*domus*), 2 gardens, 19 lands (including Mallomland, Rughedland and Stodhirdland) and 1 *frisc' Sancte Elene*
beyond Colyerchar[b]	22-25 burgages, Robert (?) of Hedlam's hall called Howelhall, 1 forge, 2 shops, 5 lands (including Rughedland)

([a]) *Hic incipit ad le Palace*; ([b]) *Hic finitur Colyerchar.*

Table 1 Properties listed in an early 15th-century rental of Gateshead. Source: DUL, CCB B/21/38.

and only 25 burgages paid more than 2d. This means that the bishop's returns from borough rents were much lower than might be expected, and that most of his income from Gateshead came from rents of land. In spite of the presence of the borough, in fact, the bishop's income from Gateshead was lower than that from the adjacent village of Whickham.[76]

[76] This can be demonstrated from the receiver general's accounts from 1416-17 to 1539-40: DUL, B/1/1-10; B/2/11-24; B/3/25-34; B/4/37-46; B/5/47-60; B/6/61-9; B/7/70-1.

The burghal nature of the settlement ensured that a large proportion of its people would depend on trade and craft activities rather than agriculture for their livelihood. Even without a comprehensive list of residents and their occupations, it is possible to identify some of their activities from details to be found in charters relating to the borough, which name both tenants of properties in Gateshead and Pipewellgate and the witnesses who attested transfers of property. At times between 1320 and 1349, the year of the Black Death, the inhabitants included Richard of *Gousill*, the stonecutter,[77] Robert del Holme, the mason,[78] and Hugh, the carpenter,[79] all in the construction industry. Charters of these years also record land that had previously belonged to John the quarryman[80] and Alexander Audri the quarryman.[81] The bynames of Robert Hwuer or Huver and John Colier[82] suggest employment digging for coal.[83] The food trades are represented by Roger the miller[84] and Richard the baker.[85] There was employment in the Tyne fisheries mentioned in Boldon Book and later sources, though the right of men of the bishop and prior to trade freely in the fish they caught was challenged by the burgesses of Newcastle, who wanted to restrict their trade to the Newcastle market.[86] In 1383 the bishop's fisheries were worth £20 a year, nearly as much as the manor and borough of Gateshead combined.[87] There was probably also a local salt-making industry, since references to a salt well recur from the late 13th century onwards in the place-names *Saltwellmedow* or *Saltwellmead*, *Saltwellside* and *Saltwellstroth*.[88] From the textile and clothing trades the residents of Gateshead and Pipewellgate included John Camber (that is, comber),[89] Gilbert the weaver,[90] Robert the dyer,[91] John the dyer,[92] Peter the dyer,[93] Adam the dyer,[94] William of Spredden, dyer,[95] William Litster (that is,

77 DCM, 3.3.Spec.11 (1332), 2.3.Spec.20 (1335), 2.3.Spec.26 (1335).
78 DCM, 2.3.Spec.18 (1349), 3.3.Spec.22 (1349).
79 DCM, 3.3.Spec.23 (1349), 4.3.Spec.28 (1349).
80 DCM, 3.3.Spec.11 (1332).
81 DCM, 2.3.Spec.45a, b (1348), 3.3.Spec.19 (1344), 3.3.Spec.24 (1348), 3.3.Spec.34a, b (1349).
82 DCM, 2.3.Spec.11 (1335), 3.3.Spec.35, item 6 (1339). But Sir John Colyer, chaplain, occurs in 1344 (3.3.Spec.19).
83 DCM, 2.3.Spec.40-1 (1325), 2.3.Spec.42 (1326).
84 DCM, 3.3.Spec.26 (1349).
85 DCM, 3.3.Spec.25 (1348).
86 DCM, Cartularium III, fo.3-3v.
87 Brand, *Newcastle*, vol.1, p.477; Greenwell, *Bishop Hatfield's Survey*, p.89.
88 *Saltewelmedue* (*c*.1299): Fraser, *Records of Anthony Bek*, no.62, p.55. *Saltwelsyde*, *Saltwelstroth*, *Saltwelmed* (*c*.1383): Greenwell, *Bishop Hatfield's Survey*, p.88.
89 DCM, 3.3.Spec.35 (1339); Oliver, *Early Deeds*, no.167, p.109 (1342).
90 Surtees, *History*, vol.106, note g (1324).
91 DCM, 2.3.Spec.42 (1326); Welford, 'Local muniments', p.124 (1323).
92 DCM, 3.3.Spec.1 (1337), 3.3.Spec.6 (1337).
93 DCM, 2.3.Spec.11 (1335), 2.3.Spec.12-13 (1348); 3.3.Spec.19 (1344), 3.3.Spec.26 (1349), 4.3.Spec.2 (1348).
94 DCM, 3.3.Spec.23 (1349).
95 DCM, 2.3.Spec.18 (1349), 3.3.Spec.22 (1349).

dyer),[96] Isolda Litster,[97] Walter Litster son of Elias the tailor,[98] Richard the fuller,[99] and Stephen Nedeller.[100] The widow and son of Roger the cobbler of *Boormore* (unidentified) suggest the presence of leather trades; by 1339 Roger's widow was remarried to Benedict of Lynn the apothecary.[101] Other occupations practised in Gateshead in this period are represented by Stephen Pedler,[102] Gilbert Bower (that is, bowyer),[103] Robert the smith,[104] Thomas of Crayke the smith,[105] John Horner,[106] John Lardener,[107] the daughter of Henry Chaundeler,[108] and Walter Potter.[109] The bursar of Durham Priory had some dispute with a potter or potters of Gateshead in 1335-6.[110] It is not always certain that bynames with a craft element were descriptions rather than inherited surnames, but in a number of cases the craft designation is secondary to some other byname (as in the case of Benedict of Lynn the apothecary or Thomas Crayke the smith), and is therefore presumably descriptive. It is also likely that Walter Litster and Elias the tailor pursued the crafts by which they were identified, since Walter had not inherited the byname by which his father was known. The number and variety of such occupational bynames is higher than would be expected in a rural community, and indicates a different occupational structure. Some of these crafts are more specialised than would normally be found in a small borough, and suggest that Gateshead benefited from the rapid growth of population and consumption in Newcastle. Likely though this proposition is, given the easy connection between the two towns across the Tyne Bridge, which was rebuilt in stone after having burned down in 1248,[111] it cannot be substantiated more fully.

Many townsmen derived some of their income from agriculture, but the agrarian development of Gateshead proves difficult even to outline; the meagre details of the bishop's estate supplied by the survey of 1183 bear so little

[96] DCM, 2.3.Spec.12-13 (1348); Oliver, *Early Deeds*, no.167, p.109 (1342).
[97] DCM, 2.3.Spec.12-13 (1348).
[98] DCM, 3.3.Spec.27 (1346).
[99] Oliver, *Early Deeds*, nos 147 (1323), p.98; cf. no.167, p.109.
[100] DCM, 2.3.Spec.11 (1335).
[101] DCM, 3.3.Spec.35, items 5, 6 (1339). Ralph the tanner is recorded in an undated charter from earlier in the century: 3.3.Spec.35c.
[102] Welford, 'Local muniments', p.124 (1323).
[103] DCM, 3.3.Spec.3 (1329). The widow of William Bower occurs in a charter of 1349: 3.3.Spec.23.
[104] Oliver, *Early Deeds*, no.147, p.98 (1323).
[105] DCM, 3.3.Spec.28 (1335); for Thomas's occupation, see 3.3.Spec.26-7.
[106] DCM, 2.3.Spec.18 (1349), 3.3.Spec.22-3 (1349); Oliver (ed.), *Early Deeds*, no.167, p.109 (1342).
[107] DCM, 2.3.Spec.11 (1335), 3.3.Spec.28 (1335); Welford, 'Local muniments', p.124 (1323).
[108] DCM, 3.3.Spec.26 (1349).
[109] DCM, 2.3.Spec.11 (1335), 3.3.Spec.1 (1337), 3.3.Spec.6 (1337), 3.3.Spec.7 (1337), 3.3.Spec.8 (1336), 3.3.Spec.11 (1332), 3.3.Spec.28 (1335); Welford, 'Local muniments', p.124 (1323).
[110] Fowler, J.T. (ed.), *Extracts from the Account Rolls of the Abbey of Durham*, 3 vols, SS, vols 99, 100, 103 (1898-9, 1901), vol.2, p.529.
[111] Luard, H.R. (ed.), *Matthaei Parisiensis Monachi Sancti Albani Chronica Majora*, 7 vols, Rolls Series (London, 1872-83), vol.v, p.35; Mackenzie, *Descriptive and Historical Account*, pp.205-6.

relationship to those of the Hatfield Survey of about 1383 that few meaningful inferences can be drawn. We can fairly deduce that the cultivated acreage of the manor was increased by land taken in from woodland and heath during the 12th and 13th centuries. Boldon Book refers to demesne land newly cleared on the instructions of Hugh du Puiset. The Hatfield Survey lists 'exchequer lands' totalling perhaps about 180 acres,[112] which was probably land cleared for cultivation between 1183 and the 14th century. Even with this addition, though, the fields of Gateshead manor listed in the Hatfield Survey contained only about 630 acres in 1383. Comparison between this acreage and the implied eight ploughteams and more of 1183 is complicated by the absence from the record of 1383 of land vested in the burgesses, which in 1814 amounted to 157 acres.[113] The bishop had granted other land away. In particular, in 1249 Bishop Nicholas of Farnham had endowed St Edmund's hospital with 'all the old demesne of Gateshead', which may mean the two ploughlands on the demesne in 1183. In that case the demesne lands of 1383, totalling 149 acres, must have been reconstituted either by clearing new land or by absorbing land previously in the hands of freeholders. The acreage recorded in the Hatfield Survey, together with these additional allowances for the burgesses' lands and the 'old demesne', would push the total arable acreage of Gateshead around 1300 to over 1,000 acres, but the unknowns are too numerous for this conclusion to be at all certain.

Gateshead had some characteristically burghal institutions, even though it was a seigniorial borough subject to the exercise of lordship by the bishops of Durham. The best attested officer was the bailiff, who often witnessed charters relating to property in the borough, but a second borough officer (a *serviens* or 'serjeant') is also in evidence in about 1300.[114] The bailiff, who also supervised the running of the manor of Gateshead, was appointed by the bishop to hold a court in the borough and to collect rents; these were the terms on which John Boterell held the office for a year from Michaelmas 1415.[115] The earlier existence of a borough court is attested by a charter of 1297 that was witnessed 'in [the] full court of Gateshead'.[116] In the 16th century these borough courts were fortnightly.[117] There was a clerk of the courts in 1353.[118]

[112] Greenwell, *Bishop Hatfield's Survey*, pp.88-9. The exchequer arable lands for which acreages are given total 112.875 acres rented for £3 4s. 8d. (averaging 0.57 shillings an acre), but no size is recorded for some other exchequer lands whose rents totalled £1 18s. 4d.
[113] Surtees, *History*, vol.2, p.106.
[114] John de Malum, *tunc seruiens eiusdem ville*: DCM, 3.3.Spec.15-17.
[115] Brand, *Newcastle*, vol.1, p.478.
[116] DCM, 3.3.Spec.35b.
[117] Anon, 'Market and fair', p.227.
[118] Robert Godybour, *capellanus, clericus curie ville de Gatesheued*: DCM, 2.3.Spec.14.

Even if bailiffs were reappointed annually, they might serve for more than one year. Gilbert Gategang was bailiff in all known instances between 1288 and 1308[119] and Hugh of Higham on all the known charters from 1335 to 1338.[120] The only instance from this period in which we can even approximately date the handover of office from one bailiff to another is in 1348, the year of the Black Death, when a change is more than usually likely to have taken place at an uncustomary time of year. But for what it is worth, Peter de Lewe was replaced by Walter of Lumley sometime between 3 August and 1 November,[121] which is compatible with a new office year beginning at Michaelmas, as in John Boterell's time, and as in Newcastle.[122] The list of

57 A later seal of Gateshead 'borough'.

Gateshead bailiffs includes both Waleran of Lumley and John of Carlisle on 26 July 1349,[123] but this seems to be the result of some clerical error. There is no other suggestion in records before the 1360s of more than one bailiff in office at a time, unlike Newcastle, where they elected a mayor and four bailiffs annually. Some bailiffs were of sufficient importance to figure in the history of Newcastle as well as in that of Durham. Hugh of Higham was elected one of the Newcastle bailiffs in 1325, perhaps in 1326, and every year from 1327 to 1335. He was MP for Newcastle in 1331, and was elected mayor there in 1335 and 1337. Waleran of Lumley was elected a bailiff of Newcastle in 1330, 1331, 1333 and 1334, and as mayor in 1339. Both Hugh of Higham and Waleran of Lumley were 'urban gentry'; they described themselves as Newcastle merchants, but were armigerous.[124] The Gategang family perhaps originated in Newcastle, where the surname is to be found in records of the 13th and 14th centuries. Alan Gategang held buildings there from Durham Priory and attested Newcastle charters in the 1220s and 1230s.[125] Sibyl Gategang was prioress of the nunnery of St Bartholomew in Newcastle in 1331,[126] and in 1337 Richard Gategang, like

[119] DCM, 2.3.Spec.33 and 34 (1288), 3.3.Spec.35, texts 1 and 2 (1296), 2.3.Spec.28 (1308).
[120] DCM, 2.3.Spec.11, 3.3.Spec.28 (1335), 2.3.Spec.26, 3.3.Spec.2 and 8 (1336), 2.3.Spec.19, 3.3.Spec.1 and 7 (1337), 4.3.Spec.1 (1338).
[121] DCM, 2.3.Spec.12, 13, 3.3.Spec.25.
[122] Oliver, *Early Deeds*, p.200.
[123] DCM, 3.3.Spec.22, 4.3.Spec.28.
[124] DCM, 2.3.Spec.36, 37; Oliver, *Early Deeds*, 211-13; Hunter Blair, C.H., 'The mayors and lord mayors of Newcastle upon Tyne, 1216-1940, and the sheriffs of the county of Newcastle upon Tyne, 1399-1940', *AA*, 4th series, vol.18 (1940), pp.4-5.
[125] Greenwell, *Feodarium*, p.2, note; Oliver, *Early Deeds*, nos 183, 396, 401, pp.116-17, 193-5.
[126] Smith, D.M. and London, V.C.M., *Heads of Religious Houses, England and Wales, II: 1216-1377* (Cambridge, 2001), p.589. For an undated reference to her from about the same time, see Oliver, *Early Deeds*, no.339, pp.176-7.

Hugh of Higham in 1339, collected wool there on behalf of Edward III.[127] However, the political influence of the Gateshead Gategangs apparently did not stretch into Newcastle. Other Gateshead bailiffs have no known Newcastle connections. Peter de Lewe, who is probably the same person as Peter the dyer,[128] does not occur in Newcastle deeds, and had no identifiable property interests across the Tyne.

While he was prominent as the bishop's officer in Gateshead in the late 13th century, Gilbert de Gategang acquired a large power base in both borough and manor. At a time when he was probably bailiff, about 1299, he became the principal freeholder in Gateshead as a result of what looks like a conscious policy on the part of Bishop Anthony Bek, who augmented Gilbert's existing lands by a grant to him and his wife Sybil of 80 acres of 'new waste' in the fields of Gateshead. The interpretation to be placed on the expression 'new waste' is uncertain, but it must mean something different from the numerous grants by 13th-century bishops of moorland waste, and probably signifies older freehold land that for some reason had come into the bishop's hands. This grant was augmented by a further 47 acres of 'new waste' in 1310.[129] The 127 acres conveyed by these two grants can easily be identified amongst the lands of Gateshead manor in 1383. The area was almost as large as that of the bishop's own demesne, and constituted 89.4 per cent of the freehold land of the manor at that date.[130] A further 33 acres of land in and beside the *Aldepark* was acquired by John Gategang from Bishop Richard of Kelloe in 1312.[131]

The Gategang family also acquired an independent lordship in Gateshead, and it may be for this reason that family members were no longer chosen as bailiffs after the last known instance in 1308. The way in which Hugh du Puiset had developed the borough as far back as the mid-12th century had a lasting effect on its institutions. Thorald of London's intermediate tenurial status between the bishop and the tenants of Pipewellgate allowed his successors to exercise lordship there through several centuries, and his title had been acquired by the Gategangs by the later 1340s, when Alan de Gategang was calling himself 'lord of Pipewellgate'.[132] A separate court was held for the tenants of Pipewellgate at this time.[133] The rights of Alan's son William in Pipewellgate, according to a deed

[127] Fraser, C.M., 'The life and death of John of Denton', *AA*, 4th ser., vol.37 (1959), p.313; Hunter Blair, 'Mayors', p.4.
[128] Oliver, *Early Deeds*, p.109.
[129] Fraser, *Records of Anthony Bek*, nos 62, 152, pp.55-6, 60.
[130] These lands are the 80 acres held by William Gategang (the grant of *c*.1299), together with the 44 acres held by John de Topcliff (the grant of 1310): Greenwell, *Bishop Hatfield's Survey*, p.88.
[131] Hardy, *Registrum Palatinum*, vol.2, pp.1,161-2.
[132] DCM, 2.3.Spec.45a, b, 3.3.Spec.24, 3.3.Spec.31.
[133] Surtees, *Newcastle*, vol.2, p.105, note a.

of 1388, comprised lands, tenements, rents, the services of free tenants, demesne, courts, wards, reliefs, marriages and escheats.[134] When in that year Durham Priory acquired eight messuages in Pipewellgate, and rents totalling 6s. 6d., the transfer was authorised by William Gategang, not by the bishop.[135] Numerous charters relating to property there were dated and witnessed 'at Pipewellgate' rather than 'at Gateshead', and the witnesses often included the bailiff, or steward, of Pipewellgate.[136] John Scot of Pandon occupied this office continuously for at least 17 years between 1332 and 1349.[137] The Gategang family did not live in Pipewellgate; in the early 15th century the family heir had a hall in the main borough of Gateshead in the street called Walden Chare (see Table 1).

After the Black Death

It is not possible to follow the fortunes of Gateshead through the tribulations of the 14th century – the war with Scotland, the famines of 1315-18, the recession of 1337-42, the Black Death, and subsequent epidemics when plague returned – which are likely not only to have halted the town's expansion but also to have reduced its population. Given the frequent incursions of Scottish raiders south of the Tyne after the battle of Bannockburn, Gateshead is unlikely to have remained untroubled, and its economy had probably lost ground well before the Black Death reached Durham in 1349. That disaster hit the Gateshead region with full force; in the adjacent parish of Heworth, 36 per cent of Durham Priory tenants of Over Heworth died, and at Nether Heworth the toll was as high as 72 per cent.[138] The second plague of 1361-2 was a further serious setback.[139] It was perhaps as a consequence of the resulting administrative complications and increased workload that in 1362-3, for the first time on record, two bailiffs held office together in Gateshead.[140]

Whatever the reason, this change was maintained for some time. Two bailiffs were appointed in 1365-6 and 1370-1, and presumably in other years during this period.[141] The number was increased further at some later point; there were three

---

[134] DCM, 4.3.Spec.19.

[135] DCM, 2.3.Spec.10. For the date, see Lomas, R.A. and Piper, A.J., *Durham Cathedral Priory Rentals, I: Bursars Rentals*, SS, vol.198 (1989), p.200.

[136] E.g. DCM, 3.3.Spec.20 (1332), 2.3.Sec.46 (1337), 4.3.Spec.1 (1338), 2.3.Spec.18 (1349).

[137] DCM, 3.3.Spec.20 (1332), 2.3.Spec.18 (1349).

[138] Lomas, R.A., 'The Black Death in County Durham', *Journal of Medieval History*, vol.15 (1989), p.129.

[139] Dodds, B., 'Durham Priory tithes and the Black Death between Tyne and Tees', *Northern History*, vol.39 (2002), p.22.

[140] DCM, 2.3.Spec.8.

[141] DCM, 4.3.Spec.12 and 15.

58 View of old Gateshead from top of the Bottle Bank.

bailiffs in 1437.[142] This development was subsequently reversed, again for reasons that can only be surmised. In March 1443 William Askeby, gentleman, was sole bailiff,[143] and a single bailiff remained the norm through the following hundred years. The return to a single bailiff perhaps corresponded to an administrative change, at present undatable, by which the bishop leased the borough revenues to a single lessee. William Askeby occurs in the accounts of the coroners of Chester Ward between 1447-8 and 1462-3 as leasing the borough and some associated other sources of income.[144] The bailiff of Gateshead from this point, if not earlier, until

[142] DCM, 2.3.Spec.55.
[143] DCM, 2.3.Spec.60.
[144] DUL, CCB B/44/2-7.

sometime in the 1490s, was the man who leased the borough. In 1500, for example, Thomas Waltden was described as former bailiff and lessee of Gateshead; in this capacity he had received a fee of £3 6s. 8d. in 1492-3.[145]

Epidemics and economic difficulties were accompanied by some loss of numbers, to judge from references to waste houses at various times in the 15th century. Most of Durham Priory's properties in Gateshead were acquired in 1388, so that it is impossible to trace their rents back before the Black Death, but thereafter they evidently did not maintain their value in the short term. The priory's tenement in Hillgate was described as waste in 1430.[146] The bursar's rental of 1396-7 lists 12 tenements in Pipewellgate rented to eight different tenants for £2 15s. 9d. altogether, but most of these were uninhabited in 1446, and had been for 30 years or more; almost half their rents there – £1 6s. 8d. out of a notional £2 17s. 4d. – were uncollectable because the properties were 'waste'. This implies some severe difficulties in finding tenants in the period 1397-1416, which is partly confirmed by evidence that two priory tenements in Pipewellgate were leased as waste in 1409. By 1495-6 the full rent of £2 17s. 4d. was owed by six tenants, which implies recovery at least to the late 14th-century level.[147] Such recovery was not universal, though. A list of the Gateshead properties held from the bishopric of Durham by Conan Barton at the time of his death in 1502 lists an accumulation of 37 burgage tenements of which 13 were waste and worth nothing, four of them in Pipewellgate and 14 in East Row.[148] The bishop's receipts from landmale declined from £2 12s. in the early 15th century to a fixed sum of £1 6s. 8d. at the beginning of the 16th century.[149]

Smaller numbers and decaying properties did not necessarily mean that the economy of Gateshead was contracting during the 15th century, as measured by the total income that its inhabitants managed to generate. They retained a wide range of occupational specialities and it is likely that standards of living were higher than before 1349.[150] From the later 14th century, unfortunately, our sources of information tell us little about burgesses and their families, but it is possible to find tradesmen in the 15th century carrying on a variety of craft traditions as in the past. Richard of *Huton*, tailor, acquired an interest in an acre

---

[145]   DUL, CCB B/31A, fos. 15r, 296v. The coroner's account of 1497-8, which describes him as *nuper balliuus de Gateshed*, notes that he owed £5 14s. 6d. from the lease of 1492-3: B/45/17.
[146]   Greenwell, *Feodarium*, pp.7-8
[147]   DCM, 4.3.Spec.23; Raine, J. (ed.), *Historiae Dunelmensis Scriptores Tres*, SS, vol.9 (1839), pp.ccxc – ccxci; Lomas and Piper, *Durham Cathedral Priory Rentals, I*, pp.125-6, 135-6, 200.
[148]   DUL, CCB B/31A, fo. 345v.
[149]   DUL, CCB B/21/38.
[150]   Dyer, C., *Standards of Living in the Later Middle Ages: Social Change in England, c.1200-1520* (Cambridge, 1989), pp.199, 202-3, 207.

of land in 1402.[151] John Alnwick, carpenter, owned a tenement on the east side of the High Street in 1421, when Robert Cok, potter, acquired the property next door.[152] Richard Tedford, tailor, acquired a tenement in Gateshead in 1423.[153] Table 1, summarising the information available from the early 15th-century rental already discussed, shows that the borough then contained at least four shops and three forges, two of them on Smithy Row (*le Smethyrawe*). The various services offered by Gateshead artisans continued to be of regional importance. The accounts of the master of Jarrow, 1495-6, include 7s. paid to a Gateshead cooper, John Cowper, for making, banding and repairing barrels.[154] The River Tyne offered other sources of employment. The bishop of Durham retained fisheries in the Tyne that were attached to Gateshead; in the early 16th century there were three, called *Greyare*, *Feulers* and *Helperyare*.[155] Other Tyne fisheries in Gateshead, called *Fleyare*, *Holmesyare*, *Dirtyare*, *Curteyare* and *Fulyare*, were owned by Durham Cathedral Priory, which was able to draw rents in cash, fish and fish oil.[156]

The laity of Gateshead, as in other towns, took a more active role in the ecclesiastical life of the borough in the 14th and 15th centuries. There was substantial rebuilding of the parish church in the 14th century, which was supported by the townsmen. William Sire's will of 1353 allocated £1 6s. 8d. for the fabric of the church, including £1 for the porch where his sons were buried. The number of dedicated altars with their separate endowments probably multiplied; Sire's will refers to an altar of St Catharine and an altar of the Virgin in the north porch.[157] On the other hand, the known investment in chantries, mostly before the mid-15th century, suggests that wealth was thinly distributed and that the borough as a whole enjoyed only a modest prosperity. Chantries of St Mary and the Trinity were founded in the earlier 14th century by Alan Prester, to be followed by two more founded by John Dolphanby dedicated to St John (*c.*1421) and to St Eligius, the patron saint of metalworkers, farriers and carters (*c.*1442).[158] The finances of the hospital of St Edmund seem to have become precarious in the mid-15th century, perhaps because of its dependence on income from land, since in 1448 it was appropriated by prioress and convent

[151] Welford, 'Local muniments', p.125.
[152] DCM, 3.3.Spec.35.
[153] Oliver, A.M. (ed.), *Northumberland and Durham Deeds from the Dodsworth MSS. in Bodley's Library* (Newcastle upon Tyne, 1929), Carnaby, nos.67, 68, pp.20-1.
[154] Raine, J. (ed.), *The Inventories and Account Rolls of the Benedictine Houses or Cells of Jarrow and Monk-Wearmouth in the County of Durham*, SS, vol.29 (1854), p.131.
[155] DUL, CCB B/69/1, 2.
[156] Lomas and Piper (eds), *Durham Cathedral Priory Rentals, I*, p.136.
[157] Pevsner, *County Durham*, pp.282-3; DCM, 4.3.Spec.3.
[158] Brand, *Newcastle*, vol.1, pp.489-93; Surtees, *History*, vol.2, pp.119-20.

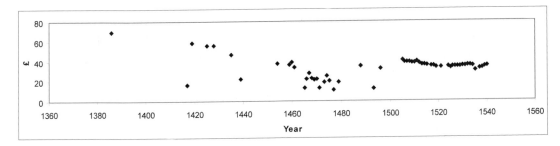

59 Payments from the bailiffs of Gateshead to the Bishop of Durham (£) as recorded in the accounts of the receiver general and those of the bailiffs, 1385/7 to 1539/40.

of St Bartholomew, Newcastle. Its annual income on the eve of the Reformation, according to an imprecisely dated rental, was £22 8s. 8d.[159] A minor interest in the coal trade between the mid-1490s and about 1520 had done little to lift the hospital's fortunes.[160]

Sparse details relating to individuals do not take us very far in understanding changes that were coming over the borough, and for that we need to assess more systematic evidence of other kinds. From the late 14th century onwards the best insight into the fortunes of Gateshead is to be derived from the estate archive of the bishops of Durham, which are meagre before this time but then become a rich if tantalising source of information. The bishop's income from Gateshead, excluding mines, had two components that can be distinguished from the accounts of the coroners of Chester Ward. The larger of these was the income from the borough, with any additional rents attached to it. In the mid-15th century these revenues were leased for a fixed annual charge of £33 6s. 8d., which included the lease of borough revenues (the *firma burgi*), rents of fisheries in the Tyne, and a windmill. This charge was raised to £35 in 1466-7 or thereabouts, probably at the time when the lease was transferred to Thomas Walker.[161] These sums were said to represent a reduction from a former level of £40.

The other source of episcopal income was from the rents of freeholdings and exchequer lands not included with the borough lease. These other rents, which had amounted to £10 16s. 3¾d. in about 1383, fell to £6 10s. 5d. by 1447-8, and

---

[159]   Knowles and Hadcock, *Medieval Religious Houses*, p.360; Surtees, History, vol.2, p.125 (excluding the revenue from Stella).

[160]   The hospital paid £5 for wayleaves to carry coal in 1504-5 and 1505-6, £10 in 1495-6, 1508-9, 1510-11, 1517-18 and 1518-19, and £12 in 1511-12, but nothing in 1509-10 or 1513-14: DUL, CCB B/3/27-47.

[161]   DUL, CCB B/44/8. In this account the sum is altered from £[33] 6s. 8d. to £35 and the name of the lessee from William Askeby to Thomas Walker.

to £4 16s. 10d. by 1483-4.[162] Though coroners continued to record them, by the 16th century they must have been normally absorbed in local costs somewhere in the system, since they were not acknowledged by the bishop's receiver general and are hard to trace elsewhere in the central accounts. They are, however, listed separately from the borough revenues in an entry in the Book of Great Receipt for 1513-14, where they total £5 18s. 2d.[163]

Unfortunately the bishop's receipts from Gateshead during the later 15th century, as recorded in the coroners' accounts, were subject to modification by the episcopal estate administration before any final total was incorporated in the receiver general's account, and it is not now possible to identify how or why these adjustments were made. In 1460-1, for example, the coroner's roll implies that the borough returned £33 6s. 8d. to the bishop and that in addition the net receipt of rents of free and exchequer lands amounted to £6 10s. 1d., but both the bishop's general receiver's account and his Book of Great Receipt of that year record a total receipt of £33 18s. 4d.[164] The two accounts diverge much more widely from this time on. In many years the receipt recorded by the general receiver is so low that it is plain that the borough farm was not being received in full in the bishop's exchequer.[165] These discrepancies mean that it is not possible to use the two sets of accounts to produce a composite data set, and, more seriously, that it is difficult to interpret either series. The plummeting figures recorded by the receiver general do not necessarily mean that the bishop's gross income from Gateshead had collapsed. They may only signify that large sums of money had been paid out from the Gateshead revenues before they reached the bishop's exchequer. There is some evidence to suggest that this was the case. In 1462-3, when Edward IV was still having to battle for control of the North, the coroner recorded that, on the authority of the Earl of Kent and the king's council at Durham, he had spent £18 on the wages of men to guard the bishop's tower, which defended the southern end of the Tyne Bridge.[166] Perhaps this sum was recorded by the receiver general as a reduction from the income paid from Gateshead rather than as a general charge on the estate. On other occasions the lessee of Gateshead made purchases on behalf of the bishop. The coroner's account of 1469-70 records an instance when the bailiff of Gateshead bought glass in bulk for the bishop's use for £6., and paid 7s. 6d. for

[162] DUL, CCB B/45/2, 15.
[163] DUL, CCB/26/3, fo. 51. The bailiff's account is separately recorded on fo. 69v.
[164] DUL, CCB B/1/10; B/26/1; B/44/5.
[165] See also Arvanigian, M., 'Free rents in the palatinate of Duham and the crisis of the late 1430s', AA, 5th series, vol.24 (1996), pp.102, 108.
[166] DUL, CCB B/44/7.

its carriage to Durham.[167] These stray examples from the coroners' accounts may have been matched by similar allowances elsewhere in the accounting system, and the figures in the receiver general's accounts may correspond to the cash sums ultimately received in Durham rather than sums that had been collected in Gateshead. Such uncertainties make it impossible to say just how badly rents and other dues from the people of Gateshead were affected by economic recession and episodes of political instability during the later 15th century.

From Michaelmas 1496 onwards, however, evidence of the bishop's income from Gateshead is more easily interpreted.[168] The bishop's administration stopped leasing Gateshead borough, and instead arranged for it to be administered by a 'bailiff and improver' (*balliuus et appruator*), which presumably means the officer in question was expected to increase the bishop's income.[169] That this represents a real change is suggested both by formal deduction of the borough revenues from the sums charged to the coroner's accounts, and by the survival of a long series of bailiffs' accounts for Gateshead from the year 1501-2.[170] The receiver general's policy was now better geared to our purposes, since it can be shown that the figures recorded in his accounts were the net sum for which the bailiff of Gateshead was answerable, normally at least without deductions of any expenses or other payments. This means both that we have a good idea of what the bishop actually received from his Gateshead assets, and also that figures from missing receiver generals' accounts can be estimated from the bailiffs' accounts to improve the data set. The sudden increase in revenues at the end of the 15th century may be no more than an indication that these conventions were newly established. On this understanding, the level of income from sources other than mining was permanently lower after about 1435 even if the figures from the later 15th century exaggerate the severity of the decline (Figure 59).

Table 2 shows how the bailiff's receipts were made up in 1509-10. The sum of £38 6s. 8d. that can be calculated from the bailiff's account corresponds exactly to the net receipt from Gateshead recorded in the receiver general's account for that year. The bulk of the bishop's income from Gateshead was made up of the rents from 21 enclosures and other miscellaneous parcels of land under the general heading 'meadows and pastures' which had previously been included in the *firma burgi*. They are listed in sufficient detail to show that they do not include the free and exchequer land rents recorded on the coroner's roll. As Figure 59 shows, by this time the bishop's income from Gateshead had

[167] DUL, CCB B/45/12. The payment is described as for *iij wawes vitri*.
[168] The transition can be dated from DUL, CCB B/31A, fo. 154v.
[169] DUL, CCB B/45/17.
[170] DUL, CCB B/69/1-36.

stabilised at around £35 a year. The apparent dip in rent income during the second and third decades of the 16th century is largely explained by mining activity that impinged on the agrarian life of the borough, and does not signify economic recession. The most noteworthy feature of these figures is their failure to show any increase, though they were predominantly derived from leasehold rents, despite the upward trend of prices during the 1530s.

Although the low receipts from Gateshead recorded by receivers general in the later 15th century cannot be safely used as indices of economic crisis, there can be little doubt that, ignoring income from mining, the bishop's income from Gateshead had declined during the 15th century, and that the contrast in Figure 59 between the figure for 1385-8 and those of the early 16th century is significant, at least for the sources of revenue recorded in the Hatfield Survey, if not for additional income from mining and quarrying, which cannot be assessed for the 1380s. Table 3 compares the bishop's income in 1509-10 with the evidence of the Hatfield Survey to show how the separate items of income had changed over this period of about 127 years. But though the bishop's income from these sources had fallen, its decline cannot be interpreted to imply the economic decline of Gateshead. Some minor losses of rent can be accounted for by the extension of mining operations over land previously used for agriculture, though this can hardly be a principal reason for declining income, since the one item that had risen, the lease of the borough, largely comprised rents of land. The chief difficulties, as Table 3 clearly shows, were losses of

60　View over Hill Gate and the waterfront, a detail from Buck's view.

revenue from mills and fisheries. The two water mills that had fetched a rent of £16 13s. 4d. were derelict by 1435, and remained untenanted 'for want of water'.[171] The lease of the bishop's fisheries in the Tyne, worth £20 a year in about 1383, was later incorporated with the lease of the borough revenues, and so cannot be assessed until the components of the borough lease can first be separated out in 1501-2. These fisheries were then leased for a combined rent of only £7, soon afterwards reduced to £5 because no one would take them at the higher rent.[172] These rent reductions may have resulted, at least in part, from the increasing use of the River Tyne and its banks for the purposes of the coal trade. They cannot have represented as severe a loss to the people of Gateshead as they did to the finances of the bishop, since the employment they created was of only minor significance.

To set against the evidence of these traditional revenues, the bishop's accounts record alternative sources of income. The later medieval economy of Gateshead had exceptional sources of development, because of the easily worked mineral deposits that it shared with Whickham nearby. Coal had become an important commodity for Newcastle merchants during the 13th century. From the early 14th century there is evidence of coal-working south of the Tyne, and from that time coal began to contribute something to incomes in Gateshead. A few personal bynames suggest the involvement of Gateshead families in mining activities, as we have seen. Some of the town's early 14th-century bailiffs engaged in the coal trade as entrepreneurs. Hugh of Higham held a colliery from Durham Priory in the west field of Elswick. Walter of Lumley's father, Gilbert, mined coal at Great Lumley by licence of the Bishop of Durham in 1339. Impressionistic evidence suggests an early 14th-century expansion of the coal trade that contributed to the resilience of Tyneside in the face of political and environmental misfortune.[173]

Though we do not know when Gateshead's own coal deposits were first explored, there was demonstrably a period of heightened activity after the Black Death. There were exceptionally extensive workings in Whickham in 1356, leased by the bishop at £333 6s. 8d. a year, and Gateshead had already begun to attract the attention of the principal commercial coal interests.[174] In 1364 John Plummer, burgess of Newcastle, began operations in Gateshead in partnership with Walter of Hesleden, burgess of Gateshead. The two men were trustees of

[171] Greenwell, *Bishop Hatfield's Survey*, p.89; DUL, CCB B/44/1, and subsequently.
[172] DUL, CCB B/69/1, 2.
[173] Galloway, R.L., 'An account of some of the earliest records connected with the working of coal on the banks of the River Tyne', *AA*, new series, vol.8 (1880), pp.173-6, 179-80.
[174] Hatcher, J., *The History of the British Coal Industry, I: before 1700* (Oxford, 1993), pp.72-3.

	£	s.	d.
Leases of meadows and pastures	27	11	0
Leases of two fisheries	5	6	8
Lease of watermill		10	0
Lease of bakehouse	2	0	0
Landmale paid by burgesses	1	6	8
Income from 25 borough court sessions	1	12	4
	38	6	8

Table 2 The bailiff of Gateshead's payments to the bishop of Durham's receiver general, 1509-10. Source: DUL, CCB B/69/8

	c.1383	1509-10
	£	£
Rents of free tenants and exchequer lands	10.82	5.91
Mills	16.67	0.50
Fisheries	20.00	5.33
Borough with demesnes, pastures and meadows	22.00	32.50
Totals	69.49	44.24

Table 3 The bishop of Durham's income from Gateshead (excluding mining) in c.1383 and 1509-10. Sources: Greenwell (ed.), *Bishop Hatfield's Survey*, pp.88-9 and Table 2 (above), but the free and exchequer rents in 1509-10 (not entered in the bailiff's account) is taken from a list of 1513-14 in the Book of Great Receipt of that year (DUL, CCB B/26/3, fo.51).

the bishop. John Plummer had served as joint bailiff of Gateshead with William of Bedingham in 1362-3, and he was again bailiff, this time jointly with Walter of Hesleden, for the year 1365-6.[175] It may be, indeed, that the appointment of two bailiffs in Gateshead during the 1360s had more to do with the positive challenges of coal-working than with the negative problems of plague and depopulation. In 1364, for an annual rent of £5, the bishop allowed John and Walter the right to mine coal in Gateshead for 24 years, provided they operated only one pit at a time. He promised them timber from his park at Gateshead both for the mine workings and for building new staithes on the river. In 1367

[175]   DCM, 2.3.Spec.8, 4.3.Spec.15.

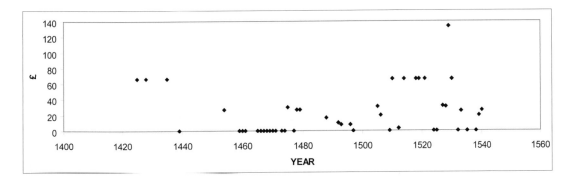

61 The Bishop of Durham's income (£) from coal-working in Gateshead, 1424-5 to 1539-40.

the bishop appointed Nicholas Coke of Newcastle as keeper and vendor of the bishop's coals within the manors of Gateshead and Whickham, in return for an annual salary of 13s. 4d., indicating some independent interest in coal-working in Gateshead on the bishop's part. And then in 1368 Roger Fulthorpe and others are recorded as digging coal on Gateshead Moor.[176] Higher workings of this sort were shafts driven in to seams exposed on the steeply rising fell side.

These various operations, implying some concerted new initiative, must have created employment, both in mining operations and in the transport of coal from the pit to the staithes. Their success, and perhaps their novelty, is suggested by the opposition they met from rival interests across the Tyne. In 1367 Plummer and Hesleden petitioned the king for help in a dispute with men of Newcastle, and were granted letters patent to protect their interests.[177] Coal mining required new carriageways at various points in the town; a lane called Collier Chare (*Colierchare*), first referred to in 1402 and 1409, which accommodated 11 burgage tenements at the time of the early 15th-century rental (Table 1), was probably a route between coal workings and the principal borough street.[178] Since the rental credits the heirs of Waleran of Lumley with one of these burgages, its origins are likely to go back at least as far as the 1350s.[179]

Revenues from coal mining in Gateshead made a considerable addition to the bishop's income from Gateshead. To judge from his rents from coal mines (Figure 61), activity was at its height in the years about 1424-35, 1513-20 and again in 1528-30. Little is known of the first of these periods, except that the lease was

---

[176] Mackenzie, *Descriptive and Historical Account*, p.747n; Wilcock, D., *The Durham Coalfield, Part 1: the 'Sea-Cole' Age*, Durham County Library Local History Publications, vol.14 (1979), p.10.
[177] Galloway, 'Account', pp.191-4, 203-4, 205-6, 207.
[178] Welford, 'Local Muniments', p.125 (1402); Walton, *Greenwell Deeds*, no.279, p.124 (1409).
[179] DUL, CCB B/21/38.

held in 1434-5 by Robert Swynburn and his partners.[180] In the second period, which followed the opening of three pits in a close called the Cornfield,[181] the enterprise was leased to a three-man consortium, Robert Adthe, William Thomlinson and William Inskip; Adthe was the bishop's clerk of works.[182] The high point of 1528-30 followed the opening of a pit on Gateshead Moor below the beacon.[183] On this occasion the principal lessee of the workings was a London merchant called John Brewke, though William Inskip was involved once more, perhaps as the more active partner.[184] In each of these periods the bishop leased the Gateshead rights for £66 13s. 4d. a year, a sum that appears to have been regarded as the fair rent whenever Gateshead's resources were fully leased. It represents an expected annual output of the order of 5,000-8,000 tons.[185] The three pits in the Cornfield produced about 5,735 tons between 20 August 1511 and 17 June 1512, when they were managed for the bishop rather than leased.[186] The only higher coal rent ever mentioned was in 1528-9, when new workings were expected to render a rent of £133 6s. 8d. This was perhaps over-optimistic, and certainly unsustained.[187]

In some years, as in 1511-12 when the receiver general's account records only £3 6s. 8d. from coal mining in Gateshead,[188] the figure was low because for much of the year the pits were worked directly for the bishop rather than leased. This means that Figure 61 cannot be used as an exact index of output. It nevertheless suggests that Gateshead's coal was not a source of sustained development and that its contribution to urban employment and incomes was erratic. In many years the bishop's mines were not fully leased, or not leased at all, for want of a tenant or because new investment was needed before work could proceed. The third quarter of the 15th century seems to have been a particularly barren period, since no income from coal rents in Gateshead is recorded in the receiver general's accounts between 1458-9 and 1473-4.[189] There was a partial revival of activity from 1474-5, when the bishop had a new pit opened on land belonging

---

[180] DUL, CCB B/1/5.
[181] DUL, CCB B/4/41, 45. The former rent owing from this close was reduced in 1510-11 and 1511-12 and then written off from 1512-13: CCB B/69/10-24.
[182] All three names are given in DUL, CCB B/4/45.
[183] DUL, CCB B/5/60.
[184] DUL, CCB B/6/63, 65. Only Brewke is mentioned as lessee in these two accounts.
[185] This is estimated from some bishop's mining accounts of Railey and Grewburn (CCB B/79/10-12), using comments on medieval weights and measures in Hatcher, *History*.
[186] DUL, CCB B/31C/220204/2, fo.94v. This records 229 keels of coal, each keel containing 20 chalders. The estimate of weight assumes the chalder weighed 25 tons: Hatcher, *History*, p.567.
[187] *Et de ... firma omnium minerarum carbonum domini apud Gateshed que modo dimittuntur Willelmo Inskip de Gateshed pro cxxxiij li. vj s. viij d. per annum non respondet hic eo quod r[eddita] est inde alibi domino [apud] London' per [Iohannem] Brake mercatorem ibidem*: DUL, CCB B/6/61.
[188] DUL, CCB B/4/41.
[189] For mid-15th century contraction of coal-working, and subsequent recovery, see Pollard, A.J., *North-Eastern England during the Wars of the Roses: Land, Society, War and Politics, 1450-1500* (Oxford, 1990), pp.75-7.

to the nuns of Newcastle,[190] but rents from mining were low again during the 1490s, and even the strong revival of activity in the early 16th century was not sustained. Other property owners in Gateshead exploited coal reserves by the late 15th century. From the late 1480s the prioress of Newcastle nunnery often paid a rent for wayleaves, and so did the master of St Edmund's Hospital from Michaelmas 1494.[191] Their activity was probably no more continuous than that of the bishop; from time to time they declined to license their wayleaves, and their activity declined significantly after 1520, even before the bishop assigned their former interests to the consortium of 1528-30.[192] Despite its discontinuity, mining activity in Gateshead encouraged investment in the infrastructure of the coal trade. From the late 15th century we hear of the bishop's staithes on the Tyne in Gateshead. One tenant paid 10s. for *stathleve* at Gateshead in 1487-8,[193] and another paid 13s. 4d. to lease a staithe there in 1490-1.[194]

Apart from mining, Gateshead had other distinctive mineral resources that supplemented the incomes to be made by craftsmen supplying the local market. The abrasive sandstone of Gateshead Fell was outstandingly good for the commercial manufacture of grindstones. This trade, for which Gateshead became internationally known in more recent times, was already established before 1435-6, when the coroner's account records an untenanted grindstone quarry from which no rent had been received.[195] A master forester's account of three years later records a more complicated situation; a quarry called *Cokewaldquarrell* was being worked on Gateshead Moor at an annual rent of £1 6s. 8d. to the bishop, and two others there called *Chilsid* and *Outlyers* were lying idle.[196] Newcastle's 15th-century customs records show that grindstones were already a regular export from the Tyne, though they do not allow an assessment of Gateshead's importance as a source.[197] As with coal mining, quarrying activity was low during the mid-15th-century depression, but it revived during the 1470s; there was a grindstone quarry on Gateshead Fell in 1476-7. Like coal mining, quarrying for grindstones was subject to stopping and starting; no one would lease the quarry in 1483. But quarrying had resumed in the late 1480s and early 1490s 'at the head of Gateshead', presumably on Gateshead High Fell.[198]

[190] DUL, CCB B/2/22.
[191] DUL, CCB B/3/30; B/31A, fo.77r.
[192] DUL, CCB B/6/61, 63.
[193] DUL, CCB B/3/30.
[194] DUL, CCB B/3/29.
[195] DUL, CCB B/44/1.
[196] DUL, B/83/1.
[197] Wade, J.F. (ed.), *The Customs Accounts of Newcastle upon Tyne 1454-1500*, SS, vol.202 (1995), pp.18, 27-9, 34-5, etc.
[198] DUL, CCB B/14, 25, 29, 30.

A new quarry was opened up in 1495, where grindstones were made on site and shipped from bishop's staithe. It was managed by Newcastle entrepreneurs, who produced 60 chaldrons of grindstones of various sizes in the first year of operations and 32 chaldrons in the second year; they were sold at 9s. a chaldron.[199] If the chaldron used was of four or six quarters,[200] 60 chaldrons was in the order of about 2,472-3,884 cubic feet of worked stone. There was a slate quarry on Gateshead Fell in 1438-9, but it was not then in operation, and was not a recurrent feature of the local economy.[201]

In short, then, the economic performance of Gateshead in the 15th and early 16th century, even taking mineral working into account, fell well short of the sort of burst of new energy that was once held to mark a transition between medieval and modern times. Levels of mining activity in the early 15th century were not obviously higher than those a century earlier, and may have been lower. The evidence of the bishop's revenues contain no hint of sustained development in any aspect of industry, mining or trade, and it is impossible to identify a period of economic transition, unless we so describe the burst of new mining activity in the later 14th century. On the other hand, Gateshead had evidently renewed its economic base in difficult times, and by 1540 was even better placed than before the Black Death to respond to the challenges of national and international markets. There were many aspects of the mining and quarrying activities of Gateshead about which we know nothing, and there were no doubt qualitative developments of geological knowledge, technology, infrastructure and organisation that elude our records. The period after 1349 launched Gateshead, as well as Whickham, as prominent centres of mining and quarrying activity, and these were to be of vital importance two centuries later in enabling the borough to participate in the economic revival of north-eastern England.

[199] DUL, CCB B/31A, fos.127v, 159v.
[200] Hatcher, *History*, p.565.
[201] DUL, CCB B/83/1.

7

The Development of Trinity House and the Guildhall before 1700

GRACE MCCOMBIE

Trinity House and the Guildhall are Newcastle's only surviving and complete secular buildings of the late medieval and early modern period. Trinity House, in Broad Chare, has been since 1505 the office and meeting hall of the Masters and Mariners of Newcastle upon Tyne. No other medieval domestic site in Newcastle has such great significance. The slow pace of alteration to Trinity House has preserved it so that evidence of earlier buildings lies within and below the present structures, and many, although not all, of the relevant records have survived to provide historical information. The present Guildhall occupies the sites of three medieval buildings: (from west to east) a house, the town hall, and a hospital with hall above. They were replaced by the 1655-8 Town Court and Chamber (the seat of government of the town), and the 1620 meeting hall of Newcastle's most powerful Company, the Merchant Adventurers, rebuilt in 1823. On the south side of Sandhill, it stood between the medieval bridge and the Lort Burn. By 1700, Newcastle's mercantile trade and sea transport were managed from these two buildings.

Trinity House

'The modest stuccoed Tudor façade does not reveal that behind it is a secluded court which transports one to some small Dutch town.'[1] Pevsner as usual got straight to the heart of the matter – in this case, the secluded courtyard. The shape of the site is the first clue before you even look at the buildings. This is now known to be a medieval courtyard house, a rare survival, possibly the only surviving example of that urban type in the northern counties, and certainly unique on Tyneside. The Guild of the Blessed Trinity acquired this property in 1505. A 16th- or 17th-century list records deeds that are now lost, and takes the building's

---

[1]   Pevsner, N., *The Buildings of Northumberland* (1957), p.244.

62 The Exchange, or Guildhall, Sandhill, as depicted in the early 19th century by William Collard.

history back as far as 1430-1.[2] The site was just west of the Pandon Burn. To the east was the vill of Pandon, added to Newcastle in 1299. To the north, the land rose steeply to the plateau on which the church of All Saints' was built, and Pilgrim Street led northwards on the east side of the Lort Burn, which now runs below Dean Street and the lower part of Grey Street. In the past the Tyne spread across the valley, lapping over ground which was eventually raised, forming the Quayside chares. Newcastle's story is one of the streams and valleys and river around which the town grew. What is seen today is a dense mass of old and new streets, and buildings of all periods, echoing the streets of earlier centuries.

Although Pevsner was probably the first to bring these buildings to the attention of a wider audience, within Newcastle they have always been appreciated – though more for their place in the history of the Master Mariners and the port of Newcastle, than for their architectural importance. Until the River Tyne Commission was established in 1850, the Company's members advised

[2] McCombie, G., 'The Buildings of Trinity House, Newcastle upon Tyne', *AA*, 5th series, vol.13 (1985), pp.163-85.

Newcastle's Council on the river's condition, especially providing measurements of its depth, and licensed the river and sea pilots that were essential for safety of men and vessels and cargoes. They set up and managed coastal buoys and markers, and most important of all, under Henry VIII's charter of 1536, built lighthouses at [North] Shields, one beside the river and the other on the high ground: if a navigator kept the two in line, he was heading into the safe channel, away from the rocks and sandbanks at the mouth of the Tyne. The expense of construction and maintenance was financed by collecting dues from all ships which came into the port of Newcastle.[3]

The Newcastle Company of Masters and Mariners, its precise title changing through time, seems to have begun as a secular guild dedicated to the Holy Trinity. Once it had acquired property, those buildings and the Company itself were often simply referred to as 'Trinity House'. It was certainly in existence before the acquisition of its present site, for in 1505 one of the three copies of that deed was to be put in the chest kept in All Saints' Church, and the 1524 deed mentioned below named 'the fraternitye and guylde of the blessed trinitye founded and established in the church of Allhallowes'.[4] It was incorporated in 1536 by charter from Henry VIII as a fraternity or guild of masters, pilots and governors of ships in honour of the Blessed Trinity.

'The Fellowship of Masters and Mariners of Newcastle upon Tyne' acquired their present site from Ralph Hebborn of Hebborn on 4 January 1505 (sometimes mistakenly said to have been in 1492, the seventh year of the reign of Henry VII).[5] Then in 1524 they acquired 'lofts and cellars' on the north side of the earlier property. Among the records of Trinity House is a paper endorsed, 'A Breviat of the Evidence belonging to the Trinitie House' in a 16th- or early 17th-century hand.[6] The first document named, dated 9 Henry V, relates to a tenement owned by John Johnson of Newcastle. Another describes the house as 'anciently called Dalton's Place', and the fifth concerns John Dalton and his wife acquiring the property in the seventh year of Edward IV's reign. Two months later they sold it to Thomas Hebborne of Hebborne (Hepburn near Chillingham). The Breviat was annotated in 1818 by 'TH' (probably the Secretary of the House), who scrawled 'lost' in the margin beside the details of all but one of the documents listed. The exception is the last, which relates to a 1524 transaction, and is marked 'remains'.[7] By it, another Thomas Hebborne had granted them further 'lofts and cellars' on

3   TNA C66/668; see also *CSPD*, vol.xi, 943, p.376.
4   TWAS GU/TH/51, formerly TWAD 659/3.
5   E.g. Brand, *Newcastle*, vol.2, p.322. For a suggested explanation of this error, see Knowles, W.H. and Boyle, J.R., *Vestiges of Old Newcastle and Gateshead* (1890), p.198.
6   TWAS GU/TH/35/3 (formerly TWAD 659/1).
7   GU.TH/51 (formerly TWAD 659/3). Quitclaim. Land at Dalton Place, 20 September 1524.

the north side of their property: those lofts and cellars were probably the upper floors of the stone building on the north side of Trinity Yard.[8]

Astonishingly, the house that was there in 1431 still stands, although modified. Fragments of its ancillary buildings are buried in the buildings around you as you stand in Trinity Yard or walk through the alley to the low yard to the south. The stone house on the north is the oldest visible structure. Between the time it was built, perhaps the 14th century, and 2008, when Trinity House's warehouses in Broad Chare became the newly enlarged Live Theatre, buildings have grown, been partly demolished, redeveloped, partly demolished, rebuilt, restored – ad infinitum, layer upon interlocking layer.

No record or other evidence is known to exist for the preceding period in which the Masters and Mariners of Newcastle upon Tyne are believed to have conducted their meetings in All Saints' Church. we only know about the deed of 1505 and its copy from just one early surviving document in the records of the House: an agreement that the men who signed the deed would build a chapel, alms houses and meeting hall on the property bought from Ralph Hebburne that same day, 4 January 1505. The document is in poor condition, but it was more legible in the early 1800s when the Secretary of Trinity House transcribed it, and his transcription was published in 1854.[9] It is still in the possession of the Master Mariners and is deposited, with most of their historic records, in Tyne and Wear Archives.[10]

The site is that of a medieval courtyard house, a rare survival, probably unique in the northern counties, and a very important part of Newcastle's history. It has three yards: Trinity Yard next to Broad Chare, the high yard at the west, and the low yard at the south. This last is reached by a gate opening off Trinity Chare, and can also be reached from Trinity Yard by an alleyway running from the main yard and turning between the south wall of the banqueting hall and the north wall of the former school to the gate into Trinity Chare. The three yards are described below as they were in 2008, followed by what is known of the site as it was before 1700.

Trinity Yard

This principal yard is entered from its east side by an alleyway leading from Broad Chare. The medieval stone house stands on the north side of the yard, its rear wall set against Dog Bank which climbs to All Saints' Church. Going

---

[8]   McCombie, 'Trinity House', p.163.

[9]   Richardson, G.B., *A descriptive catalogue of the charters, deeds of property & records belonging to the master, pilots, and seamen of the Trinity House of Newcastle-upon-Tyne* (Newcastle, 1854), pp.8-11.

[10]   TWAS GU/TH/8 (formerly TWAD 659/2). Order of the Fellowship of Masters and Mariners of Newcastle, 1505.

63 Trinity House, comprising three houses built in the 1680s, a gate and a chapel.

clockwise round the yard, the north side is the three-storey stone house, and the east side has a yard wall to a house in Broad Chare; next, on the first floor, is the 1850 secretary's office, now an exhibition room, then a broad flight of steps of 1800 to the entrance to Trinity House. A corridor to the south range bridges the entrance alleyway. The south side has a 1721 first-floor corridor from the gatehouse to the banqueting hall, and then the 1721 banqueting hall itself. Adjoining it, the west side of the yard has alms houses dated 1787 on a large plaque. Their ground floor rooms are reached from doors opening onto the yard; rooms above are reached from the yard behind, the High Yard. The north end of this range abuts the stone house.

The High Yard

A paved platform at first floor level west of the 1787 alms houses is reached by a flight of steps from the west end of the alley between the banqueting hall and the former school. At its west side there were further alms houses, designed by John Dodds and built in 1795 by William Burnup, and demolished in the 20th century. They replaced an older set of alms houses marked 'widdows houses' on a 1770 survey of Trinity House.[11] Below the yard's paving stones are brick-vaulted cellars reached from the ground floor rooms on the west side of Trinity Yard. The date of the High Yard itself is uncertain. Part of the space it occupies is marked 'Great coal yard' on the 1770 survey.

The Low Yard

Once a garden and a bowling green, later a raff yard, the yard lies behind the three Broad Chare properties which are now the premises of Live Theatre. They were built as warehouses in the 1840s to replace the three gabled houses shown on James Corbridge's map-margin illustration in 1723. Those houses were themselves built in the 1680s, replacing older houses. As with the entire Trinity House complex, fragments of many phases survive within the present structure. On the north side of the yard a three-storey brick building has its ground floor partly hidden by the present yard surface. It was built in 1753 to house the school which the house had established in 1712 so that the sons and apprentices of the brethren could be taught reading, writing and arithmetic. The yard level was raised when a block of alms houses was built in 1782 on the east side of the yard, replacing brew houses shown in 1770. On the south side of the yard the small brick structure was built for the convenience of the old men from the alms houses as they returned from the *Three Indian Kings Inn* (long demolished). Off the south-west corner, two-storey alms houses on Trinity Chare were built on the site of a brew house which Trinity House bought in the later 18th century because it needed more alms houses.

As repairs and changes have been made to the buildings, information has come to light about the medieval phase, and post-medieval developments are also better understood as research precedes development. Parts of present-day Trinity House have substantial medieval/early modern fabric, and it is known that throughout the complex, medieval fabric is incorporated into later structures.

The Stone House

The ground floor of the three-storey stone house was part of the 1505 transfer of property; the floors above are the 'lofts and cellars', transferred in 1524. The whole house is now identified as 'No. 6 Trinity House'. In the 18th century it was used as a rigging loft, where the brethren of the house could set out the hemp rigging needed for their sails. Non-members could use the facility if they

---

[11] See McCombie, 'Trinity House', Fig 1.

paid a fee. It is also known as the Dog Bank building, for its north wall lies against the cliff that street climbs. A large stone at the centre of the Dog Bank elevation is the hearth stone of the first-floor fireplace. There are no openings on that side, although it can be seen that there was once a door, now blocked, near the west end. The south elevation, now stripped of the render which covered it until the 1960s, shows

64 Trinity House, gate and chapel, detail from Corbridge's map.

earlier openings, some blocked and fitted with more recent doors and windows. The medieval door was at first floor level: its pointed arch can be discerned in the masonry above the second window from the east. It was reached by a long straight flight of stairs, shown on the 1770 plan. The lower part of the flight was turned through 90 degrees when the present curving stairs were built for the 1800 entrance; later, the ground-floor door and the stairs at the east end were inserted, and a window inserted in the door opening. Clear evidence of its age is provided not only by the first floor door and its shape, but also by the medieval rere arches of two ground floor doors (their external appearance is entirely of c.1800), and by the massive projection near the east end, a small window at first floor level indicating the presence of a closet. The closet door in the first floor hall has a medieval lintel; the projection must be a garderobe chute, and its extension up to eaves level may be evidence of collecting rain water to flush it. The roof structure has not been surveyed but is of the type found elsewhere in Newcastle (White Hart Yard in Cloth Market, and 25 the Close) in a 16th- or 17th-century context. The gables have medieval-style overlapping stone copings, that at the west with an apparently medieval finial. This is certainly the house sold in 1467 to John Dalton, known as Dalton's Place, and the ground floor sold in 1505, the upper floors in 1524, to the Mariners.[12] The Trinity and High Yards and all their structures are on land belonging to that town house.

The Chapel

It was not uncommon for important medieval town houses to have a chapel, which may have been a room within the house or may have been

---

[12] The significance of this complex is highlighted by the very interesting tree-ring dating work that has been done so far, but that must be part of a fuller survey of the early fabric of Trinity House.

a separate structure. One of the signatories of the 1524 document was 'Robert Ellison Chapelayn'. The present chapel of Trinity House was extensively refurbished in the 1630s and repaired in 1656. It is not clear from the documents if there was an earlier chapel on this site. Until the 1547 dissolution of the chantries, the Mariners had their own chantry chapel in All Saints' (or All Hallows) church. Among their earliest surviving records are references to paying the priest £4 a year, paying for the altar cloths, and

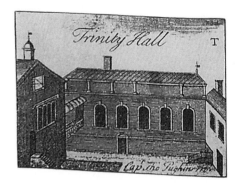

65 Trinity Hall (courtyard), detail from Corbridge's map.

finally, in 1550, 'for 'takyn downe the trinite alter and for bringing yt home'.[13] It is possible that the chapel in Broad Chare was on the south side of Trinity Yard, for in 1721 it was decided to build the new meeting room – the banqueting hall – 'over the cellars of the old chapel'. The precise meaning of 'over' was not as clear then as it is now – it need not have meant 'above'. The documents do make it certain that work was carried out to the present chapel in the 1630s. The 1723 illustration shows it had a stone-mullioned window to the yard, and a flight of stone steps climbing up its west wall to a door beside the window. This wall was modified in 1800 to build the present classical entrance. Inside, however, it can be seen that the chapel roof runs through from this west wall to the east gable on Broad Chare. Ten trees were felled in Walker Wood in 1651 to make those trusses, which are still there, with slightly bowed tie-beams. The chapel fittings – pews, pulpit, reading desk, west screen – date from 1635 when planks were bought for making them, and Richard Newlove was paid one penny for each carved cherub's head decorating them; there is also extensive use of applied fretwork.[14] There is much fine mid-17th-century carving in Newcastle and while this is not figurative and allegorical (c.f. the 'Newcastle school' overmantels such as that in the Merchant Adventurers' Hall, see below) it is accomplished work and enriches the small chapel.

[13] TWAS GU/TH/20/10 (formerly Trinity House mss 'Old Account Book 1530-1560'). 'For takyn downe the trinite alter and for bringing yt home xˢ iiᴰ'.
[14] TWAS GU/TH/21/10 (formerly Trinity House mss 'Payments 26 March 1634 – 30 December 1639') passim.

The South Range

Analysis of the visible fabric of Trinity House shows that there may have been another medieval hall on the south side of the yard, for the ground-floor cellar or undercroft below the Election Room, situated between the Gatehouse and the Banqueting Hall, has, in its west wall, three blocked stone arches. The new hall built in 1721 now fills the south side of the yard. There is no record of the building previously on that site. Nor is there any information about the designer and builders of the Banqueting Hall, but there is a tantalising note, made in the middle of the 18th century, of the contents of drawers in Trinity House; one item was a book of all the expenses of building that hall in 1721.[15] That book's whereabouts is not now known, but if found, it could give valuable information. The sash windows are remarkable, with elliptical heads and broad glazing bars; fine early Georgian sashes, and the earliest complete set in Newcastle.

The present Broad Chare is much wider than the medieval street. It covers the old chare, and spreads across the site of Stony Hill (open ground near Trinity House) and Spicer Chare to the Quayside. The present road surface covers the sites of the houses of the east side of Broad Chare and the west side of Spicer Chare. 'Broad' because it was wide enough for a cart – about the width of the present footpath – compared with other chares, which were only wide enough to allow one person to walk down them. Trinity Chare and Plummer Chare today show the narrowness of the old lanes.

South of the Trinity House gatehouse there are three large brick warehouses, now the premises of Live Theatre. In the 16th century, Trinity House received rents for three houses and yards which may have been on this site. The tenants were given notice in February 1678 (old style; 1679 by modern reckoning) and new brick houses were built.[16] Those new houses are shown in the margin of James Corbridge's map of Newcastle, as are the Chapel frontage and Trinity Yard. They were four storeys high, with 10 windows on each upper floor below shaped gables facing the street. The northernmost gable is wider than the others and covers two windows; north of the houses is the gateway to Trinity Yard. Those houses later became warehouses and were rebuilt, incorporating some older fabric, in the 1840s; the warehouses have been adapted for the Live Theatre which now uses the Election Room undercroft as a lounge: the three medieval arches are visible above a suspended part-ceiling.

[15] TWAS GU.TH/35/2 (formerly TWAD 659/665): 'Schedule of contents of Trinity House Drawers A-Q 1738'.
[16] TWAS GU.TH/9/1 (Formerly Trinity House mss. Order Book. Orders 3 March 1604-16 October 1689).

66 The Guildhall interior depicted by W.H. Knowles in 1890.

The Guildhall

The Guildhall, on Sandhill, was neither Newcastle's first town hall nor its last. Newcastle had prospered because of the coal trade. Exports from Newcastle – that is, from the River Tyne – grew rapidly. In the 17th century Sandhill was at its commercial heart, with merchants' houses along its edges and in nearby streets, and convenient for access to the town quay and the bridge to Gateshead and County Durham. The Town Wall ran along the quay from Sandgate to Sandhill, abutting the medieval Maison Dieu (east of the Guildhall); its first floor hall became the Merchant Adventurers' hall. There was thus a continuous barrier preventing vehicle access from the street to the town quay and, with the defended bridge, protecting Newcastle from southern and river-borne attackers.

Many of the town's merchants living near the water probably stored at least some of their goods in their houses and outbuildings: wills and inventories mention storage in cellars and lofts in the Quayside area. For example, Robert Lambe's inventory of February 1586 describes the contents of his shop, and also describes the contents of 'the cellar in Allhallowe

Banck' ... as 'wainskotts, English iron, soap, sweet soap, pitch, alum, sugar loaves, weights, small deals, and spruce deals'.[17] Historians of Newcastle are clear about the high status of the people who lived near the river in earlier centuries. In 1649 William Gray (in his *Chorographia*) said that there were 'many stately houses of merchants and others' in the Close (west of Sandhill), and that Sandhill was 'very convenient for merchant adventurers, merchants of coales ... In this market place is many shops, and stately houses for merchants, with great conveniences of water, bridge, garners, lofts, cellars and houses of both side of them.'[18]

Henry Bourne's *History of Newcastle* was published in 1736, three years after his death. He described Sandhill as 'that part of the Town where the chief Affairs of Trade and Business are transacted,' and said that the area was changing: 'Of late Years these Houses [in the Close] have been forsaken, and their wealthier Inhabitants have chosen the higher Parts of the Town ..., The insides of the houses speak magnificence and grandeur; the rooms being very large and stately, and, for the most part adorned with curious carving'. He recorded that on the south side of Sandhill stood 'the ancient hospital called the *Maison Dieu*' ... dedicated to St Katharine and founded by Roger Thornton in the reign of Henry IV, and that the hall and kitchen above the hospital were granted to the town's use in 1456 by [a later] Roger Thornton. Bourne also says that the hospital was conveyed to the town in 1629, quoting from the (now lost) Milbank manuscript. This reportedly noted that after the Reformation, the mayor and burgesses of Newcastle acquired part of St Katherine's Hospital, a building of stone, covered with lead, near the Tyne, and east of the Town's Chamber. Usefully, he described the Merchant Adventurers' hall as being 'adorn'd with the Arms of several generous benefactors, and some of the most curious carv'd Work in Wood'.[19]

John Brand, in his 1789 *History of Newcastle*, dedicates a fine illustration of the building to the Governor of the Merchant Adventurers.[20]

The Guildhall Exterior in 2009

The Guildhall that we see today on Sandhill is not a simple structure. It appears to be entirely of the late 18th and early 19th centuries, but appearances are deceptive.

[17]   Surtees Society 1860; LVII Inventory Robert Lambe, of Newcastle, pp.119-21.
[18]   Grey, William, *Chorographia, or a survey of Newcastle upon Tyne 1649*; 2nd edition Society of Antiquaries of Newcastle upon Tyne (1813), pp.20 and 22.
[19]   Bourne, *Newcastle*, pp.123-6.
[20]   Brand, *Newcastle*, vol.2, facing p.217.

E. Edwards delin.　　　　　　　　　　　　　　　　　　　　　　　　*J. Fittler sculp.*

To Sir Matthew White Ridley Bar.ᵗ　　　*M. P. Alderman and Governor of the Company of Merchant Adventurers*　　　*of Newcastle upon Tyne, This View of the Exchange of that Town, engraved at his Expence, is most respectfully inscribed by his very obliged & most devoted*　　　*faithful humble Servant. John Brand.*

67　The Guildhall as depicted in Brand's *History* in 1789.

It has replaced three separate earlier buildings and in addition has received many alterations. It can be thought of as being now made up of two distinct blocks: the D-plan eastern block, and the almost-rectangular western block. All is cased in ashlar but changes of style and of the way the stone is dressed indicate the many stages it has gone through to arrive at this form. The rectangular block, at west, lies between the main entrance and the lane called Watergate and is the oldest part. At its core is a building of 1655-8 by Robert Trollope but that has since been entirely refaced and its age can only be recognised from the interior. The D-plan block, east of the main entrance, is of 1823, and has a curved east end.

The north front has three storeys, the top one very much smaller than the two below. At west, five windows, at east, one, and between them a five-window projection with its three central bays pedimented. The central bay has a wide door from Sandhill. That five-bay entrance projection is part of a refurbishment designed in 1794 by William Newton and David Stephenson, the design strongly resembling that of Newton's Fenkle Street Assembly Rooms of 1786, which must have impressed the town council.[21] West of it is the rectangular block; east of it the D-plan block, a complete rebuilding of 1823 by John Dobson. The pedimented entrance bay ties the two together, indeed it successfully hides the fact that there are two buildings, further united by their Palladian style with top windows much smaller than those of the principal, first, floor. West of the projection a single-storey extension of 1897-8 fills the angle between the entrance block and the original building line, and introduces a new motif to the building, with vermiculation on the pilasters.

The south front was refaced in 1809 by John and William Stokoe in a classical style corresponding to the Stephenson and Newton work on the ground floor, with seven tall first floor windows separated by pilasters. John Dobson's 1823 work carried this style two more bays along the front to the river, but at the curved east end changed into a fully developed Greek Doric colonnade with triglyph frieze (and two upper floors). In 1823 that was open, for it held the fishmarket, transferred to this covered space from Sandhill. The two roofs over the building mark the separate parts quite clearly: the six western bays have a steeply pitched roof, hipped at the west; the eastern bays have a low-pitched roof.

The north entrance bay, facing Sandhill, was built 1794-6 by David Stephenson and William Newton, using an Adam-style pedimented unfluted giant Ionic order. West of the entrance bay, the north ground floor elevation seen now is the aisle added in 1897-8 by Armstrong & Knowles, who clad the 17th-century ground-floor arcade in sandstone, removing all Trollope's details and creating an internal colonnade supporting the wall above.[22] That wall was refaced and its old mullioned windows replaced with sashes. Also in the 1790s the present cupola was built over the entrance bay to replace Trollope's charmingly eccentric flèche, shown in engravings. The south front is less often illustrated in the 19th century, but it is certain that it was refaced in 1809 by John and William Stokoe, copying the north front but without any projection.[23]

The Early Development of the Building

To understand the building as it was before 1700 one must consider the past uses of the site. Although King John granted Newcastle a Guild Merchant in 1216, and a Guildhall was first mentioned in 1400, its location was not named.

[21] TWAS DNCP, 16/1.
[22] TWAS T186/17758.
[23] TWAS Calendar of Common Council, 1807, 25 March.

Sandhill had on its south side the bridgehead with the bridge chapel, and east of that there were houses. Next to the easternmost house was the Town House, where the mayor and burgesses of Newcastle managed both town and port. Gray established the relationship of the structures in his time, the Merchant Adventurers' hall being above the old Maison Dieu, and both adjoining the Town Court. He did not mention wood carving, but described the Merchant Adventurers' hall as 'stately'.[24]

The chamberlains' accounts show that the town house was often repaired, until eventually, in 1509, it was rebuilt. There were payments for masons' work, and trees, wood-nails, lead, laths were bought, until on 25 May the last payment was made for materials for the new house.[25] Stone, timber, wainscot (panelling) and laths had been bought, suggesting that the town house had stone walls, perhaps with timber superstructure, and panelled rooms. Brand quotes Leland who mentioned 'a square haul place' for the town.[26] Gray described that rebuilt Guildhall in 1649: 'In this Sandhill standeth the Towne-Court, or Guild-Hall ... where the major keepeth his court every Munday, and the sheriffe hath his county-court upon Wednesday and Fryday ... Under the towne-Court is a common Weigh-House for all sorts of commodities ... Neer this is the Town-House, where the Clarke of the chamber and chamberlains are to receive the revenues of the towne for coale, ballist, salt, grindstones, &c. Next adjoining is an Almes-House, called the Mason de Dieu, builded by that noble benefactor Roger de Thornton. Above which is the stately court of the merchant adventurers, of the old staple, resident at that flourishing city of Antwarpe.'[27]

In its turn, the 1509 building became inadequate. A competition seems to have been held, for the winning design was declared to be that by Robert Trollope, a mason from York. The rebuilding of the Town Hall in the 1650s was part of Newcastle's massive post-Civil War recovery, as were major changes to the houses on the north side of Sandhill. It is possible, even probable, that the Scottish artillery set up on Windmill Hills bombarded Sandhill and other parts of the town that were within range. When the Scots invaders had left, perhaps the citizens set about repairing and improving their houses and, despite no reference to such damage having so far been found in the Council's records, their town house. The houses on the north side of Sandhill seem to have been heightened and certainly

[24] Grey, *Chorographia*, pp.20-2.
[25] Fraser, C.M., *The Accounts of the Chamberlains of Newcastle upon Tyne, 1508-1511*, Society of Antiquaries of Newcastle upon Tyne (1987), pp.xxv, 61, 63-4, 78-9, 71-4, 77-8, 80, 86, 95.
[26] Brand, *Newcastle*, vol.1, p.29, n.t.
[27] Grey, *Chorographia*, p.21.

were given splendid carved overmantels at that time.[28]

Bourne said that of the total cost of £10,000, Alderman Weimoth [?Weremouth] gave £1,200. Bourne obtained information from the Town Clerk about the cost of building: in 1659 Robert Trollope was paid £9,771 and the following year a further £500. The town had paid Phineas Allen for houses which were demolished to make way for the enlarged new building, longer than its predecessor.[29]

The design was accepted in 1655 and construction lasted until 1658. In the ground floor there was the town exchange where there was a weigh-house, and where merchants met to

68   The Guildhall, a detail from Corbridge's map.

discuss business deals. It had an open arcade to Sandhill, and was sheltered by a windowed wall on the side towards the river. Above was the Town Court, and the town council chamber. On the south side, overlooking the river, one first-floor window was circular, with a sundial in its glass. Adjoining on the east was the Maison Dieu, and above that was the meeting place of the most powerful town guild, the Merchant Adventurers. The present plan was thus established: the Town Court running east-west at the west, with all the uses continuing as before, and the east end adjoining the Merchant Adventurers. The appearance from the river is captured in Buck's view of 1745: the Merchants' Court a crenellated tower, Trollope's Town Court a long hall with round turrets at each end. On the Sandhill side, Trollope managed the junction with the old east part with an ingenious stair-tower projection. As illustrated by Brand in 1789, it had twin flights of stairs with fat turned balusters set in classical arches, an upper large pointed arch, and round-arched loggias at the top. The tower rose between the loggias, to an octagonal turret and spire. Trollope's Town Court was more classical in composition if not in detail, simply five bays and two storeys above the arcaded Exchange. All arched openings were strongly rusticated.

[28]   Heslop, D., McCombie, G. and Thompson, C., *Bessie Surtees House: two merchant houses in Sandhill*, Newcastle upon Tyne (1995), p.25.
[29]   Bourne, *Newcastle*, pp.123-5.

On the north side the Sandhill stair tower gave access to the Town Court and offices to west, and to the Merchant Adventurers' hall to east, from a double stair, with balustraded open arches in the outer bays. Between them the stair tower, with arched ground floor entrance and balustraded first-floor opening and first-floor arches, rose to a clock stage. Above the clock were louvred openings. The weather vane on top of the spire was perhaps connected to a wind indicator inside the Town Court, and in Brand's illustration has a bird's nest on its top. The two-bay side walls of this stair projection, or at least that on the west which is shown in Brand's illustration, have ground floor windows and balustraded openings above to the stair and its landing. There was a shallow third level with mullioned windows. West of the stair tower, the north ground floor had rusticated columns and five round rusticated arches. On the first floor, the second bay west of the tower has unusual tracery of late Gothic style in a two-storey pointed-arch opening; other openings have casements. On the top floor there are smaller second-floor mullioned windows. East of the tower, what can be seen in the engraving has plain details of ground floor arches and upper eight-pane windows under a hipped roof, apparently leaning against a higher building with a hipped roof. The importance of the first floor, with the town's court and the council chamber, is indicated by its greater height and larger windows.

Trollope, after he won the design competition, put various suggestions to his clients, the mayor and burgesses of Newcastle. He asked 'whether your worships will have all the court paved with black and white marble or no. If we board it, your worships will never hear one another speak ...'.[30] The floor was perhaps made as he suggested, for that paving, restored, is still in place in the eastern, flat part of the court room; the date of the present furnishing of the boarded west area, with benches for judges and jury, is not known.

East of Trollope's stair tower was a very different building, which was not part of the town hall and not used for any of the town's offices. As Bourne said, it had held the Maison Dieu, or St Katharine's Hospital, founded by Robert Thornton.[31] By 1621 it had been remodelled, if not rebuilt, as the meeting hall of the Merchant Adventurers. The old hospital and the meeting hall above it were removed in the 1820s for the construction of the present east end by John Dobson, with a ground floor fish market (replacing open stalls on Sandhill) below the town's offices. Dobson copied the 1809 south front for his south side eastern bays, the first of which seems to have replaced a stair turret seen on the Buck view of 1745.

[30]   Common Council book of orders 1650-1659, TWAS MD/NC/2/2, f. 289.
[31]   Bourne, *Newcastle*, p.124.

The Present Interior of the Guildhall

Much of Trollope's building survives inside this classical shell, but the 1655-8 staircase was removed in 1794-6 when his stair tower was demolished. (The 1796 stair was itself altered in the late 19th century.) In a niche on the inner wall is a 17th-century statue of Charles II in Roman costume, which once stood on the gate tower of the old Tyne Bridge. The upper landing leads to the Town Court which was once regularly, and is now occasionally, used as a courtroom. Squares of black and white marble form the main floor, designed by Trollope but reset since the 17th century. Bourne described the Court as 'a very stately Hall', with lofty painted ceiling, a checkered marble floor, raised benches at the west end for the magistrates, and a spectators' gallery on the north side. Brand also described the raised benches, the windows on the south side, and the ceiling 'adorned with various paintings'.[32] The only paintings now on the ceiling are those of the heraldic shields decorating the hammerbeam roof. Oddly, no 18th-century account mentions the form of the roof; perhaps it was ceiled at eaves level and not as, at present, a higher level; or perhaps the roof structure was not thought worth mentioning. Bourne is the only 18th-century writer to mention the north gallery. The present arcaded gallery may not be the earlier one since there was a 19th-century decision to make a gallery in order to improve the ventilation.[33]

The court's fittings, balustrades, arcaded benches, and panelled gates and partitions, all look as though they are from the 18th century, but no documentary evidence for their date has yet been found. (Some elements may date from the 20th century.) At the centre of the north side there remains a 17th-century pointed arch of Trollope's, seen only from within the building; it has lost the Gothic tracery shown in Brand's illustration. From the lobby below that arch there is a 17th-century door at the east to a small ante room with a Tudor-arched window to the main court; at the west side of the lobby there is another such door with some original fittings and patterned raised and fielded panelling. The west door opens onto the 'Town's Chamber', the former council room, now known as the 'Mayor's Parlour'. It is a remarkable survival: the walls with painted panels, the ceiling with plaster decoration where a 'branch' motif is arranged in crosses in the interstices of richly moulded strapwork. At the west end of the room a large pedimented chimneypiece has Corinthian pilasters, and has been narrowed by the insertion of an early 19th-century chimneypiece. Late 18th-century alterations to the windows have been managed without damaging the interior.

[32] *Ibid.*, p.125; Brand, *Newcastle*, vol.1, p.29.
[33] Minutes of Common Council, MD.NC/3/3, f. 77, 15 December 1841.

At the east end of the Town Court a huge lugged doorcase leads to Dobson's reconstructed Merchant Adventurers' Court of 1823-5. It is a tall, square room of a quite different and astonishing scale. Dobson is said to have copied the 17th-century ceiling detail (the usual strapwork) but rather naughtily included the date 1620, which has been the cause of confusion. Significant Merchant Adventurers' meeting hall fittings were preserved and reinstated by Dobson. The timber chimneypiece he also copied, incorporating rearranged carvings from the magnificent original overmantel dated 1636, now recognised as one of the finest examples of the 17th-century Newcastle school of woodcarving. Its large reliefs show the Miraculous Draught and the Judgement of Solomon; smaller representations of the planetary deities are above. Anthony Wells-Cole has identified the sources of the biblical scenes as engravings by the Bolswert brothers after Rubens, the deities and side figures from a suite designed by Maarten de Vos and engraved by Crispijn de Passe the elder (whose work was also the source of plaster decoration at No. 28 the Close).[34] The wall frieze incorporates reused 17th-century carving.

The ground floor Exchange is the most altered part of the western block of the building. Nineteenth- and 20th-century alterations have removed all trace of its former structure, leaving only the fact that there are columns to support the floor above to indicate the earlier form.

Conclusion

It is both astonishing and satisfying that two major buildings in Newcastle's maritime and civic history should survive on their medieval sites. At the east end of the medieval Quayside, the courtyard of Trinity House is set back. Its membership still consists of those who are trained in managing ships, the House still carrying out duties with regard to the examining of deep-sea pilots. At Quayside's west end, where it joins Sandhill, the narrowed river no longer flows beneath the windows of the Guildhall, but Trollope's fine building, with Dobson's 1823 structure adjoining it, proclaims the importance of the site, with the river beside it; it is also a reminder that before the 20th-century Civic Centre was built, it was beside the river that the town's council and the Merchant Adventurers met to govern the town and manage its trade.

---

[34] Wells-Cole, A., *Art and decoration in Elizabethan and Jacobean England* (1997), pp.193-6.

8

The Reformation Era in Newcastle, 1530-1662

CHRISTINE M. NEWMAN

The Early Years of Reform

Medieval Newcastle was very receptive to the 'new religious impulses' which reached the town from other parts of the country and from abroad. The Lollard heresy had briefly penetrated the town by the beginning of the 15th century although the attempt by Richard Wyche to establish a Lollard network in Newcastle was quickly suppressed, signalling the end of the threat in the locality. Indeed, there was no evidence of a later 15th- or early 16th-century re-emergence of the heresy, as in some other parts of the country.[1] Neither, before 1530, was there any indication, in Newcastle, of the influence of early Protestant thought which, spreading from the continent, had begun to make an impact upon certain sections of the educated elite and the London merchant community from the early 1520s.[2] Nevertheless, by 1531 the stirrings of reform had reached the town, most probably through the medium of the port's international trading links. In November of that year the Newcastle merchant, Roger Dichaunte, was called before Bishop Tunstall in order to answer a charge of heresy. Upon being found guilty, Dichaunte confessed his guilt and abjured his heretical beliefs, some of which were clearly influenced by the new continental reformist ideas as well, perhaps, as by elements of old Lollard beliefs. They included a denunciation of the sacrifice of the Mass which, Dichaunte argued, 'stirreth the ire of God and crucifieth Christe of newe', a condemnation of the notion of purgatory and the saying of prayers for the dead, and a belief in the concepts of predestination, justification by faith alone and the priesthood of all believers.[3]

---

[1]   See above, pp.12-13.

[2]   Cross, C., *Church and People, 1450-1660* (1987), p.58.

[3]   Hinde, G. (ed.), *The Registers of Cuthbert Tunstall, Bishop of Durham, 1530-59, and James Pilkington, Bishop of Durham, 1561-76*, SS, vol.161 (1952), pp.34-6; Dickens, A.G., *Lollards and Protestants in the Diocese of York, 1509-1558* (1982), pp.14-15; Stevens Benham, L.M., 'The Durham Clergy, 1494-1540', in Marcombe, David (ed.), *The Last Principality: Politics, Religion and Society in the Bishopric of Durham 1494-1660* (1997), pp.23-4; Welford, *Newcastle and Gateshead*, vol.2, pp.123-4.

There is no evidence to indicate whether, at this time, Dichaunte's appetite for religious reform was shared by any of his fellow townsmen although, interestingly, Newcastle was one of the few places in the North to stand firm for the Crown in the Pilgrimage of Grace, the great northern rebellion which broke out a few years later, in October 1536. The town's support was regarded by the government as crucial in bolstering royal authority in the region and the King was informed how the town, 'and chiefly the mayor himself', had served him well in resisting the rebels.[4] The Pilgrimage certainly bore the outward trappings of a religious crusade although, as modern research has shown, its causes were far more complex and motivated by a multiplicity of grievances, social, economic and political as well as religious.[5] Nevertheless, as is made clear by the case of the two Franciscan Observant friars who sought to re-enter their convent during the revolt,[6] religious concerns were certainly at play in the town during this time. As Robert Brandling, the mayor of Newcastle, made clear, support for the friars was so strong that the town's governors had little choice but 'to suffer them to enter their house ... since by this action, we thought to keep the town without strife, since it hangs upon this town to stay a great part of the country'. At the same time, Brandling stressed his own opposition to this course of action and made clear how he had little time for '... our ungodly and dissembling knaves the Friars Observants ...'.[7] Given Brandling's vehement denunciation of the friars it is probable that his own religious beliefs were inclined towards reform. However, in view of his position as a prominent merchant and leading member of Newcastle's governing elite, he may also have been guided by a strong sense of expediency which saw no future in the rebel cause. His continued loyalty to the Crown ensured that Brandling was rewarded some years later when, during the Scottish wars of the late 1540s, he was one of the 'forty eight of the chief men of the army' to be knighted by the Duke of Somerset after the battle of Pinkie in 1547. Brandling represented the borough of Newcastle in the Parliaments of 1545, 1547, 1550, 1553, 1555, 1563 and remained, perhaps, the most prominent member of the town's governing body until his death in 1568.[8]

Given the confused nature of religious belief in the later years of the Henrician regime, the pace of reform was, inevitably, limited – in the North

---

[4]   *LP*, vol.11, p.486; Bush, M., *The Defeat of the Pilgrimage of Grace* (1999), pp.215-6.
[5]   See for example, Bush, M., *The Pilgrimage of Grace: a study of the rebel armies of October 1536* (1996); Hoyle, R., *The Pilgrimage of Grace and the Politics of the 1530s* (2001); Newman, C.M., *Robert Bowes and the Pilgrimage of Grace* (Papers in North Eastern History, no.7, 1997).
[6]   See above, pp.86.
[7]   *L&P*, vol.11, p.547; Bush, *Defeat of the Pilgrimage of Grace*, p.216; Welford, *Newcastle and Gateshead*, vol.2, pp.157-8.
[8]   Bindoff, S.T., *The Commons, 1508-1558* (1982), pp.486-7.

East, as in many other parts of the country. Despite the efforts of Thomas Cromwell, the King's chief minister, to encourage reform by making available the vernacular bible so that the population could study the Scriptures for themselves, progress was slow – a state of affairs not helped by the shortage of suitable priests who could '... sincerely, plainly and diligently preach the Gospel, the people so hungrily desirous to hear and learn'. This report, sent to Cromwell in November 1538, further advised him that many northern towns, including Rotherham, Leeds, Bradford, Halifax and Manchester, were lacking even 'one faithful preacher'. It went on to note that 'Newcastle and the country round is also destitute of good pastors'.[9] Within a few years, however, the spiritual fortunes of the town were to be dramatically transformed so that, for a few years at least, it was to become a 'notable centre of Protestantism'.[10]

The ultra Protestant regime of Edward VI, controlled at first by the young King's uncle, the Duke of Somerset and later by John Dudley, Duke of Northumberland, quickly sought to impose a programme of radical religious reform. An Act for the dissolution of the chantries and guilds was passed in the regime's first Parliamentary session which sat during November and December 1547, thus authorising the royal commissioners to confiscate the endowments of these institutions. Since these provided the main channels by which the laity, through the performance of their devotional and intercessory activities, participated in the life of the Church, the impact upon lay religious culture within the localities was undoubtedly profound. The shortage of clergy caused by the deprivation of the priests who served these foundations was, similarly, a further cause for concern in many communities, despite the Act's provision for the placing of such individuals.[11] Indeed, in Newcastle there had been some 25 endowments for priests to serve in chantries and other allied foundations and of these only five are known to have secured appointments as assistants in the town's churches.[12] These were the men who would be expected to shoulder much of the day-to-day burden of work within their parishes. However, many such priests were insufficiently educated and often conservative in belief, presenting the new regime with the problem of how to advance its programme of radical religious reform. In the case of Newcastle, help arrived in the guise of two Scottish preachers whose influence was to bring about the town's transformation into a centre of extreme Protestantism. The first to arrive was the former

---

[9]   *LP*, vol.13, pt 2, p.953.
[10] Cross, *Church and People*, p.93.
[11] Cross, *Church and People*, p.90; Duffy, E., *The Stripping of the Altars* (1992), pp.454-5.
[12] Welford, *Newcastle and Gateshead*, vol.2, pp.253-7, 260; Wilson, B.N., 'The Changes of the Reformation Period in Durham and Northumberland' (Ph.D. thesis, University of Durham, 1939), p.183.

Dominican friar and later Protestant martyr John Rough, who arrived in the town in 1547.[13] The second – the man destined to make the greater impact – was the charismatic Scottish Reformer, John Knox.[14]

John Rough's reputation in Scotland as a Protestant preacher had gained him the patronage of the Governor, the Earl of Arran, during the period of the Earl's short-lived flirtation with a pro-reform policy.[15] In 1546 Rough moved to St Andrew's, to act as chaplain to the Protestant rebels who had seized the castle following the murder of Cardinal Beaton. He became closely associated with John Knox, following the latter's arrival in St Andrew's in April 1547 and is credited with persuading Knox to become a Protestant preacher.[16] In the summer of the same year, Rough, who, during the 1540s, had become an agent and pensioner of Henry VIII, crossed the border into England in order to gain the patronage of the new Protestant government of Edward VI, headed by the Duke of Somerset.[17] Somerset duly renewed Rough's pension of £20 and sent him, as a preacher, to the border town of Berwick. In January 1548 he was preaching in Dumfries and from there he moved to Newcastle where he is known to have married a Scottish bride. Whilst in Newcastle he also attracted the attention of the Archbishop of York, Robert Holgate, who offered Rough a benefice in the town of Hull, 'where hee continued until the death of that blessed and good king, Edward VI'.[18] Sadly, little is known of Rough's ministry whilst in Newcastle and of the nature of his teachings. However, from his earlier preaching, it seems Rough was a staunch supporter of vernacular Scripture. Moreover, in 1547, whilst in St Andrew's both Rough and John Knox were summoned by the archbishop-elect of St Andrews to answer for their heretical beliefs which included the condemnation of the pope as an Antichrist, the assertion that the New Testament was the sole source of religion and that man could add nothing to it, an attack on Mass as an 'abominable idolatrie, blasphemous to the death of Christe and a profanation of the Lordis Supper', a denial of the existence of Purgatory and of the efficacy of praying to the saints and for the souls of the departed, and the suggestion that churchmen were not, necessarily, entitled

---

[13]   Greaves, R.L, 'Rough, John', *Oxford Dictionary of National Biography* (2004) (hereafter, *DNB*). Rough did not survive the Marian persecution of Protestants and was martyred at Smithfield in December 1557.

[14]   Dawson, J.E.A., 'Knox, John', *DNB*.

[15]   For the political background of the period see Head, D.M., 'Henry VIII's Scottish Policy: a Reassessment', *The Scottish Historical Review*, vol.61 (1982), pp.19-20.

[16]   Knox was later to note that whilst Rough was not a learned man, he was nevertheless praiseworthy for his simple and vehement condemnation of 'all impiety'. Laing, D. (ed.), *The works of John Knox*, Wodrow Society (1846-64), vol.1, pp.187-8.

[17]   Knox, *Works*, vol.1, pp.538-41; Edington, C., 'John Knox and the Castilians: a crucible of reforming opinion?' in Mason, R.A. (ed.), *John Knox and the British Reformations* (1998), pp.32-3, 36-7.

[18]   Greaves, 'Rough'; Dickens, *Lollards and Protestants*, pp.197-9; Knox, *Works*, vol.1, p.188 (n.474), 539.

to tithes. Rough was not a particularly educated man and in St Andrews he had relied to a great extent upon Knox's assistance in preparing his sermons.[19] Nevertheless, he appears to have shared many of Knox's religious opinions and some of these, at least, undoubtedly found their way into the sermons he preached to his Newcastle congregation.

Whilst Rough was preaching in the North, John Knox was serving his time as a prisoner of the French, the French fleet having captured St Andrew's Castle in July 1547. Sentenced to work on the galleys, he was released in February 1549 and came to England. His reputation as a staunch Protestant and virulent opponent of Catholicism ensured that he, too, received a warm welcome from the increasingly hard line reformist government of Edward VI which, keen to recruit able preachers to send to the more religiously conservative parts of the

69 Title page from a 1559 copy of John Knox's *Epistle to the inhabitants of Newcastle and Barwicke* (1558).

country, awarded Knox the sum of £5 and dispatched him to Berwick to serve as a preacher there. In Berwick he quickly attracted a ready-made congregation of Scottish Protestant refugees, who, seeking sanctuary, had made accommodation with the English regime during the period of Anglo-Scottish warfare in the late 1540s, known as the 'Rough Wooing'.[20] Whilst his radical liturgical innovations and charismatic preaching delighted his loyal band of Protestant followers, Knox incurred the wrath of the theologically conservative Bishop of Durham, Cuthbert Tunstall, in whose diocese Berwick lay. Particularly offensive to Tunstall was Knox's denunciation of the concept of the sacrifice of the mass and his denial of the existence of the Real Presence in the sacrament, issues which, due to the

[19]   Knox, *Works*, vol.1, pp.193-4; Edington, 'John Knox and the Castilians', pp.36-7.
[20]   Dawson, J., 'Anglo-Scottish protestant culture and integration in sixteenth-century Britain', in Ellis, S.G. and Barber, S. (eds), *Conquest and Union: Fashioning a British State, 1485-1725* (1995), p.97.

ambiguous nature of the 1549 Act of Uniformity, remained hotly debated points of theological debate. Indeed, one of the innovations Knox had introduced was that of seated Communion and the replacement of the Communion wafer with ordinary bread. As a result, in April 1550, Knox was summoned to Newcastle to appear before the Council of the North, in order to defend his opinions. This he did, stressing the necessity of scriptural validation as a prerequisite for all religious practices. This 'rigid biblical model' of belief was to form the basis of his teaching thereafter.[21]

This public exposition and defence of his beliefs brought Knox even greater celebrity, thereby serving to silence his critics, and he continued preaching at Berwick until the spring of 1551 when he was transferred to Newcastle, where he was to preach in the church of St Nicholas whose congregation included members of the town's ruling elite. The town was also home to a substantial community of fellow Scots, thus providing Knox with another ready-made congregation of loyal followers.[22] In December 1551 he was appointed as one of the six royal chaplains to Edward VI, requiring him to spend part of his time in London. Knox, nevertheless, retained his connections with the locality, not least, perhaps, because he had formed a close association with the Bowes family and in particular with Elizabeth Bowes, wife of Richard, captain of Norham Castle, whose daughter, Marjorie, Knox was later to marry.[23] In 1553 his preaching ministry was cut short by the death of Edward VI and the accession of the Roman Catholic Mary Tudor.[24] Nevertheless, during Knox's ministry in Berwick and Newcastle he instituted what was probably a unique and certainly highly radical form of worship that amounted to nothing less than, 'an alternative, publicly unauthorised religious rite, regularly celebrated in a public place'.[25] In 1558, in a letter to the inhabitants of both towns, Knox himself prompted them to recall those days, when they had been, 'partakers of the Lord's Table, prepared, used and ministred in all simplicitie … as Christ Jesus dyd institute and as it is evident that Sainct Paul dyd practice'.[26]

---

[21] Knox, *Works*, vol.3, pp.29-70; Dawson, 'Knox'; Welford, *Newcastle and Gateshead*, vol.2, p.272.

[22] Dawson, 'Knox'. The number of Scots living in Newcastle primarily because of Knox's presence there was a cause of concern to the Duke of Northumberland, by this time the predominant power within the government, and in October 1552 he suggested that Knox be given the bishopric of Rochester in order to remove him from the North. Welford, *Newcastle and Gateshead*, vol.2, pp.287-9.

[23] Collinson, P., 'John Knox, the Church of England and the Women of England', in Mason (ed.) *John Knox*, pp.74-96; Newman, C.M., 'The Reformation and Elizabeth Bowes: a study of a sixteenth century northern gentlewoman', *Studies in Church History*, vol. 27 (1990), pp.325-33.

[24] Although away from the region at the time of Edward's death, Knox returned to the North until the beginning of 1554 when he went into exile. Dawson, *Knox*.

[25] Collinson, 'John Knox', p.88.

[26] Quoted in Collinson, *Knox*, p.88. See Knox's *Epistle to the Inhabitants of Newcastle and Barwicke* (1558) in Knox, *Works*, vol.5, p.480.

Knox's ministry in the North coincided with the attempt, by the Duke of Northumberland, the predominant power within the Edwardian regime, to deprive Bishop Tunstall and dissolve the diocese of Durham in order to extend and consolidate his own authority within the North.[27] According to the Duke's plan, the see of Durham was to be replaced by two new ecclesiastical jurisdictions, the bishoprics of Durham and Newcastle upon Tyne, the former to be endowed with lands and property to the value of 2,000 marks and the latter, one thousand. Newcastle was also to become a city, befitting its new status. A church, to be called 'the cathedral church of Newcastle-upon-Tyne and the see of the bishopric thereof', was also to be provided as was the creation of a suitably endowed dean and chapter.[28] The dissolution of the diocese of Durham was sanctioned by an Act of Parliament in 1553 and, although the Act did not provide for the establishment of the two new bishoprics, it gave authorisation for these to be created by Letters Patent. A second Act, sponsored by the burgesses of Newcastle, provided for the annexation of the Bishop of Durham's borough of Gateshead to Newcastle.[29] As such, for slightly more than a year from March 1553, the diocese of Durham did not exist, although the creation of the two new bishoprics and the plan for the annexation of Gateshead was not followed through. There is no way of knowing whether Northumberland's plan would, ultimately, have succeeded if Edward VI had lived. In the event, the young King died in July and in line with the re-establishment of Catholicism under Mary, the see of Durham was restored, Bishop Tunstall was reinstated and the Edwardian Acts pertaining to the dissolution repealed.[30]

The Establishment of Protestantism

The Marian regime was characterised not only by the restoration of Catholicism but also the persecution of Protestants, resulting in the executions of nearly 300 men and women who were burned for heresy during the course of the reign. These were, however, concentrated almost exclusively in the south for although some northerners were among the victims there was only one execution across

[27]   The episode is discussed in detail in Loades, D., 'The Dissolution of the Diocese of Durham, 1553-4', in Marcombe (ed.), *Last Principality*, pp.101-16; Trevor-Roper, H.R., 'The Bishopric of Durham and the Capitalist Reformation', *Durham University Journal*, new series, vol.8 (1945), pp.45-58; *Victoria County History of Durham*, 4 vols (1905-2004) (hereafter, *VCH Durham*), vol.2, pp.164-5.

[28]   Welford, *Newcastle and Gateshead*, vol.2, pp.288, 297.

[29]   Newton, D., *North-East England, 1569-1625* (2006), p.104; Loades, 'Dissolution of the Diocese of Durham', pp.105-6, 108; Welford, *Newcastle and Durham*, vol.2, pp.293-9, 305-9.

[30]   Loades, 'Dissolution of the Diocese of Durham', pp.105-6, 108; Welford, *Newcastle and Gateshead*, vol.2, pp.293-9, 305-9.

the whole of the northern counties.[31] In reality, since Protestantism had so little time to make an impact, many of the region's inhabitants, as elsewhere, probably reverted easily to the old forms of religious observance, a state of affairs that changed little during the early years of Elizabeth's reign. Indeed in 1560 it was reported that, despite an injunction ordering their removal, many altars were still standing in the Newcastle area.[32] The task of breaking down this resistance to change and re-imposing Protestantism, as enshrined in the 1559 Elizabethan religious settlement, fell, in the first instance, upon the shoulders of the new Bishop of Durham, the zealous Protestant James Pilkington, translated to the see in 1561.[33]

The Bishop's difficulties were not eased by the perennial problem of the shortage of suitable priests. In 1563 a report sent by Thomas Randolph, the Queen's ambassador in Scotland, warned her secretary of state, Sir William Cecil, of the threat from Scottish Catholic priests who, following the establishment of Protestantism in Scotland were taking refuge across the border. One in particular, John Black, a former friar, having been banished from his homeland, had found shelter in Northumberland in the home of 'the old Lady Percy', mother of the Earl of Northumberland, where he said Mass at Easter and ministered to as many as came.[34] The following year, in a report to the Privy Council, the Bishop confirmed his own fears regarding this ongoing threat. As he pointed out, the Scottish priests were prepared to take smaller wages than others and continued to do great harm in perpetuating the survival of papist beliefs. This was not the only threat, however, for Pilkington also expressed concern over the great number of scholars from the region who, having gone overseas to study in Louvain, were sending back Catholic books and writings and apparently shipping them through Newcastle. The Bishop revealed that the young men were being supported by '... the hospitals of ... newcastell', with the '... wealthiest of that towne' and this shire as it is judged ... be[ing] their nere cousins'.[35] Pilkington's accusations probably centred on the hospital of St Mary the Virgin, in Westgate, whose master, John Raymes, a former fellow of St John's College Cambridge, had been presented to the living in 1558 by his

---

[31] Cross, *Church and People*, pp.112-3; Dickens, *Lollards and Protestants*, pp.221-2; Guy, J., *Tudor England* (1990), p.238.

[32] Marcombe, D., '"A Rude and Heady People": the local community and the Rebellion of the Northern Earls', in Marcombe (ed.), *Last Principality*, pp.131-2; Wilson, 'Changes of the Reformation Period', p.456.

[33] For his career see David Marcombe, 'Pilkington, James', *DNB*.

[34] *CSP Foreign* (1563), p.381; Marcombe, '"A Rude and Heady People"', p.137; *VCH Durham*, vol.2, pp.35-6.

[35] Bateson, M. (ed.), 'Collection of Original Letters from the Bishops to the Privy Council, 1564', *Camden Miscellany*, vol.10 (1895), p.6; Howell, R., *Newcastle upon Tyne and the Puritan Revolution* (1967), p.64. A number of English Catholic academics had settled in Louvain and it had become a centre for Catholic literature and propaganda. Bossy, J., *The English Catholic Community, 1570-1850* (1975 repr. 1979), p.12.

uncle, John Swinburne of Chopwell, in County Durham, an avowed papist who had been fined in 1562 for harbouring a priest.[36] Both men were subsequently implicated in the Northern Rising of 1569 with Swinburne, a prominent rebel, later being attainted for treason, although he managed to escape to Flanders, where he died in exile. By 1567 Raymes, too, had sought refuge in Louvain, but was back in the North by 1569 when he was committed to Durham gaol during the time of the rebellion.[37] The hospital was granted a new charter in 1611, when it was refounded as an alms house for poor, unmarried old men. The preamble to the charter noted how the original charters, grants and letters patent concerning the ancient foundation of the hospital were lost at the time of Raymes's arrest in 1569.[38]

Despite the evidence of papist activity in the town, the Bishop of Durham's written return to the Privy Council in 1564 noted that, in terms of religious conformity, the ruling elite of Newcastle, unlike much of the North East, was obedient to the laws and diligent in its governance.[39] We have no way of knowing whether the influence of Knox lay behind the townsmen's conformist stance although, as has been suggested, the Reformer's charismatic ministry in Newcastle may well have lain foundations sufficiently strong to survive the years of the Marian regime.[40] At the same time, however, as in 1536, there may also have been a degree of political pragmatism at work in the collective mind of a wealthy merchant clique which saw little advantage in antagonising the ruling regime.[41]

Nevertheless, Bishop Pilkington and his successor, Richard Barnes, appeared to be aware of the town's potential in terms of the legacy of religious reform bequeathed to the town by Knox. As such, during their respective episcopates, much emphasis was placed upon resurrecting and revitalising its reformist heritage. To this end, a succession of ultra Protestant preachers was appointed as vicars of Newcastle.[42] The incumbent upon Pilkington's arrival in the North was William Salkeld, who had been vicar of St Nicholas' since 1553. However, immediately upon his death in 1568, the prominent Scottish preacher John

---

[36] At the Dissolution the hospital fell into the hands of the Corporation who maintained it and appointed its masters. The advowson was granted to patrons who took it in turn to present their candidate. Welford, *Newcastle and Gateshead*, vol.2, pp.235-6, 514; Marcombe, "'A Rude and Heady People'", pp.135, 137.

[37] Sharp, C. (ed.), *The 1569 Rebellion; being a reprint of the Memorial of the Rebellion of the Earls of Northumberland and Westmoreland (1840)* (1975), pp.33, 263-4; Brand, *Newcastle*, vol.1, p.81; Welford, *Newcastle and Gateshead*, vol.2, 329, 414, 514.

[38] The Royal Grammar school, endowed by Thomas Horsley, a former mayor of Newcastle, was also situated here, having previously been sited in St Nicholas' churchyard. Brand, *Newcastle*, vol.1, pp.86-7.

[39] Bateson (ed.), 'Letters from the Bishops', p.67.

[40] See the discussion in Newton, *North East England*, pp.127-8.

[41] See above, p.190.

[42] Howell, *Newcastle*, p.79.

Mackbray (or Macbrair) was appointed to the living.[43] A committed Protestant, Mackbray had fled to Frankfurt to escape the Marian persecutions where he began preaching to the English congregations of exiles based there. Upon his return to England in 1559 he preached at St Paul's Cross on a number of occasions and, by 1564, was serving as chaplain to John Best, Bishop of Carlisle (who held the patronage of the vicarage of Newcastle). In 1565 he moved to the diocese of Durham, having obtained a preferment as vicar of Billingham which, thereafter, remained in his hands.[44] Mackbray, who was inducted to the vicarage of St Nicholas in November 1568, was, reputedly, a friend of John Knox, and was, apparently, as gifted in the art of preaching as his eminent predecessor. Indeed, he was one of the prominent preachers enlisted by Bishop Barnes, in 1578-9, to participate in a special programme of sermons designed to further eradicate 'evidence of ignorance and Catholicism' across the diocese.[45] Barnes, troubled by the slow pace of religious reform within his diocese, sought to establish a number of other measures, including one to improve the standard of preaching, especially amongst the unbeneficed clergy, many of whom were poorly educated. As a result some 96 clergymen across the diocese were required to undergo an oral examination based upon St Matthew's Gospel.[46] The number of clergy in Newcastle, as listed at the episcopal visitation of 1577, was small with John Mackbray, as vicar, having only one curate, Thomas Kay, to assist him at St Nicholas'. The curate of All Saints', Cuthbert Ewbanke, also had an assistant, but George Gray at St John's and Bartholomew Cowghram at St Andrew's managed their cures alone.[47] In July 1578, at a visitation held by Robert Swift, chancellor of the diocese, in St Nicholas' Church, the town's curates were all examined – in Latin, if they knew the language, or else in English. Thomas Kay,[48] Cuthbert Ewbanke and Bartholomew Cowghram had not finished their studies and were given until Michaelmas to complete the task (although it is not clear whether the matter was taken any further.) Only George Gray showed no evidence of

[43] Hinde (ed.), *Registers of Cuthbert Tunstall ... and James Pilkington*, p.168; Knox, *Works*, vol.1, p.530; Bourne, *Newcastle*, p.73 (where his name is given as 'Magrey'); Welford, *Newcastle and Gateshead*, vol.2, p.301, 422.

[44] Brand, *Newcastle*, vol.1, p.303; Welford, *Newcastle and Gateshead*, vol.3, pp.16-17; Longstaffe, W.H.D. (ed.), *Memoirs of the life of Mr Ambrose Barnes, late merchant and sometime Alderman of Newcastle upon Tyne*, SS, vol.50 (1866), p.284.

[45] Raine, J. (ed.), *Injunctions and Ecclesiastical Proceedings of Richard Barnes, Bishop of Durham*, SS, vol.22 (1850), pp.85, 92.

[46] Tillbrook, M.J., 'Aspects of the government and society of County Durham, 1558-1642' (Ph.D. thesis, University of Liverpool, 1981), vol.2, pp.442-3.

[47] Raine, *Injunctions*, p.42. The visitation records also mentioned four schoolmasters, Humphrey Gray and Thomas Boswell who presumably taught at the Royal Grammar School. The school, endowed by Thomas Horsley, a former mayor of the town, was, at this time, situated in St Nicholas' churchyard, later moving to St Mary's Hospital. Brand, *Newcastle*, vol.1, pp.86-8.

[48] He died in 1586. His short will is printed in Welford, *Newcastle and Gateshead*, vol.3, p.36.

70   St John's vicarage.

compliance in respect of the required tasks and was pronounced contumacious by the Chancellor.[49]

At the time of Mackbray's death in 1584, the congregation of St Nicholas' Church, as in the past, was once again swelled by the arrival of a number of Scottish exiles, who had fled in the wake of the passing of the 'Black Acts', which had reinstated episcopal authority in the Kirk. During their stay in Newcastle, three of the exiles set up a Presbyterian congregation organised according to the strict Genevan mode of worship, thus consolidating further Knox's legacy of ultra Protestant reform in Newcastle.[50] It is not clear how long this state of affairs survived, but it almost certainly provided some continuity of worship for the congregation until the appointment of the new vicar. This was another ultra Protestant minister, Richard Holdsworth, who had been suspended for a while in 1584 because of his nonconformity. At the beginning of 1585 he had been appointed chaplain to the puritan Earl of Huntingdon, President of the

[49]   Raine, *Injunctions*, pp.70-1.
[50]   Welford, *Newcastle and Gateshead*, vol.3, pp.27-8; Lynch, M., *Scotland: A New History* (1992), pp.230-1; Newton, *North-East England*, p.127; Howell, *Newcastle*, p.79.

ST. NICHOLAS CHURCH,
INTERIOR.

71 The nave of St Nicholas' Church stripped of Romish furniture by William Collard.

Council in the North, whose influence was undoubtedly behind Holdsworth's appointment to the church of St Nicholas.[51] The role of the Earl of Huntingdon in advancing the cause of Protestant reform within the North, both through the administrative machinery of the Council in the North and the Ecclesiastical High Commission and through his private patronage of puritan preachers, is well known.[52] In Newcastle his influence was again brought to bear, this time in favour of the radical nonconformist preacher John Udall who, in 1588, was invited by the townsmen to take up his ministry there, having been deprived of his previous position, as lecturer in Kingston upon Thames, because of his extremist Presbyterian opinions. In Newcastle he conducted his ministry in conjunction with Holdsworth and James Bamford, another preacher. However, his stay in the town was short for in early 1590 he was accused of the authorship of a tract, *The Demonstration of Discipline*, published in 1588, by the notorious

[51] Brand, *Newcastle*, vol.1, p.304; Cross, M.C., 'Noble Patronage in the Elizabethan Church', *The Historical Journal*, vol. 3:1 (1960), pp.4, 9; Welford, *Newcastle and Gateshead*, vol.3, p.109.
[52] See for example, Reid, R.R., *The King's Council in the North* (1921); Cross, M.C., *The Puritan Earl* (1966).

Marprelate Press. Summoned to London by the Privy Council, Udall was tried for disseminating a 'wicked, scandalous libel' and sentenced to death. Whilst the sentence was not carried out, he died in prison some two years later.[53]

By the closing decade of the 16th century the Corporation of Newcastle, in company with those of an increasing number of other towns, had begun to fund stipends in order to attract and retain the services of suitable preachers. This development not only allowed for the further provision of good quality sermons, in addition to those provided by the incumbents, it was also evidence of the growing assertiveness of the laity in seeking to influence clerical provision.[54] In the Newcastle accounts there is evidence of payments to lecturers from the 1590s. In February 1594 and March 1596, for instance, payments of £10 were made to the preacher, James Bamford, for his quarterly stipend.[55] In the latter year the Corporation also paid a similar stipend to 'Richard Holdsworth, preacher', suggesting that it was also supplementing his salary as vicar.[56] In 1598 another preacher, William Pierson, who subsequently married Holdsworth's daughter, was also granted payment 'of his quarterage'. By 1606 Pearson was employed as the 'afternoon preacher at St Nicholas' and was still receiving a quarterly stipend from the Corporation. Whilst his appointment as lecturer required the assent of the bishop, the town did reserve the right to nominate his replacement when the post became vacant. Initially, it seems the town's contribution was for the maintenance of a morning lecture, with the parish paying for the afternoon sermon. Subsequently, however, the Corporation increased the lecturers' salary and provided a further allowance to provide for both morning and afternoon lectures. In 1604 William Pierson was noted as both lecturer and curate at All Saints' Church where, it is suggested, the holding of a lectureship did not disqualify him from holding other preferments. The same situation seemingly pertained at St Nicholas' Church.[57]

Other preachers appeared, from time to time, in the early 17th-century records. Two of these – John Knaresdayle, who died in 1604, and Alexander Leighton, preacher at the church of All Saints' in 1610 and St Nicholas' in 1612

[53] Longstaffe, *Memoirs*, p.127; Cross, 'Noble Patronage', p.12; Cross, Claire, 'Udall, John', *DNB*; MacCulloch, D., *Reformation: Europe's House Divided, 1490-1700* (2003), p.387; Welford, *Newcastle and Gateshead*, vol.3, pp.57-8.

[54] Lamburn, D., '"Digging and Dunging": Some aspects of Lay Influence in the Church in the Northern Towns' in Wood, D. (ed.), *Life and Thought in the Northern Church, c.1100-c.1700* (1999), pp.365-80.

[55] Bamford's later expulsion from the town was noted in the pamphlet, *Christ Ruling in the Midst of his Enemies*, written in 1643 by the Presbyterian Colonel John Fenwick. Longstaffe, *Memoirs*, p.299; Howell, *Newcastle*, pp.81-2.

[56] Holdsworth died, apparently of plague, a few months later and was buried in St Nicholas' Church in September 1596. He was succeeded as vicar by William Morton. Longstaffe, *Memoirs*, pp.296-7; Cross, 'Noble Patronage', pp.4, 9.

[57] Longstaffe, *Memoirs*, p.300; Welford, *Newcastle and Gateshead*, vol.3, pp.94, 106-7, 131, 164-5. The lectureships were still in existence in Brand's time. Brand, *Newcastle*, vol.1, p.312.

NEWCASTLE AND GATESHEAD BEFORE 1700

— were described as dissenters.[58] John Shaw, lecturer at St John's Church in 1614, was paid a quarterly salary by the Corporation with the arrangement continuing for several years thereafter. At the time of his death in 1637, Shaw was curate at St John's.[59] William Swan, a lecturer, was buried at All Saints' in 1623 and in 1628 the dissenting preacher, Robert Slingsby, was buried in St Nicholas' Church.[60]

Catholic Recusancy

Whilst Newcastle was supporting a succession of godly Puritan preachers the authorities were, at the same time, seeking to eradicate the ongoing problem of Catholicism. Unlike much of the North, the town had refused to support the rebel cause during the Northern Rebellion of 1569, which had strong overtones of Catholic conspiracy. There were some piecemeal instances of support for the rebels in the town. For example, the gentleman George Lassells was granted a pardon in 1570 and, as already noted, the Catholic sympathiser, John Raymes, master of St Mary's Hospital, was imprisoned in Durham gaol. 'Young Gray', son of the schoolmaster – who was later to take refuge in Louvain – was also suspected of being sympathetic as were a number of individuals 'that are towards the Earl of Westmorland'.[61] Nevertheless, the vast majority of Newcastle's inhabitants remained loyal to the Crown. John Carvell, a captain of the garrison at Berwick who had been sent at the request of the mayor and townsmen to defend the town, reported to Cecil that '... I fynde both the Mayor, Majestrats and commonalty so willing and ready in the Quenes Majesty, our Soverayns behalf, as it wold do a man good to see them so fyrme and true ...'. Moreover, some of the town's more committed Protestants took to the streets to demonstrate against those with Catholic sympathies. The matter was only resolved when Richard Hodgson of Hebburn, 'a rank papist', was removed from the town.[62]

As with the Pilgrimage of Grace, the causes of the Northern Rebellion were complex, cutting across the socio-economic, political and religious spheres.[63] Recent research has pointed out that it was the latter theme, characteristic of the revolt's 'popular component', that was to be taken up by Protestant polemicists, providing further fodder for the 'anti-Catholic rhetoric' that was to become

[58] Welford, *Newcastle and Gateshead*, vol.3, p.94; Longstaffe, *Memoirs*, pp.300, 302-3.
[59] Brand, *Newcastle*, vol.1, p.118; Welford, *Newcastle and Gateshead*, vol.3, p.348.
[60] Longstaffe, *Memoirs*, pp.300, 302-3, 308, 313.
[61] Welford, *Newcastle and Gateshead*, vol.2, p.431; Sharp, *1569 Rebellion*, p.273; Wilson, 'Changes of the Reformation Period', p.498.
[62] Sharp, *1569 Rebellion*, pp.57-8, 77; Wilson, 'Changes of the Reformation Period', p.499.
[63] Marcombe, 'Rude and Heady People', pp.117-51.

ingrained in the national consciousness for generations to come.[64] The foundations of such rhetoric had already been set down in the writings of John Foxe, whose account of the Marian persecutions was in print, in Latin, by 1559 and in English by 1563.[65] Fears concerning Catholics were to intensify further from 1570 with the papal excommunication of the Queen and the launch, in the mid-1570s, of the determined Counter Reformation attack, spearheaded by the influx of seminary priests trained in the English Colleges at Douai (later relocated to Rheims) and Rome, to bring England back into the papal fold. They were joined, in 1580, by the first of the English Jesuits: an order whose members were regarded as the front line troops of the Counter Reformation. As a result, the penal Acts of 1581 and 1585 imposed increasingly harsh punishments on recusants and directed the full force of the treason laws against seminary priests and Jesuits.[66]

Throughout the 1580s, a decade characterised by the external threat of confrontation with Spain and internal fears of Catholic plotting, recusants were subjected to increased persecution.[67] In Newcastle the vigilance of Henry Sanderson, a customs official and free burgess of Newcastle, did much to undermine recusant activity in the locality. In 1589 Sanderson halted the activities of a group responsible for the trafficking of Jesuits and seminary priests through the port of South Shields. He also disrupted the dissemination of smuggled Catholic literature in Newcastle.[68] Sanderson was fiercely anti-Catholic, although he seems also to have been motivated as much by his desire to expand his coal-owning interests, these having been undermined by the Grand Lessees, some of whom he also denounced as papists. Sanderson was not mistaken in this for amongst the lessees was the 'rank papist' Richard Hodgson of Hebburn. Other prominent coal-owning families with recusant connections were the Jenisons, Riddells and Selbys.[69] Sanderson's success in destabilising the recusant cause was, however, undeniable and he was subsequently rewarded with leases of recusant lands and episcopal coal mines in Durham.[70]

It was at this time, too, that the first executions of seminary priests were carried out in the town. The first to die was Joseph Lambton who, at 24, was one of the youngest priests to be martyred. He had been apprehended in

[64] Kesselring, K.J., '"A Cold Pye for the Papistes": Constructing and Containing the Northern Rising of 1569', *Journal of British Studies*, vol.43 (2004), p.441 and *passim* pp.417-43; Newton, *North-East England*, p.122.

[65] Cross, *Church and People*, pp.122-3.

[66] MacCulloch, *Reformation*, p.391.

[67] *Ibid.*, pp.385-6; 391-3.

[68] James, M., *Family, Lineage and Civil Society* (1974), pp.159-60. For evidence of later recusant activity in this sphere see below, pp.292-3.

[69] Documents pertaining to the dispute are printed in Welford, *Newcastle and Gateshead*, vol.3, pp.33, 112-23, 124-5, 132-3; James, *Family, Lineage*, pp.138-41.

[70] Howell, *Newcastle*, p.40; James, *Family Lineage*, pp.159-60; Newton, *North-East England*, pp.103-4, 132, 137.

Remains of the Hospital of St Mary Magdalen, Newcastle.

72 Ruins of the dissolved hospital of St Mary Magdalen in the 18th century.

Westmorland with a fellow priest, Edward Waterson, and then transferred to Newcastle where he was put to death in July 1592. As details in the municipal accounts make clear, his execution was an extremely bloody and cruel affair. Waterson, the next to suffer, was executed in a similar fashion in January 1593.[71] In July 1594 the execution of another priest, John Ingram, took place in Gateshead and there were further executions at Durham and Darlington.[72]

Whilst such executions continued in England throughout the remainder of Elizabeth's reign, no further instances occurred in the town. On the accession of

[71] Anstruther, G., *The seminary priests: a dictionary of the secular clergy of England and Wales, 1558-1850* (c.1968-77), vol.1, pp.204-5, 371-2; Longstaffe, *Memoirs*, pp.293, 294-5.

[72] In the same month John Boste was executed in Durham whilst the Catholic layman, George Swallwell, was put to death in Darlington. Anstruther, *Seminary Priests*, vol.1, pp.43-4, 182-5.

James I hopes were high amongst English Catholics for an accommodation with the new regime, but these were soon dashed by the news of the Gunpowder Plot. Far worse, for the county of Northumberland, was the discovery that Thomas Percy, kinsman of the Earl of Northumberland and the earl's receiver for the county, was one of the conspirators. No one from the town was implicated although a number of Percy's followers were indicted before a session of gaol delivery held in Newcastle in January 1606 and subsequently executed.[73] Despite the persecution which followed in the wake of the Gunpowder Plot, Tyneside Catholics retained their commitment to their faith. Recusant numbers in the diocese of Durham overall appear to have fallen after the Plot, only to increase again during the following decade. In August 1615 the Bishop of Durham, William James, noted the 'Flocking of priests, even in a walled town like Newcastle, where, a few years ago, was not one recusant'. This, the Bishop suggested, was due to the King's leniency towards priests – an approach in line with James's royal foreign policy aims which sought peace with Spain.[74] The following year, William Morton, vicar of Newcastle and archdeacon of Durham, added his warnings regarding the dangers of popery, noting how recusants 'can import and export as they will' through the ports of Hartlepool, Sunderland and Tynemouth.[75]

As already discussed, several of the town's leading coal owners and other members of the elite had Catholic sympathies and connections, thus forming a close-knit interest group which helped shield some of the more prominent local recusants from the full force of the penal laws.[76] By such means the recusant gentlewoman, Mrs Dorothy Lawson, was able to establish what was, in essence, a Jesuit mission in her home at St Anthony's, near Newcastle on the north bank of the Tyne. Mrs Lawson was the wife of Roger Lawson esquire, originally of Brough in North Yorkshire and later of Heaton.[77] Her pedigree, one of obstinate recusancy, was impressive, with both her mother and mother-in-law featuring amongst the group of prominent Yorkshire gentlewomen who were imprisoned for recusancy by the Earl of Huntingdon in 1592.[78] Her husband, who was conformist in religion, died around 1613 and at some point thereafter she moved to St Anthony's. Here she observed a full programme of daily Masses and other

[73] Watts, S.J., *From Border to Middle Shire, Northumberland 1586-1625* (1975), pp.143-5.
[74] *CSPD*, 1611-18, p.302.
[75] *Ibid.*, 1611-18, p.395; Welford, *Newcastle and Gateshead*, vol.3, pp.107, 209, 210-11, 213-14, 231.
[76] Reid, D.S., 'The Durham Church Establishment: The Gentry and the Recusants, 1570-1640', *Durham County Local History Society*, vol.22 (1978), p.28.
[77] Palmes, W. and Richardson G.B. (ed.), *The Life of Mrs Dorothy Lawson of St Antony near Newcastle-upon-Tyne, in Northumberland* (1851).
[78] Newman, C.M., 'The Role of Women in Early Yorkshire Recusancy: A Reappraisal', *Northern Catholic History*, vol.30 (1989), p.11.

devotions for family, neighbours, servants and visitors. She also harboured a procession of priests, mainly Jesuits, including Richard Holtby, the Superior of the Society of Jesus, who was persuaded by her to lay the first stone of the new chapel erected at St Anthony's.[79] The author of the hagiographical memoir, *The Life of Mrs Dorothy Lawson*, was William Palmes, S.J., who served as her chaplain for some seven years.

In 1625, two of Mrs Lawson's chaplains were arrested and it was around this time that Bishop Neile wrote to the Privy Council, advising them of the dangerous network of recusant houses belonging to Robert Hodgson of Hebburn and others, all based along the south side of the Tyne between Tynemouth and Newcastle, and Mrs Lawson's house on the north bank of the river. As Neile pointed out, these houses were notorious for '... the conveyinge, receivinge and harbouringe of persons of all sorts ill-affected to the state'. The Bishop, however, received little help from the town Corporation for, whilst claiming to have investigated the matter, the Mayor, Thomas Liddell, reported that he and his aldermen could find '... no matter thereof but idle reports ...'.[80] However, Liddell, too, appears to have had Catholic links which perhaps accounted for his reticence to proceed against Mrs Lawson. Indeed, in 1629, Bartram Liddell, gentleman, and his wife were named in a list of recusants sent by the mayor and aldermen to the Privy Council. Also listed were Oswald Fenwick, and his wife Barbara who, as long ago as 1608, had been presented for refusing to take communion. In all, 27 recusants were named, 17 of these being women. Several were the wives of local tradesmen and one the wife of a labourer, suggesting that, in addition to its gentry supporters, adherence to Catholicism at this time was embedded in all sections of Newcastle society.[81]

Dorothy Lawson died in March 1632 and a lavish funeral was arranged by her son. The day after her death many of the town's inhabitants visited St Anthony's to pay their last respects and were 'plentifully entertained with a banquet'. Later, her remains were carried by boat to Newcastle, being accompanied by 20 or more other boats and barges. Arriving in the evening, the cortège found the streets ablaze with light and a reception party, made up of the town's magistrates and aldermen, waiting by the landing stage to receive the coffin which was taken to All Saints' Church where, 'none ... daring to oppose it', she was 'laid with Catholick ceremonies in the grave'.[82]

[79]   Palmes, *Life of Mrs Dorothy Lawson*, pp.8, 16, 30, 32-3, 39, 40.
[80]   *Ibid.*, pp.xvi, 3, 32.
[81]   Welford, *Newcastle and Gateshead*, vol.3, pp.181, 288-9.
[82]   Palmes, *Life of Mrs Dorothy Lawson*, pp.xv, 59-61.

Arminianism and the Rise of Radical Dissent

Catholic recusancy continued to pose problems for the authorities throughout the period and beyond. However, by the time of Mrs Lawson's death the English Church itself was embroiled in doctrinal controversy. The prevailing 'Calvinist consensus' was being replaced by Arminianism, with its stress on anti-predestinarianism and ritual. The diocese of Durham was one of the earliest centres of Arminianism, it having been established there by Bishop Neile, translated to the see in 1617, under whose patronage it quickly spread.[83] In Newcastle its doctrines were promoted through the endeavours of two men – Thomas Jackson, vicar of the town from 1623, and his successor, Yeldard Alvey.

Thomas Jackson, born in Witton-le-Wear, County Durham, was to become one of the leading theologians of his day. Educated at Oxford, where he proved to be a dedicated and learned scholar, he was ordained as a priest in 1605 and it was around this time that he first began to question the Calvinist teaching on election. By 1613 he had begun to publish the first in a series of commentaries on the Apostles Creed, which were to become his life's work and main theological achievement. Appointed chaplain to Bishop Neile, he quickly became a member of Neile's Durham House group of leading Arminian theologians. It was probably thanks to the Bishop's patronage that he was instituted to the vicarage of Newcastle in 1623 where he was, initially, admired for his 'excellent way of preaching which was then Puritanical'. Around this time, too, Yeldard Alvey, later to succeed Jackson as vicar, was appointed lecturer to St Nicholas' Church.[84] Jackson probably arrived in Newcastle in 1625 and was soon made aware of the town's puritan character and traditions. It was in this context that he made the famous remark about this being a town 'wherein Knox, Mackbray and Udal had sown their tares'. In 1628 he published the first part of his *Treatise on the Divine Essence and Attributes*, the sixth book in his series of commentaries, in which he rejected the Calvinist doctrine of predestination in favour of the Arminian precept of free will.[85]

However, the Arminianism of the Durham ecclesiastical establishment in general – and that of Jackson and Alvey in particular – was soon to meet with the determined opposition of the Newcastle-born preacher, Robert Jenison. Jenison, whose family had long been part of the town's governing elite, had

[83] Tillbrook, M., 'Arminianism and Society in County Durham: 1617-1642', in Marcombe (ed.), *Last Principality*, p.202.

[84] Hegarty, A.J., 'Jackson, Thomas', *DNB*; Foster, A., 'Durham House group (*act.* 1617-1630)', *DNB*; Longstaffe, *Memoirs*, pp.308-9.

[85] Hegarty, 'Jackson'; Newton, *North-East England*, pp.128, 131.

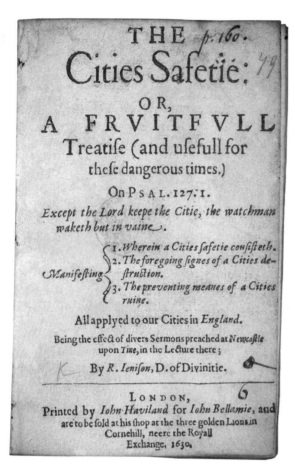

THE *p. 160.*

Cities Safetie:

OR,

A FRVITFVLL
Treatife (and ufefull for
thefe dangerous times.)

On PSAL. 127. 1.

*Except the Lord keepe the Citie, the watchman
waketh but in vaine.*

Manifefting { 1. *Wherein a Cities fafetie confifteth.*
2. *The foregoing fignes of a Cities de-
ftruction.*
3. *The preventing meanes of a Cities
ruine.* }

All applyed to our Cities in *England.*

Being the effect of divers Sermons preached at *Newcaftle*
upon *Tine,* in the Lecture there ;

By *R. Ienifon,* D. of Divinitie.

LONDON,
Printed by *Iohn Haviland* for *Iohn Bellamie,* and
are to be fold at his fhop at the three golden Lions in
Cornehill, neere the Royall
Exchange, 1630.

73 Title page from Robert Jenison's, *The Cities Safety.*

attended the town's grammar school before moving on to Cambridge where he studied at Emmanuel and St John's Colleges.[86] His tutor and mentor at Emmanuel was the puritan theologian, Samuel Ward.[87] In 1611 Jenison had been granted the mastership of the hospital of St Mary Magdalene in Newcastle.[88] He subsequently became chaplain to the Earl of Kent, returning to his fellowship at St John's after the Earl's death in 1614. Jenison had returned to Newcastle by July 1620, when he preached at the funeral of the vicar, William Morton, and in 1622 he was appointed to a lectureship at All Saints' Church. His anti-Arminian stance was immediately apparent and it was feared that he would seek the appointment of vicar of the town.[89] Following Jackson's presentation to that living, relations between the two men became strained, although not as acrimonious as later since, at this stage, Jenison was still in the process of developing his own doctrinal views. He was, however, already speaking privately of his discomfort with Arminian practices such as kneeling to receive communion and other 'popish innovations' as well as grappling with his understanding of predestination and the salvation of the elect.[90] In 1625 he published *The Christian's Apparelling by Christ*, which made clear his Calvinist

---

[86] Jenison's father, Ralph, had served both as sheriff and mayor of Newcastle, dying in 1597 whilst still holding the latter office. Robert's uncle, William, also held the offices of sheriff and mayor and was MP for the town in 1571. Welford, *Newcastle and Gateshead*, vol.2, p.525 and vol.3, pp.420-1; Howell, R., 'The career of Robert Jenison, a C17 puritan in Newcastle', in *Puritans and Radicals in North England: Essays on the English Revolution* (1984), p.113.

[87] Sheils, W.J., 'Jenison, Robert', *DNB*.

[88] Brand, *Newcastle*, vol.1, p.35; Welford, *Newcastle and Gateshead*, vol.3, p.192. The hospital, which served as an alms house, had, that year, been refounded and incorporated with St Thomas's chapel, Tyne Bridge.

[89] Longstaffe, *Memoirs*, p.307; Sheils, 'Jenison'; Brand, *Newcastle*, vol.1, p.387.

[90] Howell, *Newcastle*, p.87 and *Puritans and Radicals*, p.117.

sympathies.[91] In a later work, *The Cities Safety*, published in 1630, Jenison expressed concern for national wellbeing, a theme common to puritan writing, and voiced the fear that those cities and towns in England which, like '... Rome and other Popish cities abroad ...' had moved away from '... Christs faithfull servants and ministers ...', would be punished for their sins.[92] When Newcastle was ravaged by plague in 1636, Jenison further elaborated upon the theme of the sinful town in his publication, *Newcastles call, to her neighbour and sister townes and cities throughout the land, to take warning by her sins and sorrowes.*[93]

By 1630 Jenison, together with three prominent merchants – Sir Lionel Maddison, John Blakiston, the later regicide, and Henry Dawson – were the leaders of a distinct puritan group within the town.[94] On the other side of the religious divide, the Arminian cause was upheld by Yeldard Alvey, later to be disparagingly dismissed by William Prynne, the puritan pamphleteer and lawyer, as 'the Arminian and superstitious vicar of Newcastle'.[95] Alvey had been presented to the vicarage following the resignation of Thomas Jackson in 1630.[96] In the diocese of Durham support for Arminianism had reached its apogee by this time. Thereafter, under the more moderate episcopate of Bishop Morton, who was translated to the see in 1632, some attempts were made to reconcile Calvinists and Arminians.[97] In Newcastle, however, the animosity between the puritan preacher Jenison and the Arminian vicar Alvey intensified over the next few years, with a number of confrontations occurring. On Good Friday 1631 Jenison took to the pulpit to preach on the theme of salvation and the elect, thus challenging the Arminian doctrine of free will, and narrowly avoided being cited before the High Commission. In 1636-7 John Blakiston was brought before that court, on the citation of Alvey, charged with failing to conform to the rites and ceremonies of the Anglican Church and of accusing Alvey of making seven errors during the course of one of his sermons.[98] Henry Dawson, another

---

[91]   Sheils, 'Jenison'.

[92]   Jenison, R., *The cities safetie: or, a fruitfull treatise (and usefull for these dangerous times)*. On Psalm 127.1. *Except the Lord keepe the citie, the watchman waketh but in vaine* (1630), p.83; Newton, *North-East England*, p.130; Howell, *Puritans and Radicals*, p.119. For the plague of 1636 see below, pp.241-64.

[93]   Jenison, R., *Newcastles call, to her neighbour and sister townes and cities throughout the land, to take warning by her sins and sorrowes* (1637).

[94]   Howell, *Newcastle*, p.88 and 'Newcastle's Regicide: The Parliamentary career of John Blakiston', *AA*, 4th series, vol.42 (1964), pp.207-30.

[95]   Prynne, W., *Hidden workes of darkenes brought to publike light, or, A necessary introdvction to the history of the Archbishop of Canterbvrie's triall* (1645), p.188; Howell, *Puritans and Radicals*, p.117.

[96]   Thomas Jackson had resigned, following his election to the presidency of Corpus Christi College, Oxford. Brand, *Newcastle*, vol.1, p.305; Walker, J., *An attempt towards recovering an account of the numbers and sufferings of the clergy of the Church of England, ... who were sequester'd, harrass'd, &c. in the late times of the Grand Rebellion ...* (1714), p.188.

[97]   Tillbrook, M., 'Arminianism and Society', pp.210-11.

[98]   Howell, *Puritans and Radicals*, pp.117-18; Longstaffe, W.H.D., *The Acts of the High Commission within the Diocese of Durham*, SS, vol.34 (1857), pp.155-67.

of the Puritan leaders, was instrumental in supporting an unofficial preacher, William Morton, who lived in Dawson's house and held evening meetings there each Sunday evening to discuss the sermon he had preached earlier that day. At the beginning of 1639 information regarding these activities was passed to the Secretary of State, Sir Francis Windebank, since there was evidence to suggest that Newcastle Puritans were, by this time, in regular contact with Scottish Covenanters.[99]

In March 1639, just three months before the outbreak of the First Bishops' War, the Commissioners for Causes Ecclesiastical for the province of York cited Robert Jenison for a whole series of offences, pertaining to '… his non-observation of the rites and ceremonies of the Church as prescribed in the Book of Common Prayer'. In addition he was accused of, '… Having conference with divers of the Scotch covenanters'.[100] As a result, in September 1639, Jenison was suspended from his ministry and threatened with further proceedings should it be found that he had consorted with the Scots, as had been alleged. Given that his lectureship was in the gift of the Corporation, Windebank wrote to the mayor and aldermen of Newcastle on 9 October, instructing them, on behalf of the king, to appoint Dr George Wishart to Jenison's former posts, as lecturer at All Saints' on Sundays and at St Nicholas' on Thursdays, enjoying the same profits and advantages held by Jenison.[101]

The in-fighting between the Puritans and Yeldard Alvey did not end with Jenison's suspension. As Alvey subsequently reported to Archbishop Laud, shortly before Christmas 1639, the Newcastle Puritans had succeeded in driving away the conformist lecturer of St Nicholas', Thomas Stephenson, in order to replace him with a more amenable candidate. The Mayor, Robert Bewick, a puritan sympathiser and half-brother to Jenison, had immediately thereafter convened a meeting of the Common Council which had appointed a new candidate, John Bewick, a kinsman of the Mayor and Jenison. In early 1640, Alvey reported again, this time to the Archbishop of York, Richard Neile, informing him of the appearance in the town of two Scottish Covenanters, Sir Walter Riddell and Sir John Buchanan, who were known to be in close contact with the Puritan leaders. As the vicar pointed out to Neile, 'There is not such a watchful eye kept over these men by our mayor as is requisite in these dangerous times there should be …'. As further reports to the government suggested, Sir

[99] Howell, *Newcastle*, pp.93-100; *CSPD*, 1638-9, pp.358-60; Welford, *Newcastle and Gateshead*, vol.3, pp.368-74.
[100] *CSPD*, 1638-9, p.591.
[101] The proceedings are detailed in *CSPD*, 1638-9 and *ibid.*, 1639; Howell, *Newcastle*, pp.108-10; Dodds, M.H. (ed.), *Extracts from the Newcastle upon Tyne Council Minute Book, 1639-1656*, Newcastle upon Tyne Records Committee publications, vol.1 (1920), pp.2-3.

Lionel Maddison, another leading member of the Newcastle Puritans, appeared to be heavily implicated in this latest round of intrigues.[102]

Yeldard Alvey, together with a number of other Anglican clergymen, fled the town in the wake of the Scottish victory at the battle of Newburn in August 1640, during the Second Bishops' War. The subsequent occupation of Newcastle by the Scots, although at first greeted with some enthusiasm by the town's Puritans was not an unmitigated success. In the first place the depredations of the occupying army were soon to cause considerable resentment, as much amongst Puritans as amongst other sections of Newcastle society. Moreover, the town's Puritan ministers had all moved away before the outbreak of hostilities. William Morton, the unofficial lecturer, had departed in 1639, Robert Jenison had sought refuge in Danzig in 1640, and John Bewick, too, had left the town. Their places were taken by a number of Scottish Presbyterian ministers although the hellfire sermons preached by many of these were not to the taste of the townsmen. Little wonder that calls soon arose for the return of the ministries of the most respected and popular preachers, Jenison and Morton. In 1641 the vestry of All Saints' wrote to both men, asking them to return to the town, the latter being asked to remain until the former could make his way back to England. At the same time a petition was sent to the House of Commons, from the burgesses and inhabitants of the town, calling for Yeldard Alvey and George Wishart, amongst others, to be declared delinquents. Both men were called to answer the charges against them and Wishart was subsequently declared unfit for the post of lecturer, with a recommendation made to appoint William Morton in his stead. Morton had joined the Parliamentary army and in 1643 he and Jenison were the two divines appointed to represent Durham in the Westminster Assembly.[103]

Following the departure of the Scottish army in 1641, Yeldard Alvey and George Wishart returned to their ministries in the town. As a consequence, with Newcastle once again under Royalist control, religious life there rapidly assumed a Laudian perspective. The threat of Puritanism remained, however, and in September 1643 the Common Council ordered the disenfranchisement of 35 freemen drawn from across the social spectrum and deemed to be '... incendiaries', who '... treated with seuerall men of another nation to invade this kingdome and to possesse themselves of this Towne'. It has been suggested that the entry in the Common Council Book, which gives the names of those

[102] *CSPD*, 1639-40, pp.169-70, 324, 402; Howell, *Newcastle*, pp.91, 107; Welford, *Newcastle and Gateshead*, vol.3, pp.380-3; Dodds, *Council Minute Book*, pp.4-5.
[103] Longstaffe, *Memoirs*, pp.128-9, 330-1, 335, 336, 337; Howell, *Newcastle*, pp.130-2, 137-8, 139, 140.

disenfranchised, provides, '... the nearest thing to a list of the parliamentary Puritans of the town'.[104]

In 1643, following Parliament's decision to call upon Scottish aid and enter into the Solemn League and Covenant, the North was invaded once again, with Newcastle falling to the Scottish army in October 1644. By this time Parliament had already begun to address the issue of '... sequestring the Livings of ill-affected Ministers, and of placing good Ministers'. In August 1644 the decision was made to send four 'fit ministers' to the counties of Northumberland and Durham and, in the following December, Parliament resolved that Dr Jenison should be restored to his former positions in the town, with all advantages as he earlier enjoyed, and also to the vicarage of Newcastle thus replacing Mr Alvey, whose living was sequestered for delinquency. It also decided that the prominent divine, Christopher Love, together with William Strother, should be sent to preach in Newcastle or, if they were not available, some other suitable preachers to be appointed in their stead. This resolution was ratified by an Act of Parliament in May 1645.[105] Two new preachers, Cuthbert Sydenham and William Durant, arrived in Newcastle shortly afterwards. Although well-educated, each having attended the University of Oxford, neither man had been ordained in the Anglican Church. Sydenham seems to have been in Presbyterian orders, although he was later noted as an Independent (or Congregationalist). Their appointments were ratified by the Common Council in 1647, with Sydenham settled as afternoon lecturer at St Nicholas' and Durant as morning lecturer at All Saints'. Sydenham was also to deputise as morning lecturer at St Nicholas', in the event of Dr Jenison being unwell. Shortly afterwards two more lecturers, mentioned only as Mr Harris and Mr Sheffield, joined them although they stayed little more than a year. In the autumn of 1646 Richard Prideaux arrived in the town and was subsequently 'settled' as the preacher and minister in charge of All Saints'. Described by Brand as being 'of the Congregational judgement', modern research has, nevertheless, indicated that Prideaux was, or was later to become, a Presbyterian. He was followed in 1647 by Stephen Dockray, also a Presbyterian, who took charge at St Andrew's. He was also deputed to assist the now ailing Jenison. Thomas Woolfall arrived in the same year and was appointed as preacher and minister in charge of St John's.[106]

[104]   TWAS, MD.NC/1/1, fols 49, 50, 51, printed in Dodds, *Council Minute Books*, pp.27-8, 29-30; Howell, *Newcastle*, pp.95, 147-9.
[105]   *CJ*, vol.3, pp.408, 714; *LJ*, vol.7, p.395. Christopher Love had preached in the town on an earlier occasion, in 1641, when he famously attacked the Book of Common Prayer and Laudian ceremonial practices. Longstaffe, *Memoirs*, p.128; Vernon, E.C., 'Love, Christopher', *DNB*.
[106]   Howell, *Newcastle*, pp.221-8; Dodds, *Council Minute Book*, pp.44, 60, 66, 67, 69, 71-3; *CJ*, vol.5, p.97, Longstaffe, *Memoirs*, pp.343, 349, 350; Brand, *Newcastle*, vol.1, p.388.

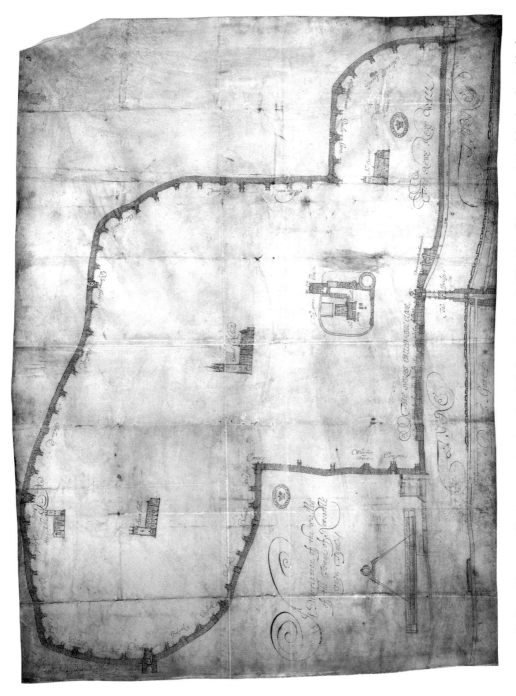

74 A plan of the city walls, drawn up in 1638, shortly before the Scottish War, identifying the principal landmarks visible from Gateshead fell.

It was Prideaux at All Saints', Dockray at St Andrew's, and Woolfall at St John's who, together with Dr Jenison at St Nicholas', were largely responsible for overseeing the establishment of Presbyterianism in Newcastle. The Book of Common Prayer had already been replaced in 1645 by the Directory for Public Worship and in 1646 Parliament ordered the setting up of Presbyterian *classes* across the country, with the episcopate being officially abolished soon afterwards. However, the shortage of ministers, coupled with difficulties in appointing sufficient numbers of suitable elders within each of the town's parishes, meant that the change to a Presbyterian system of church government was not an easy one.[107] By 1648 some headway had been made in the town although by this time the system itself was already proving unworkable. Interestingly, unlike many parts of the country, the town's Presbyterian and Independent ministers seem to have worked together in relative harmony. Nevertheless, the balance of power was shifting towards the Independents even before Cromwell – seen as the 'Independents' champion' – assumed power in 1651. The Toleration Act, passed in September 1650, effectively killed off the Presbyterian religious settlement of 1646, seeking as it did to '... grant relief to "religious and peaceable people ..."'.[108] The impact of change was soon felt in Newcastle for, in the following November, Cuthbert Sydenham was granted permission by the Common Council to establish a Congregational Church in the town, based in St Nicholas' Church and thus operating alongside Jenison's Presbyterian model.[109] On the same day, the Council sought to provide relief for the elderly Dr Jenison by granting him for life his salary of £140 a year. Acknowledging that Jenison was '... now growen Olde and Disinabled by many Infirmityes ...', it made known its intention of seeking to recruit the '... godly, Learned and able Devine ...', Samuel Hammond. At that time rector of Bishopwearmouth, the Cambridge-educated Hammond was an Independent who enjoyed the patronage of Sir Arthur Hesilrige, governor of Newcastle from 1647. He did not take up the Council's invitation straight away and it was only when Jenison died, in November 1652, that Hammond agreed to take up his ministry at St Nicholas' Church for an annual salary of £150.[110] Thomas Woolfall had also died a few weeks before Jenison, making it necessary to appoint a new minister for St John's. However, his parishioners were forced to wait some time before the town Council was able to acquire another '... pious, peaceable and able minister ...',

[107] Howell, *Newcastle*, pp.228-31; Cross, *Church and People*, pp.201-2, 204; *VCH Durham*, vol.2, pp.50-1.
[108] Collins, J.R., 'The Church Settlement of Oliver Cromwell', *History*, vol.87 (2002), p.21; Cross, *Church and People*, p.213.
[109] TWAS, MD. NC/1/2 fo. 172.
[110] *Ibid.*, fos 171, 210v, 211; Sheils, W.J., 'Hammond, Samuel', *DNB*.

to succeed him. In the end, the parishioners themselves sought out a suitable candidate and in 1654 William Cole, a Presbyterian and former minister of Kirby Kendal in Westmorland, was appointed to the living.[111]

The leading Cromwellian Independents, although willing to accept the various shades of ultra Protestant belief in general, were not in favour of toleration for radical or extremist groups, or indeed for Episcopalians and Roman Catholics.[112] Samuel Hammond, the town's principal minister (although he was not designated 'vicar') seems to have held such views for in 1653-4 he sought actively to suppress the Baptists and Quakers, who were making significant inroads in the locality. In this, Hammond was supported by the Presbyterians who, in a continuing spirit of co-operation, joined forces to fight the perceived threat. The early Baptist movement in Newcastle had drawn considerable support from army personnel, most notably Colonel Robert Lilburne, who had served as governor of the town for a short period in 1647. Also prominent was Lilburne's close associate, Colonel Paul Hobson, who became deputy governor of Newcastle, under Hesilrige, in 1648. Indeed, by the early 1650s the town had a well established Baptist congregation, led by Thomas Gower, its preacher, who seems also to have had military connections. The congregation was tolerated by the town's ministers, being permitted to use the chapel of St Thomas on Tyne Bridge. The chapel was incorporated with the hospital of St Mary Magdalene under the mastership of Robert Jenison and, later, Cuthbert Sydenham. Kept under supervision, the Newcastle Baptists seem not to have posed a threat and it was only after the establishment of a further, flourishing Baptist Church, founded in Hexham in 1651 by Thomas Tillham, that concerns regarding the congregations began to surface. The problem was resolved in 1653 when, following a scandal in which an imposter, masquerading as a Jewish convert to Christianity, was baptised into the Hexham congregation, the church's reputation was destroyed, leading to its ultimate decline.[113]

In 1654 the Newcastle ministers again formed an alliance, this time against the Quakers who had begun to make inroads following the visit to the area, in 1653, of George Fox. The movement's profile was further heightened in Newcastle by the conversion of another of Hesilrige's close associates, his secretary, Anthony Pearson. In response to the threat, two anti-Quaker pamphlets were published

---

[111] TWAS, M.D. NC/1/2, fo. 213.

[112] Collins, 'The Church Settlement of Oliver Cromwell', p.20; Sheils, 'Hammond'.

[113] Copson, S.L., *Association Life of the Particular Baptists of Northern England, 1699-1732* (Baptist Historical Society, 1991), pp.12-15; Howell, R., 'Conflict and Controversy in the early Baptist movement in Northumberland: Thomas Tillam, Paul Hobson and the False Jew of Hexham', *AA,* 5th series, vol.14 (1986), pp.81-97; Longstaffe, *Memoirs,* p.150; TWAS MD.NC/1/2, Fos 212, 220.

by the Newcastle ministers.[114] The first of these, *The Perfect Pharisee under Monkish Holinesse*, likened Quaker teachings to Catholic doctrine – and indeed they were perceived as being equally pernicious – whilst the second, *A Further Discovery of that Generation of Men called Quakers*, published 1654, was issued in answer to Quaker responses to the first pamphlet. The issue died down, to re-emerge again in 1657-8, although the town's Quakers were not deterred and, like the Baptists, survived to carry their faith through to the post-Restoration period and beyond.[115]

The Independent/Presbyterian alliance of Newcastle clergy survived, almost intact, through to the close of the Interregnum. In 1654, upon the issuing of the Ordinance for Triers and Ejectors, Hammond and Prideaux, representing both confessional wings, were appointed assistants to the commissioners for the northern counties. A potential dispute in 1656 – over Independent fears that Newcastle Presbyterians were seeking to curry favour with Cromwell, against their interests – was nipped in the bud by the Protector, who sought to reassure both parties, urging them to closer co-operation. In the same year the 'Order for settleing the Ministers in their preachinge att the severall Churches usque Death etc.,' provided a framework of guarantees and regulations for the '... better orderinge and settleinge ...' of ministers of both judgements '... for tyme to come'. The Presbyterians, Prideaux, Dockeray and Cole, thus continued to serve alongside the Independents, these being the Congregationalist ministers William Durant and Samuel Hammond. Another preacher, the newcomer John Tilsley, was appointed in March 1656 to provide Presbyterian ministry at St Nicholas' – thus taking up the position left vacant by Jenison's death – as well as preaching assistance at St John's.[116]

Reputedly, both Richard Prideaux and John Knightbridge, who had replaced Tilsley, conformed at the Restoration. The death of Stephen Dockeray, in August 1660, paved the way for the return to Newcastle of the Royalist clergyman George Wishart, who remained there until his appointment, in 1662, as Bishop of Edinburgh. Samuel Hammond also stayed on until 1662 when, refusing to subscribe to the provisions of the Act of Uniformity, he departed for the continent. By that time the clerical personnel within the town had changed, thus

---

[114]   These were Samuel Hammond, Thomas Weld, the preacher at Gateshead, Richard Prideaux, William Durant, and William Cole, the successor to Thomas Woolfall at St John's Church. For the career of Thomas Weld see Winship, M.P., 'Weld, Thomas', *DNB*.

[115]   See Howell, 'Early Quakerism in Newcastle upon Tyne: Thomas Ledgard's Discourse concerning the Quakers' and 'The Newcastle Clergy and the Quakers' in his *Puritans and Radicals*, pp.128-35, 136-61; Longstaffe, *Memoirs*, pp.383-4.

[116]   Dodds, *Council Minute Book*, pp.31-4; TWAS, MD.NC/1/2 fols 265, 266, 267, 268, 269; Howell, *Newcastle*, pp.242-3, 246, 263-4; Sheils, 'Hammond'; Cross, *Church and People*, p.215. For the workings of this Ordinance see Collins, 'The Church Settlement of Oliver Cromwell', pp.29-33.

reflecting the religious provisions of the Restoration Settlement. Nevertheless, the presence in Newcastle, during the period 1645-60, of an educated and stable preaching ministry undoubtedly ensured the survival of the nonconformist beliefs that, in future generations, would provide the foundations of the town's reputation as a major centre of religious dissent.[117]

Newcastle and the Reformation

The Reformation period in Newcastle was as complex and tortuous as in other parts of the North. Yet, its experience was far different in that, whilst much of the region showed little enthusiasm for the early stirrings of reform, it was the town's long-standing association with Protestantism which was to define the history of Newcastle and its governing elite. Without a detailed and coherent study of its elite, it is difficult to assess the reasons behind the town's religious stance and more research is clearly called for in this sphere. It has been suggested that the 'scale', 'pace' and 'complexity' of urban life in the towns and cities of later 17th-century Reformation Europe furnished their inhabitants with a 'precocious ability' to make a far wider range of life choices, including where to worship and in what manner, than were available to those in the country.[118] Admittedly such a scale of choices was clearly not available to the residents of mid-16th-century Newcastle, yet perhaps some of that same sense of self-confidence and openness to change, fostered by life in a thriving, economic, urban environment, was behind their decision to attend the preaching sessions of John Rough and John Knox. Exposure to the cut and thrust of mercantile trade had, after all, almost certainly provided Roger Dichaunte with the means and the courage to explore elements of the new reformed faith in 1531. In the later 16th century the Earl of Huntingdon clearly recognised the potential of urban centres and their residents in propagating the faith when he sought to plant Puritan preachers in as many market towns as possible. The town as a centre where godliness should thrive was a theme similarly taken up by the Newcastle preacher Robert Jenison in the 1620s.[119] The networks between the town and Scottish Protestants also need further exploration since, at crucial points during the period under consideration, the dissemination of ideas back and forth across the border played a major role in strengthening the Protestant cause. In view

---

[117] Longstaffe, *Memoirs,* pp.129, 390-2; Brand, *Newcastle,* vol.1, p.313; Sheils, 'Hammond'; Howell, *Newcastle,* pp.344-5; Wilson, K., *The Sense of the People: Politics, Culture and Imperialism in England, 1715-1785* (1995), pp.300-1, 318; Ellis, J., 'A dynamic society: social relations in Newcastle-upon-Tyne, 1660-1760' in Clark, P. (ed.), *The Transformation of English Provincial Towns, 1600-1800* (1984), pp.198, 209.

[118] McCulloch, *Reformation,* p.666.

[119] Lamburn, 'Digging and Dunging', pp.365-7; Jenison, *The cities safetie,* pp.6-9.

of the evidence, therefore, it seems clear that, when considering the case of Newcastle, generalisations about the Reformation in the 'conservative' north need to be revisited. To paraphrase Thomas Jackson, it seems that in respect of this particular northern town, Knox, Mackbray and Udal had sown their so-called 'tares' with the greatest of care.

9

The Tyneside Lobby on the Thames: Politics and Economic Issues, c.1580-1630

SIMON HEALY

Urban history tends to concentrate on the internal development of towns, factors such as population, economy, infrastructure, society and government.[1] Yet boroughs also have a relationship with the wider world: economic rivals, trading partners and the state. With livelihoods at stake, few early modern Corporations could afford to be complacent about their industries or markets, and most urban success stories were built upon the failure of numerous competitors: thus for every London there was a Sandwich; for every Hull, a Hedon; for every Newcastle, a Gateshead.

English towns also measured their performance against their most voracious competitor, London, which during the early modern period handled two-thirds to three-quarters of England's exports, and much internal trade besides. Huge quantities of cloth passed through Blackwell Hall in London en route to the continent, while most sugar, spice and silk imports (plus a significant proportion of less exotic goods) were handled by London-based merchants. Some regional industries escaped this trend towards metropolitan control: the Derbyshire lead trade came to be handled by Hull merchants; the manufacture and marketing of Norwich worsteds was dominated by local men; and much of the trade in Yorkshire kerseys remained in the hands of northerners.[2] The Tyneside mining industry was the largest industrial concern to remain outside the orbit of London's merchants, a considerable achievement in light of the fact that London comprised the largest market for Newcastle coal. The key to this success lay not in the realm of economics – other key national industries such as the broadcloth trade ultimately fell into the hands of the Londoners – but of politics, the subject of this essay.

---

[1]   See examples such as Palliser, D.M., *Tudor York* (1979); Dyer, C., *The City of Worcester in the 16th Century* (1973).
[2]   Kiernan, D., *Derbyshire Lead Industry in the 16th Century*, Derbyshire Record Society, vol.14 (1989); Evans, J.T., *17th Century Norwich* (1979); Heaton, H., *Yorkshire Woollen and Worsted Industries* (1965).

The Hostmen's Monopoly

Newcastle coal, often called 'seacoal' because it reached its customers by sea, was shipped to London in modest quantities throughout the later Middle Ages; demand took off during the reign of Elizabeth, as the rapid growth of the metropolis outstripped supplies of firewood and charcoal in the south east of England.[3] The Tyneside mine owners would have been unable to meet this demand without expanding production, which became possible when the Queen prevailed upon Bishop Barnes of Durham to assign her a 79-year lease of the episcopal manors of Gateshead and Whickham on 1 February 1578. This concession may have been extracted under pressure, as the annual rental of £117 15s. 8d. reflected no more than the land's agricultural value, ignoring the fact that potentially valuable coal seams ran close to the surface. Two months later the Crown assigned this lease to Thomas Sutton, Master of Ordnance in the North, who was said to have derived the foundations of the fortune he would later use to endow London's Charterhouse Hospital as lessee of the Durham mines.[4]

No production statistics survive for the five years of Sutton's tenure, but there was a considerable rise in output across the middle of Elizabeth's reign: annual seacoal shipments ran at 70-89,000 tons during the early 1570s, but had doubled to 150-200,000 tons by the early 1590s.[5] Sutton was almost certainly one of the chief beneficiaries of this increase, thereby challenging the primacy of the local coal merchants, the Newcastle Hostmen. The latter claimed a monopoly of the seacoal trade under a broad interpretation of a 1529 statute which specified that all cargoes shipped from the Tyne had to be loaded onto keels (barges) at the staithes (wharves) of Newcastle by freemen, for trans-shipment to colliers anchored at North and South Shields, near the mouth of the river.[6] Some of the Hostmen were more directly rivals to Sutton, leasing mines on the south bank of the Tyne, and in December 1581 one of their number, Alderman William Riddell of Newcastle, secured a Crown lease of abandoned mines situated on ex-monastic lands within the manor of Gateshead – presumably separate from the rights included in the episcopal lease. It is likely that there was some negotiation between Sutton and the Hostmen over a compromise: in April 1582 Bishop Barnes increased

---

[3]   Hatcher, J., *History of the British Coal Industry*, vol.1 (1993), pp.31-55.
[4]   Nef, J.U., *Rise of the British Coal Industry*, vol.1 (1966), pp.150-2; Hatcher, *Coal Industry*, vol.1, pp.77-8; TNA, C54/1046; *CPR*, 1575-8, p.433.
[5]   Hatcher, *Coal Industry*, vol.1, pp.487-8.
[6]   *Statutes of the Realm*, vol.3, pp.302-3; *Records of the Company of Hostmen of Newcastle-upon-Tyne*, SS, vol.105 (1901) pp.xxx-xxxi; Newton, D., *North-East England, 1569-1625: governance, culture and identity* (2006), p.38. The London Corporation complained about the Hostmen's claims under this statute in 1595: see Tawney, R.H. and Power, E. (eds), *Tudor Economic Documents*, vol.1 (1924), p.268. See also Diana Newton in this volume.

75   Shipping in the mouth of the Tyne, 1655.

the term of the Crown's lease of Gateshead and Wickham manors to 99 years; but this extension was not passed on to Sutton, who surrendered his lease in November 1583.[7]

Sutton passed his lease to the Hostmen for at least £5,500 – 46½ times the annual rental due to the bishop, or more than twice the normal market price. The surrender allowed the episcopal leases of 1578 and 1582 to be assigned to two Hostmen, Alderman Henry Anderson and William Selby, a grant known to posterity as the Grand Lease. It was later claimed that this lease was to have been held in trust for the Newcastle Corporation, but the lessees and other Hostmen who invested in the venture retained control in their own hands, an act of self-aggrandisement which became a source of tension for years thereafter.[8] Circumstantial evidence suggests that the lessees' profits were large at the outset, and grew apace: the rising supply of coal was outstripped by voracious demand from London, which drove up the prices charged at Newcastle from 4s. per chaldron before 1578, to 6s. under Sutton, and 8-9s. under the Grand Lease. In short, the Hostmen enjoyed the enviable position of producing more coal, while being able to charge their customers more for it.[9]

This rapid increase in both turnover and profits naturally attracted the attention of rival interests. A projector suggested the imposition of duties on coal shipments in 1590, while in the following year, complaints about the poor quality of coal supplies led John Thornborough, Dean of York, to propose a surveyorship of coals at Newcastle, charging a fee of 2d. per chaldron. This project was supported by the Exchequer official Peter Osborne, but was apparently vetoed by Lord Admiral Howard, who claimed admiralty rights over the Tyne; yet continuing problems with the quality of coal led to the revival of the surveyorship project at intervals over the next 40 years (see below).[10] In 1594 the London Corporation submitted a more comprehensive protest to the Privy Council about the excessive prices they were charged at Newcastle, the poor quality of the coals offered for sale, and the fact that English colliers were not given precedence over foreign buyers during times of shortage. This may have prompted Sir Thomas Wilkes, one of the Privy Council clerks, to petition for a monopoly of coal exports a few months later, although the Council turned this or a similar scheme down in July 1595.[11] The

[7]   *CPR*, 1580-2, p.205; *CPR*, 1582-3, p.67; TNA, C54/1142; Newton, *North-East England*, pp.37-9.
[8]   Nef, *Coal Industry*, vol.1, pp.151-2; Hatcher, *Coal Industry*, vol.1, pp.513-14. And see Newton in this volume.
[9]   Hatcher, *Coal Industry*, vol.1, pp.487-8, 573; Tawney and Power, *Documents*, vol.1, pp.267-9, of which another copy is in *Company of Hostmen*, pp.2-4.
[10]   Nef, *Coal Industry*, vol.2, pp.213-15; Tawney and Power, *Documents*, vol.1, pp.271-7; Corporation of London Record Office (hereafter CLRO), Remembrancia I/615. See also Diana Newton in this volume.
[11]   CLRO, Remembrancia 2/132-4 (printed in *Company of Hostmen*, pp.2-9); *CSPD*, 1595-7, p.68; *Historical Manuscripts Commission report on the manuscripts at Hatfield House* (hereafter *HMC Hatfield*), vol.5, p.267.

Londoners continued their protests for another 18 months, complaining bitterly about the activities of the Hostmen, who, they claimed, dictated prices, quality and times of sale to their customers – charges which were doubtless true. In this they perhaps hoped to make common cause with other Newcastle interests, who, resentful of the Hostmen's domination of the Corporation, tendered their own complaints to the Privy Council and Council in the North.[12] A draft proclamation which survives in Lord Treasurer Burghley's papers may have been intended to address these grievances, but it was never implemented.[13]

In November 1598 one of the Londoners' lobbyists, Henry Sanderson – customs searcher at Newcastle – approached the new Lord Treasurer, Lord Buckhurst, with a fresh plan to impose a levy on coal shipments from the Tyne.[14] His memorandum was probably the inspiration behind an export duty of 5s. per chaldron, which was farmed to Bevis Bulmer the following summer for 12 years at an annual rent of £3,000; meanwhile, another charge of 12d. per chaldron on coastwise shipments was assigned to Richard Connock, at an unspecified rent. The legal status of such duties was doubtful – impositions on cloth and wine had been questioned at the start of Elizabeth's reign, while a similar duty on currant imports became a *cause célèbre* in 1606 – and complaints were received from as far afield as Liverpool and Dublin, while some colliers refused to give bond for payment before sailing from the Tyne.[15] The Hostmen, too, initially resisted these charges, but ultimately endorsed them for their own benefit: on 22 March 1600 letters patent were sealed granting corporate status to the Hostmen's Company – membership of which was essentially coterminous with the partners in the Grand Lease. Under this charter the Hostmen secured a monopoly of shipping coal and grindstones from the River Tyne, and were exempted from the 1529 statute requiring all merchants to load cargoes at Newcastle. The first act of the newly incorporated Company, in partnership with the borough Corporation, was to confirm the duties on Tyneside coal, following which the existing farms were cancelled; a fresh grant was made to Bulmer on 23 June 1600, at a rate of £3,000 a year for the export duty (as before), and £3,200 a year for the levy on coastal shipments.[16]

[12]   *CSPD*, 1595-7, pp.501-2; CLRO, Remembrancia 2/105, pp.135-9, 153, 161; *APC*, 1598-9, pp.357-8. And see Newton in this volume.
[13]   Tawney and Power, *Documents*, vol.1, pp.277-81, tentatively dates this draft to 1592, but it seems to fit better with the later complaints.
[14]   A 12d. per chaldron levy on coal shipments landed at Plymouth had been proposed in 1592: Dietz, F.C., *English Crown Finance, 1558-1641* (1932), p.69. Taxing shipments at source was, of course, more efficient.
[15]   *HMC Hatfield*, vol.8, pp.413, 419; vol.9, p.34; TNA, E122/111/40-41; TNA, E211/195; Hall, G.D.G., 'Impositions and the courts', *Law Quarterly Review*, vol.66 (1953); BL, MS Lansdowne 156, fos 426, 432-4.
[16]   *Company of Hostmen*, pp.10-19; TNA, E210/10238; TNA, E211/40; TNA, SP46/42, fo.28.

Challenges to the Monopoly, 1600-10

The Hostmen's charter secured their control of the Tyneside coal trade: from 1600 Company members monopolised the carriage of coal from riverside staithes to the colliers, forcing gentry mine owners and masters of ships to use their services as middlemen.[17] Not surprisingly, other parties to the coal trade resented this stranglehold, and intermittently attempted to overthrow the Company's monopoly. However, the Hostmen were almost invariably able to overcome such protests with the Crown's backing, because none of their rivals were able to offer any concession equivalent to the seacoal farm, which (including the annual rent and occasional entry fines) yielded almost £340,000 to the Treasury between 1600 and 1640.[18]

One of the earliest challenges to the Hostmen came from Newcastle freemen excluded from the Company's original membership, who must have lost business when the coal trade shifted from the town's staithes to colliery wharves along the Tyne. In the summer of 1602 George Rande and other Newcastle merchants who were not Hostmen breached the Company's monopoly by loading colliers on their own authority. Two Hostmen were expelled from the Company for breaching its rules (presumably in lending their keels to the interlopers), and a strict cartel was established in February 1603 which centralised production, quality control and sales into four 'quarters' or partnerships, with annual production quotas fixed for each mine owner. The intention seems to have been for the Hostmen to avoid fluctuations in supply or quality which might induce their customers to deal with independent mine owners, thereby sustaining a high but supportable sale price of 8-10s. per chaldron.[19] Which is to say, the cartel aimed to nurture the goose that laid the Hostmen's golden eggs.

Other interests within the town were quick to respond to this cartel: in September 1603 William Wearmouth, a merchant rather than a Hostman, was elected as mayor of Newcastle. He may be presumed to have been the promoter of a lawsuit before the Council of the North at York, which protested about the operations of the Hostmen's cartel. The merchants must have been aware that the Crown was unlikely to surrender the seacoal levy, hence their Bill also offered a secondary complaint that, whereas the Hostmen had formerly charged modest entry fines of £1 13s. 4d., since the charter of 1600 they had demanded £10, £20, £30 or more from outsiders seeking membership, sums which excluded

---

[17] As appears by the rules set down in *Company of Hostmen*, pp.29-42.
[18] Figures from Exchequer receipts in TNA, E401.
[19] *Company of Hostmen*, pp.43-8; Nef, *Coal Industry*, vol.2, pp.110-15; Hatcher, *Coal Industry*, vol.1, pp.522-3.

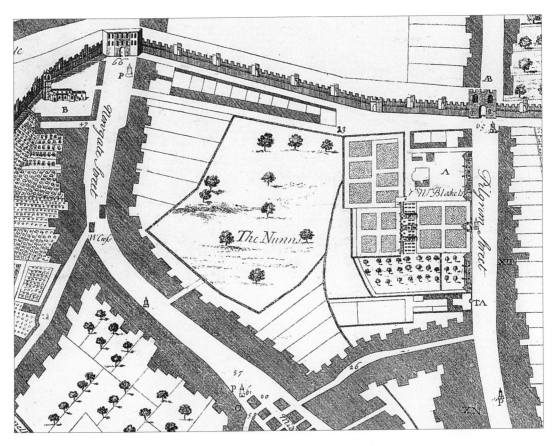

76 Anderson's Place in Corbridge's map. Built on the site of the Greyfriars and the nunnery by a leading coal merchant in the early 17th century, it was bought and developed by Richard Grainger between 1834 and 1840.

small tradesmen from their ranks. In December 1603 the Council of the North decreed that henceforth freemen of other Newcastle guilds would pay only £2 13s. 4d. for admission to the Company. The town charter was duly amended to reflect this agreement, and over the next 15 months, 25 outsiders joined the Hostmen's Company.[20]

The Newcastle dispute was not the only challenge the new Hostmen's Company faced in its early years. The London Corporation unsuccessfully protested about rising seacoal prices in 1601, then tabled a Bill for 'explanation' of the 1529 Newcastle Act in the 1604 Parliamentary session. This was designed to overthrow the Hostmen's cartel arrangements, thereby allowing

---

[20] *Company of Hostmen*, pp.20-7, 242-3, 267; TWAS, ZAN/M13/B34; Hatcher, *Coal Industry*, vol.1, pp.517-18.

their customers greater choice over both price and quality. However, with two Hostmen – Sir George Selby and Henry Chapman – serving as Newcastle's MPs, the Bill was rejected at its second reading in the Commons on 30 May.[21] The Londoners continued to put pressure on the Hostmen over the summer, complaining that they were receiving short measure from their suppliers on the Tyne. Their petition was sent to Lord Chief Justice Popham for arbitration, who placed the blame upon the keelmen who carried coals from the staithes to the colliers. In February 1605 the Hostmen responded by organising a fresh cartel providing closer supervision of the keelmen by their own officials, and they also fined a transgressor to reinforce their point.[22] However, this new cartel was attacked in its turn by the Londoners, who boycotted the Tyneside coalfields for two months; in July 1605 the Privy Council quashed the Hostmen's cartel, and offered the London Corporation a small additional concession by waiving the duty on 4,000 chaldrons of coal provided annually for the benefit of poor Londoners.[23]

The main dispute, about the activities of the Hostmen's cartel, remained unresolved in October 1605, when the parties argued their case before the Privy Council once more. The Londoners insisted that the cartel arrangements forced them to pay higher prices for lower quality coals, to which the Hostmen responded that greater demand forced them to carry coals from mines further from the riverbank, increasing their transport costs. Nothing was decided at this meeting, and the Corporation's threat to sue the Hostmen in Star Chamber or King's Bench similarly came to nothing.[24] In February 1606 the Londoners revived their 1604 Bill, this time in the Lords rather than the Commons, briefing Lord Chancellor Ellesmere and Lord Treasurer Dorset privately, doubtless in hope of securing a favourable reception. However, the rival interests were ordered to attend the committee, where the Hostmen argued their case with sufficient vigour to ensure the Bill was dropped on 10 March. The Lords' committee ordered a fresh draft, but despite support from the London Corporation, no such Bill was tabled before the end of the session, over 11 weeks later.[25]

After 1606 the London Corporation abandoned their quest for a legislative solution to their dispute with the Hostmen, perhaps because the Company

[21] CLRO, Remembrancia 2/181, p.202; CLRO, Repertory 26/2, f.343; *CJ*, vol.1, 182b, 228b. The Bill was presumably similar to that tabled in 1606, for which see TNA, SP14/18/60.I.

[22] *CSPD*, 1603-10, p.161; CLRO, Repertory 26/2, fos 463r-v, 529; *Company of Hostmen*, pp.49-56.

[23] *CSPD*, 1603-10, p.312; *Company of Hostmen*, p.56; TNA, SP14/18/60; CLRO, Repertory 26/2, fo.546v; Repertory 27, fos 10, 18, 29v-30v, 36v, 38v, 54v-5; CLRO, Journal 26, fo.364v.

[24] CLRO, Repertory 27, fos 108, 110, 117, 146v. The Hostmen's answer is probably that printed in *Company of Hostmen*, pp.58-61.

[25] CLRO, Repertory 27, fos 150v, 160v, 180, 182v; *LJ*, vol.2, 368b, 370a, 372b, 392a; TNA, SP14/18/60, 60.I, 60.II.

abandoned their attempts to establish a strict cartel for over a decade. However, in March 1610 Sir Edwin Sandys, a vociferous advocate of free trade, raised the question of the seacoal duty in the Commons as part of a wider dispute about the Crown's claim to impose duties upon maritime trade without statutory approval. The levy was cited by several MPs as evidence that impositions would eventually be extended from foreign to domestic trade, and included in the grievance petition to the Commons submitted to King James I in July 1610. Sir Julius Caesar, Chancellor of the Exchequer, protested that the seacoal duty was 'not defended by any of the King's counsel to be lawful', but James, who could not afford to lose this revenue, simply ignored the question in his answer to the grievances. As a sop to the Hostmen's critics, he did waive the duty on coal shipments from Sunderland and Blyth, a trivial matter of some £200 a year.[26] The Sunderland trade, inaugurated by the London Corporation in 1605-6 following an enquiry to George Bowes, a mine owner in the Wearside, had reached over 11,000 tons in 1609 – but this was less than five per cent of the Tyneside output. However, the tax break conceded in 1610 ensured that Wearside production grew to over 30,000 tons annually in succeeding years.[27]

Disputes over the Surveyorship of Coals, 1616-26

Having co-opted many of their Newcastle rivals into their own ranks, and seen off the Londoners, the next threat the Hostmen faced came from a projector with powerful backing at Court, who proposed a remedy for the long-standing dispute over the quality of Tyneside coal. Geologically, coal deposits vary widely in purity and calorific content; during the 17th century poor quality 'pan-coals' were generally sold as fuel for saltpans or limekilns. However, one of the benefits of the Hostmen's monopoly was that it allowed them to insist their customers accept a proportion of pan-coals, earth and stone 'mingled' with their seacoals.[28] Dean Thornborough had raised the issue in 1591, but the Privy Council first confronted the problem in March 1605, when they instructed the Newcastle Corporation to appoint the soldier Sir William Constable as measurer of coals, a position he relinquished to the Hostmen for £50 in 1610.[29] Another surveyorship for London, where the Corporation had

---

[26]   The grounds for this decision was that neither Blyth nor Sunderland was actually situated on the River Tyne, the jurisdiction covered by the Hostmen's charter.
[27]   CJ, vol.1, 416a, 428a; Foster, E.R. (ed.), *Proceedings in Parliament 1610* (1966), vol.2, pp.108-9, 146, 267-8, 336; LJ, vol.2, 639b; CLRO, Repertory 27, fo.120v; Hatcher, *Coal Industry*, vol.1, p.493.
[28]   Nef, *Coal Industry*, vol.2, pp.240-1.
[29]   CSPD, 1603-10, p.207; *Company of Hostmen*, p.246. Constable was a soldier and courtier from Yorkshire, uncle of the man who signed Charles I's death warrant in 1649.

also complained about the Hostmen's mingling of coals, was granted to the courtier Sir Thomas Somerset in 1605. However, the City had long appointed its own 'seacoalmeters' to gauge the quantity and quality of the coal arriving in the Pool of London, who charged a fee of 4d. per (London) chaldron to the buyers.[30] To preserve their own rights, the Corporation quickly bought up Somerset's patent in return for a life annuity of £160.[31] Where two patentees had succeeded in extorting money, others were sure to follow, and in 1606-7 and 1612 Chancellor of the Exchequer Sir Julius Caesar received memoranda about the measuring of seacoal, salt and grain in the outports from a 'Mr Buck', who was noted to be a servant of the Scottish courtier Lord Hay.[32]

The quality of coals had thus long been a bone of contention when, in February 1616, Andrew Boyd, a client of the new Lord Steward, the Duke of Lennox, was appointed surveyor of coals for Newcastle, Sunderland and Blyth. It is hard to avoid the suspicion that the primary motive behind this grant was financial: the mine owners were to pay a fee of 4d. per (Newcastle) chaldron to the surveyor. This promised an annual revenue of around £2,000, from which the Crown was to receive a nominal rent of £26 13s. 4d.[33] The Hostmen, understandably vexed at the prospect of sacrificing profits to furnish a pension for a Scottish courtier, sent two of their number, Sir George Selby and Sir Thomas Riddell, to lobby against this grant. They successfully argued that the Company had not been consulted when the patent was first proposed, but, having reopened the question, their counsel in London advised them to play for time, warning that James's sensitivity about challenges to his prerogative, and the prospect of imminent changes to the bench of judges, made the Crown's lawyers reluctant to oppose Lennox's patent.[34] At the end of the year, Attorney-General Sir Francis Bacon brought a test case against half a dozen Hostmen in Star Chamber for mingling of coals. The London coal merchants, doubtless angered by a fresh attempt by the Hostmen to reform their cartel, queued up to testify against their suppliers in court, but the Company secured the support of the mariners who shipped their coal to London, whose guild, Deptford Trinity House, petitioned the Privy Council for another hearing. This complaint was referred to the London Corporation, who favoured the Hostmen, doubtless because a victory for Boyd would have seen the 4d. levy passed on to the Londoners.[35]

[30]   CLRO, Repertory 26/2, fos 308, 458; Repertory 27, fos 5v, 40r-v, 42, 45v, 76, 89, 234r-v, 292r-v; Journal 26, fos 359, 382-5; Nef, *Coal Industry*, vol.2, pp.251-8.
[31]   *HMC Hatfield*, vol.17, p.126; CLRO, Repertory 27, fos 45v, 68. Somerset was Master of Horse to Queen Anne, see TNA, LR6/154/9.
[32]   BL, MS Lansdowne 152, fos 42-8. This was probably George Buc of the Revels Office.
[33]   TNA, C66/2076/11; Nef, *Coal Industry*, vol.2, pp.241-2; Hatcher, *Coal Industry*, vol.1, pp.488, 493.
[34]   *Company of Hostmen*, p.62; *APC*, 1615-16, pp.519-20; TNA, SP14/87/61, 66.
[35]   TNA, STAC 8/21/2; *Company of Hostmen*, pp.63-7; Harris, G.G. (ed.), *Trinity House of Deptford Transactions*, London Record Society, vol.19 (1983), pp.25-7; *APC*, 1616-17, pp.135-6, 138-9; CLRO, Remembrancia 4/50-3, 55, 59.

Despite this decision, the Privy Council prevaricated once again, urging Boyd to file his own Star Chamber suit to ascertain whether the mingling of coals rendered them unusable. The Crown's original case against the Hostmen eventually came to judgement in May 1618, when the defendants were found guilty, fined £20 apiece, and shamed by having the verdict read publicly at Newcastle on two market days. However, the Crown stretched credibility by interpreting this as a definitive decision in favour of Boyd's patent, ordering customs officials to enforce payment.[36] This enraged the mariners, who, lobbying 'in multitudes without any counsel at all' – in other words, as an unruly mob – succeeded in intimidating the Privy Council into suspending the patent in October 1618. Boyd belatedly filed his Star Chamber case on 9 February 1619, but a week later the order to enforce payment was cancelled, and the patent was allowed to lapse.[37]

A new patent was drafted for Boyd in July 1619, but this does not appear to have reached the Great Seal.[38] However, in Parliament on 5 May 1621 the MP Robert Snelling of Ipswich, where much of the east coast collier fleet was based, complained that Boyd's patent had been revived and assigned to another of Lennox's servants, Roger Langford. The Commons ordered the patent to be suspended once again, and referred it to the committee for grievances, but nothing was decided before the end of the session in December.[39] This confrontation suggests that tensions over the surveyorship were still simmering, and in April 1622 further controversy arose when the London coal merchants raised fresh protests about the mingling of coals, and the Hostmen formed a new cartel, headed by Sir Peter Riddell. Boyd took advantage of the situation with a petition to be allowed to sue for payment of arrears of his 4d. duty (presumably those dating from 1618), and in August the Privy Council ordered the reinstatement of his position as surveyor. Lord Keeper Williams was reluctant to reopen this dispute, but in February 1623 Lennox prevailed upon him to seal a fresh patent to Roger Langford, a poorly written document which, from internal evidence, seems to have been drafted in 1619-20.[40]

The summer of 1623 saw further recriminations, with accusations that the Hostmen forced their customers to buy cargoes of which one-third comprised 'such coals as are not saleable'. Most ominously, the Company's accusers

[36] APC, 1616-17, pp.165-7; Nef, *Coal Industry*, vol.2, pp.243-4; TNA, E159/454; TNA, STAC 8/56/10; TNA, SP14/98/29.
[37] APC, 1618-19, pp.272-3, 276, 373; TNA, STAC 8/56/10.
[38] CSPD, 1619-23, p.58; McClure, N.E. (ed.), *Chamberlain Letters*, vol.2 (1939), p.243. Langford's patent, enrolled in 1623 (C66/2270/17), was apparently unaltered from the 1619-20 grant, as it cites the Treasury commission of 1618-20 as its authority, not Lord Treasurer Middlesex.
[39] CJ, vol.1, 609a.
[40] CSPD, 1619-23, pp.372, 406; APC, 1621-3, pp.189, 263, 318-19; *Company of Hostmen*, pp.67-70; Spedding, J. (ed.), *Life and Letters of Francis Bacon* (1861-74), vol.7, p.404; TNA, C66/2270/17.

77 The Exchange at the Newcastle end of the bridge, from which the Hostmen ran their cartel; a detail from Buck.

included the mariners who had supported them in their previous dispute in 1617-18. This change of heart was prompted, as the mariners explained to the Privy Council, by the Hostmen's decision to abolish the custom of giving overmeasure, or 'gift-coals', whereby the colliers received up to 20 per cent in excess of the coal they paid for, which served as both compensation for the mingling with poor quality coals, and as a means of evading full payment of the various coal duties. The Council once again ordered the dissolution of the Hostmen's cartel, and awarded a fresh patent for the surveyorship of coals to two further Lennox nominees, the Exchequer official Sir Robert Sharpeigh, and Alexander Haitley. This grant specified that the 4d. per chaldron fee was to be paid by the mariners, but passed on to the wholesale coal merchants of London.[41] Sharpeigh's patent raised protests from another group of courtiers, the farmers of the 12d. per chaldron seacoal duty, before it reached the Great Seal. They complained, quite plausibly, that this new duty would reduce their revenue, but Lennox responded that the accurate measuring of cargoes and the increase in quality which Sharpeigh's efforts aimed to promote would more than offset any decrease in trade. The new surveyors eventually gave the farmers a bond of £1,000 to guarantee that they would be compensated for any decrease in trade arising from the new charge.[42]

[41] *APC*, 1621-3, pp.471-2, 503-4; *CSPD*, 1619-23, pp.563, 587; TNA, C66/2310/11.
[42] Centre for Kentish Studies, U269/1/OE524, U269/1/OEc257.

The surveyorship was always likely to become an issue in the 1624 Parliament, but Lennox's death, just as the session convened in February, handed the initiative to the Hostmen. It was presumably at their instigation that a complaint was submitted to the Commons' grievances committee, from which the eminent lawyer Sir Edward Coke reported on 13 March that 'there are 40 surveyors for this business, who are as so many flies to afflict the poor subjects'. Sharpeigh's patent was suspended pending further investigation, which was, after much delay, scheduled for 20 May. Sir John Suckling, Comptroller of the King's Household, informed the committee of James's opinion that revocation was unnecessary, as the patent included a proviso allowing six Privy Councillors to cancel the grant if it proved harmful. However, a cursory investigation established that the patent had been procured by 'promises and threats': it was condemned upon a vote, and included in the grievance petition delivered on the final day of the session.[43]

While King James undertook to cancel Sharpeigh's patent, nothing was done until February 1625, shortly after the postponement of the next Parliamentary session, when James broke his promise with a proclamation confirming the 1623 grant to Sharpeigh. Charles's first Parliament, in the summer of 1625, which was curtailed by political wrangles and the plague, found no time to debate this minor issue, but both sides returned to the fray in the 1626 session. A Bill to prevent the use of false measures for seacoals, doubtless promoted by Sharpeigh's backers, received two readings in the Commons on 16 and 20 February, but failed to emerge from committee. A rival measure, to punish Sharpeigh and strike down his patent, received its first reading on 27 March, but with the Duke of Buckingham's impeachment dominating the Commons' agenda, the second reading was delayed until 1 June, and this Bill was still in committee at the dissolution two weeks later. This level of prevarication suggests that most MPs were reluctant to offer any ruling on the dispute.[44] Meanwhile, the grievance committee summoned Boyd to explain his continued failure to cancel the bonds he had taken from mariners in 1618-19; no definitive decision was recorded over this question, and it seems likely that the investigation was curtailed at the dissolution.[45] The merits of Sharpeigh's patent were argued before the judges in November 1626, when a delegation from the Hostmen's Company apparently succeeded in laying it to rest.[46]

[43]   *CJ*, vol.1, pp.711-12, 790a, 794-6. The patent was revocable if the grantees abused their powers: TNA, C66/2310/11.
[44]   Larkin, J.P. and Hughes, P.L. (eds.), *Stuart Royal Proclamations* (1973-83), vol.1, pp.619-25; Bidwell, W.B. and Jansson, M. (eds.), *Proceedings in Parliament 1626* (1991-6), vol.2, pp.53, 72, 374; vol.3, pp.340, 342.
[45]   Bidwell and Jansson, *Proceedings*, vol.3, pp.319, 321-3.
[46]   *Company of Hostmen*, pp.71-2.

Further Challenges to the Monopoly, 1621-5

The dispute over the surveyorship was the most protracted challenge the coal trade faced during the early Stuart period – largely due to Lennox's involvement – but it was by no means the only one. Boyd's initiative encouraged a consortium of projectors searching for old Crown debts on behalf of Lucy, Countess of Bedford,[47] to secure a patent for arrears of a long-forgotten clause of the statute for the measuring of coals (9 Henry V cap.10) imposing a duty of 2d. per chaldron on all shippers purchasing Tyneside coal who were not Newcastle freemen.[48] In Michaelmas term 1620 the patentees pleaded their case via an Exchequer lawsuit, but the Newcastle Corporation protested that the 2d. levy had been transmuted into a charge to maintain the town walls.[49] During the 1621 Parliament, Solicitor-General Sir Thomas Coventry asked for a proviso exempting this ancient statute from the Concealments Bill;[50] the Hostmen had apparently endorsed this initiative, as the Newcastle MP Sir Thomas Riddell signified his assent. However, the farmers of the main seacoal duty had clearly not been consulted, as the lawyer Sir Thomas Trevor (brother of the seacoal farmer Sir John Trevor) objected that the 2d. levy had never been collected. As the Bill committee was not instructed to consider Coventry's motion for exemption it seems that it was dropped, but in any case, the Concealments Bill was lost at the dissolution.[51]

Lady Bedford's patentees took their suit back to the law courts in 1622, but efforts to bolster their case by searching medieval records at Newcastle and in the Exchequer proved inconclusive.[52] At the same time, the farmers of the 12d. seacoal duty laid an Exchequer suit against the Hostmen for inaccurate measuring of coals, a move clearly designed to cause trouble in the parallel dispute over Lennox's patent for the survey of coals (see above). The prosecution was quickly dropped, which suggests that it was little more than retaliation for the Hostmen's failure to consult the farmers over the 1621 proviso.[53] In the 1624 Parliament, a Bill to confirm the 2d. duty was introduced into the Commons, but at its second reading on 29 April, the Newcastle MP Sir Peter Riddell insisted that this duty

---

[47]   The Countess's late father, John, Lord Harrington of Exton, had been owed large sums for his outlay as governor of Princess Elizabeth in 1603-13.

[48]   TNA, C66/2180/5; *CSPD*, 1619-23, p.61; McClure, *Chamberlain Letters*, vol.2, p.275. Details of the patent are recited in TNA, E112/113/215, but the original cannot be found in TNA, C66.

[49]   TNA, E112/113/215.

[50]   The proviso stipulated that any Crown title or revenue not enforced for 60 years would be deemed to have lapsed.

[51]   *CJ*, vol.1, p.567. The diarist John Pym garbled this debate: Notestein, W., Relf, R.H. and Simpson, H. (eds), *Commons' Debates 1621* (1935), vol.4, p.180.

[52]   TNA, E112/113/215; TNA, E126/2, ff.244v-5, 248v; TNA, SP46/164, f.92; Centre for Kentish Studies, U269/1/OE319.

[53]   TNA, E112/113/222.

had long since been assigned to the Corporation, and attacked its attempted revival as another 'pretermitted custom'.[54] This made it obvious that the Hostmen had altered their views since 1621, and therefore it is hardly surprising that the Bill never emerged from committee.[55] The Countess's pursuit of this revenue apparently ended there, although an Exchequer decree of June 1625 hinted at forfeitures for breaches of the statute of 9 Henry V, which raises the possibility that she was paid to drop her claim.[56]

Lady Bedford's dispute was never more than a minor irritant to the Hostmen, but another confrontation in the 1621 Parliament constituted a more serious threat to the Company's privileges. This came from one of the gentry mine owners of County Durham and Northumberland, a group whose interests lay almost entirely at the mercy of the Hostmen's Company. Their dilemma is illustrated by the experience of Henry Percy, 9th Earl of Northumberland,[57] who, like most of his neighbours, habitually leased his collieries at Newburn and Tynemouth to a Hostman. In 1616, following a lawsuit over rent arrears, he appointed his own manager, but when he came to sell his coals, he was offered only 6s. 6d. per chaldron; moreover, the purchaser insisted on an oversupply of 20 per cent as 'gift-coals', which reduced the actual price to 5s. 2½d. per chaldron. He eventually struck a deal at a slightly lower price, which barely covered his costs, and abandoned the enterprise altogether when one of his mines flooded.[58] Thus, while the Hostmen were charging 8-10s. per chaldron to the London colliers, they were paying their gentry suppliers around 5s., little more than they could have obtained for pan-coals, the one trade gentry mineowners could legitimately pursue without infringing the Hostmen's monopoly.

Under such circumstances, it is hardly surprising that the Hostmen were eventually challenged by the gentry mine owners; in fact, the chief curiosity of the 1621 campaign was that its protagonist – Robert Brandling of Felling, County Durham – apparently acted alone. Brandling, who owned land on both sides of the Tyne, may have been the first man who paid £10 to join the Hostmen's Company after it was chartered,[59] but he was excluded from the Company's cartels arrangements of 1603, 1605 and 1617 (see above). In August 1620 he complained to the Privy Council about primage duties charged upon coal

---

[54] The pretermitted custom was a duty the Crown had imposed on cloth in 1619, which came under heavy attack during the 1624 session.

[55] *CJ*, vol.1, pp.693-4, 769b; Northamptonshire Record Office, FH51, fo.83.

[56] TNA, E126/3, f.58.

[57] While Northumberland was a great magnate, he spent most of James's reign in the Tower of London under suspicion of complicity in the Gunpowder Plot.

[58] Hatcher, *Coal Industry*, vol.1, pp.519-21.

[59] *Company of Hostmen*, p.267. Brandling had several namesakes in the area, but as a mine owner he was the most likely to seek Company membership.

78 A warehouse and house on the Close dating from the late 16th century.

shipments by the Newcastle Corporation, the hugely discounted rates at which the Hostmen leased coal mines under the Grand Lease, and the fact that gentry mine owners were prevented from using ballast from incoming ships to build staithes along the Tyne.[60] Brandling reinforced these complaints by refusing to pay primage, for which the Newcastle Corporation swiftly prosecuted him in the Exchequer.[61]

The Privy Council did nothing about Brandling's complaint, and would probably have left the matter to the courts, but for the fact that Brandling was returned to the Commons as MP for Morpeth in December 1620.[62] He was doubtless the sponsor of a Bill to abolish primage rates at Newcastle, which received its first reading on 27 February 1621, but as nothing further was heard of this measure, Newcastle's MPs may be presumed to have smothered it. On 26 March, the day before the Easter recess, Brandling retaliated with a

---

[60] TNA, SP14/116/74, reprinted in Notestein, *Commons' Debates*, vol.7, pp.87-9. For the ballast regulations, see Welford, *Newcastle and Gateshead* (1884-7), vol.3, pp.214-19.

[61] TNA, E112/113/225.

[62] Brandling owned a small estate, Newminster Priory, just outside Morpeth (TNA, C142/753/5), which he purchased for £1,001 in 1609 (TNA, E401/2412).

motion to investigate the Hostmen's patent. Solicitor-General Heath sprang to the defence of the seacoal farm, warning 'that this may concern the King'; he called to hear the Newcastle men, but Christopher Brooke, MP for York, noted that they had already gone home, whereupon the patent was referred for investigation after Easter. Brandling's timing had been faultless: he clearly hoped to start an investigation during the vacation, when a number of committees were scheduled to continue sitting; but the delay secured by Heath and Brooke sufficed to frustrate Brandling's complaint, which never resurfaced on the floor of the House. When the Newcastle Corporation learned of this plot, they retaliated in a rather petty way, by presenting Brandling for failure to maintain his staith at Felling.[63]

The Hostmen attempted to settle their dispute with Brandling in April 1622, when they co-opted his eldest son, Sir Francis, into their new cartel arrangements.[64] However, his brother, John Brandling, continued to trade without joining the Hostmen or paying primage for the sales he made to non-freemen; he was prosecuted, but only ran into serious trouble a year later, when he began refusing to pay the 12d. per chaldron seacoal duty, and incited others to follow his example. For this John Brandling was brought to heel in the Exchequer court, which, in Michaelmas term 1623, also widened the scope of its enquiry to rule upon the lawfulness of the Hostmen's monopoly of the Tyneside coal trade.[65] Thus on 9 April 1624 it may well have been Sir Francis Brandling, then MP for Northumberland, who presented a complaint against the Hostmen's charter to the House of Commons' committee for grievances.[66] This was immediately endorsed by Sir Edward Coke, an outspoken opponent of the monopoly patents which constituted one of the most contentious features of Jacobean finance;[67] he had promoted a Monopolies' Bill which quickly passed the Commons and was sent to the House of Lords. At a conference between the two Houses on 8 April Attorney-General Sir Thomas Coventry called for a proviso to protect the Hostmen's charter, but his plea was brushed aside by Coke.[68] Whoever tabled the petition against the Hostmens'

---

[63] *CJ*, vol.1, pp.529, 575a; Notestein, *Commons' Debates*, vol.4, p.196; *CSPD*, 1619-23, p.245; Nef, *Coal Industry*, vol.2, p.129.

[64] *Company of Hostmen*, p.69. Sir Francis is not known to have joined the Hostmen's Company, but the membership records for the time may be incomplete.

[65] TNA, E112/113/226, 234, 236; TNA, E126/3, fos 58-9.

[66] TNA, SP14/166, fo.79; Northamptonshire Record Office, FH51, f.57.

[67] For a survey of Jacobean monopoly patents and their fiscal significance, see Cramsie, J., *Kingship and Crown Finance under James VI and I, 1603-25* (2002).

[68] Kyle, C.R., '*Lex Loquens*: Legislation in the Parliament of 1624' (Ph.D. thesis, Auckland University, New Zealand, 1993), p.65. The Bill, aimed at patents granted to private individuals, was unlikely to have affected the Hostmen's incorporation, but the Crown obviously wanted to take no chances with the seacoal duty.

charter the following morning thus had an impeccable sense of timing, and under the circumstances, Brandling must be regarded as the prime suspect.

At another conference in May, Coventry asked that the Hostmen be allowed to secure statutory confirmation of their incorporation, which Coke was prepared to allow. However, when this was reported back to the Commons, Brandling moved for gentry mine owners to be granted admission to the Hostmen's Company, 'whereby better coals may be served to the commonwealth'.[69] This concession might have served as the basis for a deal, but with only 10 days left until the end of the session there was no time in which to pass a Bill. Parliament, due to reconvene in the autumn, was adjourned twice and then dissolved by the death of King James, and when the case for admitting mine owners to the Company was eventually argued in the Exchequer court (as part of John Brandling's case) on 18 May 1625, it was rejected by the judges. The Hostmen's monopoly was finally confirmed by Exchequer decree on 23 June, just as the first Parliament of the new reign met. Sir Francis Brandling had again been returned for Northumberland, perhaps with the intention of revisiting this issue, but the plague and political disputes shortened the session, and kept private business off the agenda.[70]

War and Disruptions to Trade, 1625-9

The outbreak of war with Spain in the autumn of 1625 wrought an abrupt change upon the perspectives of those with vested interests in the Newcastle coal trade, as the arrival of enemy privateers off the east coast caught the Royal Navy unawares and brought shipping to a standstill: coastal shipments of Tyneside coal fell by 40 per cent in 1624-5, and did not fully recover until the end of the decade. This caused howls of protest in the 1626 Parliament, not least from Newcastle's MPs: on 25 February Sir Peter Riddell complained that 'this interruption has undone the country', leaving 8,000 unemployed; he also asked, pointedly, what the Crown was doing with the £8,300 annual revenue from the seacoal farm. Two days later, Sir Henry Anderson quoted letters he had received from some of the 2,500 English prisoners held at the Spanish base at Dunkirk, and lambasted the Royal Navy's incompetence.[71] Secretary of State Sir John Coke attempted to pre-empt such

---

[69] *CJ*, vol.1, 703b, 706a; Kyle, '*Lex Loquens*', p.73.

[70] TNA, E126/3, ff.58-60. The adjournment of Brandling's Exchequer case on 4 February 1625 came shortly after the proclamation of 19 January postponing the next Parliamentary session: Larkin and Hughes, *Proclamations*, vol.1, pp.617-18. See also Diana Newton in this volume.

[71] Stradling, R.A., *The Armada of Flanders: Spanish maritime policy and European war, 1568-1668* (1992), pp.43-5, 59-60; Hatcher, *Coal Industry*, vol.1, pp.488-9; Bidwell and Jansson, *Proceedings*, vol.2, pp.130-1, 142. And see Newton in this volume.

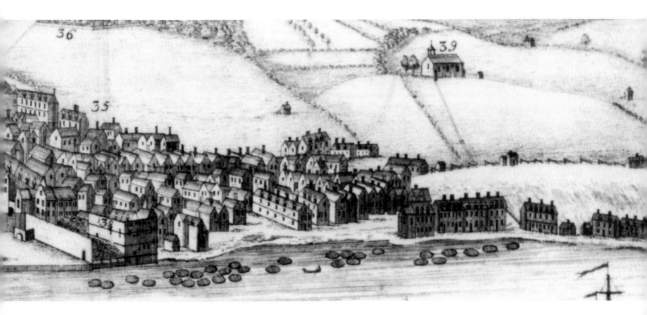

79   Keel boats gathered at Sandgate, a detail from Buck.

complaints on 25 February, citing a plan drafted by Deptford Trinity House which recommended that 10 colliers be hired and equipped with ordnance. He proposed funding the scheme via an additional levy of 12d. per chaldron of coals, but to avoid the prospect of London coal merchants passing the cost on to their customers he suggested 'that there might be [a] magazine of coals erected wherein the traders may have a stock, and thereby reasonable gain and the price kept low' – a London cartel not dissimilar to those previously implemented by the Newcastle Hostmen.[72]

Some of those who clamoured for action were merely using this crisis to attack the Duke of Buckingham, who was responsible for coastal defence in his capacity as Lord Admiral. However, coal shortages constituted a genuine grievance in London at the end of a long winter, and when the Lords debated coastal defence on 1 April, Lord President Manchester and Bishop Neile of Durham, both allies of the Duke, voiced pleas for action which could hardly be dismissed as mere partisanship. Buckingham protested that the £22,000 allocated for coastal defence in the naval budget was hopelessly inadequate, and mentioned that 'some have thought of an imposition on coals. They [that?] did anciently belong to the Admiralty, now the Lord Mayor has it' – by this, he presumably meant the 4d. per chaldron levy collected by the London seacoalmeters (see above). The Lords appointed a committee to consider this issue, but questions of

[72]   *Trinity House Transactions*, pp.67-8; Bidwell and Jansson, *Proceedings*, vol.2, pp.127, 130.

supply properly belonged to the Commons, and if this committee met at all, its deliberations were lost amid the furore surrounding the Duke's impeachment.[73] With plans for a coastal squadron already in train, Buckingham needed to procure funds somehow, and on 2 May he sent Edward Nicholas, his secretary for naval affairs, to present the London Corporation with an offer 'to undertake to store the City with seacoals if he may be contracted withal for them at some reasonable price'; this offer of a cartel was apparently declined.[74]

Coal shipments did, in fact, resume along the east coast during the summer of 1626 under armed escort, but the Crown's interest in prerogative finance grew apace after the angry dissolution of Parliament in June. Deptford Trinity House suggested that the armed colliers which protected the trade should fill their holds with coal, allowing them to profit from their convoy duties.[75] In February 1627, perhaps to deal with the vagaries of wartime trading conditions, the Hostmen organised another cartel, which raised 6d. upon every chaldron shipped in order to provide compensation of 16d. per chaldron for those who failed to sell their full quota of coals. Thus, four months later, when the Crown imposed a further levy of 6d. per chaldron on seacoal shipments from Newcastle and Sunderland to raise money for convoys, the cartel merely adjusted its duty to 12d. per chaldron. This innovation raised only £952 before being abandoned on 27 November, allegedly because 'the loss of shipping & mariners is found so great that there is more need to bethink how to cherish the trade than to give them any discontent'. However, it may not be coincidental that it ceased on the day the judges handed down their ruling in the Five Knights' case – the test case for the Forced Loan.[76] Naturally, the quest for other revenues continued: on 29 December the masters of Deptford Trinity House, acting on King Charles I's instructions, asked the London colliers how much they would be prepared to pay for convoy guards, to which they responded that, having armed themselves and organised a convoy system on their own initiative, they required no further assistance.[77] The assumption that the coastal defence levy on seacoals would prove controversial was vindicated on 7 May 1628, when Sir Peter Riddell cited it in the Commons as a grievance. The customs farmer Sir John Wolstenholme was summoned to attend with the relevant paperwork, but nothing came of this investigation; in June, when MPs framed a remonstrance against Buckingham, Riddell renewed his objections, though with no greater success.[78]

[73]   Bidwell and Jansson, *Proceedings*, vol.1, pp.241-2, 248.
[74]   *CSPD*, 1625-6, pp.292, 306, 341, 350; CLRO, Repertory 40, fo.204r-v.
[75]   Cust, R., *The Forced Loan* (1987), pp.35-7; *Trinity House Transactions*, pp.83-4.
[76]   *Company of Hostmen*, pp.72-4; TNA, E351/2595; East Sussex Record Office, GLY/423.
[77]   *Trinity House Transactions*, pp.89-90.
[78]   Johnson, R.C., Keeler, M.F., Jansson, M. and Bidwell, W.B. (eds), *Commons' Debates 1628* (1977-83), vol.3, pp.310-11, 319; vol.4, pp.293, 211.

The final threat to the seacoal trade during the wartime years came from an implausibly ambitious scheme contrived by the projector John Shotbolt *alias* Battalion, which he showed to Buckingham on 3 July 1628, only days after the end of the Parliamentary session. The plan was that the Crown would become 'the sole merchant of coals' in place of the Hostmen. Seacoals would thereafter be shipped to 16 staple ports between Scarborough and Southampton in regular convoys, with a squadron of 10 armed ships to provide escorts. Shotbolt effectively advocated a nationalisation of the Tyneside coal industry, the profits from which were to fund a permanent squadron for coastal defence. The audacity of this scheme delighted both the Duke and the King, but at one of the initial meetings someone – probably Chancellor of the Exchequer Sir Richard Weston – observed 'that the King was unprovided to stock the business'. Shotbolt spent several months persuading Lord Mayor Sir Hugh Hammersley and four other London aldermen to invest £60,000 in the scheme, but in December Weston suspended talks until after the new Parliamentary session.[79]

While evidence of an ambitious new scheme for prerogative finance would undoubtedly have alarmed MPs, Weston deliberately neglected to mention that he was also negotiating with the existing seacoal farmers for a renegotiation of their lease, the yield of which had been reduced by the wartime disruptions. On 22 April 1629, shortly after the angry dissolution of Parliament, the seacoal farmers signed a new contract which reduced their annual rent by 17 per cent, in return for which they made a cash payment of £11,000 to the Crown. Shotbolt, apparently unaware of this fact, spent a further nine months flogging a dead horse before he abandoned his project.[80] For all that King Charles and Buckingham had been (briefly) interested in this scheme, it seems likely that Weston always intended to use it as a stalking horse to procure the best terms from the existing seacoal farmers; if the latter had been under any real threat, they would almost certainly have made common cause with the Hostmen, who were apparently kept in the dark throughout the course of the negotiations.

Conclusion

While the Hostmen were based in Newcastle and the adjacent coalfields, the capital flows they managed with such conspicuous success came from all over England and north-western Europe. Thus it is hardly surprising that most of the battles for control of the Tyneside coal trade and its profits were fought elsewhere: at Court, in Parliament, in the law courts, or on the high seas. The

[79] BL, MS Stowe 326, fos1, 7-8.
[80] East Sussex Record Office, GLY/426, 429-31; *CSPD*, 1628-9, p.475; BL, MS Stowe 326, fo.1.

best measure of the Hostmen's success is the fact that early modern Newcastle became an independent centre of capital formation – on a modest scale, when compared with London, but at least on a par with other regional centres such as York, Norwich, Bristol or Exeter.[81] It also escaped the fate of towns such as Southampton, Ipswich, Weymouth or Coventry, which became satellites of the metropolis, colonised by Londoners and their capital.

Two further observations should be made. First, the Newcastle Corporation became dominated by an oligarchy whose involvement in the world of high finance gradually detached them from the mariners and coal miners who formed the vast majority of the population – but then, this would presumably have happened more rapidly and decisively if the Londoners had managed to secure control of the Tyneside coalfields. Finally, the oligarchy enjoyed a similarly remarkable record in fighting off the gentry interlopers who came to dominate so many Corporations in the decades before the Civil Wars, thanks to the unexpected bounty of the Grand Lease, and the wisdom of those Hostmen who realised that the seacoal duty represented not a burden, but the chance to render themselves indispensable to the Crown, the better to pursue their own gain.

[81] Newton, *North-East England*, p.40. For one example of a Yorkshire gentleman looking to Newcastle as a source of capital, see *Hutton Correspondence*, SS, vol.17 (1843), pp.311-12.

'That lamentable time':
Catastrophe and Community in the Great Newcastle Plague of 1636[1]

KEITH WRIGHTSON

Introduction

1636 is not usually thought of as a major plague year in England. The experience of London tends to set the standard and the surge of plague mortality in the metropolis that year has been characterised as a 'lesser outbreak', paling in comparison to the truly devastating visitations of 1563, 1603, 1625 and 1665.[2] Newcastle upon Tyne, however, like other major east coast ports, had its own epidemic history. Outbreaks of plague in the northern city tended on the whole to follow London, implying the spread of infection through the particularly close trading links between Newcastle and the capital – above all those maintained through the vital coal trade. This was the case, for example, in 1544-5, 1570-1, 1576, 1579, 1604 and 1625. Nevertheless, it was also open, by virtue of its extensive trading connections with the Netherlands and north Germany, to other sources of infection. In 1588-9, for example, Newcastle was afflicted a year ahead of other major English cities, while London was in fact spared. Moreover, the mortality of 1588-9 was peculiarly bad in Newcastle, suggesting perhaps the direct importation of a fresh and virulent strain of the plague bacillus.[3]

1636 was another such year. In the final decade of the 16th century and in the first third of the 17th, Newcastle had suffered relatively lightly from the plague. Outbreaks in 1593, 1597, 1604 and 1625 were alarming, but limited in

[1]   This essay presents some of the findings of a larger ongoing study of the plague of 1636 in Newcastle.
[2]   Finlay, R., *Population and Metropolis. The Demography of London, 1580-1650* (1981), p.111. See also P. Slack, *The Impact of Plague in Tudor and Stuart England* (1985), p.151 and chapter 6.
[3]   Slack, *Impact of Plague*, pp.61, 62, 66. For the severity of the 1588-9 outbreak, see Bourchier Richardson, G., *Plague and Pestilence in the North of England* (1852), p.15. Slack stresses that 'the importation of a more virulent strain of the plague bacillus from outside appears to have been necessary for a major epidemic', and that the more general English outbreaks of plague tended to be the culmination of broad tides of infection sweeping across Europe: *Impact of Plague*, p.68.

their impact.[4] In 1636, however, it returned, and with a severity that, as the city's Puritan lecturer Robert Jenison put it, was 'never the like with us to that it is like to doe now'.[5]

According to Jenison, the plague came directly from Holland to North Shields, at the mouth of the Tyne, in October 1635. Thereafter it lay dormant through the winter, perhaps diffusing among the rat population of the riverside districts of the city until the advent of the warm weather that favoured the development of the rat fleas which transmitted the disease from dying rats to humans. Then, as Jenison put it, 'after some few moneths intermission, it hath broken out fearefully'. The severity of the outbreak was apparent as early as 6 May, and thereafter 'it increaseth, rageth rather, runs and spreads like wildfire'.[6]

The Course of the Epidemic

It is impossible to trace the progress of the disease through the city as fully as one might wish. The parish registers of Allhallows, the largest and most populous of the city's four parishes, containing just over half the population in 1665, break off in March 1636. Those of St Andrew's, in the north west of the city commence only in late July. The registers of St Nicholas' and St John's are extant, though St John's has a gap in registration in July and early August.[7] These registration gaps, which may in part be a result of the emergency conditions of 1636, are frustrating. Nevertheless, we are unusually fortunate in having two surviving sets of weekly figures for burials in Newcastle as a whole during the epidemic, and these, as we shall see, can go some way towards compensating for the deficiencies of the parish register record.

The first set of figures was provided by Robert Jenison as an appendix to his *Newcastles Call*, and was presumably compiled by him in early January 1637.

[4]   Bourchier Richardson, *Plague and Pestilence*, pp.17-26.
[5]   Jenison, R., *Newcastles Call, To her Neighbour and Sister Townes and Cities throughout the land* (1637), p.23. As a 'lecturer' at Allhallows' Church from 1622, Jenison was employed by the city to preach sermons. For a brief account of his career and many publications, see Sheils, W.J. 'Jenison, Robert', in *Oxford Dictionary of National Biography*, and for a fuller account of his role in the religious and political life of the city, Howell, R. Jnr., *Newcastle-upon-Tyne and the Puritan Revolution. A Study of the Civil War in North England* (1967), *passim*.
[6]   Jenison, R., *Newcastle's Call*, pp.2, 4-5, 119, 178.
[7]   The original parish registers are held at the Northumberland Collections: EP 86/1, St Nicholas; EP 9/2, All Saints' [Allhallows]; EP 13/1-2, St Andrew; EP 73/3, St John. Microfilms are also available there and at TWAS. Population estimates are based on the figures for the 1665 Hearth Tax provided in Howell, R., *Newcastle-upon-Tyne and the Puritan Revolution*, Appendix, Tables I-III, and the original returns printed in Welford, R., 'Newcastle Householders in 1665', *AA*, 3rd ser., vol.7 (1911). Welford provides details of the ward boundaries, and these have been mapped in Graham, F., *Maps of Newcastle* (1984). Since the boundaries of the four parishes did not coincide exactly with those of the wards of the city used for taxation purposes, one cannot be precise about the numbers of households living in each parish at the time of the 1665 Hearth Tax assessment. However, grouping the wards falling principally into particular parishes provides the following rough estimates of the proportion of households living in each parish: Allhallows 52 per cent; St Nicholas, St Andrew and St John, roughly 16 per cent each.

It provides 18 weekly totals of burials up to 11 September, followed by a single total for the period from 11 September to 31 December.[8] The second set of figures was entered into his family bible by William Coulson of Jesmond – a leading citizen who had witnessed the epidemic – at some time between the events described and 1658. It provides burial totals for the city for 33 weeks, extending from early May until Christmas Eve 1636.[9] These Jenison/Coulson figures can be brought into alignment with one another to provide a weekly account of burials 'within the liberties' or 'Corporation' of Newcastle from May until December 1636. This can then be compared with the registered burials in St Nicholas, St John's and St Andrew's. This makes possible a simple calculation of the burials 'missing' in the parish registration: that is, the Jenison/Coulson figures minus the registered burials (see Table 6). As will be evident, most of the 'missing' burials in May and June would have occurred in the parishes of St Andrews and Allhallows. In July they would have occurred in these two parishes and St John's. After 7 August, from which date we have unbroken registration for the other three parishes, all the 'missing' burials can be attributed to Allhallows as estimated burials for that parish. Finally Table 6 also includes (in the final column) an additional

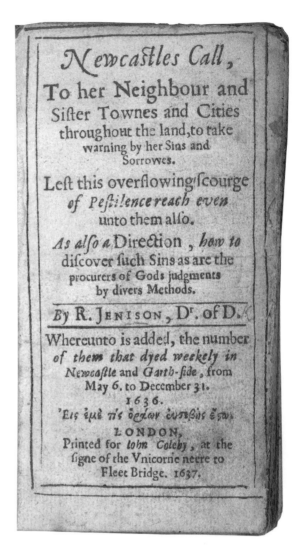

80   Title page of Jenison's *Newcastles Call*.

---

8   Jenison, *Newcastles Call*, pp.250-2.
9   Coulson's figures were published by F.W. Dendy as a note on 'The Plague in Newcastle' in *Proceedings of the Society of Antiquaries of Newcastle-upon-Tyne*, 3rd series, vol.1 (1905), p.48. Dendy points out that Coulson purchased his estate at Jesmond in 1658. Since he signed the list 'Wm. Coulson of Jesmond', this implies that 'he either did not make or did not sign the entry until that year'.

Week	Jenison/ Coulson	St Nicholas	St John	St Andrew	[?Allhallows]	'Missing'	'Garth-side'
May 1-6	-	1	2	-	-	-	
7-13	59	2	4	-	-	53	
14-20	55	1	6	-	-	48	
21-27	99	4	4	-	-	91	
28-3	122	0	5	-	-	117	30-5: 10
Jun 4-10	99	0	7	-	-	92	6-12: 24
11-17	162	2	6	-	-	154	13-19: 19
18-24	133	1	4	-	-	128	20-26: 34
25-1	172	8	1	-	-	163	27-3: 40
Jul 2-8	184	4	-	-	-	180	4-10: 75
9-15	212	7	-	-	-	205	11-17: 66
16-22	270	7	-	7	-	256	18-24: 60
23-29	366	14	-	-	-	352	25-31: 60
Aug 30-6*	337	23	-	40	-	274	1-7: 29
7-13	422	28	32	62	[300]	300	8-14: 17
14-20	346	32	41	47	[226]	226	15-21: 18
21-27	398	44	41	55	[258]	258	22-28: 13
28-3	386	41	47	61	[237]	237	29-4: 14
Sep 4-10	325	36	52	56	[181]	181	5-11: 11
11-17	202	30	35	43	[94]	94	12-18: 7
18-24	197	38	31	34	[94]	94	19-25: 4
25-1	122	17	24	30	[51]	51	26-2: 6
Oct 2-8	197	8	22	20	[147]	147	3-9: 2
9-15	65	7	14	18	[26]	26	10-16: 2
16-22	37	3	7	13	[14]	14	Oct 17: 4
23-29	28	4	3	13	[8]	8	
Nov 30-5	39	6	7	6	[20]	20	
6-12	17	2	7	2	[6]	6	
13-19	22	6	3	3	[10]	10	
20-26	13	1	4	2	[6]	6	
27-3	10	0	10	2	-	-2	
Dec 4-10	12	2	1	2	[7]	7	
11-17	3	0	0	4	-	-1	
18-24	5	1	0	2	[2]	2	
25-31	-	1	0	2	-	-	

Table 6 Progress of the plague in Newcastle, 1636 (burials). Notes: * = one extra day in order to match Jenison/Coulson figures; − = no registered burials (break in parish registration): St Nicholas, St John and St Andrews figures from parish burial registers. 'Missing' burials = Jenison/Coulson figures minus registered burials. Allhallows figures in square brackets are estimates: the Jenison/Coulson totals minus the registered burials in all other parishes.

set of figures provided by Jenison for those 'Buried in *Garth-side* in *New-castle* this present yeare, 1636' for 20 weeks from 30 May to 17 October – an issue to which we will return.

The figures presented in Table 6, together with the evidence provided by the parish of residence of plague victims whose wills have survived, enable us to trace the progress of the epidemic with some confidence. Clearly, the city authorities were aware that the plague had broken out by the end of the first week of May. The Jenison/Coulson figures show that significantly elevated levels of burials were being reported in the remainder of that month.[10] They continued to climb in June and July and peaked in the seven weeks between 23 July and 10 September – each of which saw well over 300 – before subsiding slowly in September and more markedly from mid-October.[11]

That was the general pattern. But there is also a more specific story to be told. As Table 6 indicates, there is no evidence of exceptionally severe mortality in St Nicholas' or St John's parishes in May and June 1636. St Nicholas', in fact, usually saw around eight or nine burials a month in normal years in the early 1630s, and St John's around ten. The St John's figures are certainly somewhat elevated, but not yet drastically so. As for St Andrew's, we simply do not know. Nevertheless, it seems reasonable to suppose that in May and June, and possibly for much of July, the escalating burials reported by Jenison and Coulson came principally from the parish of Allhallows.[12] This is consistent with the surviving wills which indicate death from the plague. With the single exception of the will of a man who lived in Castle Garth and was buried in nearby St Nicholas' churchyard on 29 June, the plague wills of May and June come from inhabitants

---

[10]   Comparison with pre-plague burial registration suggests that Newcastle's four parishes usually witnessed a total of around fifty burials a month in the early 1630s, which suggests a fairly high crude death rate as a normal reality. From the second week of May more than 50 burials a *week* were being reported.

[11]   The absolute peak, in the week of 7-13 August, saw over 400 burials.

[12]   Allhallows usually saw around twenty-five burials a month in 'normal' years. If the 'missing' burials came mostly from Allhallows, then it was already witnessing ten times that level in May and over 20 times that level in June.

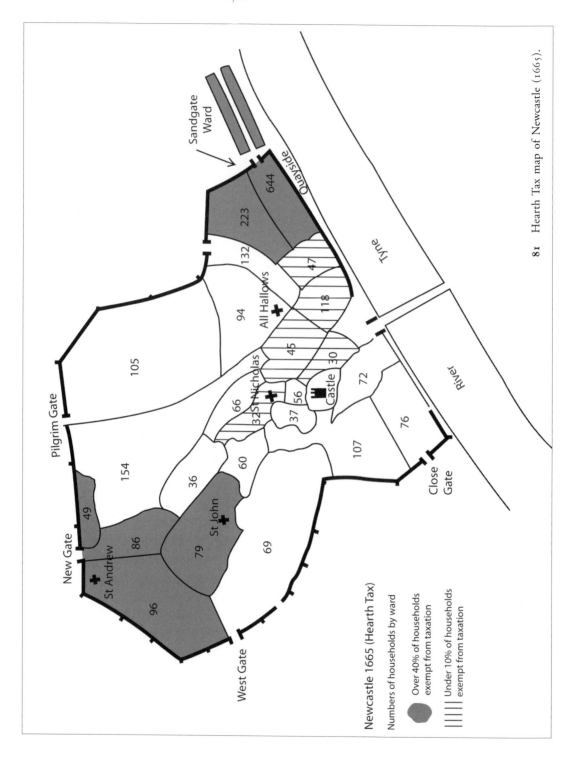

Sandgate Ward

Quayside

Tyne

River

644

223

132

47

118

94

All Hallows

105

45

30

St Nicholas

72

56

Castle

66

32

37

76

60

107

Pilgrim Gate

154

36

49

St John

79

St Andrew

86

69

96

New Gate

West Gate

Close Gate

Newcastle 1665 (Hearth Tax)

Numbers of households by ward

Over 40% of households
exempt from taxation

Under 10% of households
exempt from taxation

81   Hearth Tax map of Newcastle (1665).

of Allhallows, and more specifically the Sandgate area.[13] John Reay, for example, was a Sandgate miller. Thomas Dodds was 'of Sandgate, keleman'. William Grame, 'skipper', was another keelman who, being 'visited with the plague of pestilence', declared his will on 31 May 1636.[14]

Sandgate was the most populous of the city's 24 wards: in 1665 it contained a quarter of all households. It was also by far the poorest, with 79.2 per cent of householders being exempted from taxation that year. It was described in 1649 as 'populous all along the water side; where ship-wrights, sea-men, and keel men most live', and as an area of the city characterised by densely packed housing in 'many narrow streets or chaires'.[15] One of the city's great middens, or public dunghills, was located there – just outside the Sand Gate itself – with another close by, near Pandon Gate.[16] If the optimum conditions for plague, as Paul Slack observes, involved 'a large number of people in close proximity to one another, to dirt, and to rats', then the Sandgate and its neighbouring wards in the riverfront areas of Allhallows fitted the bill.[17] Nor was there anything new about that. In the late summer and early autumn of both 1603 and 1604, Allhallows had witnessed unusually high numbers of burials, many of which were explicitly attributed to 'plague', though no such waves of burials occurred in the registers of St Nicholas' or St John's. Allhallows was the established epicentre of infection in Newcastle.

In 1636, however, the epidemic spread. In St Nicholas' parish – which included the relatively wealthy wards of the riverside west of Sandhill, the western half of the Side and the central axis of the town up to the Bigg Market – plague was certainly present as early as May: on 8th and 12th of that month the parish clerk marked individual burials 'pl'. But it was slow to take hold. Burials remained relatively few throughout May and early June and some weeks saw none at all. In the final week of June they began to increase and six of

[13]   The exception was William Robinson. He had made his will earlier, but the inventory indicates that he and his wife died of the plague. The parish clerk also noted 'pl' beside his burial entry. Though not a wealthy man, he was one of some distinction. His will describes him as a 'painter and Deputy Herald' by profession. Henry Bourne, alluding to an early 17th-century manuscript known to him, mentions that William Robinson lived in a house in Castle Garth 'who was Deputy Herrald under Norroy, *King at Arms*. This Man wrote in a Book the Arms of all the Mayors of this Towne ... until his Time'. This may have been one of the '6 books of Armes' mentioned in his inventory: DUL, DPRI/1/1636/R9/1-2; Bourne, H., *The History of Newcastle upon Tyne: or, the ancient and present state of that town* (1736), p.121.

[14]   DUL, DPRI/1/1636/R2/1-2 (John Reay); DPRI/1/1636/D3/103 (Thomas Dodds); DPRI/1/1636/G8/1-2 (William Grame).

[15]   W[illiam] G[ray], *Chorographia, or a Survey of Newcastle Upon Tyne* (1649), pp.37, 49.

[16]   There were also middens at the West Gate, and the Close Gate, and a vast one, which served the upper town, by the castle wall. Excavations indicate that in the course of the 16th century some four metres of rubbish was deposited in the castle ditch. Bourchier Richardson, *Plague and Pestilence*, p. xv; Harbottle, B., Ellison, M. et al, 'An excavation in the Castle Ditch, Newcastle-upon-Tyne, 1974-6', *AA*, 5th series, vol.9 (1981), pp.88, 93-4.

[17]   Slack, *Impact of Plague*, p.159.

82 Mortality was high in the neighbourhood of Newgate. The gate in the early 19th century, by T.M. Richardson, snr.

the eight burials recorded were designated 'pl'. Then, after a further pause, the mortality took off in the last week of July. As might be expected, wills made by plague victims resident in St Nicholas' multiplied in July and continued to appear in August and September as the disease raged. The absolute peak in burials came in the two weeks 21 August-3 September, which typically saw five to seven burials a day, and occasionally ten or eleven. It began to subside after 25 September, which was the first day without burials since 25 July, and by October burials were down to the levels of late June and early July. Two of the four burials in the final week of October were marked 'not of ye plague' – one can sense the relief of the clerk who noted that fact – and by November it was largely, though not wholly, over. The final plague will for the parish was made on 5 November by Robert Mallabar, barber surgeon, who was buried in St Nicholas' on the eighth.[18]

In St John's parish – which included the western sector of the upper town, the suburban strip outside the West Gate and the nearby settlements of Elswick and Benwell – the first signs of plague came a week later than in St Nicholas' in the form of a cluster of burials on 14-18 May from the family of Leonard Trumble, blacksmith: first his daughter, then his son, then his wife. But as in St Nicholas', the mortality was slow to take off. The absence of burial registration for five weeks in July and early August makes it impossible to date the eventual eruption with precision, but by the second week of August the epidemic was raging and from then until September St John's typically saw five to seven burials a day, with as many as 17 and 19 on the worst days (1 and 8 September). The first surviving plague will for St John's, that of James Wilson, clockmaker, was made on 12 August. The last, that of Ralph Rowmaine, a tanner who was buried on 2 October, was written on 29 September. In St John's, however, high mortality continued for two weeks longer than in St Nicholas', and faded more slowly. Few days passed without burials before mid-October, and burial totals remained somewhat elevated even in November. The last gasp of the epidemic came only on 1 December with the burial of '7 poore things out of the Warden Close'. Presumably these bodies had just been discovered.[19]

When the plague reached St Andrew's – comprising the northern sector of the upper town, with concentrations of housing in High Friar Chare, the eastern part of Newgate Street, upper Pilgrim Street, and in the Gallowgate suburb beyond New Gate – cannot be determined. It was present on 8 July when John Laverrock made his will, and had probably taken hold by 21-2 July when seven people were buried. By 31 July, from which date there is continuous burial registration, the mortality was heavy, and it continued to be so for nine weeks before gradually diminishing in October. In the worst weeks St Andrew's saw eight to 10 burials a day, and on the very worst days 15 or 16, and significantly high mortality is evident for four weeks longer than was the case in St Nicholas' and two weeks longer than in St John's. Absolute numbers of burials were also somewhat higher in St Andrew's than in St Nicholas' or St John's – 388 in the nine weeks from 7 August to 1 October, as compared to 266 and 303 respectively. Since the populations of the three parishes were roughly proportionate, it seems

---

[18]   Northumberland Collections, EP 86/1 (Newcastle, St Nicholas). For Mallabar's will, see DUL, DPRI/1/1637/M2/1.

[19]   Northumberland Collections, EP 73/3 (Newcastle, St John); DUL, DPRI/1/1637/W9/1 (James Wilson), DPRI/1/1636/R12/1-2 (Ralph Rowmaine). The Warden Close was near a postern north of the West Gate, and was listed by Gray among the suburban districts of the city: Gray, *Chorographia*, p.40. Perhaps the bodies of these anonymous victims had been found during a post-plague search of the area.

possible that the severity of the mortality in St Andrew's was related to the relative poverty and dense housing of the wards around New Gate. Whatever the case, from late August onwards the burial registration suggests that the parish clerk was becoming overwhelmed. Novel forms of differentiation began to appear in the register that reveal both his knowledge of his neighbours and its limits. Persons of rank and office were designated by a pointing finger in the margin. Of lesser folk, some were local characters well enough known to him to be accorded the intimacy of such designations as 'Robert Toddericke … which had the honchback', 'Gorge the dyer', 'Gorges the fiddler', or 'William Nichollsone to a nickname Mr Mare'. Other entries were truncated, consisting only of a depersonalising surname – 'Nycksone', 'Dawson', 'Hunter' – or occupation – 'Munders made', 'Brands made'. Still others – 56 in all – were wholly anonymous save for their condition: 'a powre one', 'a powre child' and the like. When he noted '3 day o' on 3 October, the first day without burials since 31 July, he was clearly looking for signs of hope. He had to wait 12 more days before he could add 'none the 15' on 15 October, and a few days more until '19 none & 20', but while numbers fell thereafter, he did not mark a burial 'not of the plage' until 25 November.[20]

Meanwhile, the 'missing' burials that can be attributed to Allhallows – comprising the whole south-eastern sector of the town and suburban Sandgate – suggest that the mortality in that parish probably peaked in August, continued at a diminished but still very severe level in September, and then fell back after the first week of October. That the plague remained present, however, is suggested not only by the figures but by the fact that more plague wills survive for Allhallows in October and early November than for the other parishes combined.

We have, then, a picture of an epidemic beginning in Sandgate in May, engulfing Allhallows in June and July, taking off in St Nicholas' in late July, and in St John's and St Andrew's by early August at the latest, and raging generally through August and September. From late September and throughout October it gradually retreated, subsiding first in St Nicholas', then in St John's and St Andrew's, and finally in Allhallows. All this confirms Paul Slack's argument that plague mortality had 'a distinct urban topography', being 'concentrated in clearly distinguishable areas of each town, in the fringe parishes which were chiefly, though not wholly, inhabited by the laboring

---

[20] Northumberland Collections, EP 13/1-2 (Newcastle, St Andrew); DUL, DPRI/ 1/1637/L4/1 (John Laverrock). Five more wills survive for St Andrew's up to 7 October.

poor'.[21] In 1636 the plague affected the whole of Newcastle but, as elsewhere, it was only 'superficially indiscriminate'.[22] In the period from 7 August to 15 October, during which the plague raged throughout the city and for which we have burials or estimated burials for all parishes, the proportion of all burials registered in St Andrew's (16 per cent) was close to the parish's estimated share of the city's population. St John's, with 13 per cent of burials, was under-represented, and St Nicholas' (10 per cent of burials) was markedly under-represented. Allhallows, with 61 per cent of burials was seriously over-represented.[23] And when we consider that Allhallows had almost certainly produced most of the burials in the earlier months of the epidemic, it must have been massively over-represented in the mortality as a whole. That even this may not be the whole story is suggested by further consideration of the weekly figures provided by Jenison for those 'Buried in *Garth-side* in *New-castle*', between 30 May and 17 October.

These figures have usually been taken to refer to the town of Gateshead.[24] There are, however, good reasons to question that attribution. In the first place, Jenison refers to '*Garth-side* in *New-castle*'. As a local man he would have known very well that Gateshead was *not* in Newcastle.[25] Secondly, while Gateshead was often referred to as 'Gateside' in this period, it was never, to the best of my knowledge, called 'Garth-side'. Finally, the parish registers of Gateshead show that the plague did indeed reach the town. Normal burial registration ceased on 22 June and was followed by a list of 'The names of those that died in the infection of the plaige & is buried in the Church yard this year: 1636 since the first begyninge being aboute the first of June'. The names are numbered, and can be grouped by month, but not by week since precise dates of burial are not given. Up to 30 September, when normal registration resumed, exactly 200 names were listed. Jenison, however, gives weekly figures for 'Garth-side' totalling 515 burials. Clearly, 'Garth-side' was not Gateshead.[26]

Where, then, was '*Garth-side* in *New-castle*'. One possible candidate is the Castle Garth or yard, which was jurisdictionally part of the county of Northumberland, but physically located in Newcastle, on the hilltop south of St Nicholas' Church.

[21] Slack, *Impact of Plague*, pp.143, 153.
[22] *Ibid.*, p.192.
[23] Using population distribution derived from the 1665 hearth tax, as described in n.7 above: Allhallows 52 per cent; St Andrew's, St Nicholas' and St John's, 16 per cent each.
[24] Welford, *Newcastle and Gateshead*, vol.3 (1887), p.337; Shrewsbury, J.F.D., *A History of Bubonic Plague in the British Isles* (1970), p.382; Howell, *Newcastle-upon-Tyne and the Puritan Revolution*, p.7.
[25] See below, p.295.
[26] TWAS, Microfilm 1139 (Registers of Gateshead, St Mary), fo. 163 ff.; Jenison, *Newcastle's Call*, pp.251-2.

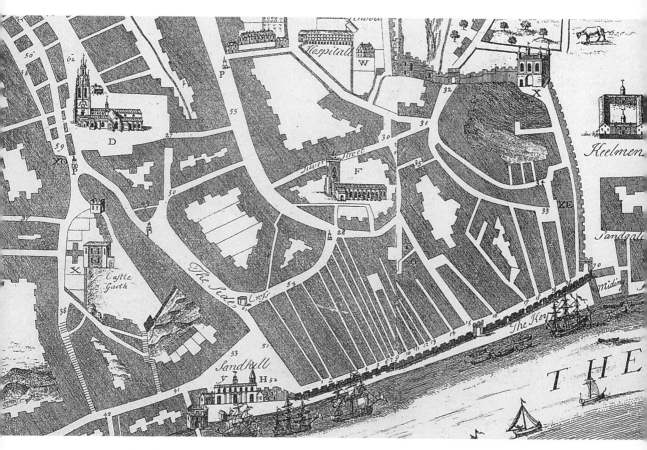

83 The dense settlement and narrow chares of Allhallows, where the plague was most virulent. Detail from Corbridge's map.

Bourchier Richardson, writing in 1852, believed that a mass grave had been located there in 1636.[27] However, the timing of the reported burials casts doubt on this possibility. Two thirds of them took place in June and July before major mortality erupted in neighbouring St Nicholas' and St John's parishes. And if the dead came from the riverside sections of Allhallows where the mortality was already high, the Castle Garth, some distance away and on top of a steep hill, seems a less than convenient place of burial. A better possibility might be the 'Place called the Garth-Heads', an open 'Place of Pleasure and Recreation' described by Henry Bourne as reachable by a lane to the right beyond Pandon

[27]   That belief, however, seems to have been based solely upon inference from Jenison and Bourchier Richardson's own experience of seeing 'vast numbers of skeletons' uncovered during railway excavations in the area: Bourchier Richardson, *Plague and Pestilence*, pp.28-9. It is now thought that these were most likely from the Anglo-Saxon cemetery now known to have been located there.

Gate: in other words to the north of the extra-mural part of Sandgate.[28] A burial ground established there would have been well placed to accommodate the bodies of plague victims from Sandgate without the walls in the early months of the outbreak. This seems to be the most likely identification of '*Garth-side in New-castle*'. But whatever the case, it seems clear that the 515 burials in Garth-side must be added to the Jenison/Coulson total of 5,116 burials if we are to appreciate the full scale of the mortality in the city and its immediate environs, producing a grand total of 5,631.

That figure gains support from a further estimate of the mortality made by the Mayor and aldermen of Newcastle in a letter written in the first week of October to the Mayor of Berwick, thanking him for a contribution to the city's relief funds. 'The number of the dead is not so manye this last weeke as formerly', they wrote, 'being but one hundred twentie two. The great death of people that hath beene, which doth amount to verie neare 6000 persons since the beginning wee feare is cause that there dye fewer now; there being not so many people left in the towne as there was'.[29] Whatever the merits of this causal reasoning, they were right about the drastic reduction of the city's population. If at least 5,600 died in all, and that may be an underestimate, then around forty-seven per cent of the population of the city died in the epidemic of 1636. A third of the population of Norwich had succumbed in the outbreak of 1579. London lost roughly 24 per cent of its people in 1563, 23 per cent in 1603 and almost 18 per cent in 1665. The absolute numbers dying in these metropolitan outbreaks were of course far higher than those suffered in Newcastle. In proportionate terms, however, the Newcastle epidemic of 1636 may have been the most devastating culling experienced by any English city in this period.[30]

Reactions to the Plague

Globally, such mortality was of course catastrophic. But the burden of sickness and death was not evenly distributed. As we have seen, it weighed heavier in particular districts. More, it was most keenly felt by particular families, for as is

---

[28]   Bourne, *History*, p.153. Garth Heads is clearly marked on Charles Hutton's map of the city, drawn in 1770 – lying between the Carpenters' Tower and the Keelmen's Hospital.

[29]   Raine, J., 'A Letter from the Corporation of Newcastle upon Tyne', *AA*, vol.2 (1832), pp.366-7. The letter is undated, but the numbers of burials reported the previous week is identical to that given by Coulson for 25 September to 1 October. The letter must therefore have been written in the week following. This also serves to confirm the source of Coulson's (and Jenison's) figures.

[30]   Slack, *Impact of Plague*, pp.16, 150-1. Shrewsbury observed that the Newcastle outbreak was 'undoubtedly one of the most disastrous visitations by bubonic plague ever sustained by any town of comparable size in the British Isles': *History of Bubonic Plague*, p.384.

84 St Andrew's churchyard, one of the burial grounds.

well established, plague deaths tended to cluster in individual households.[31] In all three Newcastle parishes for which registration survives it is clear that the majority of burials fell into surname clusters which testify to the devastation of particular households. In St John's, where the parish clerk habitually ascribed those buried to a householder – such as 'Judith Fenwick wife of Edward tayler'; 'a child of Edward Fenwicks taylor'; 'George Kirkhouse his maid' – it is possible to be precise. The burials recorded came from at least 256 male-headed households which lost at least one family member or servant. But 55 per cent of them came from the 92 hardest hit of such households: those which lost two, three, four, or five members.[32]

[31] Slack, *Impact of Plague*, p.177. For an example of such clustering in the mining parish of Whickham, four miles upriver from Newcastle, see Wrightson, K. and Levine, D., 'Death in Whickham', in Walter, J. and Schofield, R. (eds), *Famine, disease and the social order in early modern society* (1989), p.141.

[32] Households headed by widows were not counted, since it was not possible to be sure whether the women concerned had been widowed during the registration gap of July and early August. In all, of the persons buried, 50.5 per cent were adults; 39.5 per cent were described as the son, daughter or child of a householder; 8.3 per cent were servants. The remainder could not be placed.

This reality is also graphically revealed in probate evidence. When William Grame, 'skipper', made one of the earliest plague wills in the Sandgate on 31 May, he had a pregnant wife and two children. His inventory, made in November, records the costs of 'his beryall and 3 children thear berryalls'.[33] John Collingwood, cordwainer of St Nicholas', made one of the last such wills, in late October, and his inventory tells us that the plague took 'himself his children and servants beinge 7 in number'.[34] Some households were closely connected. The administrators of the estate of Ambrose Haddock, buried in St Andrew's on 10 October, paid funeral charges for 'the said deceased and of six others of his familie who died all of the plague in his house (besides Ellyson's children who were under his tuicon)'. The latter were the three daughters of George Ellison of St John's, buried 3 September, who had been entrusted by their dying father to his friend and brother-in-law Ambrose.[35]

Such clustering of mortality among people in close proximity was partly attributable to the nature of the disease and its vectors – rats and fleas. But it may also have been accentuated, as some contemporaries alleged, by the policies adopted by urban magistrates to combat plague. No minutes of decisions made by the Corporation of Newcastle survive for the 1630s, but it is clear that the mayor and aldermen were active in enforcing the usual plague orders.[36] The progress of the epidemic was closely monitored, as we have seen. Meetings of the city's many guilds were cancelled – the Masons, in a significant choice of phrase, being 'disperst in the tyme of the great sicknesse'.[37] Relief was provided for 'the poorer sort'.[38] Efforts were made to keep trade going on the Tyne, though presumably beyond the boundaries of the afflicted city.[39] At the same

---

[33]   DUL, DPRI/1/1636/G8/1-2 (William Grame).
[34]   DUL, DPRI/1/1636/C6/1-10 (John Collingwood).
[35]   Administration account for Ambrose Haddock: DUL, DPRI/1/1637/H1/1-2. The burials registered in St Andrew's suggest that Ambrose's household suffered two visitations – one in late August/early September, and another in early October. One of the Ellison girls scarcely outlived her father, though she did outlive her namesake, and possible godmother, Isobel Haddock, who had witnessed her will: DUL, DPRI/1/1636/E3/1-3 (Isobel Ellison).
[36]   For the development of plague orders (including the segregation of infected households) see Slack, *Impact of Plague*, 204ff.
[37]   Bourchier Richardson, *Plague and Pestilence*, p.31.
[38]   Jenison praised the action of the city magistrates in 'disposing the revenues of our Chamber weekly, in great summes for their reliefe': *Newcastles Call*, pp.169-70. The surviving chamberlain's accounts confirm the expenditure on 'the reliefe of the poore and infected people' and the money raised in loans from the mayor, aldermen and others 'toward the reliefe of the infected people': TWAS, 543/26, fo.264.
[39]   The chamberlain's accounts provide weekly lists of payments made for vessels using the Tyne. These show that trade continued throughout the crisis, though activity dropped severely in July, August and September. Nevertheless, the coal trade continued with coastal and foreign vessels, and grain and malt from eastern England or the Baltic were landed almost every week. The epidemic meant a sharp, but temporary decline in Newcastle's trade, rather than a total stoppage, and overall receipts for October 1635 to October 1636 (the accounting year used) were only 14 per cent down on the previous year: TWA 543/26, *passim*.

time, however, they imposed quarantine within the city: 'keeping the unclean from the cleane', as Jenison put it.[40]

Two forms of isolation were adopted. There are references to houses being 'spared upp', or 'shutt up for suspicion of the plague' from mid-June, and from July onwards accounts of 'nuncupative' [word of mouth] wills being declared by isolated testators 'through a casement', or 'a partition of dales' [a thin wooden wall], or 'att the testators doore'.[41] How tightly these houses were 'shutt up' is not clear. Some people could open a door. The merchant John Stobbs of Pilgrim Street could not, however. When Margaret Hindmers arrived to be his 'keeper' on 8 September, he spoke to her from an upstairs window and 'willed her to goe to a smyth and get his helpe to put her in att a window … which she did accordinglie'.[42] Meanwhile, by early August at the latest, some of the sick were being isolated in 'lodges nere unto the towne' (on the Town Moor, to the north of the city) which were staffed by 'watchmen' and 'clensers'. There were 10 people lying sick in the lodge in which Jane Young died in late September, some of whom, as in other cases, lived to give evidence of her final wishes 'after ther comeinge home'.[43]

All this conveys a strong sense of the distancing, separation, enclosure and confinement occasioned by fear of infection. As Paul Slack puts it, 'plague was especially destructive because it was divisive'. The threat of contagion placed immense strain upon ties of neighbourhood and friendship, the bonds between householders and their servants and apprentices, and even the obligations of kinship. 'Above all, the sick themselves were shunned. Fear of the plague produced fear of its victims.'[44] Robert Jenison would have agreed. He wrote vividly of how 'the noysomnesse and contagion' of the plague 'makes a man a stranger in his own house, to his dearest friends; yea, as it were an enemie to them, and an instrument of death to wife, children, friends; and it deprives a man of comforters in his greatest agonie and need; and at length of life, and of an Honorable burial'.[45]

There is certainly evidence of fear. Witnesses of the wills of confined testators conventionally spoke of how they came 'so neare to his house as they durst', or 'as nigh unto his doore as the[y] durst adventure'. Thomas Hayton's will was unsigned because the notary and witnesses 'durst not goe into the

---

[40] Jenison, *Newcastles Call*, p.237.
[41] DUL, DDR/EJ/CCD/2, Folder 20.i.1637-6.v.1637, fos 6v, 7, 9, 17, 23v, 26-26v, 36v; Folder 19.v.1637-17.vi.1637, fos 85, 108; Folder 22.vii.1637, fos 47ff.
[42] DUL, DDR/EJ/CCD/2, Folder 20.i.1637-6.v.1637, fo. 33.
[43] DUL, DDR/EJ/CCD/2, Folder 20.i.1637-6.v.1637, fos 18v-19; Folder 19.v.1637-17.vi.1637, fos 96v-97.
[44] Slack, *Impact of Plague*, pp.19, 20, 287-94.
[45] Jenison, *Newcastles Call*, p.35.

85 Seventeenth-century houses and Black Gate, near St Nicholas' where plague mortality was relatively light.

house to him'. The scribe of Robert Walker's took dictation from a healthy servant girl placed at the window to convey Robert's words, since he was 'not able to speake unto him' directly 'without the danger of his health'.[46] And as the severity of the outbreak first became clear, many of those with the means and opportunity to do so must of course have engaged in the most effective means of distancing themselves from infection, fleeing the city. Robert Jenison, who seems to have been one of them, had much to say about the lawfulness of flight.[47]

Plague thus distanced and divided. Fear of infection could threaten the abandonment of obligations and the breakdown of social bonds. Throughout Europe the authors of plague tracts such as Robert Jenison's *Newcastles Call* were at pains to stress this in order to reinforce their moral messages. They elaborated what has been termed a 'dystopic vision' in which outbreaks of plague were represented as 'catastrophic collisions with the life and values of the Christian community', in which 'the very principles of collective sociability seemed threatened'.[48] Yet the surprisingly neglected evidence of probate records and testamentary litigation provides an alternative perspective. These records yield stories of the plague pushed up from inside the experience itself which reveal repeatedly how the ties of family and community could hold firm.

This is evident firstly among the testators themselves. People feared the contagion, but they knew that it might reach them, and that knowledge bred anxiety regarding their responsibilities in the face of the 'social disturbance' that might be occasioned by their deaths. Some looked ahead. John Stobbs made a will on 6 June, when in perfect health, and when questioned by his neighbours explained that 'the times were dangerous which moved him thereunto'.[49] 'Aboute a fortnight before his death', William Robson, a chapman, 'gott his goods inventared' as a means of protecting his family in the event of his death.[50] On 22 July, as the infection took off in St Nicholas' parish, Jane Glasenby, spinster, wrote her wishes in a letter to her brother George at Riding Mill in Northumberland – adding on the outer wrapper 'Brother Georges I praye yw lay this safelye up and be carfull that it be not brockene up tell yw heare further from me'.[51] And when the plague came, such anxieties were the more pressing. Ten days after his goods were inventoried, William Robson was

[46] DUL, DDR/EJ/CCD/2, Folder 20.i.1637-6.v.1637, fos 7, 23, 26, 33v.
[47] Jenison, *Newcastles Call*, pp.222-8.
[48] Jones, C., 'Plague and its metaphors in Early Modern France', *Representations*, vol.53 (1996), 108ff.
[49] DUL, DDR/EJ/CCD/2, Folder 19.v.1637-17.vi.1637, fo.95v. John Stobbs was buried on 21 September.
[50] DUL, DDR/EJ/CCD/2, Folder 20.i.1637-6.v.1637, fo.3.
[51] DUL, DPRI/1/1636/G7/1 (Jane Glasenby).

gravely sick and anxious to 'declare his mind', saying 'he was much indebted' and that 'he would have his wife to pay all his debts and to take all he had', but concerned that 'all that he had was to[o] little for his wife', and wondering which 'friends' might discharge his obligations 'in caise that both he and his wife should then dye'.[52]

Those men who made wills, commonly by word of mouth when they were already sick, were principally concerned with providing adequately for their widows and children, and in the event of their deaths, for the descent of property to close kindred. William Grame was typical in leaving everything to his wife, son and daughter, and then 'if it please God to call my said wife and children', to his brother, his uncle, and his cousin in equal shares. He was unusual only in adding that 'whereas my said wife is now with child my will and mind is that iff it please God shee be safely delivered of a child, that the same shall have a full proportionable part of my said goods'. William Cooke likewise gave thought to what he could provide 'if the child that my wife is with come forward'.[53]

But there was more to it than meeting immediate family obligations. Many people facing death in isolation chose to leave small sums of money, or specific items of clothing or domestic goods, 'for a token' to people close to them in affection, or to whom they owed debts of gratitude. Ann Milborne, widow, left such tokens to two brothers, her sister-in-law, two nieces, two female cousins, the two daughters of a male cousin, and one Jane Foster, probably a servant. Typically, these gestures were disproportionately directed towards other women of significance in her life. Margaret Hutchinson, another widow, similarly left nine tokens in the form of items of clothing, all of them to women.[54] Thomas Clark left a suit of clothes and 20s. to 'his man Edwards', 'in lew of his Mothers love in entertaineing my daughter Margarett att Table'. (We learn from his subsequent inventory that the child had been sent to Rothbury for safety.)[55] John Heslop of Pudding Chare, armorer, left tokens of weaponry to five friends. George Robson, 'musitian', refered to in the parish register as 'Gorges the fiddler', left a treble viol to one musical friend, and a recorder and flute to another. To Jane Browne, his 'deare supposed freind' and 'elected wife', he gave his few household goods and his former wife's apparel 'if it were six times as much and my blesseng'.[56]

---

[52] DUL, DDR/EJ/CCD/2, Folder 20.i.1637-6.v.1637, fos 2v-3.
[53] DUL, DPRI/1/1636/G8/1 (William Grame); DPRI/1/1636/C10/1 (William Cooke).
[54] DUL, DPRI/1/1636/M6/1 (Ann Milborne); DPRI/1/1637/H20/1 (Margaret Hutchinson).
[55] DUL, DPRI/1/1636/1-4 (Thomas Clark).
[56] DUL, DPRI/1/1636/H9/1 (John Heslop); DPRI/1/1636/10/1-2 (George Robson). Robson's three children had been buried in St Andrew's on 2 September; he was buried on 7 October. Whether his first wife died in the plague or earlier is uncertain.

86 Old housing on the Side, the main route from Sandhill up to St Nicholas' and the market place.

Not a few, in particular women, also expressed a desire to be buried near loved ones: 'soe neere unto my mother and sisters as conveniently may be'; 'soe neare unto my late husband as possibly I may or can'. And where, as was sometimes the case, these people had shortly pre-deceased them, the effort to restore severed ties in death, despite the sometimes chaotic nature of plague burials, is striking. Elizabeth Cooke asked to be buried in St Nicholas' churchyard 'neare unto the hawthorne tree there'. We cannot know what that spot meant to her, but clearly its significance was powerful enough for her to make a point of it.[57]

All this involved recognition of obligations and attempts to meet them, acknowledgements of connections, and attempts to hold and preserve them. At a time of dreadful uncertainty these focused and eased the mind. The clerks and scriveners who listened to and took down such final wishes – standing beneath windows, or outside doors, or on one occasion from a vantage point on the city wall – were in fact the principal professional providers of comfort to the dying. (In contrast, I have found few references to a physician or a clergyman attending a plague victim – a duty from which the clergy were in fact exempted because of the danger involved.)[58] The people who hurried through the streets to fetch them were commonly kinsmen of the sick. The witnesses who were called to gather before doors or outside windows, to give ear, and then add their signatures and marks, were usually neighbours or special friends – sometimes brother guildsmen – who could usually testify to having known the deceased for years. John Hunter had known Thomas Holmes for 20 years. Thomas Finlay was both a 'nere neighbour' to Robert Moore and the brother of one of Moore's tenants.[59]

Some of these people subsequently died themselves. Some lived to tell the tale in probate hearings. They knew that they were at risk, but in contrast to the dystopic vision of the plague tracts, the evidence is that they contained their fear and behaved well. People still visited the sick, as was their neighbourly duty. Robert Jopling shouted up to John Stobbs to ask if he needed anything, and John 'desired [him] to buy him some fish as allsoe a pint of wyne with other necessaryes', which he promptly did. The three neighbours called by William Cooke to hear his will also stood outside, but William understood. He 'desired

[57] DUL, DPRI/1/1636/M6/1 (Ann Milborne); DPRI/1/1637/1 (Katherine Hayton); DPRI/1/1637/C8/1 (Elizabeth Cooke).

[58] Christopher Foster, curate of St Nicholas', witnessed the will of George Wilkinson on 10 August and that of James Wilson two days later. Toby Watson, a barber surgeon, was also present on the latter occasion: DUL, DPRI/1/1637/1-2 (George Wilkinson); DPRI/1/1637/1 (James Wilson).

[59] DUL, DDR/EJ/CCD/2, Folder 20.i.1637-6.v.1637, fos. 6v, 15v, 23v; DPRI/1/1636/M9/1-2 (Robert Moore).

them to goe into a neighbours house' afterwards, and 'there to drinke twoe or three pottes of beere' in recompense.[60]

Nor did everyone keep a safe distance. Steven Colterd went into the room where his neighbour Robert Walker lay sick to hear his will, while the scribe waited outside, and subsequently 'drew so togeather and had conference togethear divers times' with Robert, who 'talked very sensibly' till near the end. Ann Tayte had known Ann Mills's family for 20 years as a neighbour in Sandgate, and 'haveing beene formerly visited and recovered of the plague' herself, and 'hearing that [Mills] lade sicke of the same desease ... did as a neighbour goe to visitt her'. She found her 'lyinge sicke in a chamber', where they had 'some speeches'. Jane Robinson, a 23-year-old widow, 'being a neighbour to ... Jane Young and knoweing that she was visited with the plauge and that she was in a lodge on the towne more of Newcastle did goe to visitt her'. 'Having bene former[ly] in the like lodge her selfe', she knew what it meant.[61]

To have been sick and to have recovered perhaps gave such courage, but there were also healthy people who sheltered the sick when there was no one else to care for them. Henry Finlay harboured a fellow weaver whose 'wife and children were lately dead' – and paid for it with his own life. Margaret Humphrey sheltered her niece. Isobel Middleton did not turn out her lodger, the 'waterman' Robert Moodie, when he fell sick, but cared for him until his death. He left her his few goods, and the censorious later drew their own conclusions.[62]

Many kinsfolk are described as having 'bestowed' 'care and paines' on the sick, often hiring a 'keeper' (usually a poor widow willing to take a chance for 6d. a day) or perhaps 'a woman to sarve them with watter and meat and drink'.[63] Some neighbours did the same. Robert Jenison was of the opinion that in addition to public relief, 'some good help and assistance made freely by kind neighbours' was a principal reason why 'multitudes of the poorer sort' were 'competently provided for; not the sick or infected only, but such as are impoverished through want of imployment in their manuall Crafts and Callings'.[64]

Finally, after an interval of some five to 14 days, there were those who accompanied the dead to the grave. Thomas Hayton's wife was herself dying

[60] DUL, DDR/EJ/CCD/2, Folder 20.i.1637-6.v.1637, fos 4v, 34.
[61] DUL, DDR/EJ/CCD/2, Folder 20.i.1637-6.v.1637, fos 6v, 11v, 18v.
[62] DUL, DDR/EJ/CCD/2, Folder 20.i.1637-6.v.1637, fos 5, 5v, 6v, 7, 10v-11v, 15v.
[63] Variants on the phrase occur in many depositions and wills: e.g. DUL, DPRI/1/1637/H10/1 (Katherine Hayton); DPRI/1/1637/L4/1 (John Laverrock); DDR/EJ/CCD/2, Folder 20.i.1637-6.v.1637, fo.18v. Keepers figure, or are alluded to, in many depositions, and the costs of their services are listed in inventories: e.g. DUL, DDR/EJ/CCD/2, Folder 20.i.1637-6.v.1637, fos 3-4, 7, 33, 37; DPRI/1/1636/G7/2 (Jane Glasenby); DPRI/1/1637/L4/3 (John Laverrock); DPRI/1/1636/2-4 (Thomas Clark).
[64] Jenison, Newcastles Call, p.170.

when he was buried in Allhallows churchyard on the afternoon of 9 July. The grave was dug by William Bayles, appointed by the mayor 'to be a grave maker and alsoe a burier [of] the dead', but at least two others were there: Luke Courser, the local joiner who made the coffin, and Grace Shipley, a 'near neighbour'.[65] John Laverrock was buried from the lodges for 18s. attended by four 'carriars', a 'caller' and 'the clerk'. His cousin Elinor arranged it. Jane Glasenby had mourners who were served with wine, beer, mutton and bread (at a total cost of 24s.). And other funerals were also of appropriate dignity. The cordwainer John Collingwood's family were buried at an average cost of almost £4 each. Robert Greenwell's funeral also cost £4. That of Robert Mallabar, a barber surgeon, cost £6.[66] The implication is that in Newcastle, as elsewhere, people both resented and ignored plague regulations restricting attendance at funerals.[67] Some burials, even at the height of the infection, remained occasions on which at least a few kin and neighbours gathered to affirm their bonds to the dead and to one another.

Conclusion

The story could be continued into the aftermath: the 'clensing' of houses (another job undertaken by poor women); the inventorying and valuation of goods by groups of neighbours or fellow craftsmen; the administration of wills by surviving spouses, adult children, siblings, uncles and cousins, or unrelated 'trusty friends'; the quarrels that sometimes erupted amongst those who had, or believed themselves to have, legitimate claims on the estates of the dead. The plague cast a long shadow in its impact on social relationships, and that, too, speaks to their continuing strength.

In retrospect it all melded into a single experience: 'the plague time'; 'that lamentable time', as some survivors remembered it.[68] I have tried to convey something of the horror of that experience, while at the same time providing glimpses of the personal and familial dramas from which it was constituted; stories that show that it was less destructive of social relationships than is often imagined. As Paul Slack has observed, the social impact of plague depended above all upon the pre-existing quality of social relations: in families, among neighbours, between rulers and ruled, rich and poor.[69] Plague could and did

[61] DUL, DDR/EJ/CCD/2, Folder 22.vii.1637, fos 37, 104.
[66] DUL, DPRI/1/1637/L4/3 (John Laverrock); DPRI/1/1636/G7/2 (Jane Glasenby); DPRI/1/1636/C6/3-10 (John Collingwood); DPRI/1/1636/G12/3 (Robert Greenwell); DPRI/1/1637/M2/3 (Robert Mallabar).
[67] Slack, *Impact of Plague*, pp.296-7.
[68] DUL, DDR/EJ/CCD/2, Folder 22.vii.1637, fo. 104; DPRI/1/1637/H1/1 (Ambrose Haddock).
[69] Slack, *Impact of Plague*, p.294.

divide people: laying bare the fissures in the social order; enhancing social distance; forcing cruel choices. But the dystopic perception of contemporary plague tracts, a discourse of overheated moralists and nervous elites, freighted with religious and political messages, surely distorts more than it illuminates. It ignores the role of the social in the imperative of survival; people's capacity – and need – to hold together in circumstances of almost unimaginable stress. In Newcastle in 1636, as in Albert Camus' fictional Oran, 'what we learn in time of pestilence' is that 'there are more things to admire in men than to despise'.[70] Plague might indeed expose the fragility of the ties that bind a society, but it also provides testimony to their strength.

[70] Camus, A., *The Plague*, trans. S. Gilbert, Vintage International edition (1991), p.308.

Newcastle and the World Beyond Tyneside: 1550-1650

DIANA NEWTON

In November 1597 a Newcastle merchant made his will whilst lying on his sickbed in the town of Elbing, near Danzig, in Prussia.[1] He was Henry Riddell, a younger son of William Riddell, who was a Merchant Adventurer and soon to be entered (fourth of 48 members) on the new charter issued by Queen Elizabeth to the Company of Hostmen in 1600. His mother was a member of another leading business family in Newcastle. She was the daughter of Bertram Anderson and her brother, Henry, was to appear (listed third), on the Hostman's charter. Henry Riddell had promised marriage to Elizabeth Liddell, whose father, Thomas, was also a Merchant Adventurer and was to be the seventh member to be admitted to the Company of Hostmen. Thus, Henry Riddell was part of the highest echelons of Newcastle's mercantile society.

Having first disposed of his body and his soul, Riddell dealt with his material bequests. He gave £20 to his host and hostess, 'Essender of Elbing', and an angel each to several Englishmen, who were at hand to witness the will, and to the servants who had ministered to him. He went on to make generous provision for his friends and family in Newcastle as well as leaving £50 to Elizabeth Liddell. Amongst those who benefited most handsomely were Charles Horsley and Richard Hodgson. Horsley was apprenticed to Henry's father in 1590 and, apparently, was also present when Henry made his will, according to another of those present in Elbing when he later gave evidence during a dispute between Horsley and Elizabeth Liddell, who was now described as the wife of William Sherwood.[2] Horsley himself was admitted to the Hostman's Company in 1604, and he apprenticed Roger Chamber, in 1607, whose brother, Richard,

---

[1] DUL, Durham probate records (hereafter DPR)1/1/1599/R4/1-2 and printed in *Wills and Inventories*, iii, SS, vol.112 (1906), p.167.

[2] *Records of the Company of Hostmen*, SS, vol.105 (1901), p.266; *Wills and Inventories*, pp.iii, 167n; Elizabeth Liddell married William Sherwood in February 1599, following the death of his first wife a couple of months before. *Wills and Inventories,* iv, SS, vol.142 (1929), 101n.

went on to marry Horsley's daughter, Frances.[3] Richard Hodgson was a member of another long-standing mercantile family. This was a tight-knit network of Newcastle families whose trading activities took them far away from the town, where they formed temporary communities, such as that at Elbing when Henry Riddell made his will.

Finally, Henry Riddell remembered in his will the newly installed vicar of St Nicholas', Newcastle, William Morton, and John Snaithwaite, who preached there, as well as making provision for the poor of Newcastle. Yet, despite his clear attachment and sense of obligation to his family and to Newcastle, including its principal parish priest, he elected to be buried 'in the great church at Elbinge'. This was unusual. But remaining in Germany appears to have been a deliberate decision on his part, for it was accepted practice, in early modern England, to delay the funeral in order to accommodate the return of a body from abroad for burial. Moreover, the funerals of Newcastle's 'great and good' were deemed so important that the Merchant Adventurers passed an Act in 1553 that the body of any of its members (and their wives) must be accompanied to their burial by every brother of the fellowship, on being warned by the 'byddell' [beadle].[4] Yet, Henry Riddell's apparent contentment not to be brought home, as well as his means of disposing of his goods, suggest he was as emotionally connected to Elbing as he was to Newcastle.

Another will, that of John March, of Redworth, in County Durham, and Merchant Adventurer of Newcastle, dated 13 February 1591, but with subsequent codicils, made many bequests, including to his business associates in Newcastle and to each of his tenants at Redworth.[5] He made arrangements for the education and welfare of his nephew and heir and other relatives who were still minors. He also left £5 to the poor of Newcastle and another £5 to be paid annually to the poor of Heighington parish, within which Redworth lay. A monument in Heighington parish church testifies to this last bequest. Yet, his trading concerns encompassed the Baltic, for amongst the debts owing to him was an 'account of Rychard Stottes, mayd at Elvinge, 1590, whereby there is resteinge oweinge in the east countrye 378 florence, is in Englishe money 75l 12s'.

These two wills may be isolated cases but they do reveal an interesting truth about Newcastle's citizens and the relations with their near neighbours as well

[3]   *Company of Hostmen*, p.267; *Records of the Newcastle Merchant Adventurers* (hereafter *Merchant Adventurers*), ii, SS, vol.93 (1899), pp.219, 230, 267; *Wills and Inventories*, pp.iv, 181.
[4]   Llewellyn, Nigel, *The Art of Death: Visual Culture in the English Death Ritual*, c.1500-c1800 (1991), pp.15-16; TWAS, GU/MA/3/2, Merchant Adventurers' records, fo.11.
[5]   DUL, DPR1/1591 and printed in *Wills and Inventories*, ii, SS, vol.38 (1860), pp.188-200.

as with their trading partners across the North Sea and the Baltic. As a port and a regional centre, the world beyond Tyneside was of crucial importance to Newcastle. Yet this is an aspect of its history that has been little written about for the early modern period.

City Merchants and the County Gentry

Relations with their immediate neighbours were important to Newcastle's chief inhabitants as the mercantile community had long interacted with the landed

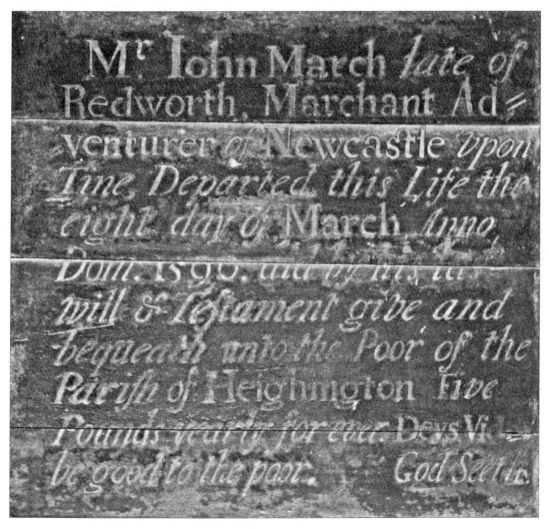

87   Memorial brass of John March in Heighington parish church.

families of the town's hinterland.[6] Marriages were made between the county gentry and the townspeople of Newcastle; there was a buoyant property market on Tyneside and beyond in which Newcastle citizens were engaged; and, the ease with which Novocastrians moved between Newcastle, Durham and Northumberland, was demonstrated by their involvement in local government and administration across the urban and county divide.

Exemplifying this interaction was Henry Riddell's uncle, Henry Anderson, who married Fortuna, daughter of Sir Cuthbert Collingwood of Eslington, of the prominent Northumberland family, and then bought an estate in County Durham.[7] He and his son, also Henry, served variously as mayor of Newcastle, sheriff of Newcastle and of Northumberland, alderman, MPs for Newcastle and for Northumberland, and commissioners of the peace for Durham. Henry Anderson junior went on to be knighted in 1603. It was perhaps no coincidence that Sir Thomas Calverley, of County Durham, who had married an Anderson, was one of the very few county gentlemen who sat on both Durham and Northumberland's commissions of the peace. Another leading coal entrepreneur, Sir Thomas Riddell of Gateshead, regularly served on the commissions of the peace for Counties Northumberland and Durham; sometimes at alternate sessions and on one occasion on both. He was married to Elizabeth, daughter of Sir John Conyers of Sockburn, near Darlington in the south of County Durham, thereby allying himself with one of the most ancient, wealthy and influential families in Durham. He was pricked sheriff of Newcastle, was mayor, and sat as its MP. He was knighted in 1616 and, after 1625, he became a justice of assize. Thus, it was members of the urban oligarchy rather than the landed gentry who were to be found straddling the counties of Durham and Northumberland. A further instance of the synthesis between town and county was the selection of Sir Henry Anderson and Sir William Selby, of Newcastle, as deputy lieutenants of Durham, by Bishop Neile, who was appointed lord lieutenant in 1617. For this was an office that traditionally confirmed the prestige and standing of the county gentlemen.

---

[6] For the earlier history see above, pp.128-35.

[7] For genealogical details, see Dugdale, Sir William, *Pedigrees Recorded at the Visitations of the County Palatine of Durham made by William Flower … in 1575, Richard St George … in 1615, and by William Dugdale … in 1666*, ed. Joseph Foster (1887); Surtees, Robert, *The History and Antiquities of the County Palatine of Durham* (1816-40). For office holders, see: *Libris Pacis* in BL, MS Egerton 2345; BL, MS Lansdowne 737; TNA, C/66/1468v; BL, MS Add. 38139; Hunter Blair, C.H., 'The mayors and lord mayors of Newcastle-upon-Tyne, 1216-1940, and the sheriffs of the county of Newcastle-upon-Tyne, 1399-1940', *AA*, 4th series, vol.18 (1940); Hunter Blair, 'The sheriffs of Northumberland to 1603', *AA*, 4th series, vol.20 (1942), p.89; Hunter Blair, 'The sheriffs of Northumberland 1603-1642', *AA*, 4th series, vol.21 (1943); Hunter Blair, 'The members of parliament for Northumberland, 1559-1831', *AA*, 4th series, vol.22 (1945); Hunter Blair, 'The members of parliament for Newcastle upon Tyne, 1559-1831', *AA*, 4th series, vol.23 (1945); supplemented by biographies in *Durham Quarter Sessions Rolls 1471-1625*, SS, vol.199 (1991).

88 Bessie Surtees' house, a timber-framed merchant's house of the mid-17th century, containing elements of an earlier building once owned in the mid-15th century by Robert Rodes.

Sir George Selby from Newcastle married a Selby from Northumberland, the Riddells took wives from Durham as well as from Newcastle, while the Northumberland gentleman, William Fenwick, married, as his second wife, Margaret Selby from Newcastle. The Newcastle Liddells bought Ravensworth Castle and thereafter styled themselves as being from Ravensworth, but continued to marry wives from Newcastle. And links were forged between the Brandlings of Gosforth and families from Counties Durham and Northumberland by the marriages of Robert and his son, Francis, to ladies from Durham and Northumberland, and Ursula Brandling to William Carr of Ford, in the north of Northumberland. Finally, both James Clavering and his son, John, of Axwell in Durham, married Newcastle ladies, as did the Bishop of Durham, William James. The incidence of marriages between traditional county families and citizens of Newcastle was not high, but they did take place.

Nor can assumptions automatically be made that Newcastle marriages were considered inferior to those contracted amongst the county elites. The proto-social commentator, Sir Thomas Smith, writing in the 1560s, might have pronounced that 'citizens and burgesses' ought to be confined to the cities or corporate towns where they dwelt because 'in the shyres they be of none accompte'.[8] But, in 1579, a dialogue between two advocates of urban and rural life, entitled *Cyvile and uncyvile life*, took a different view.[9] It addressed the enduring conflict between urban and rural elites for supremacy in the civility stakes: a civility that was demonstrable by the display of social grace and refinement. One of the arguments upon which the contest turned was that a country upbringing resulted in the sons of gentlemen developing certain enduring social flaws that took some ironing out. They were left with such 'clownish speech, and other ungentlemanly jestures, as is a good while (yea many times never) that those rusticities bee leafte'. The country-educated gentlemen were so inferior to those raised in the city 'that you shall even at the first sight, perceave by their speech, jesture, and behaviour that their educations are diverse'. But, above all, for the Novocastrians, being a citizen of Newcastle was very desirable indeed by the late 16th century, when Newcastle had become exceptionally prosperous.

It has been argued that urban associations of the merchant elites were distinguished as 'a matter chiefly of power and association', limited mostly to prestigious property-owning associations and links with fashionable society

---

[8] Smith, Thomas, *De Republica Anglorum*, ed. M. Dewer (1982), pp.70-3.
[9] *Cyvile and Uncyvile life: a Discourse where is Disputed, what Order of Lyfe best beseemeth a Gentleman*, in Hazlitt, W. Carew (ed.), *Inedited tracts: Illustrating the Manners, Opinions, and Occupations of Englishmen During the 16th and 17th Centuries*, Roxburgh Society (1868), pp.68-9, 84, 87-8.

that were useful for marriage purposes.[10] Certainly, there were opportunities for prosperous Newcastle merchants to participate in the Tyneside property market. For example, alongside traditional families, such as the Ogles and Lumleys, in the 1560s, were to be found the Claverings, Andersons, Chapmans and Shaftoes, dealing in property in Axwell, Swalwell, Whickham and Gateshead, into the 1630s and beyond.[11] Alexander Davison, who first appeared in the Newcastle Hostmen records in 1617, was buying lands in County Durham from at least 1615, and in the course of 1625 purchased property worth thousands of pounds.[12] The shrewd manipulation of the property market could result in the meteoric rise of a family's fortunes. In 1583 the relatively insignificant Thomas Cole, a cordwainer of Gateshead, who also lent money to his neighbours in Gateshead and Newcastle and further afield in Berwick, bought a small tenement in Gateshead from a Berwick merchant and his wife. He continued to buy up property on Tyneside and by 1608 had acquired a half-share of a 21-year lease on coal mines in Whickham. His nephew, Ralph, described variously as butcher, gentleman and esquire, was involved in similar enterprises: lending money, buying property and leasing coal mines. The Coles dealt with the principal citizens of Newcastle and Gateshead, including the Selbys, Andersons, Tempests and Lumleys, as well as the Darcys of Witton Castle in County Durham.[13] In 1604-5, Ralph, the nephew of an artisan, was elected to the Company of Hostmen, was sheriff of Newcastle in 1625 and mayor in 1633.[14] By the 1630s he was conducting individual business transactions to the tune of £14,000,[15] and had bought the estate of Brancepeth, once a seat of the earls of Westmorland.[16] Thus, the long tradition of Newcastle citizens buying lands in the country continued into the 16th century and beyond.

In the 1570s and '80s, the merchants Christopher and Henry Mitford, father and son, and Robert Lewen, purchased property in Hartley from the Northumberland Delaval family. While others bought estates from the Crown, such as the merchant Robert Brandling, who bought Newminster Abbey, near Morpeth, in 1609.[17] But, it must be stressed, buying a country estate did not mean a rejection of urban roots. For instance, the Andersons were described as

---

[10] Barry, Jonathan, 'Bourgeois collectivism? Urban associations and the middling sort', in Barry and Brooks, Christopher (eds), *The Middling Sort of People. Culture, Society and Politics in England, 1550-1800* (1994), p.103.

[11] DRO, D/CG/ 7/1-61, MS Clayton and Gibson.

[12] *Company of Hostmen,* 66ff; DRO, D/Gr 364-380, Greenwell deeds.

[13] DRO, MS Brancepeth, D/Br/F 7 – 44.

[14] *Company of Hostmen*, pp.53, 54.

[15] DRO, D/Br/F 45.

[16] Welford, *Newcastle and Gateshead*, vol.3 (1884-7), p.340.

[17] NRO, MS Delaval, 1/DE/1/15-19; NRO, MS Blackett-Ord, M.1/2.

being from Newcastle and Haswell, and, in a catalogue of the principal gentry as late as the reign of Charles I, were still designated as 'Anderson of Newcastle'.[18] Moreover, every property deal conducted by the Newcastle merchant elite involved lands with coal mines and staithes, or riverside wharves at which coal was landed onto keel boats, and 'keelrooms'. Only very occasionally did these transactions, that were sometimes vast, include mansion houses.[19] This suggests that it was the valuable commercial prospects of acquiring land that was its primary attraction, with social cachet – if indeed that ever was a consideration – a far less significant concern.

The county gentry and urban oligarchy could be found periodically occupying residences close to each other in the town. In the 1640s William Gray noted that 'some gentlemen of Northumberland had their houses' in the 'many ancient buildings, houses and streets' in the 'ancient towne of Pampden', while the Sandhill was occupied by 'stately houses for merchants', and other gentlemen had houses on Westgate Street.[20] This interface was reinforced with the increasing numbers of apprentices in Newcastle's trade companies and guilds who were the sons of those styling themselves gentlemen, and by the early 1600s they composed about a third of all the Merchant Adventurers's recruits.[21] Amongst these was Robert Ewbank, who was apprenticed to Oswald Mitford in 1649. Not only was he the son of Toby Ewbank of Eggleston, in County Durham, he was also the grandson of the prebendary, Henry Ewbank, thereby representing the confluence of the county, clerical and commercial communities.[22] As a result, a more distinctively elite sociability evolved and added attractions drew people in to the town with the result that Newcastle emerged as the social and cultural centre for the north-eastern counties.

Horse races were held regularly in Newcastle at Killingworth Moor from at least 1621.[23] And, there is no reason to assume that Newcastle, like its counterparts elsewhere in the kingdom, did not attract an influx of visitors from the surrounding countryside when the assize judges arrived or when the quarter sessions were sitting. They would all require entertainment. The account books of Newcastle have abundant evidence of payments to musicians, poets, players and other performers right up to the outbreak of the Civil War in 1642. These

---

[18]   BL, MS Lansdowne 865, fos 97ff.
[19]   For example, James Clavering's purchase of 1629 included coal mines, staithes and four mansion houses. DRO, D/CG/ 7/16.
[20]   William Gray's *Chorographia or a Survey of Newcastle upon Tyne: 1649*, pr. Newcastle (1818).
[21]   Brooks, Christopher, 'Apprenticeship, social mobility and the middling sort, 1550-1800', in Barry and Brooks, *Middling Sort*, pp.54-62.
[22]   TWAS, GU/MA/3/1 f.145r.
[23]   King, Rebecca, 'Aspects of sociability in the north east of England, 1600-1750' (Ph.D. thesis, Durham University, 2001), p.134.

included travelling entertainers, such as the king of Scotland's musicians in 1559, a Scottish poet in 1596, and waits (or officials bands of singers maintained by particular towns) from as far afield as Boston in Lincolnshire and King's Lynn, in Norfolk in 1598, 1608 and 1616.[24] The east coast connections which were part of the North Sea networks, established as a result of Newcastle's trading interests since at least the 14th century, meant that its culture was increasingly exposed to external influences.

At the end of the 16th century, such influences were reinforced by the regular arrival of travelling players in Newcastle. Professional actors periodically touring the country can be traced back to the 15th century, but from 1559 the practice was closely regulated, and persisted long after permanent, purpose-built theatres were erected in the capital.[25] Their plays were written and designed to be staged anywhere; and it is not inconceivable that they incorporated local and topical references (just as stand-up comedians employ on tour today). Queen Elizabeth's players came to Newcastle in 1591 and 1593, and Queen Anne's in 1615.[26] In addition, those of the Lord Admiral, and of the earls of Derby, Hertford, Huntingdon, Leicester, Lincoln, Pembroke and Sussex, played at Newcastle, as well as Lords Batholomew, Darcey, Dudley, Monteagle, Morley, Ogle, Stafford and Willoughby's players, between 1575 and 1615.[27] This is a significant proportion of the 37 Greater Men's companies that have been identified as active outside London between 1559 and 1645. The records indicate that Newcastle made payments to 39 companies of touring players over a period of 40 years. Although that was considerably fewer than Bristol, Coventry, Gloucestershire, Devon, Somerset and Norwich, it was comparable to Cambridge, Dorset, Shropshire, Sussex and York, and was significantly more than Chester, Cumberland, Westmorland, Cornwall, Herefordshire and Lancashire, who were included on only a handful of tours.[28] That so many of the leading companies were prepared to travel as far as Newcastle suggests a clear demand. Newcastle was visited by players almost every year, between 1575 and 1600, for which there are records; sometimes by two or three different companies, and, in

---

[24] TWAS 543/19, Chamberlains' account books, fos 150, 12, 112, 116, 543/21, fos 246, 285, and printed in Anderson, J.J. (ed.), *Records of Early English Drama: Newcastle upon Tyne* (hereafter, *REED: Newcastle*) (1982), pp.129, 115, 125, 148, 149.

[25] Keenan, Siobhan, *Travelling Players in Shakespeare's England* (2002), pp.2-3, 13-14 and *passim*; Gurr, Andrew, *The Shakespearian Playing Companies* (1996), p.36.

[26] TWAS, 543/18, fos 199, 150, TWAS, 543/22, fo. 269, and printed in *REED: Newcastle*, pp.79, 92, 148.

[27] See *REED: Newcastle*, *passim*.

[28] See tables 9.1 and 9.2 compiled from the REED collections by Keenan, in *Travelling Players*, pp.166-7.

1593, by no less than six.[29] The 'visitors' also included the exotic, for in 1607 Newcastle was treated to a play 'wch had the baboone'.[30]

As part of the touring circuit, the inhabitants of Newcastle were exposed to the same cultural influences as their sophisticated metropolitan counterparts. This marks a significant difference between older religious festivities, such as the Corpus Christi Day celebrations, which were firmly located in the physical space of the town where they were devised and performed, and the peripatetic secular touring theatre that replaced them. It was also an extension of the Newcastle/London nexus which was already well established between their respective commercial elites. Far from being an isolated backwater, Newcastle was a receptor and conduit for a national culture, which spread beyond the town into the north-eastern counties. Because, while the size of audiences can only be a matter of speculation, it is extremely unlikely that touring companies ventured as far north as Newcastle for a single performance; especially given that they were mostly there in the winter months. It could, therefore, be assumed they reached a much wider audience than the citizens of Newcastle. Nor was the experience restricted to the town's elites. Entry to some of the plays was free, making them accessible to everyone in the town, irrespective of status. There are references to free plays in Newcastle in the chamberlains' account books, such as the payment of £3 to the Earl of Sussex's players for putting on a free play (commanded by the mayor) in September 1593.[31] Thus, Newcastle's external connections, and its place in a wider national culture, made it a vibrant focal point at the end of the 16th and the 17th centuries.

The Mercantile Elite

From childhood, the sons of Newcastle's commercial elite were trained up to take their place in the mercantile community. Hence, Newcastle was the location of a 'free school' for the education of its freemen's sons. It has been posited that, from the 16th century, English boroughs saw a flourishing school as a sound investment in helping to produce concentrations of literate people.[32] There is no reason to doubt that Newcastle shared these aspirations: for example, grounding in Latin was crucial for the industrialists of Newcastle, when that was

---

[29] In common with the rest of England, players and acting companies toured less frequently by the middle of James I's reign. See, Keenan, *Travelling Players*, pp.183-4.

[30] TWAS, 543/21, fo. 198.

[31] Keenan, *Travelling Players*, p.40; TWAS, 543/18, fo. 150.

[32] Houston, R.A., *Scottish Literacy and the Scottish Identity. Illiteracy and Society in Scotland and Northern England, 1600-1800* (1985), pp.51-2.

89 The grammar school in St Mary's Hospital.

the language in which technical works from abroad were produced.[33] The school benefited from a particularly enlightened headmaster in the 1640s, when George Ritschel was appointed to the post. He was born in Deutschkahn, Bohemia, in 1616, though his father was related in marriage to Mrs Butler of Newcastle, whose son-in-law was Ambrose Barnes, 'one of the most colourful of the Newcastle puritans'.[34] Ritschel was educated at the University of Strasbourg, and can be subsequently traced at The Hague, Amsterdam and Leiden. He went on to share a house in Elbing with Comenius, 'one of the most advanced educational thinkers of the time', for six months. On coming to England he spent time at

[33] Mains, Brian and Tuck, Anthony, *Royal Grammar School, Newcastle upon Tyne, a History of the School in its Community* (1986), pp.3, 6.
[34] See Howell, Roger, 'A Bohemian exile in Cromwell's England: the career of George Ritschel, philosopher, schoolmaster and cleric', in his *Puritans and Radicals in North England* (1984), especially pp.162-5, 172.

Oxford, before becoming headmaster of Newcastle grammar school in 1648, where he was described as being both 'wise and successful'. Thus, the next generation of Newcastle traders were exposed to an education that would equip them to engage fully with their continental counterparts.

After school, some of the young Novocastrians left the town to further their education. Newcastle's school matched the national picture in sending at least one boy (on average) a year to Cambridge between 1550 and 1660, while the figures for Oxford were similarly respectable.[35] As well as acquiring practical expertise and constructing networks beneficial for their obligations in later life, there were also opportunities of a more personal nature. Francis Brandling, who was up at Oxford in 1611, at the same time as Edward Pitt, son and heir of Sir William Pitt, from Dorset, married, as his second wife, Edward's sister, Elizabeth, indicating that their acquaintance survived some time after they left university.[36] And Ambrose Dudley, alderman of Newcastle, who chose a wife from Buckinghamshire, might have met her under similar circumstances.

The educated youth of Newcastle then progressed from university, or went directly, to one of the inns of court, where they acquired a training in common law, necessary to discharge their supplementary duties as town governors. For instance, Henry Anderson and Thomas Calverley attended Gray's Inn and Lincoln's Inn respectively, and they were both denoted as 'my brethren in law' in William Riddell's will, in 1600.[37] Continuing the family tradition, the eldest son of William Riddell's heir, Thomas, also called William, attended University College, Oxford, and went on to Gray's Inn.[38] He married Katherine, daughter of Sir Henry Widdrington, one of the most influential Northumberland gentlemen, which was yet another example of the conjunction of the county and urban elites. But, not only was Newcastle adequately provided for in respect of common lawyers; for others, the law became their career. Mark Shafto, the third son of merchant and alderman Robert Shafto, matriculated from St John's College, Cambridge in 1616, was admitted to Gray's Inn, became a Barrister at Law and then Recorder of Newcastle in 1648, and sat as MP for Newcastle.[39] After matriculating from Queen's College, Oxford, Sir George Riddell, a younger

[35] See Venn, John (ed.), *Alumni Oxoniensis, being the Matriculation Register of the University, 1500-1714* (1891-2) and Venn, John (ed.), *Alumni Cantabrigiensis, a Biographical List of all known Students, Graduates and Holders of Office at the University of Cambridge, from the Earliest Times to 1900* (1922-7).

[36] Venn, *Alumni Oxon*, pp.171, 1,165.

[37] Foster, Joseph (ed.), *The Register of Admissions to Gray's Inn* (1889); Foster (ed.), *The Records of the Honourable Society of Lincoln's Inn, 1420-1799* (1896); DUL DPR1/1/1601.

[38] *Wills and Inventories*, pp.iv, 165n.

[39] *Wills and Inventories*, pp.iv, 160-1n.

son of William Riddell, became a notable civil lawyer, one of the 200 civil lawyers identified in England between 1603 and 1642.[40] Others travelled even further afield to complete their education. Samuel Rand, Newcastle's town physician in 1642 and again in 1652-4, left Durham for Cambridge and then went to Leyden and Groningen in the Netherlands, and Eleazer Hodgson, the son of William Hodgson of Newcastle, took degrees from Cambridge, was incorporated into Oxford, and spent the next 17 years acquiring a medical education at Padua, Bologna, Ferrara and Venice before settling in London.[41]

Newcastle's relationship with London was one that few other provincial towns could expect to emulate, and was achieved as a result of its size, its location and its dominant position within the coal industry. It has been argued that there were times when the interests of Newcastle coincided closely enough with the intentions of central policy to make a close working partnership seem appropriate and orderly – at others that the divergence was so marked as to raise questions about the application of policy to Newcastle.[42] At no time was this more apparent than during the late 16th century, when the Newcastle coal trade entered a period of its most rapid upsurge. In 1582 a very small group of local entrepreneurs appropriated this trade, by buying a 99-year lease from the Crown of all the bishop of Durham's valuable coalmines in Gateshead and Whickham.[43] They were led by Henry Anderson and William Selby, for a sum thought to be as much as £12,000.[44] They were the 'front-men' for a consortium of so-called 'grand lessees', whose precise composition is unknown; however, within 10 years, this 'grand lease' had been concentrated into the hands of a select few. In a letter to Burghley, the mayor of London described the original grand lessees as 'freehosts', numbering about sixty persons, who 'have lately compounded and made over their right to a far less number ... to about 18 or 20'.[45] What was more clear was the fact that their relationship with the capital and with central government was, on occasion, a difficult one.

In the 1590s the privy council ordered the bishop of Durham to look into the high price of coal, imposed by 'the richer sorte of the towne of New

---

[40] Levack, Brian P., *The Civil Lawyers in England, 1603-1641* (1973), p.265.

[41] Physicians and Irregular Medical Practitioners in London 1550-1640: Database (2004).

[42] Howell, 'Newcastle and the nation: the seventeenth century experience', in his *Puritans and Radicals*, p.17. See Simon Healy in this volume.

[43] For a lively account of Sutton and his coal-mine-owning enterprise see, Trevor-Roper, H., 'The bishopric of Durham and the capitalist reformation', *Durham University Journal*, new series, vol.7i, 2 (1946), pp.45-58. For a thorough treatment of Whickham, see Levine, David and Wrightson, Keith, *The Making of an Industrial Society, Whickham 1560-1765* (1991).

[44] Nef, J.U., *The Rise of the British Coal Industry*, vol.1 (1932), pp.150-4; Howell, Roger, Jr, *Newcastle-upon-Tyne and the Puritan Revolution. A Study of the Civil War in North England* (1967), pp.23-4.

[45] BL, MS Lansdowne 65, fo. 38.

Castle', whose covertous desire of excessive gain to themselves' will result in the poor being 'utterly destitute of that fuell'.[46] In a part of England that was continually claiming poverty, the urban elites of Newcastle, especially the coal owners and traders, were distinguished by their perceived wealth. Their monopoly not only attracted attention, but it was also widely challenged. At some point in Elizabeth's reign it was proposed that 'a staple of new chastel coles' should be established on the south coast, between Sandwich and Weymouth. In justification it was argued that coal was 'growen to such estimation … it is to be accompted one principall commoditie of this realme & to be used as the blessing of God bestowed … to benefite the realme & subjects thereof' – in a similar manner as salt provided for France. Not only would the Queen 'have her custome trulie answered & rather increased', but also it would bring much needed employment for her subjects and navy.[47] Other ingenious strategies were regularly concocted to tap Newcastle's wealth. In 1592 William Borough, clerk of the ships, devised a scheme to finance the completion of Plymouth Castle that included levying an extra tax on Newcastle coal. A certain Bridges further suggested that the Newcastle coal masters could bear a tax, double that proposed by Borough, to help offset the expense of repulsing the Spanish, given that Newcastle was not otherwise subject to Parliamentary taxation.[48] Although these proposals came to nothing, serious efforts were made in 1591 to regulate the export of coal and control its quality. Accordingly, a proclamation to deal with the problem was conceived. An early draft made the point that the increased demand for coal by the domestic market meant that it 'cannot conveniently be spared' for export and, moreover, that the 'better sort' was being conveyed out of the realm, leaving insufficient for 'our natural and lovinge subjects'.[49] The clause did not form part of a later draft, but it more than hints at the passions that could be aroused by coal.[50] No proclamation was finally promulgated, but there was no shortage of candidates offering to undertake the task of monitoring the export of coal and ensuring that the best remained in England; John Thornborough, the dean of York, petitioned the Queen's principal secretary, Lord Burghley, endlessly for the responsibility of overseeing coal exports.[51]

[46]   *APC*, 1595-6, 31-2.
[47]   TNA, SP 12/105/30.
[48]   TNA, SP 12/241/75; 12 /257/63.
[49]   BL, MS Lansdowne 65, fo. 22.
[50]   It also implied that their activities could be construed as tantamount (almost) to treason. BL, MS Lansdowne 67, fo. 56. An even later draft is printed in Tawney, R.H. and Power, Eileen (eds), *Tudor Economic Documents*, vol.2 (1924), p.277, who date it at 1592, and in Hughes, Paul L. and Larkin, James F., *Tudor Royal Proclamations*, vol.3 (1969), p.154, who date it at 1595.
[51]   BL, MS Lansdowne 67, fo. 50.

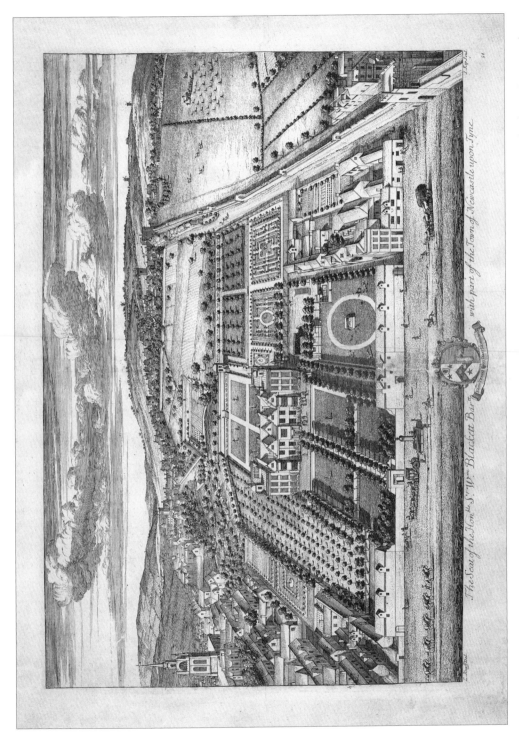

The Seat of the Hon.ble S.r W.m Blackett Bar.t with part of the Town of Newcastle upon Tyne

90 Anderson's Place, *rus in urbe*, built on the site of the Greyfriars, with the site of the former nunnery behind and Pilgrim Street in the foreground. It was later owned by Sir William Blackett.

The mayor, aldermen, and even the sheriff of Newcastle wrote repeatedly to Burghley throughout 1591 and into 1592, reciting their objections to any proposed impositions on coal.[52] They explained that it would lead to their ruin, which would impact upon the Queen, as the owner of most of the coal mines, for they would be unable to pay her rent and fines. Further duties on coal would make mining it unviable, leading to 1,500 miners and mariners being thrown out of work and raising the prospect of the consequent evils attendant on large numbers of the suddenly unemployed. The petitioners went on to declare that they would be unable to maintain the fabric of the town, which, they reminded Burghley, was the chief bulwark against Scotland. The Queen would lose customs and the Scots would step into the resultant gap in the market. The episode was not resolved until 1599, when the privy council struck a deal with the Hostmen which resulted in their being incorporated as a separate trading company.[53] In the next reign, precisely the same arguments employed in the 1590s were applied when a Bill was introduced into the 1604 session of Parliament to modify the 1529 statute, which had given Newcastle a monopoly to ship coal. The MPs for Newcastle, George Selby and Henry Chapman, prominent Hostmen, put up a spirited defense of their privileges, based on their specialist knowledge of conditions prevailing along the River Tyne. Rather disingenuously, they also warned that tampering with the statute might result in 'the danger of landing of Jesuite preestes and other daungerous persons'. But, above all, they argued, any challenge to the coal mine owners would rebound upon the king by way of lost customs and would jeopardise the supply of coal for London.[54] For it was now clear that London was critically dependent on Newcastle's coal. The Bill was rejected on its second reading.[55] Newcastle became increasingly significant to the central authorities.

Towards the end of the 1590s the privy council was obliged to become directly involved in the affairs of Newcastle's government. For the way in which the grand lessees virtually monopolised the mayoralty and shrievelty of Newcastle, and almost invariably held the town's Parliamentary seats, did not go unchallenged. Their domination of civic government was causing resentment among those who did not share their influence, resulting in a conflict which reached a climax in 1597. It appeared to be relatively straightforward. It began at the end of 1596, when Henry Sanderson, customer of the port of Newcastle, wrote to Lord Burghley about the abuses of the grand lessees,

[52]   BL, MS Lansdowne 67, fos 62 and 207; MS Lansdowne 69, fo. 68; MS Lansdowne 71, fo. 24.
[53]   Levine and Wrightson, *Making of an Industrial Society*, p.22. And see Simon Healy in this volume.
[54]   TNA, SP 14/18/79; SP 14/18/81.
[55]   BL, MS Lansdowne 65, fo. 36, and see Nef, *Coal Industry*, vol.2, p.215; *CJ*, vol.1, pp.228, 229.

and the misfortunes experienced by those he specifically designated as 'non grand lessees'.[56] He drew particular attention to the difficulties encountered by aldermen Lionel Maddison, Robert Dudley and Edward Lewen, each of whom had served as mayors of Newcastle. However, their endeavours to restore the grand lease to the entire Corporation of Newcastle, to which it was thought by some to rightfully belong, meant they had subsequently failed to achieve high office in town government.

The grand lessees, led by Henry Anderson and William Selby, wrote to Burghley's secretary (Michael Hicks), in their capacity as mayor and aldermen of Newcastle, to discredit Sanderson for the way in which he 'haithe wickedlye begun and more than uncharitablye pursued this bad begun course'. Maddison, Dudley and 14 other aldermen and burgesses responded, at great length, complaining to Burghley about Anderson and Selby's manipulation of the grand lease as well as numerous other abuses.[57] The two factions continued to lobby Burghley and his secretary, while the mayor and principal aldermen resorted to giving 'inducements' to the Queen's favourite, the Earl of Essex (whose sister was married to the Earl of Northumberland).[58] They also appealed to the privy council. The case was finally settled, on 15 December 1598, in favour of Anderson, Selby and the rest of the grand lessees.[59] No doubt the privy council felt that ensuring the continued supply of coal for the capital would best be guaranteed by retaining the goodwill and cooperation of Newcastle's major coal owners.

By the close of the 16th century, 'the oligarchical practices of the Newcastle Hostmen had legal sanction and the blessing of the Crown'.[60] King James, on the other hand, endeavoured to curb the abuses of the Newcastle coal merchants, by occasioning certain of them to be tried in Star Chamber. Theirs was a threat to the well-being of the kingdom, no less ominous than that posed by the unruly borderers, as was made plain in one of King James's last proclamations, issued on 16 February 1625. It was designed to deal with the 'many and great deceits, and abuses, done and offered unto Us, and Our loving Subjects of this Our realme of England by the Oastmen, Diggers, Getters and Traders for Coale in the Coalemines of Newcastle ...'.[61] Newcastle's coal owning oligarchy represented

---

[56]   BL, MS Lansdowne 81, fo. 104.
[57]   BL, MS Lansdowne 85, fo. 55; TNA, SP 12/263/72.
[58]   TNA, SP 12/264/117; 12/266/60; *Historical Manuscripts Commission report on the manuscripts at Hatfield House* (hereafter, HMC *Hatfield*), vol.8, p.419.
[59]   *APC*, 1595-6, pp.381-2; *APC*, 1596-7, pp.512-3; *APC*, 1597-8, pp.225-6, 627-8; *APC*, 1598-9, pp.181-2, 199, 295-6, 357-8. And see Levine and Wrightson, *Making of an Industrial Society*, p.22.
[60]   Levine and Wrightson, *Making of an Industrial Society*, p.22.
[61]   TNA, SP14/98/29; Larkin, James F. and Hughes, Paul L. (eds), *Stuart Royal Proclamations* (1973), pp.619-25.

'a great and generall abuse and enormity to Our whole Realme', right up until the end of James's reign.

Less contentiously, members of Newcastle's coal owning oligarchy also served as MPs. Furthering the interests of their county or town in the House of Commons was the fundamental obligation of occupying a county or borough seat, and Newcastle's MPs were no exception. The town of Newcastle was generally represented by members of the Company of Merchant Adventurers and then, increasingly, by members of the Hostmen's Company. Accordingly, Henry Anderson regularly sat in Parliament, following his father, Bertram, and succeeded by his son, Henry. This pattern, of fathers followed by their sons, was replicated in other families, such as the Jenisons and the Selbys, while the Riddells, Sir Thomas and his half-brother, Sir Peter, were elected to alternate Parliaments throughout the 1620s. The Newcastle members tended to be denoted, rather anonymously, as the 'burgesses of Newcastle', such as in 1604 when George Selby and Henry Chapman were commissioned to discuss the confirmation of Berwick's charter, along with the named members for Northumberland and Berwick, in 1604.[62] Chapman was appointed to the Committee for the Good of Both the Realms, selected in May that year, to treat of the union, together with the MP for Northumberland and seven members of the Council of the North.[63] But, as this committee was composed of around a hundred members, the presence of any of them was more a matter of convention than conviction. Selby and Chapmen were also appointed to the inaugural committee to meet the House of Lords, in April 1604, and again in November 1606. But Chapman was probably named simply because the Crown wanted two merchants from the north of England and two from the south.[64]

Chapman was also one of four merchants named on the commission for union, issued in May 1604, the other three being from London, York and Bristol. With trade and customs occupying a fair proportion of Parliamentary time, the presence of a member from Newcastle was no doubt considered requisite. But neither Chapman nor Selby contributed to the union debates in this or any other respect. Nor were they on the committee or the sub-committee convened to discuss commerce with the Scots.[65] As founding members of the recently incorporated Hostmen's Company, Selby and Chapman might have been

[62]   *CJ*, vol.1, pp.211, 212.
[63]   *CJ*, vol.1, pp.212-13; BL, MS Cotton Titus F IV, fos 22v-23r. It would seem that Widdrington was an unfamiliar figure at Westminster, for he was first recorded as Middrington, before being corrected.
[64]   This was pointed out to me by Simon Healy.
[65]   BL, MS Add, 26635, fo. 6v, fo. 12v.

91   A late 16th-century merchant's house on the Close.

expected to engage in a matter that seemed of direct relevance to them. On the other hand, their lack of interest could have reflected their confidence in their unassailable position in the town and beyond, and their unshakeable sense of superiority, which were beyond challenge on account of the exceptional basis of their position and wealth.

Twenty years later the picture had altered. The MPs for Newcastle, Sir Henry Anderson and Peter Riddell, as well as the MPs for Berwick were involved in debating the question of Parliamentary representation for Durham in King James's last Parliament, of 1624. Fewer than half of the 41 members commissioned to discuss the matter put in an appearance at either of the two meetings convened for that purpose, whereas Anderson and Edward Lively, member for Berwick, attended both. The members for Northumberland attended neither.[66] The fact that both Anderson and Riddell had bought estates in County Durham, however, could explain their interest in a matter with which they could closely identify, and their support for the Bill in the Commons.[67] An analysis of Commons committees attendance records in the same Parliament reveals that Anderson and Riddell were commendably diligent in other respects. Of the 16 members from constituencies throughout the wool-producing areas of England, commissioned to discuss wool exports, only the two members for Newcastle and three others turned up. Their record was considerably better than most of the 44 who were named to confer about customers fees.[68] This was more probably a determination to foster the interests of their own particular caste, however, than a demonstration of concern about the welfare of Newcastle. For the urban oligarchies were bent on preserving their own privileges – such as those possessed by the Hostmen, Merchant Adventurers and the grand lessees – against encroachments from less advantaged entrepreneurs on Tyneside and Wearside or from further afield.

By the 1640s, when divisions were far more clearly drawn throughout the kingdom, Newcastle's MPs, Sir Henry Anderson and John Blakiston, reflected that divide. Anderson, elected once again in 1640, represented a moderate position and, thus, was involved in dismantling 'Straffordian policy', with the removal of Star Chamber, ship money and the Council of the North.[69]

---

[66]   Kyle, Chris R., "'It will be a scandal to show what we have done with such a number." House of Commons committee attendance lists', in Kyle (ed.), *Parliaments, Politics and Elections, 1604-1648*, Camden 5th series, vol.17i (2001), pp.224, 217-9. Kyle, 'Commons attendance', pp.210-11.

[67]   Foster, Andrew, 'The struggle for Parliamentary representation for Durham, c.1600-1641', in Marcombe, David (ed.), *The Last Principality: Politics, Religion and Society in the Bishopric of Durham, 1494-1660* (1987).

[68]   Kyle, 'Commons attendance', pp.210-11.

[69]   Howell, Roger, 'Newcastle's Regicide: The Parliamentary career of John Blakiston', *AA*, 4th series, vol.42 (1964).

However, he was removed from the House in 1643. He was, by then, being eclipsed by the more radical Blakiston. The second son of the 'vociferous Arminian' prebendary of Durham, Marmaduke Blakiston, and brother-in-law of John Cosin, John Blakiston embraced puritanism early in his career. As the Long Parliament progressed he began to appear on an increasing number of committees and was closely involved in matters relating to religion. But, he was also deeply committed to furthering the position of Newcastle, eventually assuming responsibility for re-opening its trade once the town was reduced into Parliamentary hands. He was instrumental in fighting off the Common Council of London's bid to purchase the Grand Lease, in March 1648.[70] And he may well have been involved in the appointment of George Ritschel to the headmastership of Newcastle's grammar school. It has been argued that, while Blakiston was certainly a regicide, he was also 'one of the most active, imaginative and faithful members of parliment to have served the town'.[71] However, it would appear that, like his predecessors, he simply represented another sectional interest within Newcastle.

Overseas Connections

Newcastle had long been an important trading and commercial centre, and has been described as 'the most successful of all the "new towns" of post-conquest England'.[72] Newcastle's mercantile and industrial community was determined to protect its interests against encroachments from outsiders. In 1529 it negotiated a statute, which provided that no person should 'ship, load or unload any goods to be sold into or from any ship at any place within the river of Tyne, between the places called Sparhawke and Hedwinstremes, but only in the town of Newcastle'.[73] In effect this gave a virtual monopoly to the citizens of Newcastle, especially, 'certaine principall persons of that Towne, called Oastmen, to whom it onely apperteyned to sell and convey Coles from that Porte into any other port or place within or without the realme'.[74] It also spelt Newcastle's triumph over the bishop of Durham's ports at Gateshead and North Shields. Oastmen, or Hostmen, were 'free inhabitant householders to whom was assigned the duty of entertaining merchant strangers, of

[70]   Dodds, M.H. (ed.), *Extracts from the Newcastle upon Tyne Council Minute Book, 1639-1656*, Newcastle upon Tyne Records Committee, vol.1, pp.120, 86-7.
[71]   Howell, 'Newcastle's regicide'.
[72]   Dobson, R.B., 'Urban decline in late medieval England', *TRHS*, 5th series, vol.27 (1977), p.19.
[73]   *Statutes of the Realm*, vol.3, pp.302-3, 21. Henry VIII, *c*.18. For an earlier statute see Constance Fraser in this volume.
[74]   HMC *Hatfield*, vol.5, p.267, and see *Company of Hostmen*, p.9.

becoming answerable for their peaceful conduct, and of supervising the sales and purchases of their wares and merchandise'. The first reference to hosting in Newcastle was in the 14th century, but by 1600, and at their request, the 'guilde or fraternitie commonly called Hoastmen, for the loadinge and better disposinge of sea coles and pitt coles' (and certain other commodities), were incorporated by royal charter on 22 March.[75] William Jenison led the original 48 members as their first governor and served variously as alderman, mayor, sheriff and MP for Newcastle. He was joined by Henry Anderson and William Selby, who held similar posts, as well as members of the Riddell, Chapman, Maddison and Liddell families, who were also prominent in the government of Newcastle.

Newcastle's position as the provincial focus of the north-eastern counties of the kingdom was reinforced by its function as the principal provisioning centre for those parts. Indeed, it was the town's dual role as a market centre and as a port that was a major factor in its success.[76] For example, the wealth of Newcastle in the 15th century was heavily dependent on exporting wool to the Low Countries and importing finished goods to supply its hinterlands. The merchants of Newcastle were a strictly regulated association with a long history. Their status as a 'gild merchant' was made explicit in a charter granted to the burgesses of Newcastle by King John on 28 January 1216, which confirmed the liberties and free customs that they had enjoyed in the time of his ancestors. In 1480 three guilds (for wool, mercers and corn) combined to form the Company of Merchant Adventurers.[77] By the reign of Elizabeth they were called the Fellowship of Merchant Adventurers, with an annually appointed governor assisted by 12 assignees, who were nominated in the charter she issued on 10 May 1559. They constituted another small and exclusive Newcastle elite, whose names continued to dominate the affairs of Newcastle throughout the late 16th and early 17th centuries. The first governor appointed by Elizabeth's charter was Henry Anderson, and his assistants included Robert Brandling, Mark Shafto, Cuthbert Ellison, William Carr, Roger Mitford, Bertram Anderson and Oswald Chapman: all familiar names.

Extracts from its records show that the Merchants Adventurers of Newcastle were involved in a huge amount of business. Newcastle, rather than London, as might have been expected, also supplied luxury goods, such as wine and

[75] *Company of Hostmen*, pp.xiii, xxviii, 10-17.
[76] *The Customs Accounts of Newcastle upon Tyne 1454-1500*, SS, vol.202 (1995), p.3.
[77] *Merchant Adventurers*, vol.1, pp.xx-xxi, 281-2. And see Constance Fraser in this volume.

spices. For instance, by the 16th century, according to its records, 94 per cent of Durham priory's wine came from Newcastle.[78] In 1599 the fellowship ordained that no others could sell wine in the town, which they enforced, sometimes rigorously, by means of fines, while in 1618 a sum of 12d. was levied on every tun of wine brought into Newcastle to offset the company's debts.[79] At the same time it continued to be the provisioning centre for the wider north, at least as far as Naworth Castle in Cumberland.[80]

By the 16th century it was Newcastle's overseas trade which dominated its commercial activity, as demonstrated by Constance Fraser's comprehensive discussion of Newcastle's economic growth, up to 1536, in this volume. This was concentrated on the Tyne-Scheldt trade route, encompassing modern-day northern France, western Belgium and the Netherlands. But whereas outward cargoes were generally wool, bound for Bruges, Middleburg, Bergen-op-Zoom and Antwerp, their return cargoes were so diverse they could only have been laden in ports beyond that route, such as Gascon wine from Bordeaux.[81] Then the Tyne-Scheldt trade route underwent a prolonged depression which resulted in the final demise of the Low Countries' wool trade; albeit over a period of many years. It also meant that Newcastle ships ventured increasingly through the Sound, to engage in the Eastland trade, already established by Hull, London and Lynn; north-eastern shipping rose from none in 1500 to 52 in 1537.[82] The process was quickened by the decades of war after the 1580s in the Low Countries, which disrupted the North Sea trade and prompted the English to seek their own bases for trade from Hamburg and Elbing to the Levant and beyond.[83] In 1579 an Eastland Company of London Merchant Adventurers was incorporated, which included members of the Merchant Adventurers of Newcastle.[84] They enjoyed sole trading rights through the Sound into Scandinavia, Poland, Lithuania (except for Narva, which was the preserve of the Russian Company), Prussia and Pomerania. Twenty years later, the Eastland trade had become intrinsic to

[78] Threlfall-Holmes, M., 'Durham Cathedral Priory: consumption of imported goods: wines and spices, 1464-1520', in Hicks, M. (ed.), *Revolution and Consumption in Late Medieval England* (2001).
[79] *Merchant Adventurers*, vol.1, pp.57, 113, 123.
[80] *Selections from the Household Books of Lord W. Howard, of Naworth Castle; with Appendix of Documents Illustrative of his Life and Times*, SS, vol.68 (1878).
[81] Wade, J.F., 'The overseas trade of Newcastle upon Tyne in the late middle ages', *Northern History*, vol.30 (1994), p.35.
[82] Fudge, John D., 'Maintaining a presence: Baltic enterprise and the merchants of Lyne during the reign of Henry VIII', in Salmon, Patrick and Barrow, Tony (eds), *Britain and the Baltic* (2003); Blanchard, I.S.W., 'Commercial crisis and change: trade and the industrial economy of the north east, 1509-1532', *Northern History*, vol.8i (1973), pp.74-6.
[83] Kirby, David and Hinkkanen, Merja-Liisa, *The Baltic and the North Seas* (2000), p.96.
[84] *Merchant Adventurers*, vol.1, p.238n and vol.2, p.xix.

92 Riverside activity at Sandgate in the early 19th century.

England's prosperity, when it was one of the considerations in Lord Burghley's reflections whether to conclude a peace with Spain in 1598. For England would have trade opened for her merchants to all the countries of Spain, Portugal, Barbary and the Levant, as well as to the countries in the east, Poland and Denmark, and the maritime towns of Germany; thereby the shipping of the realm and mariners shall increase, and also the port towns that are manifestly decayed, as Newcastle, Hull, Boston, and Lynn northwards; Southampton, Pool, Weymouth, Bristol, Chester, west and southwards.[85] The Eastland trade was not enough of a consideration, however, as peace was not finally concluded until the next reign.

[85] TNA, SP12/266/3.

The expansion of trade beyond the narrow confines of medieval ports and harbours and out onto open beaches, river estuaries and such like was made possible by a smaller style of vessel pioneered by the Dutch.[86] Newcastle was quick to adapt and capitalise on this development, and it was launching smaller ships from the mid-15th century onwards. But it was another innovation, the use of lighterage, or keels with masts that could be dismantled, to connect the mines upstream from the Tyne bridge to the larger seagoing vessels, that made Tyne coal cheaper than any other; thus, securing its continuing position as the international port of the North East.[87] Most spectacular of all Newcastle's external trades was coal, which had been significant since the middle of the 14th century.[88] According to one estimate, albeit based on partial and fragmentary information, the annual shipment of coal from Newcastle increased more rapidly in the late 16th and early 17th centuries than any other period; almost twelve-fold. Another pinpoints the turning-point in the coal trade to the 1570s and '80s, with shipments in coal rising almost four-fold between the later 1560s and the later 1590s.[89] At the same time new pits were opened nearly every year in the reign of Elizabeth and the first decade of the 17th century. Although the lower Wear Valley in Durham also furnished coal, which was traded from Sunderland from around 1600, the Newcastle district towered over coal production and its trade. A poem written in the middle of the 17th century enthused:

England's a perfect World! Has Indies too!
Correct your Maps: Newcastle is Peru.[90]

In the 16th century the overseas coal trade went overwhelmingly to ports between Cherbourg and the Danish peninsula, but, with the improved accessibility of the Baltic ports, such as Danzig, Lubeck, Straslund, Stettin and Stockholm, they received an increasing proportion of the Newcastle trade in the 17th century.[91] The English east coast coal trade was also important. Tracking the passage of coal from Tyneside coalmine to the London hearth was increasingly tortuous, involving mine owner, Hostman, shipmaster, broker,

[86]   Kirby and Hinkkanen, *The Baltic and the North Seas*, p.94; Scammell, G., 'English merchant shipping at the end of the Middle Ages: some east coast evidence', *Economic History Review*, vol.13 (1960-1), pp.333-4.
[87]   Hatcher, *Coal Industry*, vol.1, p.465; Wade, 'The overseas trade of Newcastle', p.33.
[88]   See Constance Fraser in this volume.
[89]   Nef, *Coal Industry*, vol.1, p.25; Hatcher, *The History of the British Coal Industry*, vol.1, p.78.
[90]   William Ellis, 'Upon the Coale-pits about Newcastle upon Tine', *News from Newcastle*, London (1651), BL E. 622 (15).
[91]   Nef, *Coal Industry*, vol.1, pp.84-7. While he acknowledges that his figures are based on incomplete port books they do reflect broad trends.

dealer, factor and retailer.[92] It was little wonder that the central authorities and London's governors kept an anxious and watchful eye over the process, and paid such close attention to the dispute between the grand lessees and non-grand lessees in the 1590s.

But Newcastle trade was also subject to a far more menacing threat. In May 1599 the privy council received a complaint from Hull about 'the Dunkirkers', who were chasing their ships going to Newcastle for coals.[93] These were privateers (similar to pirates, but acting under licence from a sovereign power) operating out of Dunkirk and Ostende. Although not a new problem, their activities were an integral part of Habsburg state policy in the wars against the Dutch from the 1590s. For England, privateering was big business, especially after the defeat of the Armada when it helped finance the East India Company and other colonial ventures.[94] But, for their victims, the picture was not quite so positive, especially those on England's east coast, who were subject to frequent attacks which disrupted the trade between Newcastle and London. The perpetrators were not just the Dunkirkers. Their fellow Englishmen also profited from the brisk Tyneside market in the hauls of pirates and privateers, such as the East Anglian who appeared before the Admiralty Court in 1548 for having 'cummen many tymes to New Castell with dyvers prises' illicitly seized.[95] But it was the scale of the Dunkirkers' activities which caused such consternation by the turn of the century. According to the report from Hull in 1599, there were 24 great ships belonging to the Dunkirkers, plying the waters from the Sound, to Hamburg and Emden (in present-day Germany) and along the English coast. They were capable of inflicting humiliating punishment on their victims; for example, the account from Hull claimed that the Dunkirkers stripped the fishermen and mariners they captured. But they were also thoroughly pragmatic for, the report continued, they forced likely masters to be their pilots along the northern coasts.

A steady stream of complaints to the Admiralty Court and the privy council attested to the continued threat from the Dunkirkers but there were few concerted measures adopted to counter the threat. There had been a Parliamentary Act against piracy in 1535, making it a capital offence in

---

[92]   Fraser, Constance, 'The early Hostmen of Newcastle upon Tyne', *AA*, 5th series, vol.7 (1984); Hatcher, *Coal Industry*, vol.1, pp.508-9.

[93]   TNA, SP12/270/109.

[94]   Kirby and Hinkkanen, *The Baltic and the North Seas*, pp.119-20; Scammell, G.V., *The World Encompassed: the First European Maritime Empires c.800-1650* (1981), pp.458-504.

[95]   TNA, High Court of Admiralty I/34 fos 164v-6. Cited in Scammell, G.V., 'War at sea under the early Tudors – part II', *AA*, 4th series, vol.39 (1961), p.201.

93   The Hostmen's seal.

the Admiralty Court, but the Dunkirkers continued to wreak havoc on the fishing fleet of Holland. The Baltic trade did seem to get some organised protection from the *directieschepen*, which was made up of Dutch-financed and equipped warships to convoy ships through the North Sea into the Baltic. English shipowners, however, were remarkably reluctant to dig into their own pockets to pay for a fleet to patrol the seaways.[96] But when England found itself at war against both France and Spain, after 1625, minds seem to have been concentrated and the matter was finally given due attention. In January 1626 commissioners for the navy gave their opinions to the privy council regarding the danger from the Dunkirkers to ships trading with Newcastle.[97] Having consulted with the Trinity House they determined that two of the king's ships and 10 Newcastle ships would suffice to provide a convoy at a cost of £13,200. It was resolved that the way of raising the sum should be considered in Parliament. In April the question of securing the coal trade was addressed by the Committee for the Defence of the Kingdom in the House of Lords.[98] Their chief concern was the fact that the lack of coal meant that saltpetre, necessary for making gunpowder, could not be manufactured, which was a direct result of the Dunkirkers' threat to the Newcastle colliers.

Implementing the results of their deliberations seems to have been quite piecemeal, however. For example, Richard Fell, master of the *Amity* of Newcastle, was obliged to petition the commissioners of the Admiralty for payment for his three years' service in Cadiz, and then as a 'wafter for the colliers', in 1628.[99] On 13 August 1628 the privy council issued an order condemning the coal owners' failure to provide for the convoy of Newcastle colliers 'out of a desire of excessive gain', with its attendant consequences that 'both ruin themselves and

---

96   Kirby and Hinkkanen, *The Baltic and the North Seas*, pp.119-20.
97   TNA, SP16/18/59. And see Simon Healy in this volume.
98   *LJ*, vol.3, pp.546-9.
99   TNA, SP16/119/4.

weaken the kingdome by their losse, and strengthen his Majesties Enemies'.[100] This was yet another example of Newcastle not matching William Camden's 16th-century view of the town as an oasis of tranquillity and compliance in an otherwise turbulent part of the kingdom.[101] And the disquiet persisted. In May 1630, the Lord Mayor and others of London were reporting to the privy council that the Greenland fleet were 'wafting' the Newcastle ships.[102] The business, they felt, was one that 'concerned all England and should be carried with a Royal hand'. Yet, the king had already taken a hand. In March 1627 he issued a commission under the great seal to the Council of the North to compound with recusants as far south as Derby and Stafford to redress the losses suffered by the coastal trade, especially the coal trade of Newcastle, and to equip a convoy fleet.[103] In addition, he appointed Alexander Davison of Newcastle 'to receive out of the voluntary and freewill Contribution of the Owners, Buyers, and Sellers of Coals, the Six pence per Chaldron of Coals'. The mayor and others of Newcastle responded, promptly.[104] They declared that the charge for the three ships they were called upon to set forth would amount to £5,000, and that, having called together those inhabitants deemed able to contribute to such a charge, they found that by reason of the plague, decay of trade, losses in France, *and by Dunkirkers*, and also by the late loan money, they were utterly disabled, and prayed that they may not be further pressed to a charge which amounted to 90 subsidies. Tackling the threat to the Newcastle coal trade seemed to be a circle that could not be squared.

Targeting the recusants to finance measures to secure the safety of the Newcastle coal trade highlighted another threat to Newcastle. Almost from the moment that the pope issued his excommunication against England, in 1585, Newcastle was involved in the transmission of Catholic letters and material between the continent and England. For example, information from Paris to Secretary Walsingham, in December that year, reported that 'the Scotch Jesuits have their letters conveyed from Scotland into England, to one Boast, a priest in the North parts, who sends them hither by some that come from Newcastle to Dieppe'.[105] And the route between Newcastle and a number of

---

[100]   *APC*, 1628-9, p.101.
[101]   William Camden, *Britain, or a Chorographicall Account of the Most Flourishing Kingdomes, England, Scotland, and Ireland*, trans. Philemon Holland, London (1610).
[102]   TNA, SP16/166/19.
[103]   Rushworth, John, *Historical Collections of Private Passages of State*, vol.1, 1618-29 (1721), pp.417-18.
[104]   TNA, SP 16/59/55.
[105]   TNA, SP 12/29/62. The priest was John Boste, for whose activities see Questier, Michael C., 'Practical antipapistry during the reign of Elizabeth I', *Journal of British Studies*, vol.36 (1997).

French ports continued to be crucial to the Catholics, with a steady stream of reports of their activities reaching the authorities in England. On 4 April 1626, the same day that the House of Lords was debating the question of securing the Newcastle coal trade, the mayor and justices of Newcastle complained to the privy council about the Dunkirkers, and reported that one of the officers of the customs had found a bag full of popish books in the *Flying Har'*, of Hamburg.[106] Over the following weeks they uncovered a network of suspected Roman Catholics and seminary priests who were discovered on ships arriving from Calais, including Anthony Vandenhaudt, a servant of Sir Richard Hodgson, of Newcastle and Hebburn, in County Durham.[107] An ancestor of Sir Richard (another Richard Hodgson) had been described as 'a rank Papest' after a sectarian affray in Newcastle in 1569. This was an opportunity to nail the notorious family and their continental associates. However, when the detailed examinations of all the parties came to be dealt with by the sheriff of Durham, all the suspects had disappeared.[108]

There were more positive associations between Newcastle and its overseas associates. As well as the Newcastle merchants' long-standing commercial links with their Eastland counterparts, there were also connections with the exiled Bohemian protestants and they contributed to the voluntary aid for the King of Bohemia in 1620. When the radical Puritan lecturer, Robert Jenison, was dismissed from Newcastle in September 1639, he took refuge in Danzig, taking advantage of the long-standing associations between Newcastle and the Eastland region; from there he wrote bitterly of Newcastle as 'that wretched & unthankful town both to god and man'.[109] There were also benevolent and charitable links. Bertram Anderson left 'eight tons of coal to the poor of Hambrowth [Hamburg] to be taken from his staithes on the north bank of the Tyne for which they must pay for fetching it and custom and all other charges', and in September 1584 Ralph Cole wrote his will in Middleburg, in which he bequeathed twenty Flemish shillings to the poor of Middleburg 'if yt please god here to call me to his mercie'.[110] While five shillings was given to Sir William Riddell in 1653 'to buy clothes for a poore Dutch boy to whom he liberarly bestowed his Charitie',[111] thereby perpetuating his uncle Henry's philanthropy. Thus was epitomised the

[106] TNA, SP16/24/23.
[107] TNA, SP16/24/83; SP 16/26/16; SP 16/27/34.
[108] Clifford, A. (ed.), *The State Papers and Letters of Sir Ralph Sadler*, vol.2 (1809), p.64; TNA, SP16/30/36.
[109] Howell, Roger, 'The career of Robert Jenison, a C17 puritan in Newcastle' in *Puritans and Radicals*, p.121.
[110] DUL, DPR1/1571 and printed in *Wills and Inventories*, vol.3, p.58; DPR1/1586 and printed in *Wills and Inventories*, vol.3, pp.110-11.
[111] See Peter Rushton in this volume. DRO, EP/Ga.SM 4/1.

broad outlook of the Newcastle merchant, from his immediate vicinity to far beyond the River Tyne. Above all, this shows how Henry Riddell and John March were not so singular after all.

Gateshead 1550-1700
Independence Against all the Odds?

PETER RUSHTON

Introduction – Gateshead in the Mid-Sixteenth Century

'The towne of Gatesyde is as it is reported ane antyent towne or broughe belonging to the Byshope of Durhame and his predecessors', asserted one witness to a legal case brought by Newcastle's mayor and Corporation in 1578: 'by reporte tyme out of mynde of man [it] hath bene ane antyent towne', said another. Yet, somehow, it is significant that they needed to be hauled into court to prove that the place was of long-standing independence. Gateshead has always been tied to Newcastle, yet has continually had to establish its own individual identity in contrast to, or even against, its larger neighbour.[1]

When Bishop Barnes's surveyors examined Gateshead's population served by the parish church of St Mary's they gave it as 1,000 'howselinge' people, that is, worshippers or those taking communion. This was a narrow pastoral view that almost certainly excluded the children and young servants. Fifteen years later, in 1563, the community was calculated on a different basis, as consisting of more than 300 households, suggesting a markedly higher population, closer to 1,450 people overall. Despite the different methods of counting, these figures help to indicate Gateshead's relative standing in the North East in the mid-16th century. Gateshead was only slightly smaller than another place on the Great North Road, Darlington, and both shared the problems of being on a major highway where many people were on the way to somewhere else, with a local community trying to find some stability in the face of an inevitably transient population passing through. Gateshead was small by comparison with the City of Durham which had at least three times its number of people, and was completely overshadowed by Newcastle itself, which contained more than 7,500.

---

[1] Longstaffe, W.H.D., 'The Market and Fair at Gateshead', *AA*, 2nd series, vol.2 (1858), p.227. Also published separately and bound in a collection of Longstaffe's works entitled *Durham Before the Conquest* (undated, in Durham University Library), pamphlet 12, with different page numbers.

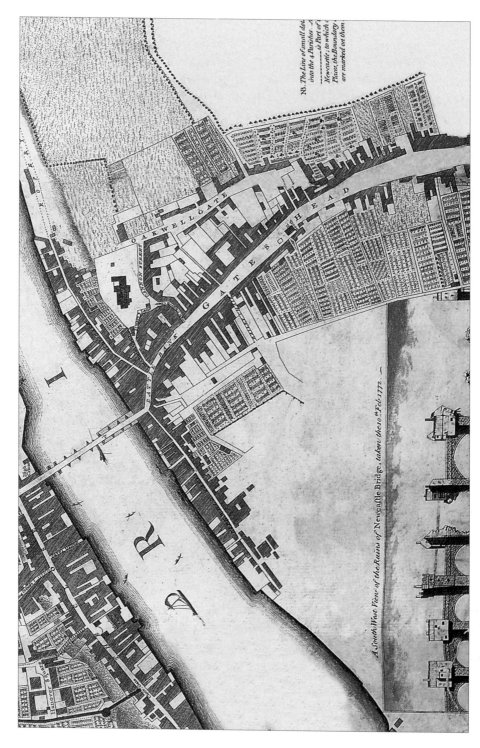

94   Map of Gateshead in the late 18th century, with a cartouche of the remains of the old bridge.

Gateshead was demonstrably in the middle rank of towns in the region.[2] Its status and organisation were complex and at times obscure: like Sunderland and a number of other places in Durham, Gateshead was both a parish, a manor and an ecclesiastical borough (that is, established by charter from the bishop), which could produce confusing overlapping lines of responsibility and some difficulties for local management. Custom rather than a logical arrangement of neat administrative structures determined how the place was run, and these traditional habits provided the continuity throughout the early modern period and well into the 18th century.[3]

In the period after the Reformation, Gateshead had an inheritance of medieval institutions and customs, some of them developing a new life, like St Edmund's Hospital, which in Elizabeth's reign was in continual danger of decay (though it was the sole caring institution remaining from the Middle Ages). Yet it was reconstituted in the early 17th century as King James's Hospital and still survives.[4] Other ancient institutions such as fairs and markets, signs of a healthy independent economy, seem to have died after the 16th century. As Robert Surtees put it, 'Gateshead, before it shrunk under the influence of Newcastle, had a borough market, which, according to depositions … was held twice a week, Tuesday and Friday'. Despite legal threats from their competitors north of the river, there is certainly evidence that in the middle of the 16th century, Gateshead had its own market days, in addition to the shops on the southern half of the bridge. By 1647, however, according to a Parliamentary survey, 'there are no faires nor market days usually kept within the mannor of Gateshead', though records were extant at that time to prove that there had once been both.

The same survey, however, revealed that there were many shops flourishing on Gateshead's half of the old bridge.[5] This situation almost certainly stemmed

[2] *The Injunctions and Other Ecclesiastical Proceedings of Richard Barnes, Bishop of Durham*, SS, vol.22 (1834), Appendix 6, pp.lxv-lxvi, survey dated 14 February, 2 Edward VI [1549]; see pp.lx-lxiii for the 'houseling' people; BL, MS Harley 594, fos 187r-195r and Fraser, Constance, 'The Diocese of Durham in 1563', in Faulkner T.E. (ed.), *Northumbrian Panorama: Studies in the History and Culture of North East England* (1996), p.93. Gateshead had 307 families compared with Darlington's 366, Durham's 959, and Newcastle's 1,747; the usual formula for deriving population being to multiple by the average household size for the early modern period of 4.75 people, suggested by Laslett, Peter, 'Size and Structure of the Household in England over Three Centuries', *Population Studies*, vol.23 (1969), p.200, and confirmed by Wall, Richard, 'Fertility, Economy, and Household in England over Three Centuries', *Population and Development Review*, vol.7 (1981), p.599.
[3] Dodds, M.H., 'The Bishops' Boroughs', *AA*, 3rd series, vol.12 (1915), pp.81-5.
[4] Manders, Francis W.D., *A History of King James's Hospital Gateshead* (1974); anon, *Collections Relating to St.Edmund's Hospital at Gateshead* (George Allan, Darlington, 1769).
[5] Surtees, Robert, *The History and Antiquities of the County Palatine of Durham* (1909), Gateshead Section, 50; Longstaffe, 'The Market and Fair at Gateshead', testifying to the vigour of both fairs and markets; Kirby, David A. (ed.), *Parliamentary Surveys of the Bishopric of Durham*, ii, SS, vol.185 (1972), p.115 and see pp.117-21 for a survey of the bridge's shops belonging to Gateshead, with 18 leases.

from Newcastle's recurrent campaigns against rival markets along the Tyne, and against the unregulated (from a Newcastle merchant's viewpoint) shops on Gateshead's part of the Tyne bridge. Newcastle tried to maintain the monopoly of its own markets, and took steps to prevent goods purchased elsewhere from being admitted to them. They also punished their own traders for selling goods outside the town. For example, the Merchant Adventurers have left detailed rules and records of their enforcement. Members (brethren, strictly speaking) could not buy goods such as the skins of sheep and lambs, nor wool, in Gateshead or elsewhere such as 'upon the bridge' (underlined emphatically in the original text) and bring them to sell in Newcastle: they had to buy them from the butchers and slaughterers of their own town. Moreover, some goods, such as all the types of corn, could not be taken out of Newcastle for sale in Gateshead, though clearly this had been difficult to enforce. Selling goods outside the town without prior permission could result in the seizure of the goods, as happened to James Butterey who lost more than £13 worth of soap (in quantity, amounting to 10 firkins) to the company for selling them to George Airey of Gateshead in 1660. Seventeen years later the company prosecuted Ayrey at Durham assizes, apparently successfully, for acting illegally as a mercer. In addition, to reinforce Newcastle's claim to control the river, steps were taken by a mayor's warrant to 'restraine the landing of goods in Gateside, and to seize all goods landed there'. The merchants were also alert to goods that were even more foreign than those supplied by Gateshead, such as imports from Holland.[6] Despite this kind of systematic exclusion, the commercial life of Gateshead expanded and was successfully re-organised in newly established guilds from the end of the 16th century.[7]

The place seems to show all the contradictions of early modern history, a mixture of old and new, traditional and freshly invented. Records of manor, borough and parish for the 16th century are few, but those surviving from the 1620s onward suggest that, despite difficulties, the problems of the community attracted careful administration and provoked attention to local need. Yet times were difficult, as Gateshead was at the centre of several disturbing events. The pattern of repeated disruptions from the Reformation to the Civil War posed great threats both to local leadership and the processes of self-government, as changes in religion and political power led to Gateshead becoming the focus of intermittent attention from central authority.

[6] *Extracts from the Records of the Merchant Adventurers of Newcastle upon Tyne*, i, SS, vol.93 (1895), pp.47, 56-7, 151, 167, 197, 207, 220-1.
[7] See later discussion of the importance of guilds.

The Politics of Coal

In the 16th century, the threats to Gateshead's independence, both economic and political, came from Newcastle. Gateshead was the southern gateway to the town, and shared responsibility for the bridge that united them. From the point of view of Newcastle's coal merchants, however, Gateshead was more than just a neighbour: it was a suburb beyond its control. Moreover, it was the solution to a central paradox for these entrepreneurs, because Newcastle was that strange phenomenon, a coal town without any coal. Gateshead had some easily accessible coal, and, more importantly, provided the ways and means of transporting it from neighbouring areas such as Whickham and more distant pits to the banks of the Tyne for loading on to ships. Gateshead's problems in the latter half of the 16th century therefore derived entirely from Newcastle's repeated attempts to take over this function of its increasingly profitable neighbour. The story has been well told by Gateshead's own historian, Francis Manders, as well as by earlier scholars. Events can be traced in detail through the records of Parliament. The first attempt was listed as the 'Bill for the Town of Gateside to be Parcel of Newcastle upon Tyne', or the Bill to have the town 'annexed to Newcastle upon Tyne'. The legislation was passed in 1553, as Manders has remarked, with indecent haste. Within a year, after Mary had acceded to the throne, the Act was repealed. Newcastle bided its time, and tried again under Queen Elizabeth in 1576.[8] The arguments for the measure were a mixture of the economic and the moral, as far as Newcastle was concerned. Gateshead was full of a 'greate nombre of handy penters, collyers, fishers, maryners, and other handycraftes menne, which by their handy workes gayne and have their chief and in manner hole lyving' in Newcastle, went the petition from Newcastle's leaders. Unfortunately, these 'handy' men came to the town 'wher they daly committed manyfolde enormetyes and disorders which escape unpunished to a very evil example in the hindrance of justice, by reason that soch offendors, by repairing to the saide towne of Gatesyde, being withowte the jurisdiction of the said haven towne of Newcastle'. Newcastle also complained that Gateshead did not keep its part of the Tyne bridge in proper repair and, worse, people were allowed to dump rubbish into the river without penalty.[9]

It is unclear how Gateshead's authorities replied to the first (briefly successful) attempt to take them over, but when in 1576 Newcastle tried again, they concentrated their rebuttal on demonstrating the orderly state of their government

---

[8]   CJ, vol. 1, p.26; Manders, Francis W.D., *A History of Gateshead* (Gateshead Corporation, 1973), p.9.
[9]   Surtees, *Durham*, Gateshead Section, pp.57-8. This is the preamble to the first Act in 1553.

and the efficient enforcement of law and order, elaborating on their own virtues in a series of petitions to both the Speaker of the Commons and Lord Burghley.

> The Towne of Gateshead is ruled by the Bayliff and Burgesses, and hath good and holsom constitution and ordinances within themselves, and is as well governed for justice as they are in Newcastle, punishing all offenders which cast rubbishe and cleansinge of their howses into the River Tyne, and therefore the suggestion which they alleage in the statute of unitinge the townes is manifestly untrew, as it is evidentlly knowen for that the South side of the River, which is towards Gateshead, is deep and more cleane than that side towards Newcastle.

The proposed law was contradictory, they pointed out, because it would put Gateshead under Newcastle's control, but the judicial structure would still involve sending cases to Durham's courts, as before. In addition, the people of Gateshead – allegedly 3,000 in total, with 400 householders – stood to see their common lands handed over to Newcastle. Newcastle would restrict their trade and close the shops on their end of the bridge (whose businesses were, as mentioned above, regarded as a threat by Newcastle's merchants). Their own customs, by contrast, were, they said, 'lawdable'. To clinch the argument, they pointed out that the north side of Newcastle was equally beyond the town's control (being in Northumberland), while Gateshead had a:

> Great nombre of substantial honest men faitfull and trewe subjects, as did appeare in the late rebellyon, some merchaunts, some drapers, and other honest artificers, whom the towne of Newcastell doth envie because they swell so nie unto them.[10]

Professions of loyalty to Queen Elizabeth and Church were a crucial element in their response. Sir William Fleetwood, Recorder of London, who also held a post in the diocese of Durham, noted in his letter of support for Gateshead that the town had no bishop or knights of the shires in Parliament to fight for them, yet was loyal to the government. The people were religious, 'godly, and good Protestants', whereas by contrast, he alleged, 'the towne of Newcastell are all papists', enflamed by ambition and malice towards its southern neighbour. In the face of this sustained campaign, the Bill was defeated.[11]

[10]   Surtees, *Durham*, Gateshead Section, pp.58-9 (he thinks this is 1575); Longstaffe, 'The Attempt to Annex Gateshead to Newcastle in 1575', *AA*, NS vol.2 (1858), pp.226-8. Much of this is also in Manders, *Gateshead*, pp.9-15.
[11]   Longstaffe, 'The Attempt', p.231; *CJ*, vol. 1, pp.114-15; See also Welford, *Newcastle and Gateshead*, ii (1885), pp.476-81.

95 Gateshead waterfront, deeper and cleaner than the Newcastle bank. Captured by W.H. Knowles in the late 19th century.

Despite this apparent setback, the managers of Newcastle achieved their aims by other means. The salt meadows (east of the town along the riverside, towards where the Gateshead Stadium now is) were leased by Bishop Tunstall to Newcastle in 1555, that is, immediately after Gateshead regained its formal independence, 'with a view, probably, to take off the opposition of the wealthy and powerful Corporation of Newcastle, who reluctantly quitted their grasp on the south side of the river', says Surtees. The lease was for an astonishing 450 years, giving Newcastle control of later industrial developments across the river. Surtees' interpretation was almost certainly correct, as the second, frustrated, attempt at a direct takeover resulted in the Grand Lease in 1583 for 99 years, which captured the even greater prize Newcastle had been seeking all along. It seems likely that attempts at a forcible merger through Parliamentary legislation were a tactic – successful on two occasions – to force the bishop into surrendering crucial assets in Gateshead and Whickham.[12]

---

[12] Surtees, *History*, p.59; Manders, *Gateshead*, p.10. See also 'Exemplification of a Lease of the Salt Meadows and Tolls of the Town of Gateshead', in *Collectanea Ad Civilem et Ecclesiasticum Comitatus Dunelmensis* (1774), and also copied in Kirby, *Parliamentary Surveys*, pp.121-2.

During the lifetime of the Grand Lease, and after, Newcastle's coal interests kept an intimate involvement in the affairs of Gateshead. This was helped by the way that a number of Newcastle merchants such as the Liddells and Clavering moved out to the Durham countryside to buy land and estates: 'well chosen estates could consolidate a family's industrial strength', and Gateshead and Whickham were the obvious place to go.[13] This gave families such as the Liddells a ready entry into the management of Gateshead, and Sir Thomas served on the vestry, called the 'four-and-twenty', and sometimes acted as churchwarden, from the early 1630s to the Civil War. He joined influential Gateshead 'coalmasters' such as Ralph and Nicholas Cole, who had rented coal assets in Axwell Houses. They were not passive nor did they dominate by working behind scenes, but became deeply involved personally in the minutiae of the parish problems discussed below. They served on the vestry and acted (when asked) for the interests of the town. Given the wealth and power of the Liddells, this participation suggests a rapid conversion to a culture of rural patronage and activism, as much as a cold-blooded desire to dominate the source of their wealth. In the 1650s, Ralph Clavering, another newcomer into Gateshead from Newcastle, represented the borough and parish in attempts to achieve a legal settlement of Baron Hilton's will. This left the parish and other places in Durham some charitable money for the poor, but proved legally unresolved and subject to expensive proceedings in London for some years (though the legacy produced a useful £24 a year for Gateshead by the 1680s).[14]

The manor of Gateshead was controlled by Newcastle under the Grand Lease and evidence suggests that the town was careful to place its people in charge of it. This may have been more symbolic than actually necessary to ensure profitable control of the coal, but it did make sure that the community understood who was in charge. During the time when the lord of Gateshead manor was in fact a plural – as the surviving records put it, the 'Lords' were the 'Mayor and Burgesses of Newcastle' – it was natural that they put their own people into office in Gateshead. In the 1650s well-known Newcastle men such

---

[13] Levine D. and Wrightson, K., *The Making of an Industrial Society: Whickham, 1560-1765* (1991), p.24; Halliday, Stuart, 'Landed Power in the Palatinate: a study of the Attainment, Maintenance and Loss of Landed Elite Status in the County of Durham between the seventeenth and nineteenth Centuries' (unpublished MA thesis, University of Sunderland, 1999) and his 'Social Mobility, Demographic Change and the Landed Elite of County Durham, 1610-1819', *Northern History*, vol.30 (1994), pp.49-63.

[14] Levine and Wrightson, *The Making of an Industrial Society*, pp.15, 23-4; DRO, EP.Ga SM. 4/1, pp.33, 122, 206; EP.Ga.SM 5/1, p.45 (£48 over two years from 1684); for the legal niceties see Rushton, Peter, 'Law in North-East England: Community, County and Region, 1550-1850', in Green, Adrian and Pollard, A.J. (eds), *Regional Identities in North-East England circa 1300-2000* (2007), p.82.

as Thomas Milbourne, Thomas Ledger and Thomas Bonner (who was mayor of Newcastle during the witchcraft outbreak of 1649-50) served as bailiffs of the borough of Gateshead, or as stewards. That both posts could be taken by outsiders reflects the way that control of the manor through the Grand Lease in effect extended over the rest of the town or, at least enabled the exercise of considerable influence. In the 1660s Sir Robert Shafto served as bailiff, and continued to do so until the Grand Lease lapsed. In 1682, the last year in the century for which we have evidence, Robert Delaval was bailiff. This period marked the highpoint of Newcastle's personal dominance of Gateshead's affairs. When records begin again in the 18th century there are no bailiffs mentioned, and there are no extant references to them in the intermediate period: it may be that Delaval was the last, as was believed in the late 18th century. From that point on, those wishing to influence Gateshead's affairs served as stewards or on the vestry. The latter was the key administrative force for most of the early modern period.[15]

These powerful families therefore provided Gateshead with a paradoxical contribution. Their members often acted in and for the community, but if any conflict arose between the town and their private interests, things had to be handled with great care by Gateshead's authorities. On a couple of occasions, when negotiating the rates for wayleaves across the town, or trying to restrict both encroachments on and collateral damage from them, the vestry used arbitration rather than direct confrontation or legal suits. In 1657, for example, accusing William Riddell's wayleave over Windmill Hills of causing spillage and spoils on the adjoining land, the four-and-twenty appointed James Clavering as their representative, while Riddell chose Albert Hodgson, both sides agreeing to a negotiated solution. More direct action was taken in 1670, when a 'company' was employed by the vestry to dig a trench across the coal ways, to stop the coal owners using it, and then to watch the ways overnight to make sure. This was in part to 'defend the Townes Interest against Mr Riddell', it was recorded, though both sides seem to have met to settle in the end. By contrast, in reply to a legal attack by Sir Henry Liddle of Ravensworth Castle, who 'indicted' several inhabitants for destroying a wall built at Low Eighton on the boundary of the town, whose precise location seems to have been the problem, the vestry had to send the stewards to pay the costs of the

---

15 TWAS, DF.OX/7/1 (John Oxberry's lists of the data in the three books of the Borough of Gateshead); Manders, *Gateshead*, p.26, interprets Shafto's appointment as a sign that the bishop had regained control by 1679, but Shafto had served since 1661; Surtees, *Durham*, Gateshead volume, 54n cites a 1772 petition from Gateshead to the bishop to appoint a bailiff, at which point it was believed that Delaval had been the last.

indictment and 'cause the same to be traversed this sessions'. They also sent in their biggest guns, including lawyer William Cotesworth, who later acquired the lordship of Gateshead manor, to attend on Sir Henry about this boundary dispute (on Gateshead Fell), with full power on behalf of the town to 'enter into securities, to abide the award and determination of such as shall be so named'.[16]

Vagrants, Paupers and Puritans

Gateshead at the level of borough and parish showed all the characteristics of the early modern 'parish state', as poet John Clare called it in the 19th century. The phrase makes the point very neatly that, for most of the period before the 19th century, the British 'state' was in fact made up of parish and county personnel, serving as everything from constable, churchwarden, overseer of the poor to justice of the peace, usually unpaid or in exchange for basic expenses. Amateur it may have been, but this organisation was remarkably effective.[17] In Gateshead there seems to have been a simple structure with a single body: for much of the 17th century, to judge from the surviving records, the four-and-twenty of the vestry in effect ran both the parish and the borough, managing the appointments of officials, and paying for many of the functions of the borough such as guaranteeing the water supply from the 'pants' or wells and springs, and ensuring the town's fields were in good condition. The four-and-twenty of the vestry – the 'most notable of the north country close vestries' – were, in effect, 'the executive body in the affairs of the town'.[18] There was a substantial supplementary bureaucracy to attend to the many community functions, and this suggests that the expenditure on these activities was a major factor in providing local employment. Officers were numerous: there were four each of churchwardens, overseers, constables, grassmen, overseers of the highways, officers 'for gathering wayne money', and two 'pant maisters' or overseers of the pants. In fact, more than two dozen men had official titled posts annually. There were also those paid to perform particular duties: in addition to a bellman who also seemed to double as a

[16]   DRO, EP. Ga. SM 4/1, pp.184-5, 225, 403; EP. Ga. SM 5/1, 191, 195; on Cotesworth, see Manders, *Gateshead*, p.26, and Ellis, Joyce M., *A Study of the Business Fortunes of William Cotesworth, c.1668-1726* (unpublished D.Phil., University of Oxford, 1975).
[17]   Hindle, Steve, 'Power, Poor Relief, and Social Relations in Holland Fen, c.1600-1800', *Historical Journal*, vol.41 (1) (1998), pp.67-96, 94; Kent, Joan R., 'The Centre and the Localities: State Formation and Parish Government in England, c.1640-1740', *Historical Journal*, vol.38 (1995), pp.363-404.
[18]   Dodds, 'The Bishops' Boroughs', pp.163-4.

grave digger, there were regular payments to a town piper, unnumbered town waits (musicians, though we do not know what instruments they played), and a 'hird' or herdsman paid an annual salary to look after the cattle on the town fields (where he was also provided with a house). By the 1650s there was also a beadle. In 1638 a 'waterman' was mentioned, paid 15s. a quarter, but it is not clear what his duties were. Other local professions received help, too, such as local schoolteachers occasionally given funds to teach poor boys. Also, the various carers of the town bull during the winter required payment (he seems to have spent the summer in the town fields), as well as the many workers hired to undertake the many routine repairs to the church and other buildings, or employed to clean and take away the heaps of rubbish. The impression is that this kind of expenditure provided a useful source of employment both for skilled craftsmen such as glaziers and stonemasons, and for the relatively unskilled of the town.[19]

The work of these officials was vital to the management of the social problems of the parish, particularly with regard to the poor. The vestry through the churchwardens spent large sums on the wandering poor, in particular, and responded to emergencies such as outbreaks of plague. Perhaps the most intriguing aspect of the poor passing through Gateshead before the Civil Wars was that substantial numbers were Irish. In 1630 alone, for example, the churchwardens record the following outgoings:

paid unto 2 Irish men wch [which] had a pass – 1s.

paid unto 2 Irish folkes wch [which] had a pass – 1s.

paid unto a Irish gentlewoman wch [which] had a pass – 1s. 6d.

paid unto six Irish folkes wch [which] had a pass – 2s. 6d.

By the 1640s the Irish seem to have changed character: though it is hard to prove beyond doubt, the records make them sound more like refugees than paupers, perhaps fleeing from the fighting at the start of the Civil War. Certainly they had only recently left Ireland. For example, on 20 August 1642, 1s. was paid 'to a poore man, his wife, 2 children who came from Ireland', and in another case in December 1s. 6d. was given to '2 gentlewomen and 3 children that had a passe from Ireland'. There were others from Ireland that winter: significantly, most had passes or a 'passport', and one was lodged in the house of a respectable parishioner, John London. It is likely that their

---

[19] DRO, EP/Ga.SM 4/1, pp.8, 88, 193.

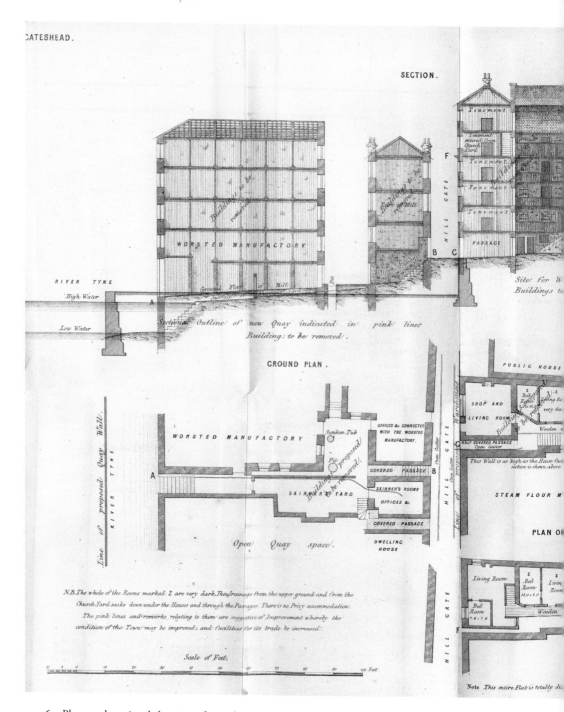

96 Plans and sectional drawing of a 19th-century slum, lying between the churchyard and the river, crossing Hill Gate.

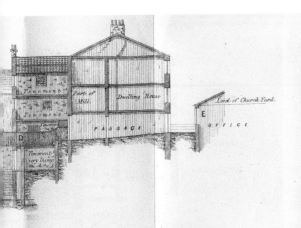

PLANS AND SECTION
OF PROPERTY
LYING BETWEEN THE CHURCH YARD IN
GATESHEAD,
AND THE RIVER TYNE,
CROSSING THE STREET CALLED HILL GATE.

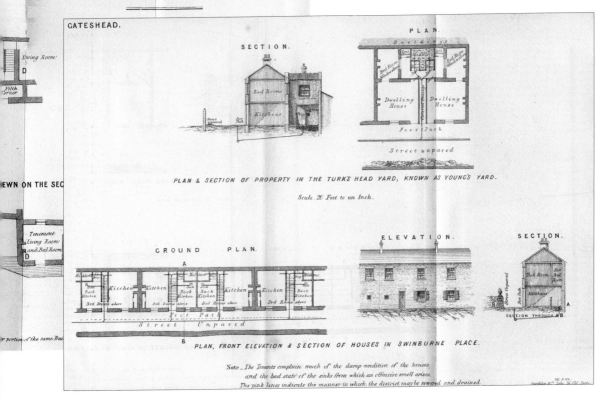

situation evoked a level of public sympathy usually lacking with regard to more ordinary vagrants.[20]

There were also routine gifts to the needy throughout the period. Soldiers in distress, or sailors who were in difficulties – such as a 'poore seaman that was shipp broken' – would receive a few pennies. The same was true of children described as poor 'scholars', and money was given to maintain children apparently without parents in other people's households, and pay for mending their clothes and shoes. In the 1620s around £45-50 a year was being collected through various sources including charities, and being distributed to the poor. In 1638 this included a 'poor Halifax man'. Others came from even further away. Five shillings were given to Sir William Riddell in 1653 'to buy clothes for a poore Dutch boy to whom he liberarly bestowed his Charitie'.[21] When plague struck in 1644, expenses rose substantially, and collections were made at the church door – one for nearly £8 in the middle of the epidemic – in July. There are signs that some kind of emergency shelters were required during this outbreak, as money was spent 'for making loudges and for the relief of the poor infected people in Bensham', expenditure that far exceeded what had been collected in routine poor rate assessments. They had no choice but to spend the money as they collected it in this emergency, 'because of the peoples impoverishment' the authorities recorded. Plague affected the soldiers in the fighting for Tynemouth Priory as well as those in the region's communities where they stayed.[22]

The four-and-twenty of the vestry, through their churchwardens, also spent considerable sums on the more unpleasant business of law and order. The routine costs of maintaining those in the town's lock-up, the tollbooth, or sending people to the county's house of correction, as happened to three 'boys' in 1631, or of moving suspects to Durham to await trial, were met by the town. In addition, there were direct costs of maintaining the stocks and whipping post, and of carrying out punishments such as public whippings.[23] In 1649 and 1650 there were also the costs of a witchcraft outbreak.

It.[Item] pd [paid] out for goeing to the justices about the witches – 4s.

It. [Item] pd [paid] the constables for carying the witches to Jaole – 4s.

---

[20]   DRO, EP/Ga.SM 4/1, pp.28-9, 119, 164.
[21]   DRO, EP/Ga.SM 4/1, pp.2, 12, 28-9, 59, 80, 87, 111, 195.
[22]   DRO, EP/Ga.SM 4/1, pp.134, 136; see Richardson, M.A., *The Local Historian's Table Book*, Historical Division, vol. 1 (1841), for the 1644 plague.
[23]   DRO, EP/Ga.SM 4/1, pp.2, 41, 47, 81, 37, 60.

It. [Item] given them in the Tolebooth & carying the witches to Durham
– 4s.

In addition there were expenses (3s. 4d.) incurred when the magistrates sat to examine the witnesses at Mrs Watson's house, and after the trials in August 1650, 6d. was spent on a 'grave for a witch'. Gateshead seems to have taken part in the general hysteria which gripped Newcastle (and parts of Northumberland) from the spring of 1649 that led to the mass executions in 1650. There were at least six witches on trial in Durham in August 1650, three of them convicted: the procedure was clearly like that initiated in Newcastle, with the accused being searched for suspicious marks, and these were recorded in the assize court records as significant pieces of information. One Margaret Rowle, it was

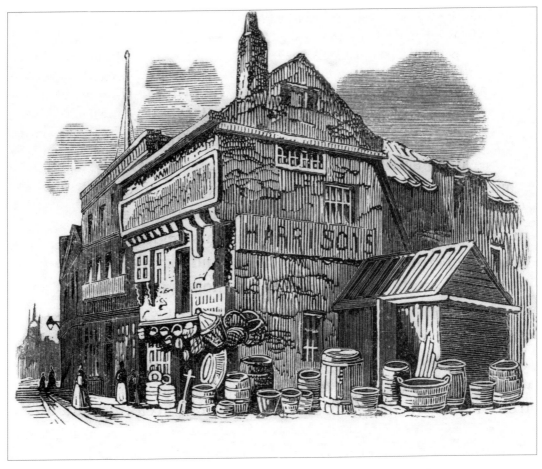

97 Gateshead High Street in 1844, with the tower of St Nicholas, Newcastle, in the distance.

reported, 'will not be searched', and yet was acquitted. It is difficult to know, however, if all, or only some of these came from Gateshead.[24]

Witchcraft and war seemed to go together, and in this the North East in the 1640s was not exceptional. War was the central feature of the 1640s, but little evidence survives of the immediate impact of the fighting. In 1640 Sir Thomas Liddell's mines had been trashed and flooded by the Scots, the engines broken and the coal seams 'drowned'. In the subsequent Scottish invasion of Gateshead that accompanied, and probably exacerbated, the plague epidemic of 1644, the parsonage and its 'necessary' houses were damaged, being described in 1647 as 'pulled down by the Scots souldiers in time of war'. Gateshead had been the centre of the Scottish attack on Newcastle, directed from their base in Sunderland, and was occupied for some months, with heavy guns placed on Windmill Hills and the way to the bridge blocked. Gateshead was the means by which forces in Newcastle could be bottled up: in July 1644 the Scots commander beat them back across the bridge, and reported that 'there is nothing without the port in Gaittsyde unpossessed by us'.[25]

In the Civil War the parish underwent other forms of disturbance. There was a shortage of parish officers in 1648, with no overseers of the pants, and only three churchwardens and three serving as surveyors of the highways.[26] In the Interregnum, old parish priests were replaced by suitably puritan ministers. In 1645 Jonathan Devereux petitioned Parliament and was approved to be 'presented to the Rectory of Gateside, alias Gateshead, in the County and Bishoprick of Duresme; and that the Commissioners of the Great Seal shall issue out a Commission or Presentation under the said Seal accordingly'. Despite this enforcement of puritan orthodoxy, Newcastle's new pro-Parliament authorities complained the very next year that, despite having arrested and imprisoned many 'malignants' (Royalists, in effect) in their town on London's instructions, some had escaped: 'yet they are lying on Gateshead

[24]   DRO, EP/Ga.SM 4/1, pp.158, 160. See also Rushton, Peter, 'Crazes and Quarrels: the Character of Witchcraft in the North East of England, 1649-80', *Durham County Local History Society Bulletin*, vol.31 (1983) pp.2-40; TNA, ASSI 47/20/6, fo.393. The convicted were: Elizabeth Borthecke for an attack on Margaret Selby; Isabella Wright on three charges of attacking Catherine Hunter, Mary Hodgson (for which she was convicted) and Joseph Greenwell; and Anne Harrison for attacking Catherine Hunter (12 August 1650 gaol delivery). None of their victims, nor any of the other three accused and their victims, appear in Gateshead's marriage records (accessed at GenUKI, transcribed by George Bell).

[25]   Sharpe, J.A., *Instruments of Darkness: Witchcraft in England, 1550-1750* (1996) and Gaskill, Malcolm, *Witchfinders: A Seventeenth-Century English Tragedy* (2005); Manders, *Gateshead*, p.16; Kirby, *Parliamentary Surveys*, vol.2, p.116; *The Taking of Gateshead Hill: And Blocking up of Newcastle, certified in a Letter from the Commissioners at Sunderland* (London, 1644; 'Published according to Order'); *A Collection of the State Papers of John Thurloe*, vol.1: 1638-1653 (1742), pp.38-50, accessed on 21 June 2007 from http://www.british-history.ac.uk. For an account of these campaigns, see Meikle, Maureen M. and Newman, Christine M., *Sunderland and its Origins: Monks to Mariners* (Phillimore, 2007), pp.121-36.

[26]   DRO, EP, Ga.SM 4/1, p.150.

side, and many other parts in an abundance'.[27] In 1650 a new minister was appointed, Thomas Weld, who had earlier returned from the Massachusetts Bay colony in America. Weld was described in Parliament on his appointment in response to a petition from the inhabitants of Gateshead as 'an orthodox, able, and pious Preacher'.[28] However much they apparently wanted him then, they – or the most influential of them – subsequently found him not to their liking as an Independent preacher (since they favoured Presbyterianism). He fell into conflict with his vestry, and petitioned the Council of State against them. Weld's petition of protest coincided confusingly with an attempt by the guild of drapers and others to have their royal charter renewed by the Commonwealth.

> Thomas Weld and Sam.[uel] Hamond, ministers and other inhabitants of Gateshead: the town is oppressed by 24 of the inhabitants, who assume without right a power to govern the rest, make bye-laws, oppress them with taxes, elect officers of like spirit, and hinder the work of reformation. Beg that these known opposers of godliness may no longer be suffered, but that godly persons in a list annexed maybe empowered to act. Also that the charter for trade now in agitation may be settled in hands recommended by justices of the peace adjoining, and aldermen and ministers of Newcastle and Gateshead, who know the inhabitants.

The four-and-twenty were, it seems, against his notion of 'godliness' and Weld could not work with them. The government recorded his petition as coming from the 'well affected', that is the loyal, of the borough of Gateshead throughout the dispute.[29] The case was referred to Robert Fenwick, governor of Tynemouth, and Henry Ogle, 'to consider how the government of the said town may best be settled'. The case was heard in detail before them and John Topping and in the meantime the vestry were to 'forbear all proceedings to any election or the supply of vacancies among themselves or the town officers'. When they eventually reported in June 1658, all 24 vestrymen were displaced for 'profanity and other crimes' and new members set up to replace them, by

---

[27] *Perfect Occurrences from Both Houses of Parliament and Martiall Affairs*, 18 December 1646 (unpaginated), 'Monday December 14, from Newcastle', letter dated 10 December 1646: there are also hints of illegal publications that would please the 'malignants and episcopall men', but not necessarily in Gateshead. Yet Thomas Weld's publications were printed there (see below).

[28] *CJ*, vol.4, pp.195-98, 211-12; *LJ*, vol.7, pp.498-500; *CJ*, vol.6, p.354; Weld, Thomas, *The Perfect Pharisee under Monkish Holiness* (1653).

[29] *CSPD*, 1657-8, pp.218, 238, 251; the latter quotes the petition (undated probably 1657); Howells, Roger, 'Thomas Weld of Gateshead: The Return of an New England Puritan', and 'The Newcastle Clergy and the Quakers', both in his *Puritans and Radicals in North England: Essays on the English Revolution* (1984), pp.83-111, 136-61, see p.101; for the progress of the guild's petition see *CSPD*, 1656-7, pp.199, 284 and *CSPD*, 1657-8, p.142.

order of the Lord Protector himself.[30] The victory was fleeting, for less than two years later both king and church were back, and a new minister, John Laidler, read the Anglican articles of faith to the congregation. All Weld left behind was his wife Judith buried in the churchyard.[31]

Despite this turbulence, many aspects of communal life had continued unchanged. The vestry had a major role in maintaining the ceremonial life of the community associated with both the church and the town lands. Just as the bellman had duties in the church, so he also provided a primary means of making public announcements, and had to be rewarded for going about warning people of forthcoming events. The bells also had to be rung on special occasions, such as when the Lord Lieutenant of the county visited, or on the king's coronation day and 'Gunpowder treason date', 5 November: the records do not speak of Guy Fawkes at all.[32] Similarly, the town's piper and waits had to be paid for regular duties: playing music both on the way to the town fields, and while the people 'scaled' or cleansed the pastures and did routine work on keeping them in good condition. They also played when everyone rode the bounds of the town (usually around Rogation, a week or so before Whitsuntide), something that was generally celebrated with food and drink – for the young and old – all of which had to be paid for. The Rogationtide ridings were still important in the early modern period, when boundaries still had to be printed on people's memories because they were not yet drawn on incontestable maps. Knowledge of the distinctions between complex units of manor, township and parish in 17th-century Northumberland were still maintained by annual perambulation.[33]

Interestingly, there is no real sign of any difference in Gateshead caused by the Parliamentary success in the Civil War: the bells were rung for Parliamentary victories against the Irish and Scots, and for the 'Lord Protector's Inauguration' in 1658 (for Richard Cromwell, following Oliver's death). The 5 November festivities naturally continued just as before, celebrating Parliament's escape from Catholic terrorism.[34] The waits and the piper still accompanied the riders of the bounds and the workers in the town fields, too: 2s. 6d. 'paid to the waits for playing music to the Townes people when they dressed the Townes

[30] *CSPD*, 1657-8, pp.330, 360; *CSPD*, 1658-9, pp.69-70; 'profaness' was the word in the copy in the vestry records in Gateshead itself, DRO, EP Ga.SM 4/1, pp.242-3.
[31] DRO, EP Ga.SM 4/1, p.265. See also in Surtees, *Durham*, Gateshead volume, pp.69 and 72 for Mrs Judith Weld buried 1656, 'who was to three Godly Ministers a good wife' said the monument.
[32] DRO, EP/Ga.SM 4/1, pp.10, 36, 114.
[33] Whyte, Nicola, 'Landscape, Memory and Custom: Parish Identities, *c*.1550-1700', *Social History*, vol.32 (2007), pp.169-70, 172.
[34] DRO, EP/Ga.SM 4/1, pp.158, 168, 191, 235.

ffeeld' recorded the churchwardens in 1654. At the riding, if anything, the level of provision of food was even greater: in 1656 the waits played and were paid 4s. for their services, but 14s. more was spent 'upon the young men and boys at the hirds house at the same time' (that is, at the house provided by the parish for the town's herdsman). The music played on after the Restoration of the Monarchy, though by the early 18th century the waits were appearing at a new local ritual: the horse races which, as elsewhere in the region, had become increasingly popular since the early 17th century. Riding the bounds may have been moved to Midsummer Day by then. The musicians, like the constables and the beadle, were dressed in coats paid for by the borough, and there are hints that these made for a distinctive civic uniform.[35] One change, which is hard to prove convincingly, is that there seems to have been less gender segregation in the church pews after 1650 than before the war. In the 1630s it seems that men sat in different pews from their wives, who were in female-only areas of the church. This reflected much earlier practices, and also helped to sustain some of the social hierarchies of small communities, with family pews ranked according to cost and the social status of their occupants. By the 1650s, as the numbers of paying pewholders fell, perhaps reflecting hostility to the Thomas Weld's Independent views, the lists contained large blanks, and there is less sign of this rigidity. Certainly there were more family groups including servants and children but the pattern is not entirely clear in the absence of any public resolutions or policy on the matter.[36]

Restoration and Revival

The population after the Restoration of 1660 was clearly much greater than a century earlier. The hearth tax records for 1674 suggests that there were more than 700 households, of which only half paid tax: this indicates a likely population of about 3,500 people. Gateshead at this time was therefore slightly smaller in size than Sunderland and the parishes at the mouth of the River Wear. In the two large wards, Bank Ward and High Ward, the number of hearth tax payers were outnumbered by those too poor to pay tax, in the former by a large margin. As in much of Durham and the North East, most houses had only one hearth, that is, they had in effect only one heated

[35] DRO, EP/Ga.SM 4/1, pp.73, 193, 206, 219, 258, 388; 'Gateshead Parish Accounts', *Proceedings of the Society of Antiquaries of Newcastle upon Tyne*, 3rd series, vol.3 (1907-8), p.249. These records are in part from TWAS DF.OX/9/1.
[36] DRO, EP/Ga.SM 4/1, pp.52-7, 226-31. And see Thomas, Keith, *Religion and the Decline of Magic: Studies in Popular Beliefs in Sixteenth- and Seventeenth-Century England* (1973), p.180.

room for all vital functions such as cooking and washing.[37] This may indicate a population who were far from secure and prosperous. Something of the scale of Gateshead's personal poverty and vulnerability emerges in the parish records in the Restoration period. For example, the single payments made by the churchwardens from charitable funds (separate from the weekly payments given to the regularly maintained poor, that is paupers, paid from the parish rates) were in some bad years in the 1660s handed out to more than 500 individuals. In a good year the numbers might be only 200 or 300, and were fewer than 200 in 1675. During the 1680s, too, numbers fluctuated from around 120 in 1681 to more than 400 in 1685, and rose from 71 people in 1683 to more than 400 two years later. The size of payments were not large – a few shillings at the most per head – but may have been an effective means of subsidising a large proportion of the relatively poor.[38] The parish administrators were also dealing with poor wanderers, having to spend money on sending poor children back to places as far away as London, in 1693. Another problem was that strangers were allegedly settling in Gateshead and adding to its burdens. According to one vestry resolution:

5 February 1682

Whereas [a] Great increase of poor people have bene of late years in the Parish by persons receiving & taking in strangers and fforeigners who by continuance of time become inhabitants [and] so chargeable to the Parish for education whereof It is ordered that if any Landlord or Owner of any house or houses in the Parish doe at any time hereafter take in or harbour any such strangers without giveing security to save the parish harmeless, and if any such stranger shall by their takeing in be troublesome or chargeable to the Parish, that upon every such person that shall so take in or entertain any such strangers shall be lyable to maintain the s[ai]d stranger or strangers so falling into decay and that such persons shall be assessed proportionately thereunto in the weikly Taxation for the year.

Like other parishes in this period, particularly those in small towns such as Corbridge and Hexham, the mobility of paupers created anxiety, and local

---

[37] Green, A.G., Parkinson, E. and Spufford, M., *Durham Hearth Tax: Lady Day 1666* (2006), pp.cviii, cxxvi cxxxv, 231. Gateshead had 727 households, of which 371 paid tax; Bank Ward 151 of which 113 paid, High Ward 145 of which 140 paid. In 1666 there had been 499 households paying tax, with no information on those not paying; in 1674 Sunderland – excluding modern Washington but including all the villages such as Hylton, Silksworth, Fulwell, Tunstall and Burdon – had 851 households, of which 406 paid tax.
[38] DRO, EP/Ga.SM 4/1, pp.288, 382; DRO, EP/Ga.SM 5/1, pp.34, 55-60.

98   St Mary's Church.

authorities everywhere tried to stop in-migration to their parishes by erecting prohibitive penalties like this against those who took in 'inmates' (that is illegal settlers, taken in as lodgers). At no time were these measures very successful. Yet in other ways Gateshead's officers were not entirely uncaring: Irish people travelling with passes to another parish received help, and in the 1690s the parish paid regular amounts of money to the 'blind drummer', who was probably employed by the community as well as receiving intermittent help from them. In 1681 they paid someone 'for watching the madwoman'. In 1693 they were willing to spend money (1s. 6d.) 'when collecting money for the slaves in Turkey'. This was part of a larger effort, widespread in England and northern Europe, to free Christians captured by Mediterranean pirates (the money might more likely have been used to liberate captives held on the North African coast under Ottoman control, in fact, than in modern-day Turkey). It was common to collect for this purpose throughout England.[39] One aspect of the officers' work that did not apparently cause them any misgivings was the repression of Quakers, which cost time and money in the 1680s. In 1683 substantial sums were spent 'when we leavyed the Quakers goods and Councell's fee', and in taking them to Durham. The following year it cost nearly £3 in 'charges paid carrying 26 Quakers to Durham'. It is unclear whether this was because they failed to pay parish taxation or because they refused to take oaths of loyalty: they might have been on their way to gaol in either case.[40]

This diversity of parish and borough business, and the frequent meetings needed to deal with it, meant that serving on the vestry was not a particularly attractive duty, for there was much tedious and detailed work to be done, and in the later 17th century there are signs of men neglecting their duties. In 1688 a 12d. fine was introduced for any vestryman who absented himself from published meetings without excuse:

> For prevention of the inconvenience which doe usually happen by reason of the wilfulness or negligence of the ffoure and twenty in not appearing when they are lawfully warned to consult and agree upon such things as are most necessary for the good and benefitt of the town.

Just in case any member might wish to challenge the imposition of a fine, a detailed record of absences from the vestry meetings had been maintained for some years previously. It is possible that many of the more ordinary men on the vestry did not have the leisure for public office. In 1685, one of the few years for which detailed lists of occupations survive, the four-and-twenty were a mixed group, including one baronet, one knight, two gentlemen, two esquires and a merchant; but there were also four blacksmiths, two tanners, a pewterer,

39 DRO, EP/Ga.SM 5/, pp.16, 99, 102, 125, 130, 148. On the poor law in the North East see Rushton, Peter 'The Poor Law, the Parish and the Community in North East England, 1600-1800', *Northern History*, vol.25 (1989), pp.135-52, especially pp.140-1 for measures against inmates. For studies of Barbary Coast pirates and raising money to buy their captives' freedom, see Vitkus, Daniel J. (ed.), *Piracy, Slavery and Redemption; Barbary Captivity Narratives from Early Modern England* (2001), pp.23-9, 360-6.
40 DRO, EP Ga. SM 5/1, pp.33, 48.

a glazier and a feltmaker. It is likely that these less affluent men found their duties time-consuming and irksome at times.[41]

In other respects, too, there could be difficulties, particularly when the respectable of the parish fell out among themselves. It emerges from a dispute between the rector of St Mary's and the local schoolmaster that the ancient part of the church called the Anchorage was used as a schoolroom. However, there was uncertainty as to who should use it: in 1693 the vestry recorded the following resolution:

> Whereas John Tennant Schoolmaster teaches school in a certain room over the vestry of the Church of St Marie in Gateshead commonly known by the name of the Anchorage, without the consent and in opposition to Mr Geo[rge] Tullie Rector of the said Parish, whom we conceive to have a right to place a schoolmaster in the room abovementioned, we therefore whose names are underwritten at a vestrie meeting the day and the year above specified do, in corroboration of the said Rector's right, if need be, join and concur with him in displacing the above mentioned John Tenant from teaching any farther in the aforementioned room.

This was signed by 14 men, including the Rector himself. The Anchorage survives, though rebuilt in the 18th century, as a two-storey structure on the north side of St Mary's Church (and was still being used as a school in the 19th century). The churchwardens had a long-standing policy from the early 17th century of keeping up the maintenance of the schoolroom and paying the schoolmaster to teach children whose parents, presumably, could not afford to pay. This was happening as early as the 1630s, and clearly education was an important part of the parish's provision throughout the century.[42]

The End of the Seventeenth Century

After the Restoration, and particularly once the Grand Lease had lapsed in 1682, Gateshead could establish itself in some ways on its own terms. The foundations of a reasonable prosperity were laid: the territory it encompassed was essential as a conduit for moving coal to the Tyne, and loading it from staithes to the keels. The overall financial basis of the borough accordingly

---

[41] DRO, EP.Ga. SM 5/1, pp.83, 49, 933-6; Manders, *Gateshead*, p.40.

[42] DRO, EP.Ga. SM 5/1, p.122; Pevsner, Nikolaus, *County Durham*, Buildings of England series, revised by Elizabeth Williamson (1983), p.283; Surtees, *Durham*, Gateshead volume, p.68; DRO, EP Ga SM 4/1, pp.103, 115.

99   Gateshead from the tower on the north side of the new bridge.

was not as bad as might be expected. Whatever the difficulties in maintaining local coal production, there was a steady income from the wayleaves across Gateshead, which provided crucial funds for the four-and-twenty's accounts. The earlier developments under the Grand Lease may have been hard to sustain, but the territory of Gateshead, as ever, was a vital means of reaching the river. Surveys from the 1680s suggest that there was much more profitable business being conducted towards the river and along the southern riverside.[43] Administratively, too, things became simpler by 1700. The triple structure of borough, parish and manor always stood in danger of confusion. The three seem to have become two, and things were managed by the steward of the manor, with its manor court, on the one hand, and the vestry of four-and-twenty on the other. The borough court had existed up to 1682, but seems to have been replaced by the 18th century by a manorial court – a court leet – dealing with the town lands and the tenants or burgesses. There were between

[43]   Hatcher, John, *The History of the British Coal Industry*, vol.1 (1993), p.80; TWAS, DF.HUG/103/1 and 2 for a map of Gateshead Park and the 'south shore staiths' of Gateshead, with a survey of the lands belonging to the Grand Lease.

120 and 140 burgesses: in 1663, of 135, 19 were women, and six married couples were treated as a single unit. According to Dodds, 'At Gateshead a bailiff was not appointed after 1681, and the borough courts ceased to be held. The halmote court of the manor of Gateshead was held yearly, however, by the leasees of the manor. It seems to have taken over the functions of the borough court, and freemen of the companies were not eligible to be jurors.' In the 18th century the court leet and its jury were the beneficiary of long lectures by William Cotesworth on their duties: among other things, they were to control community problems such as public nuisances, the pasturing of 'scabbed' horses, 'public disorderly houses', encroachments on the highways, diversion of ancient waterways, dumping of carrion and dirt, riots and unlawful assemblies. The jury was also to present to the court 'all eavesdroppers such as listen under walls and windows to hear and carry Tales amongst their Neighbours', as well as all 'scolds and other breakers of the peace'. Certainly records suggest that they maintained the instruments required for local community discipline, repairing the stocks and ducking stool, for example, at the turn of the 17th century and into the 18th.[44]

Other local institutions retained their importance into the 18th century. The guilds which had been established from the late 16th century onward provided an essential element of economic independence from Newcastle, shaping the way local men acquired skilled training and career opportunities. Dodds says that Newcastle had initially opposed any guilds in Gateshead but despite this, 'the trade companies of Gateshead were second only to those of Durham in importance' in the county. They were hardly specialist organisations, since they gathered many closely related trades together in conglomerate associations. There was, for example, a company of dyers, fullers, locksmiths, blacksmiths, cutlers, joiners and house carpenters, and another of drapers, tailors, mercers, hardwaremen, coopers and chandlers. There were two others, one for cordwainers, and another for a large group of stone-workers, such as freemasons, carvers and stone-cutters as well as nailers, plumbers and pewterers. William Cotesworth in 1683 was apprenticed to a merchant and tallow chandler, Robert Sutton, and became a member of the Drapers' Company in 1690, described by Dodds as the most powerful of Gateshead's guilds.[45] Certainly the guilds were active at the end of the 17th century, as they had been during

[44] Dodds, 'The Bishops' Boroughs', p.179; TWAS, DF.OX/7/1, pp.45-50, 51-5; DF.HUG/106/1-3; *Society of Antiquaries*, 3rd series, vol.3 (1907-8), pp.248-9; TWAS, DF.OX/9/1 (unpaginated, 22 August 1705).
[45] Dodds, 'Bishops' Boroughs', pp.153 and 156; TWAS, GU/DFL/1 (MF 2072); Dodds, E., *The Records of the Gateshead Company of Drapers, Tailors, Mercers, Hardwaremen, Coopers and Chandlers* (1907); Surtees, *History*, pp.59-60; Ellis, *A Study of the Business Fortunes of William Cotesworth*, p.5.

100   Gateshead, past and present.

the Parliamentary period, with a petition to the central government defending their commercial interests.

A petition of the Stewards and Company of Pewterers, inhabiting in the ancient Borough of Gateshead, in the County Palatine of Durham, was presented to the House, and set forth, 'That great Quantities of Tin have been exported from England into foreign Nations, at small Rates; and by mixing the same with Lead, debase the Pewter; so that, thereby, they are enabled to sell the same a great deal cheaper than the Petitioners; which tends to the Decay of Trade, and the Loss of his Majesty's Customs: And praying the Consideration of the House; and Relief in the Premises.

This kept Gateshead firmly active in the national politics of trade, and whereas they might have had common interests with others in the same business in Newcastle over this issue, they chose to express them separately. In this way they registered their distinct identity with the national authorities.[46]

At the end of the 17th century Gateshead had established a stable pattern of local administration and community life that remained until the Victorian era, when it would, like Sunderland, join the ranks of the new municipal boroughs. Things were never as exciting again, after 1700, for the period from the Reformation to the Glorious Revolution unquestionably constituted what the Chinese call 'interesting times' for Gateshead. By the 18th century both the relationship with the growing Tyneside economy and the internal relations of parish, manor and borough were orderly. Despite this picture of responsible independence, it is unlikely that Gateshead's reputation with its northern neighbour changed very much. For Newcastle, Gateshead represented both a deplorable zone of free trade that required continual efforts at containment and exclusion, and a desirable area of coal production which had to be brought under control. Was it an important asset or just an embarrassment; the 'dirty lane' that led to their town? Newcastle's politicians never knew whether to exclude Gateshead or to take it over: at different times, they tried both. As for Gateshead's image, it ended the 18th century as it had begun the 16th, as the place to which Newcastle's villains fled beyond the town council's control. It was there that the 'rogues' – those running the well-known disreputable ale-houses and bawdy houses of the quayside's hilly 'chares' near the Guildhall – fled. In the 1770s and 1780s Newcastle's frustrated authorities noted the number of no-goods who lodged in Gateshead. The infamous Bishop Auckland and Gateshead Fell gang met at the *Crown and Canon* on Gateshead Fell, it was alleged. Like the disorderly of the 16th century or the Royalist malignants of the 17th, Charles Cadwell and his wife Mary Smith, who in the early 1770s had harboured their gang of itinerant thieves, pickpockets, card sharpers and house breakers in the *Goat* on Newcastle's quayside, one of the town's well-known 'lewd houses', avoided arrest there by crossing the river, and were recorded by the town's files as 'removed to Gateshead'.[47] D.J. Rowe

---

[46]   *CJ*, vol.12, pp.585-7; See Rushton, 'Law in North-East England', for similar instances of regional unity and separate actions in Parliament.

[47]   TWAS, 616/1; Rowe, D.J., 'The North-East', in Thompson, F.M.L (ed.), *The Cambridge Social History of Britain, 1750-1950*, vol.1 Regions and Communities, p.417.

has observed that Gateshead has never forgiven the insult that it was 'a long (sometimes the adjective is "dirty") lane leading to Newcastle'. It was always more than that: it was a means of escape and refuge for those wanting to get away from Newcastle. Above all, Gateshead managed to survive all attempts at outside control, preserving its separate identity and its distinctive way of doing things. The locals achieved this despite over 200 years of pressure and blackmail, and survival was in many ways both against Newcastle – and against the odds.

Index

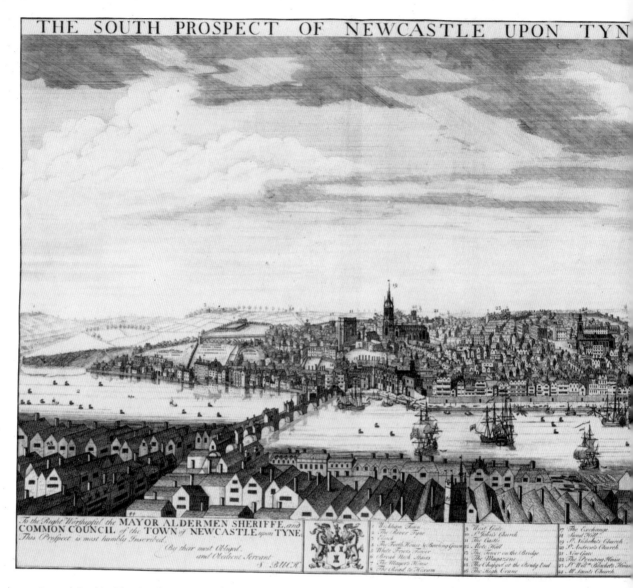

THE SOUTH PROSPECT OF NEWCASTLE UPON TYN

To the Right Worshipful the MAYOR ALDERMEN SHERIFFE, and
COMMON COUNCIL of the TOWN of NEWCASTLE upon TYNE.
This Prospect is most humbly Inscribed.

By their most Obliged.
and Obedient Servant
S. BUCK.

Samuel Buck's 'The South Prospect of Newcastle upon Tyne taken from Gateshead Church
Steeple'; the top of the tower of St Mary's, 1745.